Frontiers in Information Systems

(Volume 2)

Mathematics Applied in Information Systems

Edited by

Mangey Ram

Department of Mathematics, Computer Science and Engineering
Graphic Era Deemed to be University, Dehradun, India

General:

1. Any dispute or claim arising out of or in connection with this License Agreement or the Work (including non-contractual disputes or claims) will be governed by and construed in accordance with the laws of the U.A.E. as applied in the Emirate of Dubai. Each party agrees that the courts of the Emirate of Dubai shall have exclusive jurisdiction to settle any dispute or claim arising out of or in connection with this License Agreement or the Work (including non-contractual disputes or claims).
2. Your rights under this License Agreement will automatically terminate without notice and without the need for a court order if at any point you breach any terms of this License Agreement. In no event will any delay or failure by Bentham Science Publishers in enforcing your compliance with this License Agreement constitute a waiver of any of its rights.
3. You acknowledge that you have read this License Agreement, and agree to be bound by its terms and conditions. To the extent that any other terms and conditions presented on any website of Bentham Science Publishers conflict with, or are inconsistent with, the terms and conditions set out in this License Agreement, you acknowledge that the terms and conditions set out in this License Agreement shall prevail.

Bentham Science Publishers Ltd.
Executive Suite Y - 2
PO Box 7917, Saif Zone
Sharjah, U.A.E.
Email: subscriptions@benthamscience.org

BENTHAM SCIENCE

CONTENTS

FOREWORD 1

It gives me a great pleasure to write a foreword of the book on 'Mathematics Applied to Information Systems'. The book is indeed painstakingly compiled covering a diverse range of topics in mathematical applications in information systems to include software reliability growth models, reliability optimization in intuitionistic fuzzy environment, applications ranging from railways to retrieval of soil parameters, mathematical models for digital imaging and their applications in digital image forensics, quality issues in the design of supply chains, food safety and security, propositional logic and application of stochastic differential equation to software release modeling. I must congratulate Prof. Mangey Ram for his sincere efforts in promoting the spirit of mathematics in various application domains. I hope this book will provide the reader with an insight into the various application possibilities and encourage researchers to find solutions to various complex problems in engineering and science.

Ajit Kumar Verma
Professor (Technical Safety), ATØM
Western Norway University of Applied Sciences
Haugesund
Norway

FOREWORD 2

In this information age, editing a book on "Mathematics Applied in Information System" is very timely and commendable step. Every engineered system as well as human society deals with information flow and it has become more important with growing use of internet in every aspect of human life. The management of information, timely flow, and reliability and safety of information is becoming increasingly challenging and critical. The growing globalization and interdependence between nations and societies are entirely relying on information technology that makes reliability and safety of information sharing even more critical. The chapters included in this book cover majority of these issues and concerns. Specifically, software reliability, reliability optimization in intuitionistic fuzzy environment, mathematical models for digital imaging and their applications in digital image forensics, quality issues dealing with information flow in supply chain system, safety and security in IT based technology, food safety and security, fault-detection and correction in complex network system are some of the important topics covered in the book, which attempt to address some of the major concerns and challenges being faced my information systems. This book has compiled and edited work of several researchers who have been working hard to anticipate upcoming issue and develop appropriate tools and technologies to address these issues up-front. I congratulate editor for this timely effort to compile the work on the most challenging area.

Om Prakash Yadav
Professor
Department of Industrial and Manufacturing Engineering
North Dakota State University
USA

PREFACE

Today's challenges faced by science and engineering are so complex features that can only be solved by the help of participation of mathematical scientists to research and development in the area of mathematical sciences application in information sciences. All approaches to scientific observation and experiment, theory are needed to understand the complex phenomena investigated by scientists and engineers and each approach requires the mathematical sciences. The real world utility of mathematics remarkably significance in the life of academics, practitioners, researchers and industry leaders. In recent years mathematics applied in information system considers only original and timely contribution containing new results in various fields of applied mathematics. Advance in science and technology, however, brought about a further development of mathematical applications.

This book **Mathematics Applied in Information System** confronts various series of range in mathematics applied to information systems. Mathematics applied in various fields of software reliability relating to different aspects, reliability optimization in intuitionistic fuzzy environment, information technology, natural language processing, supply chain management, geoscience, mathematical models for digital imaging and their applications in digital image forensics have been discussed through the chapters

The Editor acknowledges Bentham Science for this opportunity and for their enthusiastic and professional support. Finally, I would like to thank all the chapter authors and reviewers for their availability for this work.

Mangey Ram
Department of Mathematics
Computer Science and Engineering
Graphic Era Deemed to be University
Dehradun
India

Acknowledgements

The Editor acknowledges Bentham Science Publishers for this opportunity and professional support. My special thanks to Dr. Faryal Sami, Assistant Manager Publications, Bentham Science Publishers for the excellent support, provided to me for completing this book. Also, I would like to thank all the chapter authors and reviewers for their availability for this work.

Mangey Ram
Department of Mathematics
Computer Science and Engineering
Graphic Era Deemed to be University
Dehradun
India

List of Contributors

Avinash K. Shrivastava   Fortune Institute of International Business, New Delhi India

Adarsh Anand   Department of Operational Research, University of Delhi, Delhi 110007, India

Ali Muhammad Rushdi   Department of Electrical and Computer Engineering, Faculty of Engineering, King Abdulaziz University, P.O. Box 80204, Jeddah, 21589, Kingdom of Saudi Arabia

Alok K. Yadav   Department of Mechanical Engineering, Graphic Era Deemed to be University, Dehradun-248002, Uttarakhand, India

Bhasker Pant   Department of Computer Science and Engineering, Graphic Era Deemed to be University, Dehradun, Uttarakhand, India

Deepika   Department of Operational Research, University of Delhi, Delhi 110007, India

Dharmendra Singh   Department of Electronics and Communication Engineering, Indian Institute of Technology Rookee, Rookee, Uttarakhand, India

Harish Garg   School of Mathematics, Thapar Institute of Engineering & Technology (Deemed University) Patiala – 147004, Punjab, India

Hemant K. Verma   Multimedia Analysis and Security (MANAS) Lab, Electrical Engineering, Indian Institute of Technology Gandhinagar, India

Hiroyuki Okamura   Department of Information Engineering, Hiroshima University, Higashi-Hiroshima, Japan

Junjun Zheng   Department of Information Engineering, Hiroshima University, Higashi-Hiroshima, Japan

Kanchan Das   East Carolina University, College of Engineering and Computer Science Greenville, North Carolina, USA

Lin Zhu Jin   Department of Information Engineering, Hiroshima University, Higashi-Hiroshima, Japan

Mangey Ram   Department of Mathematics; Computer Science and Engineering, Graphic Era Deemed to be University, Dehradun, Uttarakhand, India

Muhammad Ali Rushdi   Department of Biomedical and Systems Engineering, Faculty of Engineering, Cairo University, Giza, 12613, Arab Republic of Egypt

Nitin Khanna

Multimedia Analysis and Security (MANAS) Lab, Electrical Engineering, Indian Institute of Technology Gandhinagar, India

Ompal Singh

Department of Operational Research, University of Delhi, Delhi 110007, India

Parmod K. Kapur

Amity Centre for Interdisciplinary Research, Amity University Noida U.P., India
Department of Operational Research, University of Delhi, Delhi 110007, India

Pravin P. Patil

Department of Mechanical Engineering, Graphic Era Deemed to be University, Dehradun-248002, Uttarakhand, India

Rishi Prakash

Department of Electronics and Communication Engineering, Graphic Era (Deemed to be University), Dehradun, Uttarakhand, India

Sachin K. Mangla

Plymouth Business School (PBS), University of Plymouth, United Kingdom

Sunil Luthra

Department of Mechanical Engineering, Government Polytechnic, Jhajjar-124103

Suresh K. Jakhar

Indian Institute of Management, Lucknow, India

Tadashi Dohi

Department of Information Engineering, Hiroshima University, Higashi-Hiroshima, Japan

Vijay Singh

Department of Computer Science and Engineering, Graphic Era Deemed to be University, Dehradun, Uttarakhand, India

Vinay Verma

Multimedia Analysis and Security (MANAS) Lab, Electrical Engineering, Indian Institute of Technology Gandhinagar, India

Yogesh K. Sharma

Department of Mechanical Engineering, Graphic Era Deemed to be University, Dehradun-248002, Uttarakhand, India

Frontiers in Information Systems, 2018, *Vol. 2*, 1-33

CHAPTER 1

Software Reliability Modeling in Continuous-State Space

Tadashi Dohi*, Lin Zhu Jin, Junjun Zheng and Hiroyuki Okamura

Department of Information Engineering, Hiroshima University, Higashi-Hiroshima, Japan

Abstract: For large scale software systems with a huge number of source codes, it may be often useful to regard approximately software fault-counting processes observed in testing phase as continuous-state stochastic processes. In this chapter we introduce stochastic non-counting process models to describe the fault-detection phenomena in software testing. The time-nonhomogeneous Gaussian process and time-nonhomogeneous gamma process-based software reliability models (SRMs) are summarized, and are compared with the existing SRMs such as the geometric Brownian motion and nonhomogeneous Poisson processes (NHPPs). It is shown in numerical examples with actual software development project data that the time-nonhomogeneous gamma process-based SRMs could provide the better goodness-of-fit and predictive performances than the existing SRMs in many cases.

Keywords: Brownian motion process, Gamma wear process, Goodness-of-fit performance, Information criteria, Kolmogorov-Smirnov test, Mean squared error, Nonhomogeneous Poisson process, Predictive performance, Reliability growth modeling, Software reliability, Stochastic differential equation.

INTRODUCTION

During the last four decades, stochastic models called *software reliability models* (SRMs) have been extensively developed in executing the black-box test of software products [1-5]. The most classical but important SRMs would be nonhomogeneous Poisson process (NHPP)-based SRMs [6-8]. These SRMs are presented based on different debugging scenarios, and can catch qualitatively typical (but not general) reliability growth phenomena observed in testing phases of software products. It should be noted, however, that nobody has given

---

* **Corresponding author Tadashi Dohi:** Department of Information Engineering, Hiroshima University, Higashi-Hiroshima, Japan; Tel: +81 82 424 7698; Fax: +81 82 422 7025; E-mail: dohi@hiroshima-u.ac.jp

Mangey Ram (Ed.)

satisfactory answer for the question whether the NHPP-based SRMs were really best stochastic processes to describe software-fault detection phenomena. Of course, we know that the NHPP-based SRMs are very tractable and much attractive, because they involve only one parameter, called the *mean value function*, and can often provide nice goodness-of-fit performance. Nevertheless, the hypothesis that software fault-detection process in testing phase is governed by the Poisson law cannot be always accepted in nature. For instance, it is worth mentioning that the variance of an NHPP at an arbitrary time equals exactly its mean value. Unfortunately, such a specific property cannot be necessarily justified to describe the software fault-detection process. Several authors try to give the physical meaning for debugging scenarios or formulations by unifying the SRMs. Langberg & Singpurwalla [9] prove that the Jelinski and Moranda model [10] as a continuous-time Markov chain is involved in an exponential NHPP-based SRM as a special case by Goel & Okumoto [6]. Shanthikumar [11] shows that the NHPP-SRM can be described by a time-dependent Markov process, and obtains the almost same conclusion as Langberg & Singpurwalla [9]. Miller [12] introduces an idea of exponential order statistics and clarifies the relationship between the existing SRMs and the order statistics of software fault-detection time data. In this way, the past literature on the SRM formulation has focused on the development of new models in the specified framework and/or their unification.

From the above reason, some authors have challenged to propose plausible SRMs based on different stochastic processes. Chen and Singpuwalla [13] show that almost all existing SRMs presented in the past literature were involved in self-exciting point processes. It should be noted that a generalization of SRMs may lead to a various type of reliability growth patterns but may lose their technical tractability. For instance, even if one considers a generalized nonhomogeneous pure birth process, which belongs to somewhat wider class of stochastic processes than NHPPs, it is not always possible to obtain the transition probability in an analytical form. Recently, Ishii & Dohi [14] and Saito & Dohi [15] develop nonhomogeneous gamma process (NHGP)-based SRMs in discrete-state space and generalize the common NHPP-based SRMs with arbitrary mean value functions. Not only their results on goodness-of-fit performance but also the easy treatment of parameter estimation are emphasized there. However, since the NHGPs are also complex point processes, the analytical derivation of finite moments such as the mean and variance of cumulative number of software faults detected by an arbitrary testing time, is analytically impossible except for trivial cases. This penalizes us to use the NHGP-based SRMs in practice to evaluate the software reliability measures. Koch & Spreij [16] and Yip [17] describe the SRMs as counting processes with semi-martingale representation.

An alternative way is to approximate the software fault-counting process by a continuous-state stochastic process. For large scale software systems with a huge number of source codes, such an approach may be validated practically. Even if one assumes the NHPP-based SRMs with discrete sample paths, the average tendencies are estimated as continuous values (real numbers) through the mean value functions. Tamura & Yamada [18, 19], Yamada *et al.* [20, 21], Yamada & Tamura [22] assume that the software fault-detection process is described by the geometric Brownian motion process or its variations with time-dependent drift parameters. Lee *et al.* [23] also introduce different drift parameters, and propose two S-shaped continuous SRMs, which can be categorized into the variations of the geometric Brownian motion process, to represent different debugging scenarios. However, since the Gaussian processes in [18-23] infinitely fluctuate with up and down trends during a finite time length, and can decrease even for a sufficiently small time interval with probability one, the justification to use such non-counting stochastic processes depends on the magnitude of their variances. Unfortunately, since the geometric Brownian motion process and its variations are typical diffusion processes, the possibility of large variances can be allowed at all and, as the result, it is concluded that such a modeling is not always acceptable to describe counting phenomena.

Second, although the SRMs in the above references [18-23] obey the lognormal-like distributions with time-dependent drift parameter, it implies that the familiar central limit theorem cannot be applied to represent the asymptotic behavior and that no approximate effect for an arbitrary stochastic processes arises. Third, it is seen in [21] that the geometric Brownian motion process provides much lower Akaike information criteria (AICs) [24, 25] than the NHPP-based SRMs. However, this comparison is not fair theoretically and wrong, because the corresponding AICs are based on different likelihood information, *i.e.*, the former is calculated with the joint probability density function which is not defined as a probability, the latter is with the joint probability mass function. In other words, it is meaningless to compare the continuous-state space model with the discrete-state space model in terms of the information criteria.

In this chapter, we introduce yet alternative continuous-state SRMs, called the nonhomogeneous gamma wear process (NHGWP), in addition to another Gaussian process models which are consistent to the NHPP-based SRM. The

NHGWP is quite different from the previous NHGP-based SRMs by Ishii & Dohi [14] and Saito & Dohi [15], because the NHGPs are characterized by a Stieltjes convolution of fault-detection time distributions of NHPPs. Since the continuous-state gamma wear process is one of the Levy processes corresponding to the gamma distributions, from the well-known Levy-Khintchine representation, it can be decomposed into three parts: deterministic function of time, scaled Brownian motion and a superposition of compound Poisson processes. Abdel-Hameed [26] introduces a homogeneous gamma wear process with stationary and independent increments to describe a wear process of a device. Dufresne *et al.* [27] consider an NHGWP, which is a monotone continuous-time non-stationary Markov process with independent increments and non-decreasing sample paths, and use it to model an aggregate claim process in insurance mathematics. To describe the software fault-detection process consistently, the non-decreasing property of the cumulative number of software faults is definitely needed since the assumption of an infinite number of imperfect debugs are indeed unrealistic in actual software testing. In this sense, our NHGWP-based SRM developed in this chapter can be useful to explore the software fault-detection phenomena without unrealistic modeling assumption.

This chapter is organized as follows. In the following section, we summarize the representative NHPP-based SRMs, and carry out preliminary experiments to test the Poisson properties with the actual software fault-count data. Here, we report two statistical test results on renewal property and equity dispersion, and show that an applicability of the NHPP-based SRMs cannot be always accepted. Next, we give an alternative interpretation of the NHPP-based software reliability modeling based on the semi-martingale representation. Along with the above discussion, we introduce the existing continuous SRM based on a geometric Brownian motion process, which is proposed by Yamada *et al.* [20]. By taking account of the difference of the modeling philosophy from the existing continuous SRM, we develop two NHPP-consistent continuous SRMs with exponential curve and S-shaped curve. These new models are also based on the Gaussian processes and possess continuous sample path. Subsequently, we propose an NHGWP as an alternative continuous SRM. Numerical examples with real software-fault count data are devoted to compare our continuous SRMs with both the NHPP-based SRMs and the existing continuous SRMs in terms of goodness-of fit and predictive performances. It is shown that our NHGWP-based SRMs defined in a continuous-state space can provide relatively small AIC and Bayesian information criterion (BIC) by Schwartz [28] in many cases, and that the existing continuous SRM does not function better than our new SRMs and the NHPP-based SRMs, if it is used to predict the number of software faults detected in the future. Finally, the present chapter is concluded with some remarks with future direction.

PRELIMINARY ANALYSIS

NHPP-based SRMs

We carry out preliminary experiments to examine statistically whether the software fault detection process is governed by the familiar Poisson law. Here, we treat the representative two NHPP-based SRMs; exponential (GO) SRM by Goel & Okumoto [6] and delayed S-shaped (YOO) SRM by Yamada *et al.* [7]. Let $\{N(t), t \geq 0\}$ denote the cumulative number of software faults experienced up to time t in software testing. Then, the stochastic process $N(t)$ is said an NHPP with intensity function $\lambda(t)$, if

(i) $N(0) = 0$

(ii) $\{N(t), t \geq 0\}$ has independent increments

(iii) $\Pr\{N(t+h) - N(t) = 1\} = \lambda(t)h + o(h)$

(iv) $\Pr\{N(t+h) - N(t) \geq 2\} = o(h)$

for small $h (> 0)$, where $o(h)$ is the higher order term of h. From the above definition, the probability mass function (p.m.f.) of the NHPP is given by

$$\Pr\{N(t) = k\} = \frac{\Lambda(t)^k}{k!} e^{-\Lambda(t)}, \tag{1}$$

where $E[N(t)] = \Lambda(t)$ is called the mean value function with $\lambda(t) = d\Lambda(t)/dt$. Also it is easy to show that $E[N(t)] = \text{Var}[N(t)]$, where this statistical property is called *equity dispersion*.

Suppose that the intensity function is given by

$$\lambda(t) = \frac{d}{dt} \Lambda(t) = b(a - \Lambda(t)), \tag{2}$$

where $a\,(>0)$ and $b\,(>0)$ denote the expected initial number of software faults before testing and the fault detection rate per unit time, respectively, *i.e.*, the differential equation in Eq. (2) implies that the number of software faults detected per unit time is proportional to the product of the fault detection rate b and the number of remaining faults in software at time t. Then, the corresponding NHPP with the mean value function

$$\Lambda(t) = a(1 - e^{-bt}) \tag{3}$$

is called the GO model or simply exponential NHPP SRM. Also, if the intensity is given by

$$\lambda(t) = b(a\{1 - e^{-bt}\} - \Lambda(t)), \tag{4}$$

then we can easily obtain the following mean value function:

$$\Lambda(t) = a\{1 - (1 + bt)e^{-bt}\}. \tag{5}$$

This model is called the YOO model or delayed S-shaped NHPP SRM, and can represent a S-shaped curve on the expected cumulative number of software faults with respect to test execution time t. In this way, we often model the NHPP-based SRMs by taking account of the (deterministic or average) cumulative behavior of software faults detected in the testing phase and substituting arbitrary mean value functions into Eq. (1).

Statistical Test of Renewal Property

Suppose that n software fault detection time data $\{t_1, t_2, \cdots, t_n\}$ are observed in the testing phase. If the software fault detection process follows an NHPP with the mean value function $\Lambda(t)$, which is completely known, then it is known that the time-scale transformed data sequence $u_i = \Lambda(t_i)$, $i = 1, 2, \cdots, n$ can be regarded as a sample process from a homogeneous Poisson process (HPP) with unit intensity, $\{Y(t), t \geq 0\}$, with the mean value t and intensity 1 [29]. For this transformed data sequence $u_1, u_2, \cdots, u_n$, we can test the Poisson property with several statistical testing techniques. The simplest method is to test the renewal property of the HPP with unit intensity and to carry out the χ^2-squared goodness-of-fit test, so that the time intervals $u_1, u_2 - u_1, \cdots, u_n - u_{n-1}$ can be considered as a sample from the identical exponential distributions with unit rate. We check the renewal property of the software fault detection data, DS-1, DS-2, DS-3, DS-4, observed in real software development projects [1] (see the later section for the details). Table **1** presents the results of χ^2-squared goodness-of-fit test under the assumptions that the underlying NHPPs are described by GO model and YOO model. Although these data are often used in the goodness-of-fit test of the NHPP-based SRMs, it is known that GO model could fit DS-1 with 95% significance level and with DS-3 with both 95% and 99% significance levels. From these testing results, we cannot strongly accept the null hypothesis that the transformed data $u_i = \Lambda(t_i), i = 1, 2, \cdots, n$ are sampled from the HPP with unit intensity.

Table 1. χ^2 **goodness-of-fit test.**

(a) DS-1.

DS-1	GO	YOO
χ^2 statistics	35.771	160.171
significance level 90%	35.563	
significance level 95%	38.885	

(b) DS-2.

DS-2	GO	YOO
χ^2 statistics	223.600	1120.743
significance level 90%	94.374	
significance level 95%	99.617	

(c) DS-3.

DS-3	GO	YOO
χ^2 statistics	48.971	72.171
significance level 90%	51.805	
significance level 95%	55.758	

(d) DS-4.

DS-4	GO	YOO
χ^2 statistics	53.600	154.578
significance level 90%	27.204	
significance level 95%	30.144	

Statistical Test of Equity Dispersion

Next, we consider the equity dispersion property. As mentioned before, NHPP is characterized (but not uniquely) by the equity dispersion; $\Lambda(t) = \mathrm{E}[N(t)] = \mathrm{Var}[N(t)]$ and $t = \mathrm{E}[Y(t)] = \mathrm{Var}[Y(t)]$. In fact, the assumption of equity dispersion may be questionable from the practical points of view, because the software fault detection process is not necessarily satisfied with such a very specific condition (*e.g.*, when the expected cumulative number of software faults is given by $\Lambda(t) = 50$, its variance $\mathrm{Var}[N(t)]$ must be exactly 50). The statistical test based on the variance-time function for arbitrary point processes is developed by Cox & Smith [30]. The variance-time function $V(s)$ is defined as the variance of the number of events $Y(s)$ occurred during the time interval [0, *s*]. Divide the observation point of time t by k (> 0) segments, where $t = ks$. Further, we divide each interval s by r (> 0) segments with length τ (> 0) and make $rk - r + 1$ sub-intervals with length $s = r\tau$ as depicted in Fig. (**1**). For an arbitrary time interval s, an estimate of the variance-time function is given by

$$\hat{V}(s) = \frac{3\phi\{\sum_{i=1}^{\phi} n_i^2 - (\sum_{i=1}^{\phi} n_i)^2 / \phi\}}{3\phi^2 - 3\phi r + r^2 + 1}, \tag{6}$$

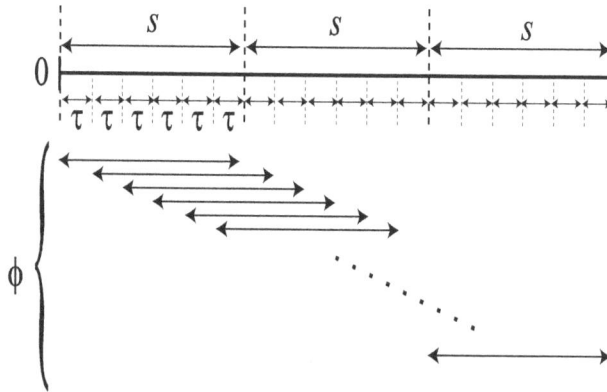

Fig. (1). Configuration of data segment.

where $\phi = rk - r + 1$, and $n_i, i = 1, 2, \cdots, rk - r + 1$ is the number of events occurred in i-th sub-interval. As a special case, if $Y(t)$ is an HPP with unit rate, then the mean and variance of an estimate $\hat{V}(s)$ are given by

$$E[\hat{V}(s)] = s, \tag{7}$$

$$Var[\hat{V}(s)] = \frac{r\tau}{3\phi}\{4r^2\tau + 3r + 2\tau\} + o(\phi^{-1}). \tag{8}$$

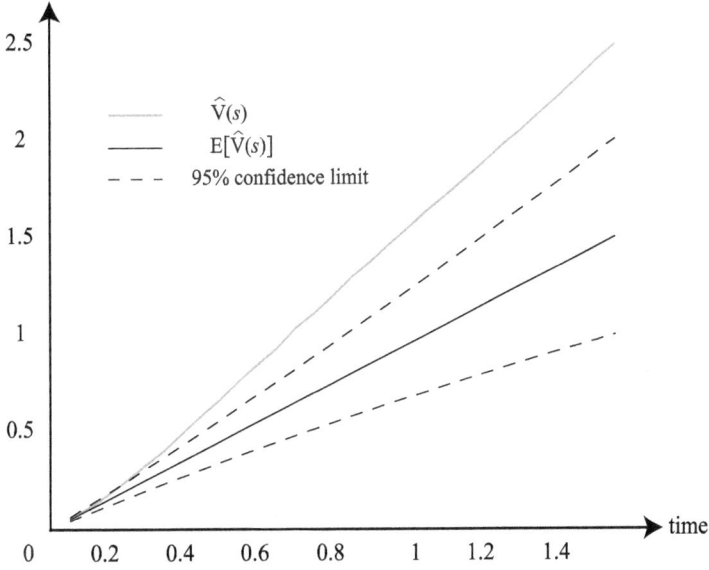

Fig. (2). Behavior of estimate of variance on GO model with DS-4.

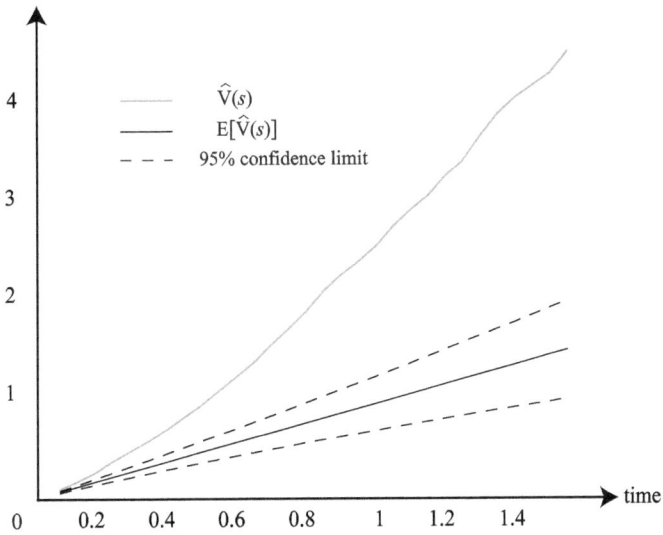

Fig. (3). Behavior of estimate of variance on YOO model with DS-4.

From this result, the 95% confidence intervals of the estimate $\hat{V}(s)$ can be approximately given by $E[\hat{V}(s)] \pm 1.96\sqrt{\mathrm{Var}[\hat{V}(s)]}$. Hence if the estimate $\hat{V}(s)$ is included in the confidence region;

$$\left[E[\hat{V}(s)] - 1.96\sqrt{\mathrm{Var}[\hat{V}(s)]},\ E[\hat{V}(s)] + 1.96\sqrt{\mathrm{Var}[\hat{V}(s)]}\right],$$

then it can be judged that the variance of $Y(s)$ is equal to the mean value s. Figs. (**2** and **3**) show the behavior of estimates of variance in GO model and YOO model with DS-4, respectively, where the dot line denotes the 95% confidence interval of the variance and $\tau = 0.05$ is fixed. If the underlying data are sampled from NHPPs with the mean value functions in Eqs. (3) and (5), the estimate $\hat{V}(s)$ will be included in the confidence region with higher probability. However, in these figures, it is observed that the sample variance is rather different from the sample mean, even when the segment interval s becomes smaller. For the other data sets, we observe the similar tendency except in DS-3 with GO model, so that the estimates of variance-time function are not included in the confidence region. From these observations, we find that the null hypothesis that the variance is equal to the mean value function may not be accepted positively in some cases, and that the NHPP assumption is still questionable in the above examples.

As the other statistical test methods of Poisson processes, we can apply the conditional uniform test, Sherman statistics, Anderson-Derling statistics and so on (for more details, see Cox and Lewis [29]), though we omit to show those results for brevity. Here, we want to emphasize through a few examples conducted in our preliminary test that we never reject the NHPP-based SRM assumption, because the NHPP, itself, can be validated from the physical meaning of software debugging theory. Nevertheless, we should recognize the statistical testing results in the above examples with only two kinds of SRMs, and consider the case where the real software fault count data may not be always described by NHPPs. In other words, the experimental results introduced here motivate us to examine the other kind of stochastic processes for describing software fault detection process.

GAUSSIAN PROCESS MODELING

Existing Gaussian SRMs in Continuous-State Space

When it is not validated that the software fault-detection phenomenon follows NHPPs, what is the second alternative? As a different modeling framework,

Yamada *et al.* [20] propose a continuous-state SRM from a different point of view. Given the constant (not mean) initial fault contents a_0 (>0), they first assume that the number of remaining software faults at time t in software testing, $S(t) = a_0 - N(t)$, is described by the following deterministic differential equation:

$$\frac{dS(t)}{dt} = -bS(t), \quad S(0) = a_0. \tag{9}$$

Note that the progress of software testing procedures in actual cases is influenced by various uncertain factors. If the fault-detection rate b is irregularly influenced by random factors such as the testing effort expenditures, the skill of test personnel, the testing tools, *etc.*, it may be regarded as a stochastic process. Yamada *et al.* [20] suppose that Eq. (9) is reformulated as a stochastic differential equation:

$$\frac{dS(t)}{dt} = -(b + \xi(t))S(t) \tag{10}$$

with a noise $\{\xi(t), t \geq 0\}$ that exhibits an irregular fluctuation. Yamada *et al.* [20] make its solution a Markov process and regard the noise factor as $\xi(t) = \sigma\gamma(t)$, where σ (>0) is a positive constant representing a magnitude of the irregular fluctuation and $\gamma(t)$ is a standardized Gaussian white noise. Substituting $\xi(t) = \sigma\gamma(t)$ into Eq. (10) yields the following stochastic differential equation of Ito type:

$$dS(t) = -\left\{ b - \frac{\sigma^2}{2} \right\} S(t)dt + \sigma S(t)dB(t), \tag{11}$$

where $\{B(t), t \geq 0\}$ is a one-dimensional Wiener (standard Brownian motion) process. The Wiener process is a Gaussian process and has the following properties:

(i) $\Pr\{B(0) = 0\} = 1$

(ii) $E[B(t)] = 0$

(iii) $E[B(t)B(t')] = \min(t, t')$.

By the use of well-known Ito's formula, it is straightforward to solve the stochastic differential equation in Eq. (11) with the initial condition $S(0) = a_0$ as follows.

$$S(t) = a_0 e^{-bt - \sigma B(t)}. \tag{12}$$

This stochastic process is called *the geometric Brownian motion process* or *the lognormal process*, and is often used to describe the stock price in financial engineering [31]. From the Gaussian property of $B(t)$, the transition probability distribution function of the process $S(t)$ is given by the lognormal distribution:

$$\Pr\{S(t) \le x \mid S(0) = a_0\} = \Phi\left(\frac{\log(x/a_0) + bt}{\sigma\sqrt{t}} \right), \tag{13}$$

where $\Phi(\cdot)$ denotes the standard normal cumulative distribution function (c.d.f.):

$$\Phi(x) = \frac{1}{\sqrt{2\pi}} \int_{-\infty}^{x} e^{-y^2/2} dy. \tag{14}$$

From Eq. (13), the cumulative number of software faults experienced by time t, $N(t) = a_0 - S(t)$, is intuitively obtained in the form:

$$N(t) = a_0(1 - e^{-bt + \sigma B(t)}), \quad N(0) = 0 \tag{15}$$

with

$$\Pr\{N(t) \le x \mid N(0) = 0\} = \Phi\left(\frac{\log(a_0/[a_0 - x]) - bt}{\sigma\sqrt{t}} \right), \tag{16}$$

provided that $b > \sigma^2/2$. Then, the mean and variance of $N(t)$ are easily given by

$$E[N(t)] = a_0(1 - e^{-\left(b - \frac{\sigma^2}{2}\right)t}) \to a_0, \quad (t \to \infty), \tag{17}$$

$$\text{Var}[N(t)] = a_0^2 e^{-(2b-\sigma^2)t}(e^{\sigma^2 t} - 1) \to 0, \quad (t \to \infty). \tag{18}$$

In this chapter, we call the above SRM the lognormal model. Yamada *et al.* [20] show with two software fault-detection time data that the lognormal model could provide higher log-likelihood comparing with two NHPP-based SRMs; GO model and YOO model. Unfortunately, it is pointed out that the maximum likelihood estimation in [20] is wrong, because the authors confuse the software fault-detection time data (complete data) with the grouped data (incomplete data). Also, they calculate some software reliability measures such as instantaneous MTBF (mean time between faults) and cumulative MTBF. The reader may find that the lognormal model mentioned above is developed under a quite different model assumption from NHPP-based SRMs. For instance, since the parameter a_0 in the lognormal model indicates a constant representing the initial number of software faults, it must be an integer value and the underlying stochastic process has a boundary at $N(t) = a_0$. This is also a different feature from NHPP-based SRMs, because the sample path of NHPP with mean value function in Eq. (3) or (5) is not bounded though the corresponding mean value function $\Lambda(t)$ is bounded, *i.e.*, in GO model and YOO model, the probability that $N(t)$ in Eq. (1) takes the larger value than a_0 is always positive. In other words, the lognormal model is similar at the first look, but not consistent to the existing NHPP-based SRMs.

Alternative Probabilistic Interpretation of NHPP-Based SRMs

It is evident that the lognormal model is not consistent with the NHPP-based SRMs. Here, we provide a more plausible framework for modeling continuous-state Gaussian SRMs. Formally, Let $(\Omega, \mathcal{F}, \mathcal{P})$ be a probability space, where $\{\mathcal{F}, t \geq 0\} \in \mathcal{F}$ be a non-decreasing family of σ-algebras. Let $\{N(t), t \geq 0\}$ be a semi-martingale process representing the cumulative number of software faults detected by time *t*. It is known that the semi-martingale process belongs to a more wide class than the self-exiting point processes [13] and involves SRMs developed in the past literature. Define an arbitrary non-negative function $\psi(\cdot)$ with Lipschitz continuity. Since the semi-martingale process can be decomposed by a martingale part and a non-martingale part from the Doob-Mayer decomposition theorem [31], suppose that the sample path of the cumulative number of software faults detected per unit time is described by the following stochastic differential equation:

$$dN(t) = \psi(t, N(t))dt + dM(t), \tag{19}$$

where $\{M(t), t \geq 0\}$ is a continuous-time martingale with the following properties:

(i) $\{M(t), t \geq 0\}$ is $\mathcal{F}_t$ measurable for all t

(ii) $E[|M(t)|] < \infty$ for all t

(iii) $E[M(s)|\mathcal{F}_t] = M(t)$ for all $s \geq t$.

As a special case, suppose that $M(t)$ is given by a martingale defined on the Poisson probability measure $\{P(t), t \geq 0\}$. Similar to Goel & Okumoto [6], if the number of software faults per unit time is proportional to the number of faults experienced before time t, i.e., $\psi(t, N(t)) = b(a - N(t))$ with given constants a and b, then we obtain

$$dN(t) = b(a - N(t))dt + dP(t), \quad N(0) = 0. \tag{20}$$

Solving this stochastic differential equation with the initial condition $N(0) = 0$, it is evident that $N(t)$ is an NHPP with the mean value function in Eq. (3) and is reduced to the GO model with $\lim_{t \to \infty} E[N(t)] = a$. Also, if the software fault-detection process is given by

$$dN(t) = b\{a(1 - e^{-bt}) - N(t)\}dt + dP(t), \quad N(0) = 0, \tag{21}$$

then the resulting NHPP-based SRM is reduced to the YOO model. In this way, an arbitrary stochastic counting process as well as NHPPs can be described by the stochastic differential equation [32]. In other words, the dynamics of software-fault detection process given in Eq. (19) provides a unified probabilistic interpretation for software reliability modeling in both continuous- and discrete-state spaces.

NHPP-Consistent Continuous-State SRMs

We provide a more natural derivation of continuous SRM which is consistent to one of the NHPP-based SRMs. In Eq. (20), suppose that the stochastic process $\{M(t), t \geq 0\}$ is given by a martingale on the Wiener probability measure, i.e., $M(t) = \sigma B(t)$, where $\sigma (> 0)$ is the scale parameter. Similar to the GO model, if

$\psi(t, N(t)) = b(a - N(t))$, then we obtain the stochastic differential equation of Ito type:

$$dN(t) = b(a - N(t))dt + sdB(t), \quad N(0) = 0. \tag{22}$$

This process is called *the mean-reverting Ornstein-Uhlenbeck process* or *Vasicek model*, and is quite popular to describe the term structure of interest rate process in financial engineering [33]. Since this is also a Gauss-Markov process, it can be solved with the initial condition $N(0) = 0$ as

$$N(t) = a(1 - e^{-bt}) + \sigma \int_0^t e^{-b(t-s)} dB(s). \tag{23}$$

From the explicit solution, it is straightforward to obtain

$$\Pr\{N(t) \le x \mid N(0) = 0\} = \Phi\left(\frac{x + a(1 - e^{-bt})}{\sqrt{(\sigma^2 / 2b)(1 - e^{-2bt})}}\right). \tag{24}$$

It is also easy to check that

$$\mathrm{E}[N(t)] = a(1 - e^{-bt}) \to a \quad (t \to \infty), \tag{25}$$

$$\mathrm{Var}[N(t)] = \frac{\sigma^2}{2b}(1 - e^{-2bt}) \to \frac{\sigma^2}{2b} \quad (t \to \infty), \tag{26}$$

so that the steady-state transition probability distribution is given by the normal distribution with mean a and variance $\sigma^2 / (2b)$.

Note that the stochastic process $N(t)$ described in Eq. (23) is not bounded at $N(t) = a$ and approaches to a asymptotically as the software testing time t goes to ∞. This is the most remarkable difference from the lognormal model in [20]. Also, only the difference from GO model is the kind of martingale. That is, we represent an additive fluctuation by a martingale defined in continuous-state space, but not discrete-state space. Comparing our model in Eq. (23) with the GO model, the scale parameter σ depends on the variance $\mathrm{Var}[N(t)]$. As a special case, if $\sigma = \sqrt{2ab}$, then the corresponding transition probability in the steady state is given by the normal distribution with mean a and variance a, and can be regarded approximately as the c.d.f. of the NHPP-based SRM with the equity dispersion. In a fashion similar to the exponential type of normal model, we consider an alternative continuous SRM with S-shaped curve in average. Suppose that the number of software faults detected by time t is described by the stochastic differential equation:

$$dN(t) = b\{a(1-e^{-bt}) - N(t)\}dt + \sigma dB(t). \tag{27}$$

From a few algebraic manipulations, we can derive

$$N(t) = a\{1 - (1+bt)e^{-bt}\} + \sigma \int_0^t e^{-b(t-s)} dB(s) \tag{28}$$

and find that $N(t)$ obeys the normal distribution with mean and variance;

$$\mathrm{E}[N(t)] = a\{1 - (1+bt)e^{-bt}\} \to a \quad (t \to \infty), \tag{29}$$

$$\mathrm{Var}[N(t)] = \frac{\sigma^2}{2b}(1 - e^{-2bt}) \to \frac{\sigma^2}{2b} \quad (t \to \infty), \tag{30}$$

respectively. To our best knowledge, this type of mean reverting process with S-shaped curve has not been studied yet in the past literature.

A much simpler approach for NHPP-consistent continuous SRMs would be to consider an additive process. From Doob-Mayer decomposition theorem, again, an arbitrary stochastic process is decomposed into a martingale part and a non-martingale part, so it is straightforward to consider the following stochastic processes:

$$N(t) = a(1 - e^{-bt}) + \sigma B(t), \tag{31}$$

$$N(t) = a\{1 - (1+bt)e^{-bt}\} + \sigma B(t), \tag{32}$$

where the mean value functions are given in the same forms as Eqs. (25) and (29). In general, if the scale parameter is given by the function of time, $\sigma(t)$, and the function $\psi(t, N(t)) = \mu(t)N(t) + b(t)$ with arbitrary functions $\mu(t)$ and $b(t)$ is Lipschitz continuous, then the linear stochastic differential equation

$$dN(t) = \{\mu(t)N(t) + b(t)\}dt + \sigma(t)dB(t) \tag{33}$$

has a unique solution with a Gauss-Markov property. Hence, we can derive the continuous SRM in the same modeling framework as analogies of the NHPP-based SRMs. However, since our purpose here is not develop so many continuous SRMs as a huge number of NHPP-based SRMs have been proposed for the last four decades, we omit to show here the other continuous SRMs. Even though more complex stochastic differential equation than Eqs. (22) and (27) is considered, it is not always to be able to get the transition probability distribution function explicitly. In such a case, it is difficult to estimate the model parameters by means of the maximum likelihood method, which is commonly used in software reliability engineering.

In this section, we have developed new SRMs with continuous sample path by changing the treatment of martingale. Strictly speaking, these continuous SRMs cannot describe exactly the actual software fault-detection process, since it should be represented by a non-decreasing stochastic counting process in discrete-state space.

In the remaining part of this section, we summarize the maximum likelihood estimation method for Gaussian process-based SRMs. Suppose that n observations of the form $(t_j, x_j)\ (j = 1, 2, \cdots, n)$ are available, where $0 < t_1 < t_2 < \cdots < t_n$ denote the observation point of time and $\{x_1, x_2, \cdots, x_n\}$ are the cumulative number of software faults detected in the time interval $(0, t_j]$. Let

$$P(t_1, x_1; t_2, x_2; \cdots; t_n, x_n) = \Pr\{N(t_1) \le n_1, \cdots, N(t_n) \le x_n | N(0) = 0\} \tag{34}$$

be the joint c.d.f. of the stochastic process $N(t)$ having the joint p.d.f.:

$$p(t_1, x_1; t_2, x_2; \cdots; t_n, x_n) = \frac{\partial^n P(t_1, x_1; t_2, x_2; \cdots; t_n, x_n)}{\partial x_1 \partial x_2 \cdots \partial x_n}. \tag{35}$$

Define the logarithmic likelihood function:

$$L(t_1, x_1; t_2, x_2; \cdots; t_n, x_n) = \log p(t_1, x_1; t_2, x_2; \cdots; t_n, x_n). \tag{36}$$

The maximum likelihood estimators $\hat{a}$, $\hat{b}$ and $\hat{\sigma}$ in continuous SRMs are defined by the values which maximize the logarithmic likelihood function. Then the first order conditions of optimality are given by

$$\partial L(t_1,x_1;t_2,x_2;\cdots;t_n,x_n)/\partial a = 0, \tag{37}$$

$$\partial L(t_1,x_1;t_2,x_2;\cdots;t_n,x_n)/\partial b = 0, \tag{38}$$

$$\partial L(t_1,x_1;t_2,x_2;\cdots;t_n,x_n)/\partial \sigma = 0. \tag{39}$$

By the use of the Bayes' formula, the logarithmic likelihood function is transformed to

$$L(t_1,x_1;t_2,x_2;\cdots;t_n,x_n) = p(t_2,x_2;\cdots;t_n,x_n|\,t_1,x_1)p(t_1,x_1|0,0), \tag{40}$$

where $p(t_1,x_1|0,0)$ is the conditional p.d.f. under the condition of $N(0)=0$. From the Markov property of the continuous SRMs, we can represent

$$L(t_1,x_1;t_2,x_2;\cdots;t_n,x_n) = \Pi_{j=1}^{n} p(t_j,x_j|\,t_{j-1},x_{j-1}). \tag{41}$$

Even if the transition probability distribution function is given, it is not so easy to solve the simultaneous logarithmic likelihood equations analytically. Thus, we numerically solve the simultaneous equations with real software fault-count data.

GAMMA WEAR PROCESS MODELING

Definition

Let $\{N(t),t \geq 0\}$ denote the cumulative number of software faults detected in software testing and be a non-decreasing stochastic process. Define the right-continuous and nondecreasing function $v(t)$ $(t \geq 0)$ with $v(0)=0$. We call $v(t)$ *the shape function* in this chapter. Let $\mathrm{Gam}(x|\,v,u)$ be the gamma p.d.f. with shape parameter $v\,(>0)$ and scale parameter $u\,(>0)$:

$$\mathrm{Gam}(x|v,u) = \frac{u^v}{\Gamma(v)} x^{v-1} e^{-ux} I_{(0,\infty)}(x), \tag{42}$$

where

$$\Gamma(v) = \int_0^\infty t^{v-1} e^{-t} dt \tag{43}$$

and

$$I_A(x) = \begin{cases} 1 & x \in A \\ 0 & x \notin A \end{cases} \tag{44}$$

for a probabilistic event A. The homogeneous gamma process $N(t;v,u)$ with shape parameter v and scale parameter u is an absolutely continuous-time stochastic process with stationary, independent gamma increments such that for any t, say, $N(t+\tau;v,u) - N(t;v,u) \sim \text{Gam}(x| v(t+\tau) - vt, u)$, where $N(0) = 0$ with probability one.

Next we consider a nonhomogeneous case, *i.e.*, the gamma process has the shape function of time. Then, $N(t;v(t),u)$ is said to be the nonhomogeneous gamma wear process (NHGWP) with independent but not stationary increments $\text{Gam}(x| v(t+\tau) - v(t), u)$. Since the c.d.f. of $N(t)$ is given by $\text{Gam}(x| v(t), u)$, the mean and variance are calculated by $E[N(t)] = v(t)/u$ and $\text{Var}[N(t)] = v(t)/u^2$, respectively. In general, the parameter u affects the dispersion property; over-dispersion $(E[N(t)] < \text{Var}[N(t)])$ or under-dispersion $(E[N(t)] > \text{Var}[N(t)])$. When $u = 1$, not only the mean value function of $N(t)$ but also the variance are exactly same as the shape function $v(t)$, so that the first two moments of $N(t)$ are equivalent to those of an NHPP with the same mean value function as $v(t)$. If $v(t) = 1$ for all $t \geq 0$, then $N(t)$ becomes a homogeneous Poisson process (HPP) with rate u. From the above discussion, the NHGWP is absolutely continuous but is nondecreasing in time with $N(0) = 0$. Since the cumulative number of software faults detected in software testing has a time-dependent nature with a saturation level, it can be approximately modeled by the NHGWP with bounded shape function $v(t) < \infty$ for all $t \geq 0$.

NHGWP-based SRMs

By substituting arbitrary functions into $v(t)$, it seems to be possible to represent many kinds of NHGWP-based SRMs. However, we do not take such stupid approaches viewed in the long history on SRM modeling during the last four decades. Instead, it is worth noting to investigate what kind of probability law can be fitted to explore the phenomena of software debugging. Of our concern is the comparison of the underlying stochastic processes for SRMs with similar shape (or mean value) functions. Although we have tried over 10 representative shape functions in our preliminary study, we focus on only two examples in this chapter; exponential SRM (Goel & Okumoto [6]) and delayed S-Shaped SRM (Yamada *et al.* [7]). More specifically, it is assumed in respective cases that $v(t) = \Lambda(t) = a\{1 - \exp(-bt)\}$ and $v(t) = \Lambda(t) = a\{1 - (1 + bt)\exp(-bt)\}$, where $b\ (>0)$ and $a\ (>0)$ are positive constants. When the goodness-of-fit property is studied for the NHGWP-based SRMs, it should be noted that the associated likelihood functions are given by the product form of the gamma p.d.f.s since the NHGWP is absolutely continuous. In other words, the information criteria such as AIC and BIC as well as the maximum log-likelihood function cannot be used for comparison with the NHPP-based SRMs in a discrete-state space. This is because the likelihood function of the NHPP is calculated with the p.m.f. and is regarded as a probability which is always less than one (in this sense, the comparison in [21] between an NHPP-based SRM and the geometric Brownian motion seems to be meaningless). Hence, the model selection between the continuous-state SRM and the discrete-state SRM will be made based on the mean squared error (MSE), if needed.

Next, we introduce the maximum likelihood estimation for NHGWP-based SRMs, where two methods (MLE-1 and MLE-2) are considered. Suppose that n software fault count data $(t_1, x_1), \ldots, (t_n, x_n)$ are available in a testing phase, where $t_i\ (i = 1, \ldots, n)$ and x_i denote the observation time and the cumulative number of detected software faults, respectively. The first method (MLE-1) is classified into a conditional maximum likelihood estimation. Given that x_n software faults were detected at time $t = t_n$, we assume that $E[N(t_n)] = x_n$. Define $\delta_i = x_i - x_{i-1}, i = 1, 2, \cdots, n; x_0 = 0$. Under the above assumption, the likelihood function in the exponential NHGWP-based SRM is given by

$$L(a, b) = \prod_{i=1}^{n} \frac{u^{a(e^{-bt_{i-1}} - e^{-bt_i})}}{\Gamma(a(e^{-bt_{i-1}} - e^{-bt_i}))} \delta_i^{a(e^{-bt_{i-1}} - e^{-bt_i}) - 1} \exp\{-u\delta_i\} \qquad (45)$$

with $u = v(t_n)/x_n = a(1 - e^{-bt_n})/x_n$. On the other hand, in the delayed S-shaped NHGWP-based SRM, we have

$$L(a, b) = \prod_{i=1}^{n} \frac{u^{a[(1 + bt_{i-1})e^{-bt_{i-1}} - (1 + bt_i)e^{-bt_i}]}}{\Gamma(a[(1 + bt_{i-1})e^{-bt_{i-1}} - (1 + bt_i)e^{-bt_i}])}$$
$$\times \delta_i^{(a[(1 + bt_{i-1})e^{-bt_{i-1}} - (1 + bt_i)e^{-bt_i}] - 1)} \exp\{-u\delta_i\} \qquad (46)$$

with $u = v(t_n)/x_n = a(1 - [1 + bt]e^{-bt_n})/x_n$. Then the optimization problem is to find the estimates $(\hat{a}, \hat{b})$ maximizing $L(a,b)$. The advantage for MLE-1 is that the end point $E[N(t_n)] = v(t_n)/u$ always equals the observation point x_n. This is useful to estimate exactly the number of software faults detected at the end of software testing. Since MLE-1 involves a restriction on the terminal value, strictly speaking, the resulting estimates are not the maximum likelihood estimates. By dropping the terminal condition of $E[N(t_n)] = x_n$, we obtain the likelihood functions for the NHGWP-based SRMs in Eqs. (45) and (46) as the functions of (a, b, u), and call the common method based on $L(a, b, u)$ MLE-2.

NUMERICAL EXAMPLES

Data Sets

In numerical examples to examine the goodness-of-fit and predictive performances in our continuous SRMs, we use 4 real project data (DS-1~DS-4) consisting of the number of software faults detected per day (grouped data), where the number of data are $(t_{42}, x_{42}) = (42, 133)$ in DS-1, $(t_{81}, x_{81}) = (81, 224)$ in DS-2, $(t_{37}, x_{37}) = (37, 351)$ in DS-3, and $(t_{71}, x_{71}) = (71, 367)$ in DS-4 [1]. Based on MLE-1 and MLE-1 (denoted by Gamma 1 and Gamma 2), we estimate the model parameters for two NHGWP-based SRMs with different mean value functions (Exp & S-shape). As competitive continuous SRMs, we assume two geometric Brownian motions (Lognormal) [20, 23] with same mean value functions (Exp & S-shape) and our four continuous SRMs (denoted by Normal1 in Eqs. (23) and (28) and Normal2 in Eqs. (31) and (32)).

Maximum Likelihood Estimation

Tables **2** and **3** present the maximum likelihood estimates of model parameters $a\,(a_0)$, b and $u\,(\sigma)$, where the models are categorized into exponential type (Exp) and S-shape type (S-shape), respectively. We find that Lognormal tends to rather overestimate the initial fault contents much more than the other continuous SRMs. In Figs. (**4-7**), we plot the expected cumulative number of software faults estimated with respective SRMs and the underlying software fault-count data. It can be found that the exponential trend curves fit the underlying data better than the S-shaped curves, and that the NHGWP-based SRMs (Gamma1 & Gamma2) fit the underlying data well visually.

Table 2. Parameter estimation of Exp type models.

Parameter		Gamma1	Gamma2	Lognormal	Normal1	Normal2	NHPP
DS-1	a	332.217	336.393	4585.09	632.502	631.429	869.502
	b	0.002784	0.002749	0.000433	0.003691	0.003687	0.002547
	$u(\sigma)$	—	0.407762	0.000616	2.75109	2.75862	—
DS-2	a	147.903	147.928	591.244	541.598	538.641	522.379
	b	0.024841	0.024868	0.018761	0.025197	0.025409	0.025103
	$u(\sigma)$	—	0.273972	0.016487	4.76159	4.82724	—
DS-3	a	89.3802	89.8052	418.583	460.882	456.758	412.565
	b	0.053966	0.054227	0.045348	0.040518	0.041034	0.044862
	$u(\sigma)$	—	0.217128	0.037268	6.50191	6.65359	—
DS-4	a	2152.72	2619.44	963.231	1351.61	1360.47	1714.29
	b	0.001374	0.001496	0.006633	0.004395	0.004361	0.00328
	$u(\sigma)$	—	0.731729	0.003191	2.56003	2.56629	—

Kolmogorov-Smirnov Test

Next, we execute the Kolmogorov-Smirnov (K-S) test with 5% and 1% significance levels. Define the K-S statistics:

$$D = \max\{D_i\} \ (1 \le i \le n-1), \tag{47}$$

$$D_i = \max\left\{ \left| \frac{H(t_i)}{H(t_n)} - \frac{y_i}{y_n} \right|, \left| \frac{H(t_i)}{H(t_n)} - \frac{y_{i-1}}{y_n} \right| \right\}. \tag{48}$$

Table 3. Parameter estimation of S-shape type models.

Parameter		Gamma1	Gamma2	Lognormal	Normal1	Normal2	NHPP
DS-1	a	1.39756	1.39762	204.772	162.961	161.257	161.902
	b	0.051712	0.051712	0.033785	0.044082	0.042297	0.046675
	$u(\sigma)$	—	0.009115	0.022152	2.74956	2.84772	—
DS-2	a	1.00712	1.00713	533.966	413.164	410.75	466.548
	b	0.041519	0.041519	0.039967	0.074396	0.075123	0.06772
	$u(\sigma)$	—	0.001881	0.024242	5.16539	5.36376	—
DS-3	a	0.764158	0.764156	386.619	361.465	358.626	359.275
	b	0.080654	0.080654	0.092737	0.116663	0.117974	0.12688
	$u(\sigma)$	—	0.001848	0.052686	6.55796	6.96427	—
DS-4	a	0.877062	0.877074	510.439	428.555	428.202	455.667
	b	0.04353	0.043531	0.033793	0.041733	0.041776	0.041112
	$u(\sigma)$	—	0.001982	0.008459	2.7265	2.78401	—

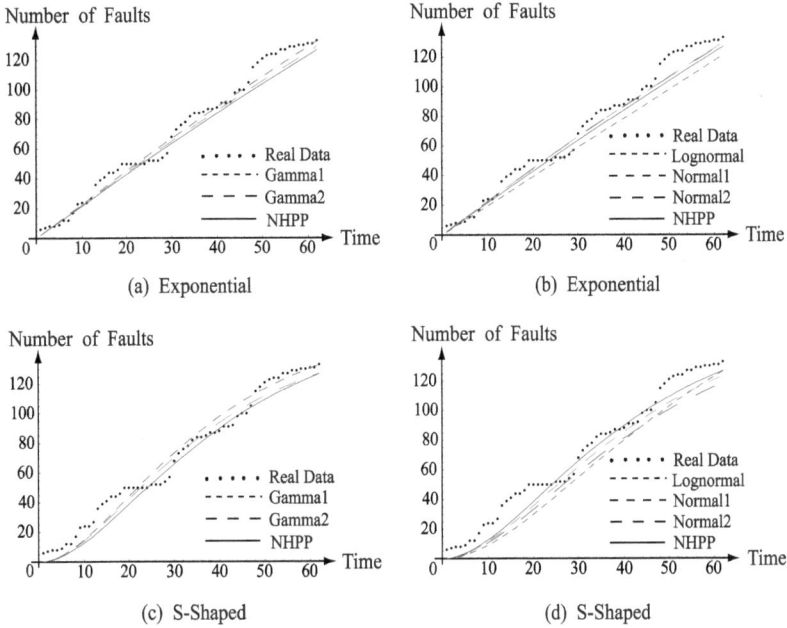

Fig. (4). Behavior of cumulative number of software faults with DS-1.

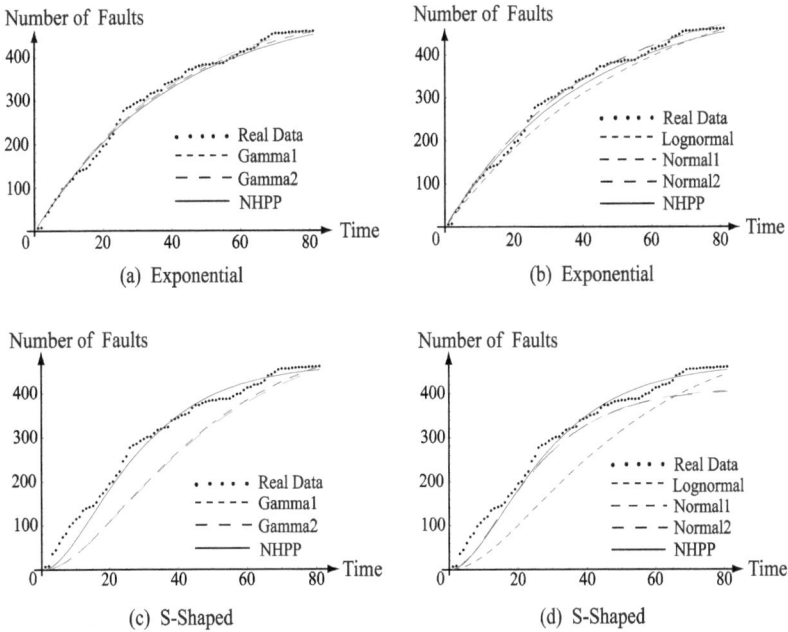

Fig. (5). Behavior of cumulative number of software faults with DS-2.

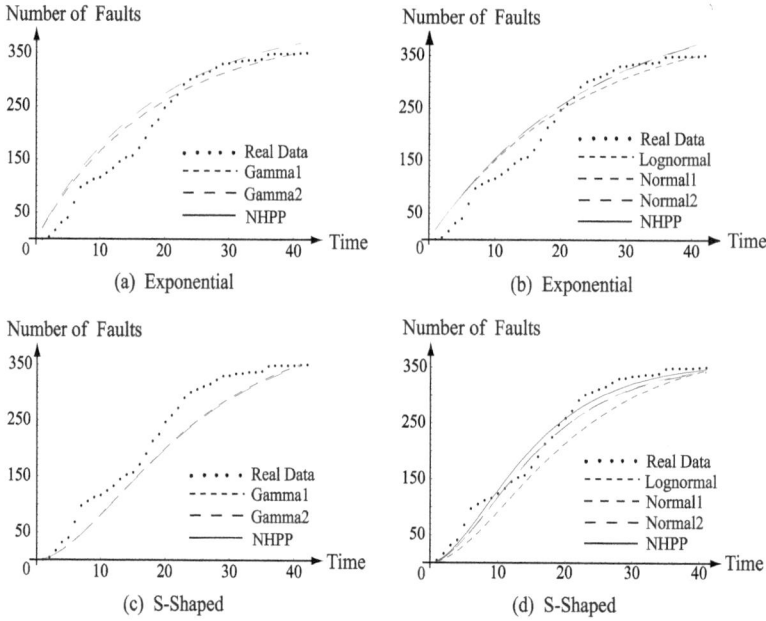

Fig. (6). Behavior of cumulative number of software faults with DS-3.

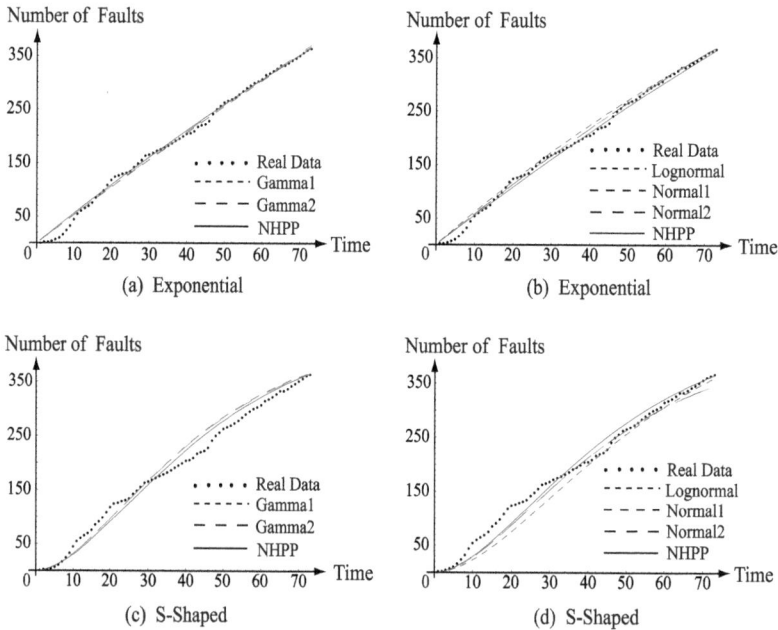

Fig. (7). Behavior of cumulative number of software faults with DS-4.

Table 4. Kolmogorov-Smirnov with DS-1.

	Model	D_{max}	Judge	$D_{0.05}$	$D_{0.01}$
			DS-1		
Exp	Gamma1	0.090103	A	0.16956	0.20343
	Gamma2	0.090259	A		
	Lognormal	0.101237	A		
	Normal1	0.090250	A		
	Normal2	0.090222	A		
S-shrap	Gamma1	0.126841	A	0.16956	0.20343
	Gamma2	0.126842	A		
	Lognormal	0.164847	A		
	Normal1	0.124763	A		
	Normal2	0.131308	A		

If D is less than the critical value with significance level α, i.e., $D < D_{n-1;\alpha}$, then the SRM assumed can fit the underlying software fault-count data. Without any loss of generality, we assume $\alpha = 0.05$ and $\alpha = 0.01$. In Tables **4-7**, we present the K-S test results, where D_{max} denotes the maximum statistics for the model, and `A' and 'R' in the tables mean the acceptance and rejection, respectively. From these results, it can be seen that three models; Gamma1, Gamma2 and Lognormal with S-shaped curves could not fit the data in DS-2 with both significance levels. Hence, it must be needed to look for the other acceptable SRMs with S-shaped curve.

Table 5. Kolmogorov-Smirnov with DS-2.

	Model	D_{max}	Judge	$D_{0.05}$	$D_{0.01}$
			DS-2		
Exp	Gamma1	0.065734	A	0.14868	0.1784
	Gamma2	0.065949	A		
	Lognormal	0.107992	A		
	Normal1	0.068543	A		
	Normal2	0.070218	A		
S-shrap	Gamma1	0.255184	R	0.14868	0.1784
	Gamma2	0.255184	R		
	Lognormal	0.266611	R		
	Normal1	0.094094	A		
	Normal2	0.095931	A		

Table 6: Kolmogorov-Smirnov with DS-3.

DS-3					
	Model	D_{max}	Judge	$D_{0.05}$	$D_{0.01}$
Exp	Gamma1	0.175798	A	0.20760	0.24904
	Gamma2	0.176932	A		
	Lognormal	0.134085	A		
	Normal1	0.152443	A		
	Normal2	0.154121	A		
S-shrap	Gamma1	0.200555	A	0.20760	0.24904
	Gamma2	0.200556	A		
	Lognormal	0.155643	A		
	Normal1	0.137708	A		
	Normal2	0.142734	A		

Model Selection

To select the best SRM fitted to the underlying data, we calculate the Akaike information criterion (AIC), Bayesian information criterion (BIC) and mean squared error (MSE) in Tables 8-10, respectively. In DS-1~DS-3, the NHGWP-based exponential SRM with MLE-1 (Gamma1) provides the best goodness-of-fit performance. On the other hand, in DS-4, the geometric Brownian motion (Lognormal) with exponential trend gives the best result in terms of AIC. We obtain the similar results on BIC as well. In order to compare the discrete SRM such as NHPP-based SRM with our continuous SRMs, we also calculate MSEs against the underlying data in Table **10**.

Table 7. Kolmogorov-Smirnov with DS-4.

DS-4					
	Model	D_{max}	Judge	$D_{0.05}$	$D_{0.01}$
Exp	Gamma1	0.073048	A	0.15649	0.18776
	Gamma2	0.073446	A		
	Lognormal	0.074592	A		
	Normal1	0.067578	A		
	Normal2	0.067475	A		
S-shrap	Gamma1	0.100708	A	0.15649	0.18776
	Gamma2	0.100711	A		
	Lognormal	0.128964	A		
	Normal1	0.088384	A		
	Normal2	0.088384	A		

Table 8. Comparison of AICs among competitive SRMs.

DS-1					
Model	Gamma1	Gamma2	Lognormal	Normal1	Normal2
Exp	200.818	202.776	204.493	217.238	217.236
S-shape	468.942	470.938	217.908	217.192	217.524

DS-2					
Model	Gamma1	Gamma2	Lognormal	Normal1	Normal2
Exp	397.552	399.530	413.164	428.914	428.810
S-shape	983.560	985.560	433.556	440.310	439.676

DS-3					
Model	Gamma1	Gamma2	Lognormal	Normal1	Normal2
Exp	227.666	229.478	236.252	245.032	245.068
S-shape	506.484	508.484	244.542	245.652	245.386

DS-4					
Model	Gamma1	Gamma2	Lognormal	Normal1	Normal2
Exp	352.392	333.062	321.120	337.638	337.668
S-shape	1007.200	1009.200	333.652	346.460	346.396

For DS-2 in which three SRMs were rejected in the K-S test, the NHPP-based SRM with S-shaped trend is best fitted, although the MSEs take rather large values comparing with the other data sets. In the comparison with MSE, Gamma 1 (Exp), Gamma2 (Exp), Normal (S-shape) and Normal2 (Exp) minimize MSEs in DS-1, DS-2, DS-3 and DS-4, respectively. From these results with real software development project data, it seems to be difficult to judge that the proposed NHGWP-based SRM is always superior to the existing SRMs. Note that the NHGWP-based SRM does not possess unrealistic properties like infinite vibrations in the geometric Brownian motion and equity dispersion of the Poisson process. It can show relatively good performance. The lesson learned from the numerical examples is that the NHGWP-based SRM should be an attractive alternative as an assessment tool in software reliability, from the viewpoints of technical tractability and goodness-of-fit performance.

Predictive Performance

The goodness-of-fit performance focuses on only the fitting ability of SRMs to the past observation experienced in software testing. Next, we concern about the prediction ability to the future with unknown fault-detection pattern. In Tables **11-14** we present the predictive log-likelihood and the predictive MSE at observation points; 25%, 50% and 75% of the whole data sets, where we estimate model parameters in each observation point, and calculate the log-likelihood and the MSE with only the remaining data, which will be observed after the observation point. When the predictive log-likelihood (mean squared error) becomes larger (smaller), the predictive performance is also greater. From these results, it can be seen that the NHGWP-based SRMs could show higher prediction performance in many cases.

Table 9. Comparison of BICs among competitive SRMs.

DS-1					
Model	Gamma1	Gamma2	Lognormal	Normal1	Normal2
Exp	205.072	209.158	210.875	223.619	223.617
S-shape	473.196	477.319	224.289	223.573	223.905
DS-2					
Model	Gamma1	Gamma2	Lognormal	Normal1	Normal2
Exp	402.341	402.319	415.953	431.703	431.599
S-shape	988.349	988.349	436.345	443.099	442.465
DS-3					
Model	Gamma1	Gamma2	Lognormal	Normal1	Normal2
Exp	231.094	234.619	241.393	250.173	250.209
S-shape	509.911	518.079	249.683	250.793	250.527
DS-4					
Model	Gamma1	Gamma2	Lognormal	Normal1	Normal2
Exp	356.973	339.933	327.991	344.509	344.539
S-shape	1011.780	1016.080	340.523	353.331	353.267

Table 10. Comparison of MSEs among competitive SRMs.

DS-1					
Model	Gamma1	Gamma2	Lognormal	Normal1	Normal2
Exp	1518.2	2970.6	9008.3	2660.9	2776.3
S-shape	3615.7	2834.4	11101.7	6658.6	10806.7
DS-2					
Model	Gamma1	Gamma2	Lognormal	Normal1	Normal2
Exp	9846.4	8229.3	47513.0	9441.6	9286.0
S-shape	338608.0	365692.0	453033.0	87550.7	90742.1
DS-3					
Model	Gamma1	Gamma2	Lognormal	Normal1	Normal2
Exp	41346.0	57401.8	19546.7	28677.5	28648.0
S-shape	50059.4	53989.4	50376.0	10058.5	10775.6
DS-4					
Model	Gamma1	Gamma2	Lognormal	Normal1	Normal2
Exp	4594.7	4458.4	7632.1	3112.1	3089.4
S-shape	23338.3	21594.1	35928.5	19842.5	19808.1

Table 11. Predictive log-likelihood with DS-1 and DS-2.

DS-1				
Shape	Model	25%	50%	75%
Exp	Gamma1	-75.957	-41.444	-16.130
	Gamma2	-77.470	-41.418	-14.920
	Lognormal	-56.251	-33.057	-19.250
	NHPP	-110.118	-117.230	-128.606
	Normal1	-81.282	-47.841	-18.968
	Normal2	-81.410	-47.837	-18.962
S-shaped	Gamma1	-287.199	-127.558	-45.210
	Gamma2	-288.520	-127.732	-45.213
	Lognormal	-592.675	-54.493	-22.279
	NHPP	-398.985	-118.440	-125.653
	Normal1	-338.528	-48.502	-18.848
	Normal2	-395.325	-48.830	-19.048

DS-2				
Shape	Model	25%	50%	75%
Exp	Gamma1	-149.653	-121.886	-60.185
	Gamma2	-153.314	-95.543	-60.948
	Lognormal	NULL	31.803	93.173
	NHPP	-293.449	-413.963	-439.464
	Normal1	-161.961	-100.013	-63.583
	Normal2	-161.750	-99.982	-60.366
S-shape	Gamma1	-532.048	-267.501	-158.567
	Gamma2	-532.396	-267.520	-158.568
	Lognormal	NULL	NULL	NULL
	NHPP	-926.687	-466.899	-463.245
	Normal1	-176.073	-103.463	-65.822
	Normal2	-175.225	-103.040	-65.493

Table 12. Predictive log-likelihood with DS-3 and DS-4.

DS-3				
Shape	Model	25%	50%	75%
Exp	Gamma1	-83.055	-86.918	-26.354
	Gamma2	-95.595	-97.741	-28.294
	Lognormal	-91.161	-58.544	-22.408
	NHPP	-228.991	-365.823	-389.026
	Normal1	-89.452	-65.342	-21.473
	Normal2	-89.326	-65.436	-21.571
S-shape	Gamma1	-249.643	-137.313	-34.790
	Gamma2	-249.944	-137.335	-34.792
	Lognormal	NULL	-71.120	-32.334
	NHPP	-1499.580	-265.492	-356.610
	Normal1	-99.782	-58.319	-19.165
	Normal2	-99.318	-58.056	-19.070

DS-4				
Shape	Model	25%	50%	75%
Exp	Gamma1	-121.892	-81.947	-36.551
	Gamma2	-123.275	-77.659	-34.976
	Lognormal	-112.835	-495.884	80.029
	NHPP	-180.157	-227.279	-304.759
	Normal1	-125.556	-78.973	-34.235
	Normal2	-127.779	-78.889	-34.363
S-shape	Gamma1	-515.892	-287.170	-128.893
	Gamma2	-516.398	-287.313	-128.904
	Lognormal	NULL	NULL	-30.623
	NHPP	-197.430	-342.623	-310.035
	Normal1	-143.360	-121.856	-38.865
	Normal2	-143.035	-121.595	-38.841

Table 13. Predictive MSEs with DS-1 and DS-2.

DS-1				
Shape	Model	25%	50%	75%
Exp	Gamma1	22763.8	570.0	966.3
	Gamma2	10698.2	586.7	762.5
	Lognormal	11140.1	582.8	890.5
	NHPP	5399.2	618.4	744.7
	Normal1	9517.6	638.5	1498.7
	Normal2	10019.3	666.4	1498.7
S-shape	Gamma1	114197.0	19147.5	189.8
	Gamma2	118609.0	20118.8	231.6
	Lognormal	2538970.0	20598.5	4061.5
	NHPP	2315000.0	3765.9	286.5
	Normal1	1520640.0	6230.6	1175.6
	Normal2	1746750.0	9406.2	1345.3

DS-2				
Shape	Model	25%	50%	75%
Exp	Gamma1	168198.0	166051.0	13942.8
	Gamma2	183025.0	107217.0	15017.7
	Lognormal	747395.0	65792.8	3766.1
	NHPP	58261.8	72067.1	6423.6
	Normal1	663372.0	28164.9	4640.8
	Normal2	663385.0	28164.8	4554.6
S-shape	Gamma1	1862800.0	81407.7	4908.0
	Gamma2	1882480.0	84806.7	5261.8
	Lognormal	1466430.0	57314.4	5464.3
	NHPP	1980030.0	137214.0	32109.4
	Normal1	2276450.0	123647.0	33271.1
	Normal2	2276490.0	123647.0	33422.6

Table 14. Predictive MSEs with DS-3 and DS-4.

DS-3				
Shape	Model	25%	50%	75%
Exp	Gamma1	318232.0	2719650.0	11546.5
	Gamma2	317031.0	112194.0	12558.1
	Lognormal	198349.0	197494.0	8715.4
	NHPP	20488.1	131927.0	17083.7
	Normal1	215321.0	83403.8	14522.0
	Normal2	215338.0	83419.6	14521.6
S-shape	Gamma1	586228.0	79762.6	4166.4
	Gamma2	590987.0	79953.5	4091.5
	Lognormal	809864.0	6458.4	1304.8
	NHPP	20172300.0	24075.8	1760.6
	Normal1	634971.0	55096.3	2458.1
	Normal2	634992.0	57202.3	2458.1

DS-4				
Shape	Model	25%	50%	75%
Exp	Gamma1	155045.0	3667.1	3197.3
	Gamma2	196090.0	3012.7	3123.9
	Lognormal	133464.0	70484.1	1842.2
	NHPP	117621.0	1682.7	2671.4
	Normal1	113051.0	9701.1	535.7
	Normal2	143866.0	9039.0	606.6
S-shape	Gamma1	755999.0	181729.0	7803.5
	Gamma2	757011.0	182753.0	7889.8
	Lognormal	49369.7	165644.0	158.9
	NHPP	114856.0	165204.0	3871.6
	Normal1	41535.5	207411.0	9231.6
	Normal2	41416.9	206689.0	9234.1

CONCLUSIONS

In this chapter we have summarized the well-known NHPP-based SRMs and the Gaussian process-based SRMs in continuous-state space, reported in the literature, and proposed a novel modeling framework of NHPP-consistent continuous SRMs and the NHGWP-based SRMs as alternatives. After showing examples that the underlying software fault-count data do not follow the Poisson law, we have performed the goodness-of-fit test and the predictive performance test with four actual software fault data, and compared our proposed SRMs with the existing ones. It is worth mentioning that the past works on continuous SRMs did not conduct a fair comparison of two different models in continuous-state space and discrete-state space. Hence, our results suggest an applicability of continuous SRMs in actual software reliability assessment. In the future, we plan to repot a more comprehensive empirical work with a number of actual software project data and to examine the other types of models except Exp and S-shape.

CONSENT FOR PUBLICATION

Not applicable.

CONFLICT OF INTEREST

The authors declares no conflict of interest, financial or otherwise.

ACKNOWLEDGEMENTS

This article is based on our conference papers presented at 2004 Asian International Workshop on Advanced Reliability Modeling (AIWARM-2004) [34] and The 2011 International Conference on Quality, Reliability, Maintenance and Safety Engineering (ICQR2MSE-2011) [35], in addition to some new materials. The authors thank the editor, Professor Mangey Ram, Graphic Era University, India, for his kind invitation to submit our article.

REFERENCES

[1]   M.R. Lyu, Ed., *Handbook of software reliability engineering.*. McGraw-Hill: New York, 1996.
[2]   J.D. Musa, *Software reliability engineering.*. McGraw-Hill: New York, 1999.
[3]   J.D. Musa, A. Iannino, and K. Okumoto, *Software reliability: Measurement, prediction, application.*. McGraw-Hill: New York, 1987.
[4]   N.D. Singpurwalla, and S.P. Wilson, *Statistical methods in software engineering.*. Springer-Verlag: New York, 1999.
[5]   M. Xie, *Software reliability modelling.*. World Scientific: Singapore, 1991.

[6]   A.L. Goel, and K. Okumoto, "Time-dependent error-detection rate model for software reliability and other performance measures", *IEEE Trans. Reliab.,* vol. R-28, no. 3, pp. 206-211.

[7]   S. Yamada, M. Ohba, and S. Osaki, "S-shaped reliability growth modeling for software error detection", *IEEE Trans. Reliab.,* vol. R-32, no. 5, pp. 475-484.

[8]   K. Okumoto, "A statistical method for software quality control", *IEEE Trans. Softw. Eng.,* vol. SE-11, pp. 1424-1430.

[9]   N. Langberg, and N.D. Singpurwalla, "A unification of some software reliability models", *SIAM J. Sci. Comput.,* vol. 6, no. 3, pp. 781-790.

[10]   Z. Jelinski, and P.B. Moranda, Software reliability research.*Statistical computer performance evaluation..* Academic Press: New York, 1972, pp. 465-484.

[11]   J.G. Shanthikumar, "A general software reliability model for performance prediction", *Microelectron. Reliab.,* vol. 21, no. 5, pp. 671-682.

[12]   D.R. Miller, "Exponential order statistic models of software reliability growth", *IEEE Trans. Softw. Eng.,* vol. SE-12, no. 1, pp. 12-24.

[13]   Y. Chen, and N.D. Singpurwalla, "Unification of software reliability models by self-exciting point processes", *Adv. Appl. Probab.,* vol. 29, pp. 337-352.

[14]   T. Ishii, and T. Dohi, *A new paradigm for software reliability modeling -- from NHPP to NHGP.* In: Proc 14th Pacific Rim Int'l Sympo Dependable Computing (PRDC-2008), 2008, pp. 224-231.

[15]   Y. Saito, and T. Dohi, "Robustness of non-homogeneous gamma process-based software reliability models", *Proc 2015 IEEE Int'l Conf Software Quality, Reliability and Security (QRS-2015),* 2015pp. 75-84

[16]   G. Koch, and P.J.C. Spreij, "Software reliability as an application of martingale & filtering theory", *IEEE Trans. Reliab.,* vol. R-32, no. 4, pp. 342-345.

[17]   P. Yip, "Estimating the number of errors in a system using a martingale approach", *IEEE Trans. Reliab.,* vol. 44, no. 2, pp. 322-326.

[18]   Y. Tamura, and S. Yamada, "A flexible stochastic differential equation model in distributed development environment", *Eur. J. Oper. Res.,* vol. 175, pp. 435-445.

[19]   Y. Tamura, and S. Yamada, "Optimisation analysis for reliability assessment based on stochastic differential equation modelling for open source software", *Int. J. Syst. Sci.,* vol. 40, no. 4, pp. 429-438.

[20]   S Yamada, M Kimura, H Tanaka, and S Osaki, "Software reliability measurement and assessment with stochastic differential equations", *IEICE Trans Fundamentals (A),* no. 1, pp. 109-116. (E77-A)

[21]   S. Yamada, A. Nishigaki, and M. Kimura, "A stochastic differential equation model for software reliability assessment and its goodness-of-fit", *Int'l J Reliability and Applications,* vol. 4, no. 1, pp. 1-11.

[22]   S. Yamada, and Y. Tamura, *OSS reliability measurement and assessment..* Springer: London, 2016.

[23]   C.H. Lee, Y.T. Kim, and D.H. Park, "S-shaped software reliability growth models derived from stochastic differential equations", *IIE Trans.,* vol. 36, no. 12, pp. 1193-1199.

[24]   H. Akaike, Information theory and an extension of the maximum likelihood principle.*Proc 2nd Int'l Sympo Inf Theory..* Akademiai Kiado: Budapest, 1973, pp. 267-281.

[25]   H. Akaike, "A new look at the statistical model identification", *IEEE Trans. Automat. Contr.,* vol. AC-19, pp. 716-723.

[26]   M. Abdel-Hameed, "A gamma wear process", *IEEE Trans. Reliab.,* vol. 24, no. 2, pp. 152-153.

[27]   F. Dufresne, H.U. Gerber, and E.S.W. Shiu, "Risk theory with the gamma process", *ASTIN Bull.,* vol. 21, pp. 177-192.

[28]   G. Schwarz, "Estimating the dimension of a model", *Ann. Stat.,* vol. 6, no. 2, pp. 461-464.

[29]   D.R. Cox, and P.A. Lewis, *Statistical analysis of series of events..* Methuen: London, 1966.

[30]   D.R. Cox, and W.L. Smith, "The superposition of several strictly periodic sequences of events", *Biometrika,* vol. 40, pp. 1-11.

[31]   B. Øksendal, *Stochastic differential equations.,* 3rd ed Springer-Verlag: Berlin, 1992.

[32]   M. Grigoriu, "The Ito and Stratonovich integrals for stochastic differential equations with Poisson white noise", *Probab. Eng. Mech.,* vol. 13, no. 3, pp. 175-182.

[33]   Q.A. Vasicek, "An equilibrium characterization of the term structure", *J. Financ. Econ.,* vol. 5, pp. 177-188.

[34]   T. Ando, and T. Dohi, "How can we estimate software reliability with a continuous-state software reliability model?", T Dohi, and WY Yun, Eds., *Proc 2004 Asian Int'l Workshop on Advanced Reliability Modeling (AIWARM-2004), ,* 2004pp. 17-24

[35]   L.Z. Jin, T. Dohi, and S. Osaki, *Continuous software reliability models – how good are they?,* 2011pp. 418-423 *In: Proc. 2011 Int'l Conf on Quality, Reliability, Maintenance and Safety Engineering (ICQR2MSE-2011),* 2011.

CHAPTER 2

Development of Software Reliability Growth Models with Time Lag and Change-Point and a New Perspective for Release Time Problem

Avinash K. Shrivastava[1,*] and **Parmod K. Kapur**[2]

[1]*Fortune Institute of International Business, New Delhi, India*
[2]*Amity Centre for Interdisciplinary Research, Amity University, Noida U.P., India*

Abstract: Over the past three decades, many software reliability growth models (SRGMs) have been proposed and used to predict and estimate software reliability. One common assumption of these conventional SRGMs is to assume that detected faults will be removed immediately. In reality, this assumption may not be reasonable and may not always occur. During debugging, developers need time to reproduce the failure, identify the root causes of faults, fix them, and then re-run the software. In this chapter, we proposed a fault dependency model considering the fault removal phenomenon as a three-stage process of removing leading, dependent and additional faults in software. Leading faults are those which can be removed upon failure, but dependent faults are masked by leading faults and can only be removed after the corresponding leading faults have been removed. Additional faults are those which are removed during the removal process of dependent fault. These additional faults can't be removed directly as they are not identified for causing failure. During the removal process of dependent faults testing team detect and remove them from the code.

Also during testing, the fault correction rate may not be constant due to change in the testing strategies; experience and skills as time proceeds. The change in detection/correction rate is known as change-point. We have incorporated the concept of change-point to model a new lag function based SRGM. Further in the existing software reliability literature the cost of model framework focuses on the detection or correction process only to calculate the release time and reliability of the software and ignoring the impact of either detection or correction process. As both detection and correction have significant impact on release and reliability prediction hence either of them cannot be neglected. In this chapter we provide a new perspective to the release time problem incorporating both detection and correction costs. Validation of the above models is done on real life software failure data sets of Tandem Computers and a numerical example is also given to illustrate the significance of new release policy.

* Corresponding author Avinash K. Shrivastava: Fortune Institute of International Business, New Delhi, India; Tel: 09891915372; E-mail: kavinash1987@gmail.com

Keywords: Change-point, Correction, Cost, Detection, Lag, Non Homogeneous Poisson Process (NHPP) Modelling, Optimization, Release time, Software reliability.

INTRODUCTION

Software testing is the process of exercising a program with the specific intent of finding faults prior to delivery to the users. Generally, fault correction is not performed immediately once a failure is detected. For each fault detected, it is reported, diagnosed, verified, and then corrected. The time between detection and correction should not be neglected. The time to remove a detected fault depends on the complexity of the fault, the skill and experience of the debugging team, the available manpower, the software development environment, and so on.

The idea of modeling fault correction processes was first proposed by Schneidewind [1]. He described the testing process as a two-stage process in which all detected faults are corrected after a constant delay of time. Later Yamada *et al.* [2] developed a Software Reliability Growth Model (SRGM) assuming fault detection and correction as two stage process. Xie and Zhao [3] extended the Schneidewind [1] model to a continuous version by substituting a time dependent delay function for the constant delay arguing that detected faults become harder to correct while testing is in progress. Following this direction researchers emphasized on the importance of the fault correction modeling and proposed faults correction models under different assumptions [4, 5].

Schneidewind assumed that the time delay is a random variable following an exponential distribution [6]. A general framework for modeling fault detection and correction processes in software reliability analysis was proposed by Lo and Huang [7] where some existing NHPP models were re-evaluated from the viewpoint of correction process. Further Xie *et al.* [8] emphasized on fault correction process described by delayed detection process with a random or deterministic delay. Kapur *et al.*[9] derived a SRGM by integration of failure observation, fault detection/isolation and fault correction/removal processes and shown a delay between the above three processes. As a result, combined fault detection and correction modelling could present more practical models for software testing process. Conventional strategy & methods of software testing allow programmers to use their knowledge to remove faults more effectively. Failure data can be recorded systematically during testing. If the software failure data set is available, programmers can use it to estimate, and predict software reliability. There are many software data set published in the literature [10-12]. In general, failure data are usually collected in two ways: Failure Count Data and Time-Between- Failure. But sometimes it is not easy to understand the possible fault dependency in software from data sets exclusively. Ohba [13] proposed an inflection S-shaped model to describe the software failure occurrence phenomenon with mutual dependency of faults. He visualized that an exponential SRGM was sometimes insufficient and inaccurate to analyse actual software failure data for reliability assessment. In fact Ohba categorizes the faults as independent and dependent faults. Kapur and Garg [14] assumed that more faults could be removed during the checking of code for identification of cause of a failure. Thus, it is a fact that different categories of faults exist in software. Kapur and Younes [15] has developed fault dependency model as a two-stage process by considering leading and dependent faults in software: Leading faults are those which can be removed upon failure, but dependent faults are masked by leading faults and can only be removed after the corresponding leading faults have been removed. Here, it has been assumed that detected dependent fault may not be immediately removed, and it lags the fault detection process by a debugging time lag. Kapur *et al.* [16] incorporated time dependent lag function into the second stage *i.e.* during modelling of dependent fault detection process. Lately, Huang and Lin [17] proposed several SRGMs that incorporate different debugging lag functions during modelling of dependent and leading fault detection process. But, software reliability growth models developed by incorporating fault dependency and various debugging time lag functions are not flexible in nature due to the fact that the various debugging time lags assumed give rise to S-shaped curve for a leading fault detection process and hence the total fault removal phenomenon is S-shaped in nature. Kapur *et al.* [18] relaxed this assumption by taking zero debugging time lag zero for independent faults, so that the total fault removal phenomenon can be given by a more flexible model. Depending upon the values of the parameters the proposed models reduce to either exponential or S-shaped or a mix of the two models. To ascertain better goodness of fit, they used power function of testing time, which incorporates fault dependency with various debugging time lag functions. Kapur *et al.* [19] assumed that the time delay between the fault detection & correction process is not negligible in case of independent faults and therefore considered debugging time lag for both types of faults. Shu *et al.* [20] proposed a fault correction model based on gamma correction lag. Jia *et al.* [21] make an in-depth analysis of real-life software testing process and proposed a Markovian SRGM considering fault correction process. Kapur *et al.* [22] developed a hazard rate based generalised framework for fault detection and correction under imperfect debugging and error generation. Peng *et al.* [23] proposed testing dependent software reliability model for imperfect debugging process considering both detection and correction. Singh *et al.* [24] proposed a two stage fault detection an d correction model for multi upgradations of software under imperfect and error generation. Kapur *et al.* [25] extended the work of Singh *et al.* [24] and proposed effort based two stage fault detection correction modelling for multi release of software. Liu *et al.* [26] developed a SRGM in which they relaxed the assumption of fault correction time from constant delay to random delay in modelling software correction processes. In all the above studies researchers assumed that faults are removed in two stage *i.e.* detection and correction. During the fault removal process testing team also removes the faults which were not discovered earlier but found during removal of detected faults termed as additional faults. We have incorporated these additional number of faults in our modelling framework. Further in the existing software reliability literature [10-12] various release time problems are defined to determine the optimal release time of the software. The simplest release time policy was suggested by Okumoto and Goel [27]. They worked on their exponential SRGM in two ways in which they considered an unconstrained cost objective in the first method and an unconstrained reliability objective for second one. Yamada and Osaki [28] examined based release time problems with cost minimization and reliability maximization objective. Kapur and Garg [29] introduced the concept of penalty cost in modelling release time problem of software. Dohi *et al.* [30] and proposed optimal software release policies with debugging time lag. Pham and Zhang [31] incorporated warranty and risk cost to the traditional cost function. Singh *et al.* [32] developed a release time problem with multiple constraints. A good survey of software release time problem is given in Kapur *et al.* [11]. But all these studies assume either detection or correction to model the cost functions. In the current work we have proposed a new cost model which considers both detection and correction of faults to determine the total cost incurred during the software lifecycle. In the next section, we propose a new SRGM considering the removal of some more bugs during the fault removal process which we term as additional number of faults. In section 2 fault detection and correction process have been discussed and it is seen how different software reliability growth models can be reinterpreted as the delayed fault detection models. Section 3 deals with notations and assumptions used for model development. In section 4 we proposed a new SRGM using fault dependency. Further in section 5 we developed a new SRGM using fault dependency and change-point. Section 6 contains the numerical illustration for the proposed model. In section 7 we propose a new cost model based on fault detection and correction and illustrate an example to show the validity of the proposed cost model. Finally section 8 provides the conclusion of the chapter.

Modeling of Fault Detection and Correction Processes

Most software reliability models have assumed that each time a failure occurs; the fault that caused it is immediately and perfectly removed. But from practical point of view, this assumption may not be suitable in an actual software development environment and detected fault is not immediately removed but it lags the fault detection process by a delay factor $\phi(t)$ The delay effect factor $\phi(t)$ *i.e.* debugging time lag function assumed to be a time –dependent function that measures the expected delay in correcting a detected fault at any time. Some existing SRGM can be reinterpreted as the delayed fault detection model. Let $m_f(t) = a(1 - \exp(-bt))$ be the mean value function of the expected number of faults detected in time [0, t] then from modified assumption the mean value function of removal process is given by

$$m_r(t) = m_f(t - \phi(t)) \tag{1}$$

$$m_r(t) = a\left(1 - \exp\left(-b\left(t - \phi(t)\right)\right)\right) \tag{2}$$

In the following subsections, some existing software reliability growth models have been reinterpreted as delayed fault detection model.

Goel –Okumoto Model [27]

This model, first proposed by Goel& Okumoto, is one of the most popular NHPP models in the field of software reliability engineering. If $\phi(t) = 0$ in equation (2), we have

$$m_r(t) = a(1 - \exp(-bt)) \tag{3}$$

Yamada Delayed S-shaped Model [2]

This model is a modification of the NHPP to obtain an S-shaped curve for cumulative number of faults detected such that the failure rate initially increases, and later decays. The software fault detection process described by such an S-shaped curve can be regarded as a learning process because the tester's skills gradually improve as the time progresses. If $\phi(t) = \left[\frac{1}{b} \log(1+bt) \right]$ in equation (2), we have

$$m_r(t) = a\left(1 - (1+bt)\exp(-bt)\right) \qquad (4)$$

Kapur-Garg Error Removal Model [14]

This model was proposed by Kapur & Garg, and its underlying concept is that there are two types of faults *i.e.* leading and dependent and dependent faults can be removed only after removing the leading faults.

$\phi(t) = \left[\frac{1}{b} \log\left(\frac{(1+\beta)\exp(-bt)}{1+\beta\exp(-bt)} \right) \right]$ in equation (2), we have

$$m_r(t) = a\left(\frac{1-\exp(-bt)}{1+\beta\exp(-bt)} \right) \qquad (5)$$

K-3 Stage-Model [16]

In this model, it has been assumed that the software testing and debugging consists of three different processes- failure observation, fault isolation and fault removal. The time lag between the failure observation and fault isolation / removal represents the severity of the fault. Harder the fault, longer is the time

lag. If $\phi(t) = \left[\frac{1}{b} \log\left(1+bt+\frac{b^2t^2}{2} \right) \right]$ in equation (2), we have

$$m_r(t) = a\left[1 - \left(1+bt+\frac{b^2t^2}{2} \right)\exp(-bt) \right] \qquad (6)$$

MODEL DEVELOPMENT

In this section, the notations and assumptions of the proposed software reliability growth models using fault dependency and various debugging time lag functions are given.

Notations

$m(t)$	mean value function of the expected number of detected/removed faults in the time interval $[0,t]$
$m_f(t)$	mean value function of the expected number of observed/detected faults in the time interval $[0,t]$
$m_r(t)$	mean value function of the expected number of removed faults in the time interval $[0,t]$
$m_1(t)$	mean value function of the expected number of leading faults
$m_2(t)$	mean value function of the expected number of dependent faults
$m_3(t)$	mean value function of the expected number of extra faults removed
a	constants, representing initial fault content, power of time
a_1	total number of leading faults
a_2	total number of dependent faults
a_3	total number of extra faults
b_1, b'_1	fault detection rate of leading faults before and after change point
b_2, b'_2	faults detection rate of dependent faults before and after change-point
b_3	faults detection rate of additional faults
p_1, p_3	proportion of leading faults before and after change point
p_2, p_4	proportion of dependent faults before and after change point
p'_2	proportion of additional faults
$\phi(t)$	delay effect factor/debugging time lag function

Basic Assumptions

The fault dependency models using debugging time lag function are based upon the following assumptions.

1. Software is subject to failures at random times caused by errors remaining in the software.
2. The fault removal process follows an NHPP.
3. Identified faults are removed perfectly. No additional faults are introduced during removal process.

4.   All detected faults can be categorized as leading faults, dependent faults and additional faults removed during debugging process. The total number of faults is finite.

5.   The mean number of leading faults detected in the time interval $[t, t+\Delta t]$ is proportional to the mean number of remaining leading faults in the system.

6.   The mean number of dependent faults detected in the time interval $[t, t+\Delta t]$ is proportional to the mean number of remaining dependent faults in the system and to the ratio of leading faults removed at time t to the total number of leading faults.

7.   The detected dependent faults may not be immediately removed, and it lags the fault detection process by a delay effect factor/debugging time lag $\phi(t)$.

   (That is $\phi(t)$ is the time delay between the removal of leading fault and dependent fault).

PROPOSED SOFTWARE RELIABILITY GROWTH MODELING USING FAULT DEPENDENCY

In this section, an attempt has been made to develop software reliability growth models incorporating dependency of the errors and various debugging time lag functions.

From assumption (6) we have the following equation

$$a = a_1 + a_2 + a_3 \text{ where } a_1 = ap_1, a_2 = ap_2 \text{ and } a_3 = ap'_2; p_1 + p_2 + p'_2 = 1 \qquad (7)$$

Where a_1, a_2 and a_3 are the number of leading, dependent and additional faults respectively.

The proposed model is the mean value function of a NHPP. *i.e.* assumption (2). Let $m(t)$ represents the mean number of faults removed in time $[t, t+\Delta t]$. The removal of leading, dependent and additional faults is also assumed to follow a NHPP. Thus $m(t)$ can be written as the superposition of the three NHPP$_s$:

$$m(t) = m_1(t) + m_2(t) + m_3(t) \qquad (8)$$

Where $m_1(t)$ is the mean value function of the expected number of leading faults detected in time $[0,t]$, $m_2(t)$ is the mean value function of the expected number of dependent faults detected in time $[0,t]$ and $m_3(t)$ is the mean value function of the expected number of extra faults detected in time $[0,t]$.

Consequently, if the number of detected leading faults is proportional to the number of remaining leading faults *i.e.* assumption (7), then we obtain the following differential equation:

$$\frac{dm_1(t)}{dt} = b_1 \times \left[a_1 - m_1(t) \right] \tag{9}$$

Solving equation (9) under the boundary condition *i.e.* at $t = 0, m_1(0) = 0$, we have

$$m_1(t) = a_1 \left(1 - \exp(-b_1 t) \right) \tag{10}$$

Equation (10) models the leading fault removal phenomenon. It is clear that the growth obtained by equation (10) is exponential, thus it is in line with the assumption of the Goel–Okumoto [27] model. In other words, the leading faults are independent of each other and randomly removed.

From assumption (8), we have the following differential equation:

$$\frac{dm_2(t)}{dt} = b_2 \times \left[a_2 - m_2(t) \right] \times \frac{m_1(t - \phi(t))}{a_1} \tag{11}$$

Earlier in literature Kapur and Younes [15] assumed that the mean number of dependent faults detected in the time interval $[t, t+\Delta t]$ is proportional to the mean number of remaining dependent faults in the system and to the ratio of leading faults removed at time 't' to the total number of faults. Following Kapur *et al.* [16] we have modified the above assumption by taking the ratio of leading faults removed at time t to the total number of leading faults. Later, Huang and Lin [17] incorporated the assumption given by Kapur and Younes [15] in their modeling. It is important to note that the dependent faults can be removed only when the leading fault is perfectly removed with a debugging time lag $\phi(t)$.

Here, we let

$$a_1 = p_1 a, a_2 = p_2 a \text{ and } a_3 = ap'_2 \ ; \ 0 \le p_1, p_2, p'_2 \le 1 \tag{12}$$

Using different removal equations discussed in section 2, solving equation (11) using different debugging time lag functions with boundary condition $t = 0, m_2(0) = 0$, and using equation (7), we obtain $m(t)$ as given below

Assuming $\phi(t) = \left| \dfrac{1}{b_1} \log(1 + b_1 t) \right|$ equation (11) becomes

$$\frac{dm_2(t)}{dt} = b_2 \times \left[a_2 - m_2(t) \right] \times \frac{a_1 \left(1 - (1 + b_1 t) \exp(-b_1 t) \right)}{a_1} \tag{13}$$

Solving equation (13) with boundary condition $t = 0, m_2(0) = 0$, we obtain

$$m_2(t) = a_2 \left(\exp\left[\frac{2b_2}{b_1} \left(1 - \exp[-b_1 t] \right) - t b_2 \left(1 + \exp[-b_1 t] \right) \right] \right) \tag{14}$$

Here we are considering the case of removing some additional faults during removal of dependent faults. These additional faults are removed during the removal of dependent faults. The corresponding differential equation is given by

$$\frac{dm_3(t)}{dt} = b_3(t) \left(ap_3 - m_3(t) \right) \frac{m_3(t)}{ap'_2} \tag{15}$$

On taking $b_3(t) = b_3$ and solving using initial condition we get

$$m_3(t) = \frac{ap'_2}{1 + k e^{-b_3 t}}, k = e^{-c} \tag{16}$$

Total number of faults

$$m(t) = m_1(t) + m_2(t) + m_3(t) \tag{17}$$

MODELLING DEBUGGING TIME LAG WITH CHANGE-POINT

During debugging phase the failure speed depends heavily on the ability of the debugger, error debugging environment, tools and techniques, *etc.* Therefore, the fault detection and removal rate is likely be neither fixed nor unruffled, *i.e.*, may vary at times called change-point [10,11]. Practical experience has shown that the fault detection and removal ability of developers and testers can change as time increases. Moreover new employees can also be done in order not to waste resources or miss the deadline. In advanced software engineering, it is always suggested to proposed and adopt fresh debugging tools and techniques, which are essentially unlike from those used previously [33]. These tools and techniques can provide continuous advancement in testing and software performance. Therefore, the time of the incorporation of new tools and techniques can be considered as change-point.

In general, the change-point is a time when the model parameters jump in the time. In simple words, it is the time when the parameter values change. In recent years, a number of SRGMs have been proposed in the literature which addressed the problem of change points in software reliability [10, 11, 34]. Firstly, M. Zhao [35] introduced the idea of change point modeling and analysis in hardware and software reliability. Kapur *et al.* [36, 37] proposed various testing effort control and testing effort functions addressing change point model (CPM) in software reliability. Kapur *et al.* [38] proposed a SRGM for error of different severity using change point modelling. Kapur *et al.* [39] proposed multiple change points in SRGM for fielded software. Zhao *et al.* [40] presents a SRGM as a function of time with environmental function and change point. Hayashida [41] &Inoue *et al.* [42-44] proposed various hazard rate models with change points for software reliability assessment. Also, some reliability Change point models have been introduced and adopted in the yesteryears, such as the Weibull, the Jlinski-Moranda de-eutrophication and the Littlewood CPM with single change point [35, 40, 45-48]. In the next section, we have developed a new SRGM using lag function with change point.

Here we are considering change point in the fault detection and removal, hence the corresponding mean value function before change-point is given by

$$m_1(t) = ap_1(1 - e^{-b_1 t}); \ t < \tau$$

$$m_2(t) = ap_2 \left[1 - e^{-\left(\frac{-2b_2}{b_1}\left(1 - e^{-b_1 t}\right) - b_2 t\left(1 + e^{-b_1 t}\right) \right)} \right]; t < \tau$$

Total number of faults removed till τ is $m(\tau) = m_1(\tau) + m_2(\tau)$. Hence the faults remaining after τ are $a' = a - m(\tau)$. And for $t \geq \tau$ the differential equation is given by

$$\frac{dm'_1(t)}{dt} = b'_1(t)\left(a' p_3 - m'_1(t)\right)$$

On solving using initial conditions we get

$$m'_1(t) = a' p_3 \left(1 - e^{-b'_1(t-\tau)}\right)$$

$$\frac{dm'_2(t)}{dt} = b'_2 \cdot \left[a' p_4 - m'_2(t)\right] \frac{m'_1(t - \phi(t))}{a' p_3}$$

On solving using initial condition we get

$$m'_2(t) = a' p_4 \left[1 - e^{-\left(\frac{-2b'_2}{b'_1}\left(1 - e^{-b'_1(t-\tau)}\right) - b'_2(t-\tau)\left(1 + e^{-b'_1(t-\tau)}\right) \right)} \right]$$

Hence the total number of faults removed by time 't'

$$m(t) = m_1(t) + m_2(t) + m'_1(t) + m'_2(t)$$

NUMERICAL ILLUSTRATION

Parameters of the proposed models are estimated on the second release data of Woods [49]. This data is observed for 19 weeks and 120 faults encountered. From the data we estimated that sixth week is the change point. The model proposed in this work is not linear, and provides additional problems in the estimation of the parameters. Technically, it's harder to find a solution for non-linear models using the least squares method and requires numerical algorithms to solve it. A software package such as SPSS, which was used here to estimate the parameters helps to overcome this problem. We estimated the parameter values using SPSS. We also calculated the different comparison criterion values *i.e.* BIAS, MSE Variance and RMSPE for the proposed model [10, 11]. The parameter estimates and comparison criteria results of the proposed models are given in Table **1** and **2**. Goodness of fit curves for each release is given in the Figs. (**1** and **2**).

Table 1. Parameter estimation results.

Parameter	a	b_1	b_2	b_3 / b'_1	b'_2	p_1	p_2	p_3	p_4	k
SRGM 1	168.82	0.032	0.022	0.367	-	0.302	0.122	0.576	-	11.54
SRGM 2	163.46	0.189	0.522	0.088	0.025	0.008	0.064	0.427	0.502	-

Table 2. Comparison criteria results.

Comparison Criteria	R^2	Bias	MSE	Variance	RMSPE
SRGM1	0.998	-0.03105	2.515532	1.629192	1.629488
SRGM2	0.991	-0.03474	47.53768	0.147375	0.151414

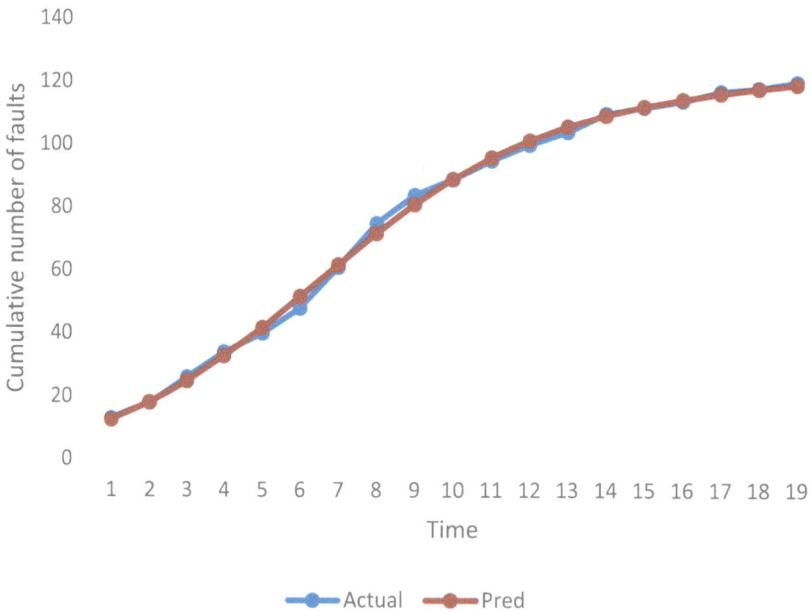

Fig. (1). Goodness of fit curve of SRGM1.

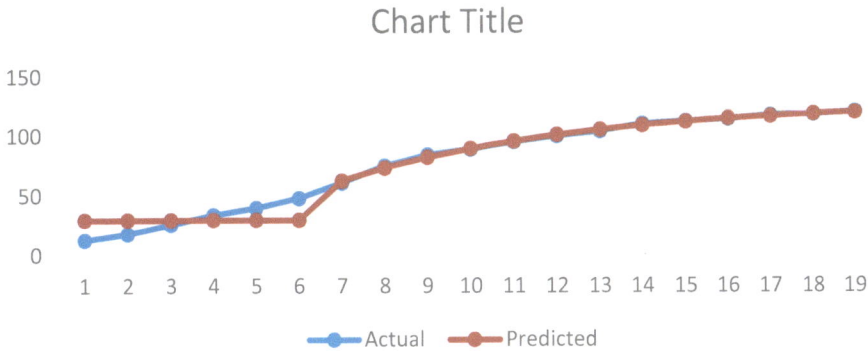

Fig. (2). Goodness of fit curve of SRGM2.

PROPOSED COST MODEL

Most of the literature on SRGMs is focused exclusively on fault detection activities, ignoring the fault correction process by assuming immediate debugging. However, in modern software systems, debugging has a signiifcant☐ impact on the actual growth times of reliability that cannot be neglected at all. SRGM are commonly used to minimize overall fault removal and testing cost of a given product, with respect to time t. The total incurred during a software lifecycle under the assumption that faults are corrected immediately after detection and used in other studies [10,11] consists of three components given by

Testing cost per unit time= $c_1 \tau$

Cost of immediate debugging after detection= $c_2 m_d(\tau)$

Cost of debugging remaining number of faults= $c_3(m_d(\infty) - m_d(\tau))$

On combining the above three components together we get the

$$Total \operatorname{Cos} t = c_1 \tau + c_2 m_d(\tau) + c_3(m_d(\infty) - m_d(\tau)) \tag{30}$$

We will use the equation (30) to analyse the impact caused by immediate debugging on cost estimation. Here we propose a cost model which consists of the following components:

Testing cost per unit time= $c_1 \tau$

Cost of detection$=c_2 m_d(\tau)$

Cost of detection$=c_3 m_c(\tau)$

Cost of debugging remaining number of faults$=c_3(m_d(\infty)-m_d(\tau))$. By considering the fault correction distribution, equation (30) becomes:

$$Total\,\mathrm{Cos}\,t = c_1\tau + c_3 m_d(\tau) + c_3 m_c(\tau) + c_4(m_d(\infty)-m_c(\tau)) \tag{31}$$

Where $(m_d(\infty)-m_c(\tau))$ is the number of uncorrected faults which includes undetected faults *i.e.* $(m_d(\infty)-m_d(\tau))$ and detected but not corrected faults *i.e.* $(m_d(\tau)-m_c(\tau))$.

For numerical study let us consider the following equations for detection and correction proposed by Lo and Huang [7]

$$\frac{dm_d(t)}{dt} = b_1(t)\big(m_d(\infty)-m_d(t)\big) \tag{32}$$

$$\frac{dm_c(t)}{dt} = b_2(t)\big(m_d(t)-m_c(t)\big) \tag{33}$$

$$m_d(t) = m_d(\infty)\big(1-\exp(-D(t))\big) \tag{34}$$

And

$$m_c(t) = \exp\big(-C(t)\big)\left\{\int_0^t m_d(\infty)b_2(s)\exp\big(C(s)\big)\big(1-\exp(-D(s))\big)ds\right\} \tag{35}$$

Where $D(t) = \int_0^t b_1(x)dx$, $C(t) = \int_0^t b_2(x)dx$ *and* $m_d(\infty)=a$

Considering $b_1(t)=b$ *and* $b_2(t)=c$ in the above equation (32) and (33) we get

$m_d(t) = a\big(1-e^{-bt}\big)$ and

$$m_c(t) = a\left(1 + \frac{c}{b-c}e^{-bt} - \frac{b}{b-c}e^{-ct}\right)$$

We have estimated the parameters of the above detection and detection/correction models using SPSS software on Woods second release data set which is mentioned above and obtained the following results. The parameter estimates of detection model are a=127.399,b=0.242 and for combined detection/correction model the parameter estimates are a=131.782, b=0.385, c=0.159. However, any set of representative values would have fit the scope of analysis without impact the finding of the study. On optimizing the two cost models given in equation (30) and (31) using MAPLE software by taking cost parameter values $c_1 = 10, c_2 = 15 \& c_3 = 15, c_4 = 30$ and using the parameter estimation results of detection and correction models we obtained the following results. The optimal release time and cost in case of immediate debugging are 19.34 weeks and Rs. 2145.75. In case of cost model not considering immediate debugging the optimal release time and cost are 30.35 weeks and 4319.94. Looking at the optimal results we see that the difference between the two release time (existing and new) is approximately eleven weeks. From this result we infer that we have underestimated the cost as well as the release time which means large number of faults are yet to be corrected. Also to remove those remaining faults large resources are required which will ultimately increase the budget. Releasing the software with existing strategy may result in more number of failure during operational phase due to low reliability of the software. On calculating the reliability using Lyu [12] method (ratio of number of faults corrected to the initial number of faults) *i.e.* $\frac{m(t)}{a}$, we observe that in case of immediate debugging assumption reliability achieved at the software release time $\tau = 19.34$ given by $\left.\frac{m_d(\tau)}{a}\right|_{\tau=19.579}$ is 99.07% weeks but actual reliability $\frac{m_c(\tau)}{a}$ achieved is 92.1%.

That means we have overestimated the reliability before software release which is a serious threat to reliability prediction and which may result in users facing more number of faults during operation. Hence firm have to face huge loss in terms of servicing cost. Also under estimating the budget may have adverse effect on budgetary and resource planning's of the firm.

CONCLUSION

In this chapter we have developed two new SRGMs using time lag. First proposed SRGM we consider the removal of additional number of faults during removal of dependent faults. While the second proposed SRGM considers the phenomenon of time lag with change-point. In the existing software reliability literature lot of work has been done in developing a cost model for a software to determine the optimal release time under different set of assumptions. But in all the existing work either detection or correction of software fault is considered to model the cost function. In this work we have proposed a new cost model considering the cost of detection and correction both to determine the time to release the software and compared with the existing cost models. The results obtained shows that it is important to consider detection and correction both in the cost model to get the better prediction of reliability achieved before release of the software. In future we will work on to develop effort based SRGM with time and change point. We will work on to extend the proposed model to incorporate the effort and change point based cost model. Various extensions of the proposed SRGMs and cost models is possible by considering different aspects of software reliability such as coverage, effort, imperfect debugging *etc.*

CONSENT FOR PUBLICATION

Not applicable.

CONFLICT OF INTEREST

The author(s) confirm that this chapter contents have no conflict of interest.

ACKNOWLEDGEMENT

Authors are grateful to Founder President Dr. Ashok K Chauhan for his research and innovation vision which inspires us all to reach newer heights.

REFERENCES

[1]   N.F. Schneidewind, "Analysis of error processes in computer software", *SIGPLAN Not.,* vol. 10, pp. 337-346.
[2]   S. Yamada, M. Obha, and S. Osaki, "S-shaped software reliability growth modeling for software error detection", *IEEE Trans. Reliab.,* vol. 32, no. 5, pp. 475-484.
[3]   M. Xie, and M. Zhao, "The Schneidewind software reliability model revisited", *In Software Reliability Engineering, 1992. Proceedings,* Oct 7, 1992pp. 184-192 *Third International Symposium on,* Oct 7, 1992. IEEE
[4]   V.B. Singh, K. Yadav, R. Kapur, and V.S. Yadavalli, "Considering the fault dependency concept with debugging time lag in software reliability growth modeling using a power function of testing time", *International Journal of Automation and Computing.,* vol. 4, no. 4, pp. 359-368.
[5]   P.K. Kapur, A.K. Shrivastava, and O. Singh, "When to Release and Stop Testing of software", *Journal of Indian Society for Probability and Statistics,* vol. 18, no. 1, pp. 19-37.

[6]   N.F. Schneidewind, "Modelling the fault correction process", *In Software Reliability Engineering, 2001. ISSRE 2001. Proceedings,* Nov 27, 2001pp. 185-190 *12th International Symposium on*, Nov 27, 2001. IEEE

[7]   J.H. Lo, and C.Y. Huang, "An integration of fault detection and correction processes in software reliability analysis", *J. Syst. Softw.,* vol. 79, no. 9, pp. 1312-1323.

[8]   M. Xie, Q.P. Hu, Y.P. Wu, and S.H. Ng, "A study of the modeling and analysis of software fault-detection and fault-correction processes", *Qual. Reliab. Eng. Int.,* vol. 23, no. 4, pp. 459-470.

[9]   P.K. Kapur, and P.C. Jha, *Gupta Deepali, and Yadav Kalpana" Identification of Different Stages in the Testing Phase of a Software Reliability Growth Model. the proceedings of Advances in Performance and safety of complex systems..* MacMillan India Ltd., 2008, pp. 850-861.

[10]   H. Pham, "System software reliability", *Springer Science & Business Media,* .

[11]   P.K. Kapur, H. Pham, A. Gupta, and P.C. Jha, *Software reliability assessment with OR applications..* Springer: London, 2011.

[12]   MR Lyu, "Handbook of software reliability engineering", *CA: IEEE computer society press,* .

[13]   M. Ohba, "Software reliability analysis models", *IBM J. Res. Develop.,* vol. 28, no. 4, pp. 428-443.

[14]   P.K. Kapur, and R.B. Garg, "A software reliability growth model for an error-removal phenomenon", *Softw. Eng. J.,* vol. 7, no. 4, pp. 291-294.

[15]   P.K. Kapur, and S. Younes, "Software reliability growth model with error dependency", *Microelectron. Reliab.,* vol. 35, no. 2, pp. 273-278.

[16]   P.K. Kapur, A.K. Bardhan, and O. Shatnawi, "Software reliability growth model with fault dependency using lag function", *Proceedings of International Conference on Quality, Reliability and Control,* 2001pp. 1-7

[17]   C.Y. Huang, and C.T. Lin, "Software reliability analysis by considering fault dependency and debugging time lag", *IEEE Trans. Reliab.,* vol. 55, no. 3, pp. 436-450.

[18]   P.K. Kapur, and V.B. Singh, *Yadav K Software Reliability Growth Model Incorporating Fault Dependency Concept Using a Power Function of Testing Time. Quality Reliability and Infocom Technology..* MacMillan India Ltd., 2007, pp. 587-595.

[19]   P.K. Kapur, V.B. Singh, and S. Anand, "Fault Dependency Based Software Reliability Growth Modeling with Debugging Time Lag Functions", *Communications in Dependability and Quality Management An International Journal,Serbia,* vol. 10, no. 3, pp. 46-68.

[20]   Y. Shu, H. Liu, Z. Wu, and X. Yang, "Modeling of Software fault and Correction Process Based on Correction lag", *Information Technology Journal,* vol. 8, pp. 735-742.

[21]   L. Jia, Y.A. Bo, G.U. Suchang, and D.H. Park, "Software reliability modeling considering fault correction process", *IEICE Trans. Inf. Syst.,* vol. 93, no. 1, pp. 185-188.

[22]   P.K. Kapur, H. Pham, S. Anand, and K. Yadav, "A unified approach for developing software reliability growth models in the presence of imperfect debugging and error generation", *IEEE Trans. Reliab.,* vol. 60, no. 1, pp. 331-340.

[23]   R. Peng, Y.F. Li, W.J. Zhang, and Q.P. Hu, "Testing effort dependent software reliability model for imperfect debugging process considering both detection and correction", *Reliab. Eng. Syst. Saf.,* vol. 126, pp. 37-43.

[24]   O. Singh, P.K. Kapur, A.K. Shrivastava, and L. Das, "A unified approach for successive release of a software under two types of imperfect debugging",

[25]   P.K. Kapur, O. Singh, A.K. Shrivastava, and J.N. Singh, "A software up-gradation model with testing effort and two types of imperfect debugging", *Futuristic Trends on Computational Analysis and Knowledge Management (ABLAZE),* , 2015pp. 613-618

[26]   Y. Liu, D. Li, L. Wang, and Q. Hu, "A general modeling and analysis framework for software fault detection and correction process", *Softw. Test. Verif. Reliab.,* vol. 26, no. 5, pp. 351-365.

[27]   K. Okumoto, and A.L. Goel, "Optimum release time for software systems based on reliability and cost criteria", *J. Syst. Softw.,* vol. 1, pp. 315-318.

[28]   S. Yamada, and S. Osaki, "Optimal software release policies with simultaneous cost and reliability requirements", *Eur. J. Oper. Res.,* vol. 31, no. 1, pp. 46-51.

[29]   P.K. Kapur, and R.B. Garg, "Cost–reliability optimum release policies for a software system under penalty cost", *Int. J. Syst. Sci.,* vol. 20, no. 12, pp. 2547-2562.

[30]   T. Dohi, N. Kaio, and S. Osaki, "Optimal software release policies with debugging time lag", *Int. J. Reliab. Qual. Saf. Eng.,* vol. 4, no. 03, pp. 241-255.

[31]   H. Pham, and X. Zhang, "A Software Cost Model with Warranty and Risk Costs IEEE Transactions on Computers",

[32]   O. Singh, P.K. Kapur, A.K. Shrivastava, and V. Kumar, "Release time problem with multiple constraints", *International Journal of System Assurance Engineering and Management.,* vol. 6, no. 1, pp. 83-91.

[33]   JD Musa, A Iannino, and K Okumoto, "Software reliability: measurement, prediction, application", *McGraw-Hill, Inc, .*

[34]   P.K. Kapur, V.B. Singh, S. Anand, and V.S. Yadavalli, "Software reliability growth model with change-point and effort control using a power function of the testing time", *Int. J. Prod. Res.,* vol. 46, no. 3, pp. 771-787.

[35]   M. Zhao, "Change-point problems in software and hardware reliability", *Commun. Stat. Theory Methods,* vol. 22, no. 3, pp. 757-768.

[36]   P.K. Kapur, J. Kumar, and R. Kumar, "A unified modeling framework incorporating change-point for measuring reliability growth during software testing", *Opsearch.,* vol. 45, no. 4, p. 317.

[37]   P.K. Kapur, A. Gupta, O. Shatnawi, and V.S. Yadavalli, "Testing effort control using flexible software reliability growth model with change point", *Int. J. Perform. Eng.,* vol. 2, no. 3, pp. 245-262.

[38]   P.K. Kapur, A. Kumar, K. Yadav, and S.K. Khatri, "Software reliability growth modelling for errors of different severity using change point", *Int. J. Reliab. Qual. Saf. Eng.,* vol. 14, no. 04, pp. 311-326.

[39]   P.K. Kapur, V.B. Singh, and S. Anand, *Software Reliability Growth Model of Fielded Software Based on Multiple Change-Point Concept Using a Power Function of Testing Time. Quality Reliability and Infocom Technology..* MacMillan India Ltd., 2007, pp. 171-178.

[40]   J. Zhao, H.W. Liu, G. Cui, and X.Z. Yang, "Software reliability growth model with change-point and environmental function", *J. Syst. Softw.,* vol. 79, no. 11, pp. 1578-1587.

[41]   S. Hayashida, S. Inoue, and S. Yamada, "Software Reliability Assessment Using Exponential-Type Change-Point Hazard Rate Models", *Int. J. Reliab. Qual. Saf. Eng.,* vol. 21, no. 04, p. 1450019.

[42]   S. Inoue, "HAYASHIDA S, Yamada S. Extended hazard rate models for software reliability assessment with effect at change-point", *Int. J. Reliab. Qual. Saf. Eng.,* vol. 20, no. 02, p. 1350009.

[43]   S. Inoue, S. Taniguchi, and S. Yamada, "An All-Stage Truncated Multiple Change Point Model for Software Reliability Assessment", *Int. J. Reliab. Qual. Saf. Eng.,* vol. 22, no. 04, p. 1550017.

[44]   S. Inoue, and S. Yamada, "Change-point modeling for software reliability assessment depending on two-types of reliability growth factors", In: *InIndustrial Engineering and Engineering Management (IEEM), 2010 IEEE International Conference on,* Dec 7, 2010, pp. 616-620. IEEE

[45]   K.C. Chiu, "An exploration on debugging performance for software reliability growth models with learning effects and change-points", *Journal of Industrial and Production Engineering.,* vol. 32, no. 6, pp. 369-386.

[46]   M. Zhao, Statistical reliability change-point estimation models.*Handbook of Reliability Engineering..* Springer London, 2003, pp. 157-163.

[47]   O. Singh, V.B. Singh, J. Kumar, and P.K. Kapur, "Generalized Framework for Fault Detection – Correction Process Incorporating Change-Point", *Communications in Dependability and Quality Management: An International Journal,* vol. 12, no. 1, pp. 35-46.

[48]   Y.P. Chang, "Estimation of parameters for nonhomogeneous Poisson process: Software reliability with change-point model", *Commun. Stat. Simul. Comput.,* vol. 30, no. 3, pp. 623-635.

[49]   A. Wood, "Predicting software reliability", *Computer,* vol. 29, no. 11, pp. 69-77.

CHAPTER 3

Stochastic Differential Equation Based Formulation for Multiple Software Release Considering Fault Detection and Correction Process

Adarsh Anand[1], Deepika[1,*], Ompal Singh[1] and Parmod K. Kapur[2]

[1]*Department of Operational Research, University of Delhi, Delhi 110007, India*
[2]*Centre for Interdisciplinary Research, Amity University, Noida, India*

Abstract: Fault detection and correction are two different and yet important activities for software developers. They both should go hand in hand for a good debugging process. The two concepts have been mathematically studied in depth and a lot seems to be in the pipeline. In the present framework, we have developed some software reliability growth models (SRGMs) that inculcate the concept of software in multi versions. The methodical approach of stochastic differential equation has been used to model the scenario that unifiedly takes care of fault detection and correction process. The proposed models are validated on Tandem data set that comprises of four successive software releases and the results obtained and authenticated by weighted criteria technique are promising.

Keywords: Convolution, Fault Correction Process (FCP), Fault Detection Process (FDP), Multi release, Non–Homogenous Poisson Process (NHPP), SRGMs, Stochastic Differential Equation (SDE), Tandem data set, Weighted criteria approach.

INTRODUCTION

The modern high technology innovations and vital business systems act as the key players in the continuous evolution. The application of software has been progressively become ubiquitous and universal. Software sequence work as the lead out for the speedy modifications in tools is affecting in different behavior.

In the past literature, different SRGMs have been proposed and developed to estimate important measures such as leftover faults, failure intensity *etc*. Most of these SRGMs are based on NHPP [1-7] and are helpful to depict the performance

---

*Corresponding author Deepika: Department of Operational Research, University of Delhi, Delhi 110007, India; Tel: +91-11-27666672; E-mail: deepika.sre@gmail.com

Mangey Ram (Ed.)

of testing procedure that includes detection and correction of faults. Firstly, the procedure of testing as a two-stage method in which there is a constant lag between detection and correction of faults is explained by Scheindewind [8]. Later, two stage procedures are also discussed by Yamada *et al.* [7]. Huang *et al.* [9] proposed a general structure from the correction point of view where a quantity of existing NHPP models was evaluated. Then, a deterministic delay between detection and correction of faults is given by Xie *et al.* [10].

A large number of SRGMs, which relate the number of failure and implementation time, have been discussed in the past literature [3, 11]. "These SRGMs assume diverse testing environment like distinction between failure and correction processes, learning of the testing personnel, possibility of imperfect debugging and fault generation, constant or monotonically increasing /decreasing fault detection rate (FDR) or randomness in growth curve" [12]. But no SRGM can be declared to be the best as the physical understanding of the testing and debugging changes due to plentiful factors *e.g.* test cases design, fault density, skills and effectiveness of testing team, accessibility of testing resources *etc*. To minimize this complexity, unified modelling framework has been formulated by various authors. Some of these approaches are based on (i) Infinite server queuing theory (ii) Random lag function (iii) Hazard rate function [3]. In 1980's [6] this work proposed Generalized Birth Process model.

In today's big business, the upgraded technologies are released in the market under different versions. Continuous up- gradation has become a requirement for the industries. "The term upgrade refers to the replacement of a product with a modified version of the same product". Software industries plan consecutive release for their construction because of two aspects; money matter and software engineering. In one progressive cycle, software companies do not endeavour to convey an absolute and ideal product due to resource restriction and time. They plan succeeding performance of system compared to preceding release by eliminating the errors from existing software [13]. "Each fault correction process is connected to a detection process as fault can only be corrected if they are detected". Of late Kapur *et al.* [4] gave a model related to multi up gradation, "considering that cumulative faults in each generation depend on all previous releases and also assume that fault is removed with certainty". Later, Anand *et al.* [14] proposed fault severity based multi up-gradation modeling considering testing and operational phase. These proposed models have the postulation that "the overall fault removal of the new release depends on the reported bugs from the just previous release of the software".

Numerous NHPP based SRGMs have been taken as a discrete counting procedure. Yamada *et al.* [15] developed that "if the size of the software system is large than the number of fault detected during the testing phase becomes large and the change of the number of faults which are detected and removed through each debugging activities becomes sufficiently small compared with the initial fault content at the beginning of the testing phase". Before the software is released in the market, a quantity of bugs are observed and eliminated throughout the testing epoch. However, when the users discover the faults then the Software Company releases an efficient version of the system. Thus in this scenario the numeral of bugs that remain in the system can be considered to be a stochastic process with continuous state space [16]. Many researchers [3, 17] developed simple software SRGM to illustrate the FDP during the testing phase by applying Itô type SDE and attain numerous software reliability measures using the probability distribution. Later on, during the testing phase of the distributed development environment they proposed a flexible SDE Model describing a FDP [18]. Lee *et al.* [19] used SDEs to represent a per-fault detection rate that include an irregular fluctuation instead of an NHPP. Therefore, in order to discuss stochastic behaviour of fault detection correction process, a stochastic model can be used in SRGMs that inculcates the concept of software coming in multi versions.

Rest of the manuscript is prearranged as follow: Firstly, assumptions about SRGM and notations have been comprised. Then we have discussed about modeling framework. Next successive sections enlighten the multi release modeling and SDE based modeling with convolution probability function and parameter estimates in each release of all SRGMs. Further, a subsection describes the ranks by weighted criteria approach [20-23] of all SRGMs. At last, conclusion followed by references has been provided.

ASSUMPTIONS

- Failure phenomenon tends to follow NHPP.
- FDP is modeled as stochastic process with a continuous state space.
- Remaining number of faults decreases with testing expansion goes on.
- There is mutually independency in all faults.
- Faults are debugged perfectly in software.

NOTATIONS

$N(t)$	A random variable which is calculating the number of bugs detected during testing time t.
$m(t) = E(N(t))$	During testing period, expected quantity of bugs detected in time 't'
$m_i(t)$	Mean value function for i^{th}(i=1 to 4) release.
a_i	Introductory number of faults for i^{th} (i=1 to 4) release.
b_i	Error correction rate for i^{th} (i=1 to 4) release.
s_i	A positive fixed value that symbolize the scale of irregular fluctuation for i^{th} release (i=1 to 4).
$\gamma(t)$	Standardized Gaussian White Noise.
$F_{di}(t)$	Distribution function for detection process used in i^{th} release (i=1 to 4).
$F_{ci}(t)$	Distributions function for correction process used in i^{th} release (i=1 to 4).
*	Convolution operator.
$\otimes$	Steiltjes convolution.
t_i	Time for i^{th} release (i=1 to 4).

SDE BASED FAULT DETECTION-CORRECTION MODELING: A UNIFIED FRAMEWORK

Let $\{N(t), t \geq 0\}$ be an arbitrary variable that denotes the quantity of software bugs observed in the software system up to testing time 't' and it is assumed that $N(t)$ takes on continuous real value. The various models of NHPP described in the past literature have considered the software FDP during the testing period in a discrete environment. However, "if the size of the software system is large, the number of faults detected in testing phase is also large and the change in the number of faults which are corrected and removed throughout the debugging process, becomes small as compared to the initial fault content at the beginning of the testing phase". Therefore, to illustrate the stochastic behaviour of the fault detection-correction process, we make use of a stochastic model in continuous time [24]. The purpose of testing is observation and elimination of errors before the release. Generally, whenever a fault is recognized the fault removal team requires an epoch of time to search the fault and alter various codes accordingly to eliminate it. Thus, in software testing the time lag between detection and correction is a regular experience [25]. The correction time of an error depends on different factors such as difficulty of the faults, skill of removal *etc*. So corrected lag cannot be avoid. Some faults which are observed but not eliminated still remain in the software. This uncover faults are caused by the removal lag and replicate the link between FDP and FCP.

One stage modeling for unification is written as [3, 26]

$$N(t) = aF(t) \tag{1}$$

Above equation can be structured as

$$\frac{dN(t)}{dt} = \frac{f(t)}{1 - F(t)}[a - N(t)] \tag{2}$$

Where $\dfrac{f(t)}{1 - F(t)}$ is the hazard rate function which is calculating the failure rate at a very small time interval *i.e.* it is the ratio of Probability Density Function and survival function.

In case of two stage testing process, first stage is detection of faults and second is correction of faults [2] is define by $F_d(t)$ and $F_c(t)$ distribution function can be written as equation (1)

$$N(t) = a[(F_d \otimes F_c)(t)] \tag{3}$$

Hence

$$\frac{dN(t)}{dt} = a(f_d * f_c)(t) \tag{4}$$

Equation (4) can be structured as follows

$$\frac{dN(t)}{dt} = \frac{(f_d * f_c)(t)}{[1 - (F_d \otimes F_c)(t)]}[a - N(t)] \tag{5}$$

Where $\dfrac{(f_d * f_c)(t)}{[1 - (F_d \otimes F_c)(t)]}$ is fault detection/fault correction rate.

It is quite rare when the rate is not known entirely, but with the constraint of some arbitrary environmental effect [10], so we have

$$r(t) = \frac{(f_d * f_c)(t)}{[1 - (F_d \otimes F_c)(t)]} + "noise" \tag{6}$$

To inculcate the concept of SDE for fault detection-correction process with convolution of probability distribution function, the linear differential equation is prearranged as

$$\frac{dN(t)}{dt} = \left(\frac{(f_d * f_c)(t)}{[1 - ((F_d \otimes F_c)(t))]} + s\gamma(t) \right) [a - N(t)] \tag{7}$$

where $\gamma(t)$ be a standard Gaussian white noise and s be a positive fixed value that symbolize the scale of irregular fluctuations [2].

The above equation can be represented as SDE of an *Itô* type.

$$dN(t) = \left(\frac{(f_d * f_c)(t)}{[1 - ((F_d \otimes F_c)(t))]} - \frac{s^2}{2} \right) [a - N(t)]dt + s[a - N(t)]dW(t) \tag{8}$$

where $w(t)$ is one –dimensional Wiener Process, which is formally defined as an integration of the white-noise $\gamma(t)$ with respect to time t *i.e.* $w(t) = \int \gamma(t)dt$. Using the fact that the Wiener Process $w(t)$, is a Gaussian process and has the following axioms:

$$P\{w(0) = 0\} = 1$$
$$E\{w(t)\} = 0 \tag{9}$$
$$E\{w(t), w(t')\} = \min[t, t']$$

Using seed value $N(0) = 0$, we obtain

$$m(t) = E(N(t)) = a[1 - (1 - (F_d \otimes F_c)(t))e^{s^2 t/2}] \tag{10}$$

MULTI RELEASE MODELING

Business is not fixed, it changes firmly with time. In dynamic scenario, update sector becomes a significant component in firms and based on these elements firms are trying to continue to exist in market by accretion of novel functionality. "First release of the software product is the main foundation of the firms so the firms have to pay more attention on it". On the other hand, at this first release testing team observes and eliminates errors as much as possible and reduces the risk of amount of error in future. And after first release firm has to arrange for subsequent version with fresh update in preceding release. They will test and scrutinize the reported errors of just prior release [27, 28].

Modeling for First Release

Presume that first version of the software is released at time $t = t_1$ and it is actuality that correcting all the bugs during first release of the software is virtually infeasible *i.e.* several faults of prior release have to be eliminated in the consecutive releases. Modeling of foremost release for two stage detection-correction procedure with SDE is written as:

$$m_1(t) = a_1[(F_{d1} \otimes F_{c1})(t)] \qquad\qquad\qquad ; 0 \leq t < t_1 \qquad (11)$$

where $(F_{d1} \otimes F_{c1})(t) = [1 - \{1 - (F_{d1} \otimes F_{c1})t\}e^{\frac{1}{2}s_1^2 t}]$

Modeling for Second Release

Considering the time for opening of second release is t_2 and testing period for second release $[t_1, t_2)$ will be operational phase for just previous release. In this epoch when there are two versions of the software $a_1[1 - (F_{d1} \otimes F_{c1})(t_1)]$, the residual faults content of the first version cooperates with new detection-correction rate. As a result of these interactions, a portion of errors which were not removed during the testing of first version of the product gets eliminated [29]. In accumulation, faults are generated to improve the quality and they are removed during the testing with new detection-correction fraction *i.e.* $(F_{d2} \otimes F_{c2})(t - t_1)$.

Hence mathematical expression of Release 2 during $[t_1, t_2)$ can be structured as

$$m_2(t) = a_2[(F_{d2} \otimes F_{c2})(t - t_1)] + a_1[1 - ((F_{d1} \otimes F_{c1})(t_1))][(F_{d2} \otimes F_{c2})(t - t_1)] \qquad (12)$$

$$=[a_2 + a_1\{1 - (F_{d1} \otimes F_{c1})(t_1)\}][(F_{d2} \otimes F_{c2})(t - t_1)] \; ; t_1 \leq t < t_2$$

where $(F_{d2} \otimes F_{c2})(t) = [1 - \{1 - (F_{d2} \otimes F_{c2})t\}e^{\frac{1}{2}s_2^2 t}]$

Modeling for Third Release

In the same way for release 3, it is assumed that faults are generated in third release due to the new lines of code and new functionalities. Time for introduction of third release is t_3 and $[t_2, t_3)$ is the testing period for third release. In this interval, $a_2[1 - (F_{d2} \otimes F_{c2})(t_2 - t_1)]$ the remaining error of the second version interacts with changed fault detection-correction rate and faults related to new functionalities are corrected with new detection-correction proportion $(F_{d3} \otimes F_{c3})(t - t_2)$. The mathematical expression for release 3 is as follows:

$$
\begin{aligned}
m_3(t) \;\; &= a_3[(F_{d3} \otimes F_{c3})(t - t_2)] \\
&\quad + a_2[1 - \{(F_{d2} \otimes F_{c2})(t_2 - t_1)\}][(F_{d3} \otimes F_{c3})(t - t_2)]
\end{aligned}
\tag{13}
$$

$$= [a_3 + a_2[1 - \{(F_{d2} \otimes F_{c2})(t_2 - t_1)\}]][(F_{d3} \otimes F_{c3})(t - t_2)] \; ; t_2 \leq t < t_3$$

where $(F_{d3} \otimes F_{c3})(t) = [1 - \{1 - (F_{d3} \otimes F_{c3})t\}e^{\frac{1}{2}s_3^2 t}]$

Modeling for Fourth Release

Based on same analogy, numerical equation for release 4 can be written by

$$
\begin{aligned}
m_4(t) \;\; &= a_4[(F_{d4} \otimes F_{c4})(t - t_3)] \\
&\quad + a_3[1 - ((F_{d3} \otimes F_{c3})(t_3 - t_2))][F_{d4} \otimes F_{c4})(t - t_3)]
\end{aligned}
\tag{14}
$$

$$= [a_4 + a_3[1 - \{(F_{d3} \otimes F_{c3})(t_3 - t_2)\}]][F_{d4} \otimes F_{c4})(t - t_3)] \; ; t_3 \leq t < t_4$$

where $(F_{d4} \otimes F_{c4})(t) = [1 - \{1 - (F_{d4} \otimes F_{c4})t\}e^{\frac{1}{2}s_4^2 t}]$

Similarly we can express the mathematical equation for $(n-1)^{th}$ and n^{th} release.

$$
\begin{aligned}
m_{n-1}(t) &= a_{n-1}[(F_{d(n-1)} \otimes F_{c(n-1)})(t - t_{n-2})] \\
&\quad + a_{n-2}[1 - ((F_{d(n-2)} \otimes F_{c(n-2)})(t_{n-2} - t_{n-3}))][F_{d(n-1)} \otimes F_{c(n-1)})(t - t_{n-2})] \; ; t_{n-2} \leq t < t_{n-1}
\end{aligned}
\tag{15}
$$

$$= \lfloor a_{n-1} + a_{n-2}[1 - \{(F_{d(n-2)} \otimes F_{c(n-2)})(t_{n-2} - t_{n-3})\}] \rfloor [F_{d(n-1)} \otimes F_{c(n-1)})(t - t_{(n-2)})]$$

where $(F_{d(n-1)} \otimes F_{c(n-1)})(t) = [1 - \{1 - (F_{d(n-1)} \otimes F_{c(n-1)})t\}e^{\frac{1}{2}s_{n-1}^2 t}]$

and

$$
\begin{aligned}
m_n(t) &= a_n[(F_{dn} \otimes F_{cn})(t - t_{n-1})] \\
&+ a_{n-1}[1 - ((F_{d(n-1)} \otimes F_{c(n-1)})(t_{n-1} - t_{n-2}))][F_{dn} \otimes F_{cn})(t - t_{n-1})] \; ; t_{n-1} \leq t < t_n \quad \textbf{(16)}
\end{aligned}
$$

$$= \lfloor a_n + a_{n-1}[1 - \{(F_{d(n-1)} \otimes F_{c(n-1)})(t_{n-1} - t_{n-2})\}] \rfloor [F_{dn} \otimes F_{cn})(t - t_{n-1})]$$

where $(F_{dn} \otimes F_{cn})(t) = [1 - \{1 - (F_{dn} \otimes F_{cn})t\}e^{\frac{1}{2}s_n^2 t}]$

MEAN VALUE FUNCTIONS FOR PROPOSED SOFTWARE RELIABILITY GROWTH MODELS

In this segment, we will depict mean value function for four proposed software reliability growth models for fault detection-correction process with stochastic differential equation. A case of Tandem computers that comprises with four successive versions has been utilized for validation.

SRGM 1

Presuming with the aim of FDP as a fixed value and FCP as exponential *i.e.* $F_d(t) \sim 1(t)$ and $F_c(t) \sim \exp(b)$; using the above equations with convolution distribution function, we get different mean value functions with different releases.

$$
\begin{aligned}
m_1(t) &= a_1[1 - \{1 - ((F_{d1} \otimes F_{c1})(t)\}e^{\frac{1}{2}s_1^2 t}] \\
&= a_1[1 - e^{-b_1 t + \frac{1}{2}s_1^2 t}] \hspace{3cm} ; 0 \leq t < t_1 \quad \textbf{(17)}
\end{aligned}
$$

$$
\begin{aligned}
m_2(t) &= [a_2 + a_1\{1 - (F_{d1} \otimes F_{c1})(t_1)\}].[(F_{d2} \otimes F_{c2})(t - t_1)] \\
&= [a_2 + a_1(e^{(-b_1 + \frac{1}{2}s_1^2)t_1})].[(1 - e^{(-b_2 + \frac{1}{2}s_2^2)(t - t_1)})] \hspace{1cm} ; t_1 \leq t < t_2 \quad \textbf{(18)}
\end{aligned}
$$

$$m_3(t) = [a_3 + a_2\{1 - (F_{d2} \otimes F_{c2})(t_2 - t_1)\}].[F_{d3} \otimes F_{c3})(t - t_2)]$$

$$= [a_3 + a_2(e^{(-b_2 + \frac{1}{2}s_2^2)(t_2 - t_1)})].[(1 - e^{(-b_3 + \frac{1}{2}s_3^2)(t - t_2)})] \qquad ; t_2 \leq t < t_3 \qquad \textbf{(19)}$$

$$m_4(t) = [a_4 + a_3\{1 - (F_{d3} \otimes F_{c3})(t_3 - t_2)\}].[F_{d4} \otimes F_{c4})(t - t_3)]$$

$$= [a_4 + a_3(e^{(-b_3 + \frac{1}{2}s_3^2)(t_3 - t_2)})].[(1 - e^{(-b_4 + \frac{1}{2}s_4^2)(t - t_3)})] \qquad ; t_2 \leq t < t_3 \qquad \textbf{(20)}$$

SRGM 2

Assuming that both FDP and FCP as exponential *i.e.* $F_d(t) \sim \exp(b)$ and $F_c(t) \sim \exp(b)$; so making use of above multi releases equations, we get mean value functions for respective releases.

$$m_1(t) = a_1[1 - (1 + b_1 t)e^{-b_1 t + \frac{1}{2}s_1^2 t}] \qquad ; 0 \leq t < t_1 \qquad \textbf{(21)}$$

$$m_2(t) = [a_2 + a_1((1 + b_1 t_1)e^{(-b_1 + \frac{1}{2}s_1^2)t_1})]$$
$$\cdot[1 - (1 + b_2(t - t_1))e^{(-b_2 + \frac{1}{2}s_2^2)(t - t_1)}] \qquad ; t_1 \leq t < t_2 \qquad \textbf{(22)}$$

$$m_3(t) = [a_3 + a_2((1 + b_2(t_2 - t_1))e^{(-b_2 + \frac{1}{2}s_2^2)(t_2 - t_1)})]$$
$$\cdot[1 - (1 + b_3(t - t_2))e^{(-b_3 + \frac{1}{2}s_3^2)(t - t_2)}] \qquad ; t_2 \leq t < t_3 \qquad \textbf{(23)}$$

$$m_4(t) = [a_4 + a_3((1 + b_3(t_3 - t_2))e^{(-b_3 + \frac{1}{2}s_3^2)(t_3 - t_2)})]$$
$$\cdot[1 - (1 + b_4(t - t_3))e^{(-b_4 + \frac{1}{2}s_4^2)(t - t_3)}] \qquad ; t_3 \leq t < t_4 \qquad \textbf{(24)}$$

SRGM 3

Assuming that both FDP and FCP as exponential with different detection-correction rate respectively *i.e.* $F_d(t) \sim \exp(b_1)$ and $F_c(t) \sim \exp(b_2)$ again making use of above equation we get the mean value functions with the concept of SDE.

$$m_1(t) = a_1\left|1 - \left(\left(\frac{1}{b_{11} - b_{21}}\right)(b_{11}e^{-b_{21}t} - b_{21}e^{-b_1 t})\right)e^{\frac{1}{2}s_1^2 t}\right| \qquad ; 0 \leq t < t_1 \qquad \textbf{(25)}$$

$$m_2(t) = \left[a_2 + a_1 \left(\frac{1}{b_{11} - b_{21}} \right) (b_{11} e^{-b_{21} t_1} - b_{21} e^{-b_{11} t_1}) e^{\frac{1}{2} s_1^2 t_1} \right.$$
$$\left. \cdot \left[1 - \left(\frac{1}{b_{12} - b_{22}} \right) (b_{12} e^{-b_{22}(t-t_1)} - b_{22} e^{-b_{12}(t-t_1)}) e^{\frac{1}{2} s_2^2 (t-t_1)} \right] \right] ; t_1 \le t < t_2 \qquad (26)$$

$$m_3(t) = \left[a_3 + a_2 \left(\frac{1}{b_{12} - b_{22}} \right) (b_{12} e^{-b_{22}(t_2-t_1)} - b_{22} e^{-b_{12}(t_2-t_1)}) e^{\frac{1}{2} s_2^2 (t_2-t_1)} \right.$$
$$\left. \cdot \left[1 - \left(\frac{1}{b_{13} - b_{23}} \right) (b_{13} e^{-b_{23}(t-t_2)} - b_{23} e^{-b_{13}(t-t_2)}) e^{\frac{1}{2} s_3^2 (t-t_2)} \right] \right] ; t_2 \le t < t_3 \qquad (27)$$

$$m_4(t) = \left[a_4 + a_3 \left(\frac{1}{b_{13} - b_{23}} \right) (b_{13} e^{-b_{23}(t_3-t_2)} - b_{23} e^{-b_{13}(t_3-t_2)}) e^{\frac{1}{2} s_3^2 (t_3-t_2)} \right.$$
$$\left. \cdot \left[1 - \left(\frac{1}{b_{14} - b_{24}} \right) (b_{14} e^{-b_{24}(t-t_3)} - b_{24} e^{-b_{14}(t-t_3)}) e^{\frac{1}{2} s_4^2 (t-t_3)} \right] \right] ; t_3 \le t < t_4 \qquad (28)$$

Where b_{1i} and b_{2i} are fault detection-correction rate obtained from convolution methodology corresponding to i^{th} release ($i=1$ to 4).

SRGM 4

Assuming that FDP as Erlang-3(b) and FCP as exponential *i.e.* $F_d(t) \sim \text{Erlang} - 3(b)$ and $F_c(t) \sim \exp(b)$; and utilizing the concept developed in above equations, we get mean value functions.

$$m_1(t) = a_1 \left[1 - \left(1 + b_1 t + \frac{b_1^2 t^2}{2} \right) e^{(-b_1 + \frac{1}{2} s_1^2) t} \right] ; 0 \le t < t_1 \qquad (29)$$

$$m_2(t) = \left[a_2 + a_1 \left(1 + b_1 t_1 + \frac{b_1^2 t_1^2}{2} \right) e^{(-b_1 + \frac{1}{2} s_1^2) t_1} \right.$$
$$\left. \cdot \left[1 - \left(1 + b_2 (t - t_1) + \frac{b_2^2 (t - t_1)^2}{2} \right) e^{(-b_2 + \frac{1}{2} s_2^2)(t - t_1)} \right] \right] ; t_1 \le t < t_2 \qquad (30)$$

$$m_3(t) = \left[a_3 + a_2 \left(1 + b_2(t_2 - t_1) + \frac{b_2^2(t_2 - t_1)^2}{2} \right) e^{(-b_2 + \frac{1}{2}s_2^2)(t_2 - t_1)} \right]$$

$$\cdot \left[1 - \left(1 + b_3(t - t_2) + \frac{b_3^2(t - t_2)^2}{2} \right) e^{(-b_3 + \frac{1}{2}s_3^2)(t - t_2)} \right] \quad ; t_2 \le t < t_3 \quad \textbf{(31)}$$

$$m_4(t) = \left[a_4 + a_3 \left(1 + b_3(t_3 - t_2) + \frac{b_3^2(t_3 - t_2)^2}{2} \right) e^{(-b_3 + \frac{1}{2}s_3^2)(t_3 - t_2)} \right]$$

$$\cdot \left[1 - \left(1 + b_4(t - t_3) + \frac{b_4^2(t - t_3)^2}{2} \right) e^{(-b_4 + \frac{1}{2}s_4^2)(t - t_3)} \right] \quad ; t_3 \le t < t_4 \quad \textbf{(32)}$$

DATA SET, ESTIMATION OF PARAMETERS, DATA ANALYSIS AND MODEL VALIDATION

As stated in earlier fragment, we have evaluated the performance of proposed model by using real data set of tandem computers [30] for four releases. The parameter estimation is presented in the above equation using non-linear least square by SPSS. Tables **1-4** depicts the estimation measures for the different parameters used SRGM-1 to SRGM -4. The connected evaluation criteria are shown in Tables **5-8**. Also Figs. (**1-4**) gives the goodness of fit between the predicted and actual values of SRGM-1 to SRGM-4. Tables **5-8** gives the results of comparison criteria for developed models which are calculated by Mean Square Error, BIAS, Root Mean Square Predictions Error, Coefficient of Determination (R^2), VARIATION [3, 6].

Table 1. Estimated results for SRGM 1.

Release	1	2	3	4
a	131.569	161.793	157.319	70.000
b	0.081	0.236	0.039	0.016
s	0.006	0.595	0.120	0.020

Table 2. Estimated results for SRGM 2.

Release	1	2	3	4
a	110	130	65	50
b	0.241	0.219	0.28	0.153
s	0.015	.01	0.106	0.010

Table 3. Estimated results for SRGM 3.

Release	1	2	3	4
a	117.30	130.0	77.0	50.0
b_1	0.113	0.001	0.045	0.060
b_2	0.990	0.990	0.760	0.880
s	0.082	0.010	0.100	0.212

Table 4. Estimation results of SRGM 4.

Release	1	2	3	4
a	110.0	130.0	62.000	45.000
b	0.362	0.343	0.511	0.305
S	0.001	0.010	0.002	0.009

Table 5. Comparison Result for Release 1.

Release 1	MSE	Bias	Variation	RMSPE	R^2
SRGM 1	15.73	0.134	4.066	4.069	0.98
SRGM 2	35.99	0.931	6.080	6.151	0.96
SRGM 3	22.49	0.885	4.780	4.861	0.97
SRGM 4	81.75	1.428	9.160	9.270	0.90

Table 6. Comparison Result for Release 2.

Release 2	MSE	Bias	Variation	RMSPE	R^2
SRGM 1	22.61	-0.490	4.860	4.884	0.983
SRGM 2	18.54	0.793	4.348	4.420	0.99
SRGM 3	22.58	6.367	13.985	15.367	0.88
SRGM 4	58.76	1.170	7.783	7.870	0.96

Table 7. Comparison Result for Release 3.

Release 3	MSE	Bias	Variation	RMSPE	R^2
SRGM 1	16.72	-0.585	4.229	4.269	0.96
SRGM 2	6.57	0.095	2.773	2.774	0.99
SRGM 3	20.42	1.074	7.182	7.262	0.95
SRGM 4	5.290	0.512	2.441	2.494	0.99

Table 8. Comparison Result for Release 4.

Release 4	MSE	Bias	Variation	RMSPE	R^2
SRGM 1	5.36	-0.06	2.41	2.41	0.97
SRGM 2	4.95	0.28	2.32	2.34	0.97
SRGM 3	5.80	0.500	6.49	6.51	0.97
SRGM 4	4.48	0.231	2.36	2.37	0.98

Above shown graphs (Figs. **1-4**) correspond to better fit for all the four releases on proposed SRGMs. As, it can be seen from Fig. (**1**) and also from Table **5** that Release-1 is performing better under exponential and constant scenario which is mathematically modeled as SRGM-1. But for other releases *i.e.* for release 2-4 it is not clear that which is performing best among the four releases. Thus, there was the need for an approach to quantify proposed SRGM on the basis of some ranking approach for three releases. To supplement, we have used weighted criteria approach for ranking the SRGMs on the basis of five comparison attributes [20-23].

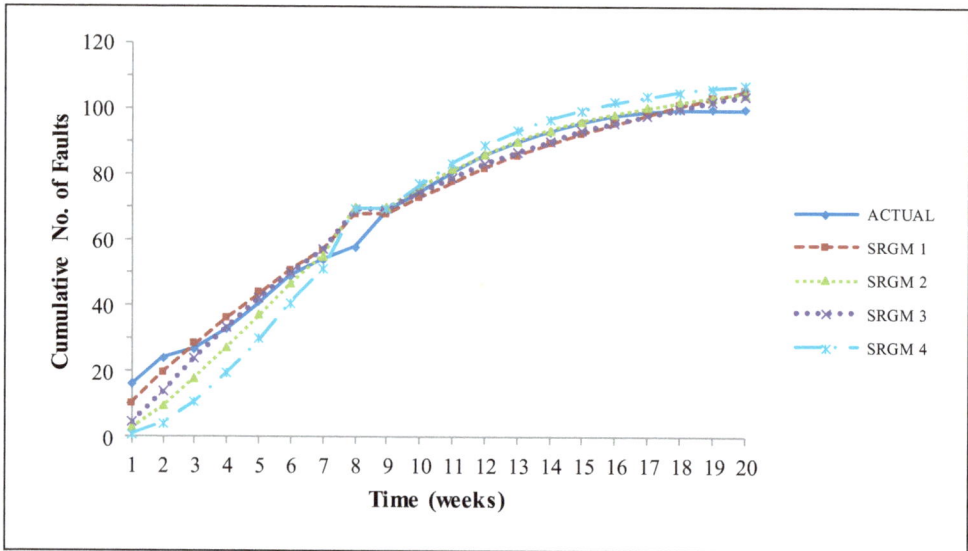

Fig. (1). Goodness of fit measure of release 1.

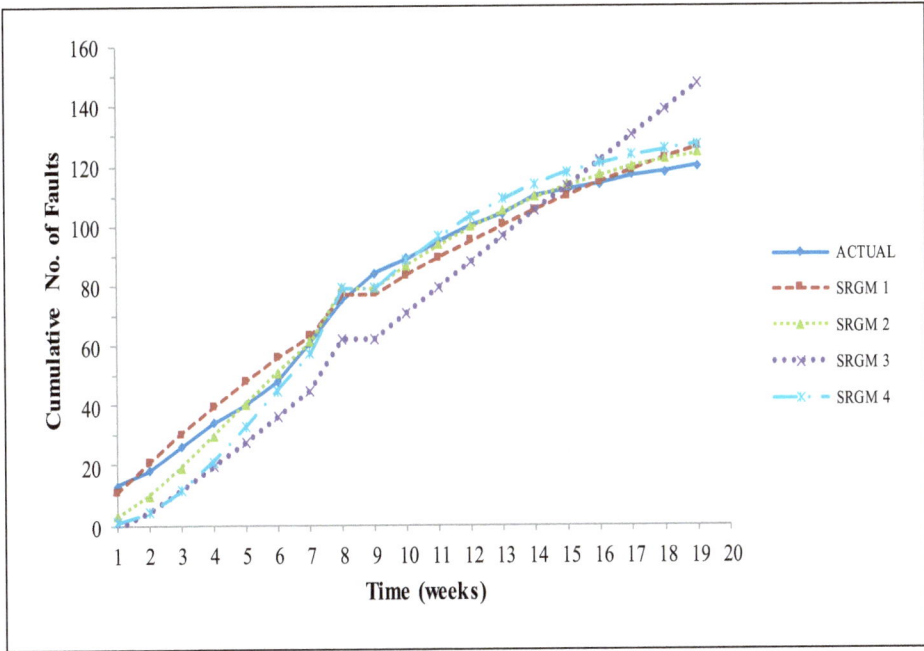

Fig. (2). Goodness of fit measure of release 2.

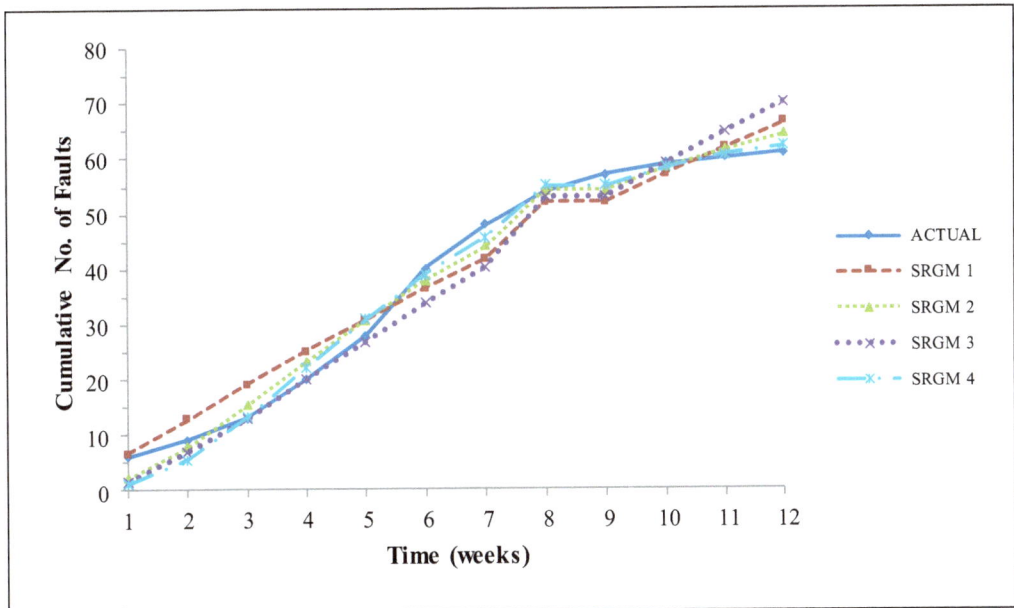

Fig. (3). Goodness of fit measure of release 3.

Making use of Weighted Criteria Approach as described in [20-23], the appropriate ranking for the proposed SRGMs is obtained. The evaluated some of weights, their values, thus obtained are presented from Tables **9-11**.

Table 9. Model Permanent value & Ranking (Release-2).

Release 2	Weighted Sum	Sum of Weighted value	Value	Rank
SRGM 1	0.2244	2.7848	12.4088	3
SRGM 2	0.1872	0.1486	0.7938	1
SRGM 3	4.1004	38.8668	9.4786	2
SRGM 4	2.1983	64.5740	29.37422	4

Table 10. Model Permanent value & Ranking (Release-3).

Release 3	Weighted Sum	Sum of Weighted value	Value	Rank
SRGM 1	2.2553	16.5502	7.3383	3
SRGM 2	0.7070	1.0346	1.4633	2
SRGM 3	5.0000	36.8925	7.3785	4
SRGM 4	0.6611	0.3385	0.5120	1

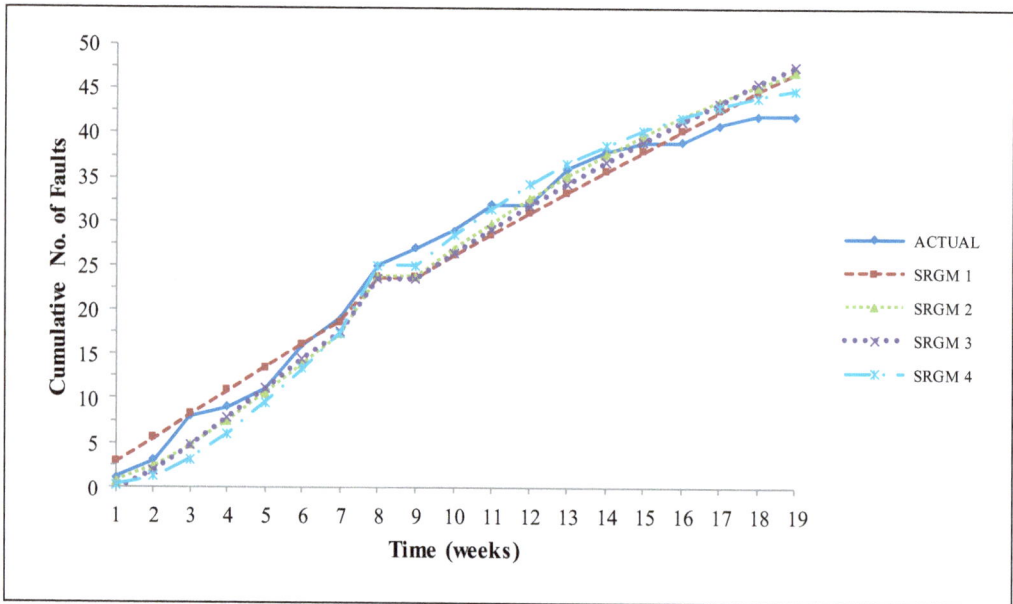

Fig. (4). Goodness of fit measure of release 4.

Table 11. Model Permanent value & Ranking (Release-4).

Release 4	Weighted Sum	Sum of Weighted value	Value	Rank
SRGM 1	1.1347	4.0902	3.6045	3
SRGM 2	1.3991	2.3714	1.6949	2
SRGM 3	5.000	20.2858	4.0571	4
SRGM 4	0.5399	0.1612	0.2986	1

On the basis of analysis performed above, the weighted criteria value approach [20-23] in identifying the ranking for different proposed SRGMs shows that SRGM-2 is at rank one followed by SRGM-3, SRGM-1 and SRGM-4 respectively (Table **9**). Further, it can be seen that in Table **10** and Table **11**, SRGM-4 is ranked one then followed by SRGM-2, SRGM-1 and SRGM-3 respectively. As releases of data set are exponential and S-shaped in nature, therefore SRGM-1 is at first position in first release and at third position in other releases (Release 2-4). SRGM-2 is at first position in release 2 similarly SRGM-3 and SRGM-4 have different ranks as we can see in above weighted approach based tables. Being at the top for both the releases (release 3 and release 4), SRGM-4 shows the better performance.

CONCLUSION

Technologies are changing very quickly and these innovations act similar to a fresh product. Due to the presence of excessive competition in market it is a must need for a software to be latest upgraded. In this paper, modeling framework captured cumulative quantity of errors removed when software was released in market multiple times. Four SRGMs for the progressive release of software using SDEs has been proposed. Capturing uncertainties produce by the stochastic fluctuations due to environmental conditions simulates stochastic process. While modeling the successive releases of the software we have considered the interaction between the errors remaining in the just prior release and the present one. This modeling improves the quality of software by reducing the faults more and more thus enabling the generation of highly reliable software. Fault removal phenomenon of SRGMs has been classified in to two categories: FDP and FCP. So as to differentiate these two categories we used convolution of probability distribution function. For consideration we reviewed standard distributions *such as* Erlang-3 stage and Exponential for detection and correction behaviours. The parameters of models have been estimated on real life four release software failure data sets. The proposed models have been produced reliable parameter estimates and goodness of fit curve has also been calculated. But the goodness of fit of proposed SRGMs does not depict any clarity on performances of the models. So, for determining the optimal rank for different SRGMs, the weighted criteria approach has been used. In this manner we were able to make use of the traditional comparison criteria in evaluating the proposed SRGMs.

CONSENT FOR PUBLICATION

Not applicable.

CONFLICT OF INTEREST

The authors confirm that this chapter contents have no conflict of interest.

ACKNOWLEDGEMENT

The research work presented in this chapter has been supported by grants to first and third author from Department of Science and Technology, via DST PURSE phase II, India.

REFERENCES

[1]   L. Goel, and K. Okumoto, "Time-dependent error-detection rate model for software reliability and other performance measures", *IEEE Trans. Reliab.*, vol. 8, no. 3, pp. 206-211.

[2]   P.K. Kapur, A.S. Garmabaki, and J. Singh, "Multi up-gradation software reliability model with imperfect debugging", *Proceedings of the International Congress on Productivity, Quality, Reliability, Optimization and Modeling (ICPQROM)*, 2011p. 136 New Delhi, India

[3]   P.K. Kapur, H. Pham, A. Gupta, and P.C. Jha, *Software reliability assessment with OR applications..* Springer: UK, 2011.

[4]   P.K. Kapur, A. Tandon, and G. Kaur, *Multi up-gradation software reliability model,* 2010pp. 468-474 *2nd International Conference on Reliability Safety and Hazard: ICRESH,* 2010.

[5]   J.D. Musa, A. Iannino, and K. Okumoto, *Software reliability: measurement, prediction, application..* McGraw-Hill: New York, 1980.

[6]   H. Pham, *System software reliability..* Springer-Verlag, 2006.

[7]   S. Yamada, and S. Ohba, "S-shaped software reliability growth models and their applications", *IEEE Trans. Reliab.*, vol. 33, no. 4, pp. 289-292.

[8]   N.F. Schneidewind, "Analysis of error processes in computer software", *SIGPLAN Not.*, vol. 10, pp. 337-346.

[9]   L.J. Hua, and C.Y. Huang, "An integration of fault detection and correction processes in software reliability analysis", *J. Syst. Softw.*, vol. 79, pp. 1312-1323.

[10]   M. Xie, Q.P. Hu, Y.P. Wu, and S.H. Ng, "A study of the modeling and analysis of software fault-detection and fault correction processes", *Qual. Reliab. Eng. Int.*, vol. 23, pp. 459-470.

[11]   P.K. Kapur, R.B. Garg, and S. Kumar, *Contribution to hardware and software reliability..* World Scientific Singapore, 1999.

[12]   "Shanti kumar JG. A general software reliability model for performance prediction", *Microelectron. Reliab.*, vol. 21, pp. 671-682.

[13]   A Anand, Deepika and Singh O. Incorporating features enhancement archetype in software reliability growth modeling and optimal release time determination. International Journal of Computer Applications (0975 - 8887) 2016; 139(4); 1-6

[14]   A Anand, O Singh, and S Das, "Fault severity based multi up-gradation modeling considering testing and operational profile", *International Journal of Computer Applications (0975 - 8887)*, vol. 124, no. 4, pp. 9-15.

[15]   S. Yamada, A. Nishigaki, and M. Kimura, "A stochastic differential equation model for software reliability assessment and its goodness of fit", *International Journal of Reliability and Applications*, vol. 4, no. 1, pp. 1-11.

[16]   O. Singh, P.K. Kapur, A. Anand, and J. Singh, *Stochastic differential equation based modeling for multiple generations of software*, 2009pp. 122-131 *Proceedings of the4th International Conference on Quality, Reliability and Infocom Technology (ICQRIT), Trends and Future Directions, Narosa Publications*, 2009.

[17]   B. Oksendal, *Stochastic differential equations: an introduction with applications. Universitext.*, 6th ed Springer: Berlin, Germany, 2013.

[18]   Y. Tamura, and S. Yamada, "A flexible stochastic differential equation model in distributed development environment", *Eur. J. Oper. Res.*, vol. 168, no. 1, pp. 143-152.

[19]   C.H. Lee, Y.T. Kim, and D.H. Park, "S-shaped software reliability growth models derived from stochastic differential equations", *IIE Trans.*, vol. 36, no. 12, pp. 1193-1199.

[20]   A Anand, PK Kapur, M Agarwal, and D Aggrawal, "Generalized innovation diffusion modeling & weighted criteria based ranking", *IEEE Explore*, vol. 9718, no. 1, pp. 4799-6896.

[21]   A Anand, and N Bhatt, "Vulnerability discovery modeling and weighted criteria based ranking", *Journal of the Indian society for probability and statistics*, vol. 17, no. 1, pp. 1-10.

[22]   A. Anand, O. Singh, R. Aggarwal, and D. Aggrawal, "Diffusion modeling based on customer's review and product satisfaction", *Int. J. Technol. Diffus.*, vol. 7, pp. 20-31.

[23]   M Anjum, MA Harque, and N Ahmad, Analysis and ranking of software reliability models based on weighted criteria value. IJ information technology and computer science: 2013; 1-14

[24]   O. Singh, P.K. Kapur, and A. Anand, *A Stochastic formulation of successive software releases with fault severity.*. Industrial Engineering and Engineering Management, 2011, pp. 136-140.

[25]   P.K. Kapur, and V. Kumar, "Testing resource allocation for fault detection and correction processes under dynamic environment", *Proceedings of the 5th National Conference,*, 2011

[26]   S.S. Gokhle, T. Philip, P.N. Marinos, and K.S. Trivedi, "Unification of finite failure non homogenous poisson process models through coverage", *Proceedings of the International Symposium on Software Reliability Engineering (ISSRE) White Plains*, 1996pp. 289-299 NY

[27]   P.K. Kapur, A. Anand, and O. Singh, Modeling successive software up-gradations with faults of different severity. Proceedings of the 5th National Conference on Computing For Nation Development 2011; ISSN 0973-7529 ISBN 978-93-80544-00-7

[28]   O. Singh, P.K. Kapur, S.K. Khatri, and J.N.P. Singh, "Software reliability growth modeling for successive releases", *Proceeding of the 4th International Conference on Quality, Reliability and Infocom Technology (ICQRIT)*, 2012pp. 77-87

[29]   A. Anand, A. Singh, P.K. Kapur, and S. Das, "Modeling Conjoint effect of faults testified from operational phase for successive software releases", *Proceedings of the 5th International Conference on Life Cycle Engineering and Management (ICDQM)*, 2014pp. 83-94

[30]   A. Wood, "Predicting software reliability", *IEEE Computer*, vol. 11, pp. 69-77.

CHAPTER 4

Mathematical Models for Digital Imaging and their Applications in Digital Image Forensics

Hemant K. Verma, Vinay Verma and Nitin Khanna*

Multimedia Analysis and Security (MANAS) Lab, Electrical Engineering, Indian Institute of Technology Gandhinagar, India

Abstract: With rapid technological advancements in the last few decades, our information and communication systems are progressively moving towards being completely digitized. Simultaneously, as a consequence of modern networking technologies, a plethora of digital information is being stored and transmitted in a couple of seconds. Highly appreciated multimedia enabled handheld devices are empowering even the common man to communicate on the go. Today, our understanding of events is highly dependent on visual information. Consequently, digital images have become a prominent carrier of information. Dependence of our lifestyles on digital images leads to the critical importance of their security and reliability. In parallel to the technological advancement, availability of software tools capable of easily manipulating digital images in a user-friendly manner is not so rare. With this, the trust we keep on digital image as proof of an event is at risk. This chapter presents an introduction to the emerging field of digital image forensics, which aims to provide authenticity and security to digital images. This introduction is followed by detailed analysis of one class of image forensic methods, methods based on color filter array interpolation. An experimental comparison of some prominent works and recent developments in this field on a common dataset has been discussed in this chapter.

Keywords: Bayer pattern, Camera classification, CFA de-mosaicking, CFA forensics, CFA pattern, Color filter array (CFA), De-mosaicking artifacts, Digital camera, Digital color imaging, Digital image forensics, Digital image forgery, Image authenticity, Image forgery detection, Image source classification, Image tampering, Information processing and management, Information technology and security, Intelligent systems, Multimedia forensics, Multimedia security, Non-intrusive image forensics, Tampering detection.

***Corresponding author Nitin Khanna:** Multimedia Analysis and Security (MANAS) Lab, Electrical Engineering, Indian Institute of Technology Gandhinagar, India; Tel: +91-7923952488; Fax: +91-7923952032; E-mail: nitinkhanna@iitgn.ac.in

Mangey Ram (Ed.)

INFORMATION SECURITY

In computing, the term *information* refers to "digital data that is processed, stored, or transmitted by a computer[1]," and *security*, according to the dictionary means "the state of being free from danger or threat" [1]. Combining these two terms forms information security, which essentially means "the state of being protected against the unauthorized use of information, especially electronic data, or the measures taken to achieve this" [1].

This celebrated concept of the modern era has its roots back in the late Roman Republic when *Julius Caesar* invented *Caesar Cipher* to prevent his secret messages from being read by unauthorized persons [2]. Information security we know today was in its infancy during the 1960s and 1970s when the concept of paperless office was introduced for the first time with the advent of computers. Since then, a vast amount of information available in business/corporate firms is stored in digital form in computer-based systems. And today, because of reduced size and cost of computing devices like laptops, tablet PCs, smartphones, *etc.* not only business firms but also a common individual of the modern era have become a contributor to this plethora of digital data containing sensitive information. This gives rise to the obvious question of security and reliability of these valuable digital information assets, answers to which lie in the policies, procedures, and standards of information security. The objectives fulfilled by information security include not only protection of information assets from threats like security breach, forgery, piracy, phishing, *etc.*, but also investigation of these threats so as to mitigate the possibilities of future recurrences of such threats. The former objective is usually achieved by techniques like encryption, watermarking, *etc.* while the latter objective mainly relies on forensic techniques to get probative facts about any potential crime. This chapter focuses on forensics aspect of information security, and presents a brief hierarchical explanation of different branches of forensics, as shown in Fig. (**1**).

DIGITAL FORENSICS

The term *forensics* derived from a Latin word *forum* meaning "a public square used for judicial business," can be summed up as "attempts to investigate crime scene using scientific methods or techniques" [1]. In a typical forensics framework, a forensic investigator first creates a model of reality based on his/her

---

[1] The term computer here is not limited to desktop PC, but it includes any electronic device capable of processing digital data.

understanding of reality and then analyses the evidence obtained from crime scene to get some probative facts about the crime. Better the model is, more reliable the probative facts are. In a *classical (analog) forensics* scenario, forensic investigator studies the physical evidence obtained from crime scene, however, in context of information security, the evidence from crime scene are digital. In such environments where the domain of evidence is digital, the forensics counterpart is termed as *digital forensics.*

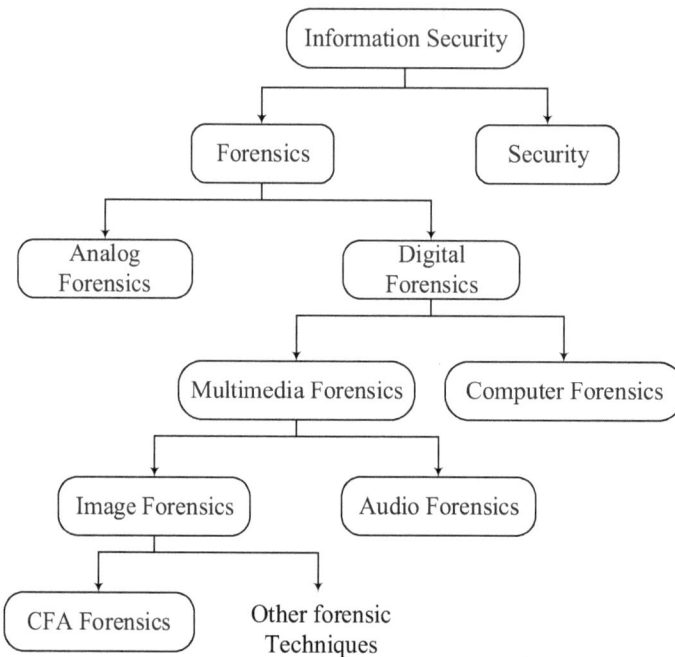

Fig. (1). Hierarchy of different branches of Forensics.

As discussed in previous section, a huge amount of information ranging from highly confidential bank databases to a photograph of a bird captured with a smartphone is being generated and stored digitally. Depending on the way digital information is generated, it is possible to classify it into two broad classes. First, when the information exists physically in analog world and is digitized by means of some sensor, *e.g.,* a painting painted by an artist in analog world and digitized by a digital camera or a scanner. And second, when the information has no physical existence in analog world but is created directly in digital form, *e.g.,* an email or SMS sent from one person to another or a computer-generated image using simulated models of physical world. Based on these two classes, digital forensics can be further classified into *multimedia forensics* corresponding to the first class, and *computer forensics* corresponding to the second class. Both computer forensics and multimedia forensics rely on digital evidence but differ in the underlying models of reality [3]. In computer forensics, where information is created digitally, the underlying model of reality is restricted to digital world. Whereas in multimedia forensics, the model of reality is derived from digital information as well as from the attributes of sensor and analog information. Rest of this chapter will specifically concentrate on multimedia forensics.

MULTIMEDIA FORENSICS

A broad definition of multimedia is, "combination of number of media to express or communicate" [1]. In the digital world, multimedia mainly refers to digital audios, images, and videos stored on digital storage such as hard disk or a DVD drive. Ever since the invention of cameras around the 18th century, images have been used to keep records of past events and presented as evidence in the court of law to reveal the truth. The rapid technological advancements within last few decades have changed our lifestyles immensely, and images have become an integral part of an individual's professional as well as personal life. With social networking platforms, sharing a photograph is now a matter of few seconds.

On one side, we are inclined to treat these images as trustworthy evidence in the court of law, while on the flip side attempts to manipulate them are also well-known. Traces of image forgery go back even to the beginning of photography, for example, a photograph doctored in the 18th century was revealed in 2015. This photograph featured General Ulysses S. Grant in front of his troops at the City Point, Virginia, during the American Civil War [4].

Till date, numerous instances of image manipulation to mislead the audience have been published and revealed in various renowned articles, newspapers, and magazines. Some recent cases include [5] where a Jewish newspaper airbrushed female world leaders out of a picture captured during a march in Paris, and [6] where India's state-run PIB tweeted an edited image of India Prime Minister surveying deadly Chennai floods in 2015, [7] in 2011 where it was claimed that former US president was photoshoped into an image, and he was not actually present in the original image, but later it was revealed that the claimed photoshoped image was actually the original image, and [8] in 2014 where the Malaysian Air's flight MH17 was featured in a satellite image to be shot down by a fighter jet. Many more instances of famous image forgeries are available at [9], and some samples of image forgery are presented in Fig. (2).

Altered Image   Altered Image

Original Image   Original Image

Fig. (2). Image Tampering Examples. Top row is tampered, and bottom is original, in the top left figure a bird is added, and in the top right figure a blue colored car is added.

This leads us to the question of security and reliability of these multimedia contents, answer to which lies in multimedia forensics. Multimedia forensics attempts to provide probative facts about authenticity and origin of multimedia content. Depending on multimedia content under investigation, this field is further classified into *audio forensics* and *image forensics*, both of which follow the same underlying principles, but differ in application scenario. Since a video can be treated as a sequence of images captured at different instances of time, for the purpose of this discussion, image forensics includes the methods applicable for forensic examination of videos as well. This chapter focuses on image forensics.

In a typical image forensics scenario, a forensic investigator first derives a model based on knowledge and/or assumptions about the capturing device (*e.g.,* a camera) and reality (*i.e.,* the scene captured) and then tests the image under investigation with this model. The definition of this model generally depends on the probative facts to be analyzed. For example, to test the authenticity of an image, the model is based either on camera processing pipeline [10-12] or on some post-processing operation typically used while making forgeries [13, 14]. In the former case, consistent presence of some signatures due to camera pipeline all over the image indicates authenticity, while in the latter case, presence or absence of some post-processing operation (*e.g.,* lossy compression, double compression) indicates about the authenticity of image under investigation.

Whereas to comment on the origin of an image, the model is based on some feature(s) of imaging device which is/are unique to every device. One such feature is sensor pattern noise or Photo Response Non-uniformity (PRNU) [15, 16]. The rest of this chapter focuses on one major class of image forensics consisting of techniques based on artifacts due to Color Filter Array (CFA) de-mosaicking, henceforth referred as CFA forensics.

CFA FORENSICS: AN OVERVIEW

Color filter array (CFA) forensics is the branch of image forensics that relies on CFA de-mosaicking signatures left by imaging device or out of camera processing software for converting RAW images into color images or for converting images obtained using one CFA de-mosaicking into another. In order to understand forensics techniques based on these signatures, one must have an understanding of CFA and CFA de-mosaicking algorithms. The following subsections give a brief description of the same.

CFA Configuration

One of the core components of a digital camera is sensor array which senses light and converts it into electrical signals. This sensor array consist a number of sensor elements arranged in a grid-like fashion. Each sensor element is a color-blind light sensitive device (*e.g.,* a CCD or a CMOS) and records the amount of light from dark to bright without any color information. In order to incorporate color information in an image, an optical filter is placed in front of each sensor element, which allows light of particular wavelengths to pass through and blocks other wavelengths. Consequently, every sensor element captures light intensity of a particular color. To get the complete color image, several different configurations of these optical filters and sensor elements are used in digital cameras. The prominent ones are as follows:

1. Color Filter Array (CFA) based single-sensor configuration

2. Color sequential sensor configuration

3. Multi-sensor configuration

Among these three configurations, the color sequential sensor captures three colors at same sensor element sequentially *via* a set of moving optical filters, and hence it is suitable only for still objects. Multi-sensor configuration which uses three different sensor elements to capture three colors has limitation of its large size and high cost. Whereas, CFA based sensor is smaller, works fine with dynamic scenes and hence used widely among various camera manufacturers. This chapter focuses on forensic techniques based on statistical features of images acquired using CFA configuration.

Fig. (**3**) shows a generic block diagram of processing pipeline of a camera with CFA based single-sensor configuration. The light coming from scene first passes through camera optics, which incorporates an optical low pass filter to avoid aliasing due to sampling by sensor array. Before striking the sensor array, light rays are passed through an array of transmissive optical filters referred as color filter array. Although a number of CFA configurations have been proposed so far, the most prominent ones are shown in Fig. (**4**).

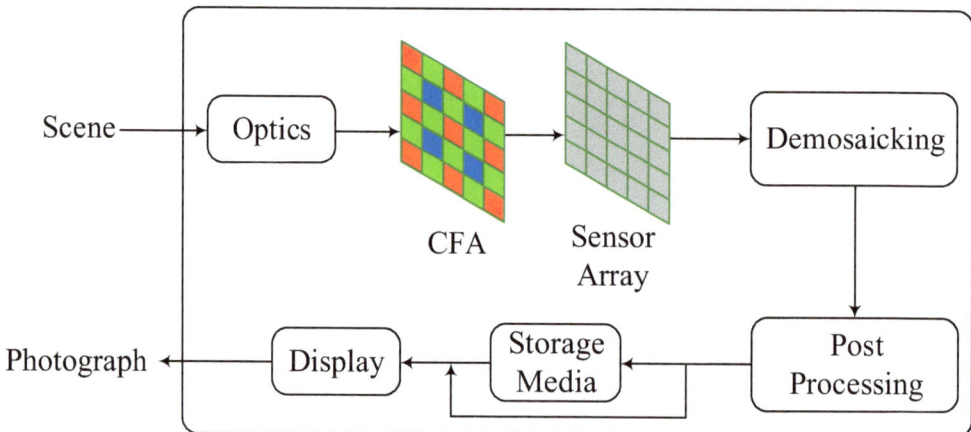

Fig. (3). Block diagram of single-sensor camera processing pipeline.

In the first CFA configuration shown in Fig. (**4a**), each optical filter denoted by R, G and B only allows light rays with wavelength corresponding to red, green and blue colors, respectively. Thus, each sensor element records either red, green or blue color sample at a particular sample location. The arrangement of red, green and blue color in every 2×2 block of CFA shown in Fig. (**4a**) is referred to as Bayer pattern [17]. As human visual perception is more sensitive to luminance which depends primarily on green light, the Bayer pattern samples green color twice and red and blue color only once in every 2×2 block. Consequently, high spatial frequencies in luminance are preserved due to sampling at a higher sampling rate. Other possible variants of Bayer pattern are shown in Fig. (**4c**).

The CMYG configuration shown in Fig. (**4b**) uses cyan (C), magenta (M), yellow (Y) and green (G) color filters. As filters corresponding to yellow and cyan colors pass more light energy in comparison to those corresponding to red and blue, this configuration provides higher SNR at low illumination. However, under normal illumination, the complex processing required with this configuration increases noise, and hence this configuration is less preferred over the first one for use in normal cameras [18]. Forensic techniques discussed in this chapter are prominently related to RGB configuration, but they can be easily extended for CMYG based configurations as well.

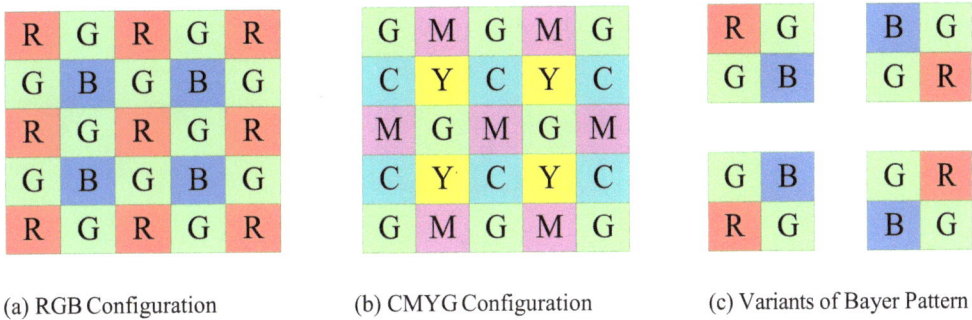

(a) RGB Configuration   (b) CMYG Configuration   (c) Variants of Bayer Pattern

Fig. (4). Color filter array configurations.

Color De-mosaicking

A digital color image has three channels, each representing one of the red, green and blue spectral bands. In a camera with RGB color filter array, each sensor element acquires only one color sample at a given sample location, and other two colors are missing.

For example, consider the color filter array shown in Fig. (**4a**), and corresponding image $\hat{I}$ (Fig. **5**) generated by the sensor array. At sample location (1,1) red sample r_{11} is acquired while green and blue samples are missing. Information related to the red, green and blue channels, as directly present in the image $\hat{I}$, is given as follows:

$$\hat{R}(m,n) = \hat{I}(m,n) \times r(m,n)$$

$$\hat{G}(m,n) = \hat{I}(m,n) \times g(m,n)$$

$$\hat{B}(m,n) = \hat{I}(m,n) \times b(m,n)$$

where,

$$r(m,n) = \begin{cases} 1 & \text{if red color is acquired} \\ 0 & \text{otherwise} \end{cases}$$

$$b(m,n) = \begin{cases} 1 & \text{if blue color is acquired} \\ 0 & \text{otherwise} \end{cases}$$

$$b(m,n) = \begin{cases} 1 & \text{if blue color is acquired} \\ 0 & \text{otherwise} \end{cases}$$

r_{11}	g_{12}	r_{13}	g_{14}	r_{15}	g_{16}
g_{21}	b_{22}	g_{23}	b_{24}	g_{25}	b_{26}
r_{31}	g_{32}	r_{33}	g_{34}	r_{35}	g_{36}
g_{41}	b_{42}	g_{43}	b_{44}	g_{45}	b_{46}
r_{51}	g_{52}	r_{53}	g_{54}	r_{55}	g_{56}
g_{61}	b_{62}	g_{63}	b_{64}	g_{65}	b_{66}

Fig. (5). Image $\hat{I}$ generated by sensor.

In order to get complete red, green and blue channels, missing color samples are estimated from neighboring acquired samples. This process of estimating missing color samples from acquired samples is called CFA de-mosaicking or CFA interpolation.

Among numerous proposed de-mosaicking algorithms there are some simpler algorithms like bilinear interpolation, and some complex algorithms like [19]. Table **1** lists some prominent de-mosaicking algorithms in the literature, and their behavior. Simpler de-mosaicking algorithms find the missing color samples by computing a weighted average of nearest acquired samples of the same color in a linear, channel-independent manner (Equations 1.1-3).

$$R(m,n) = \sum_{l,k=-\beta}^{\beta} \alpha_r(l,k)\,\hat{R}(m+l,n+k) + \varepsilon_r(m,n) \qquad (1)$$

$$G(m,n) = \sum_{l,k=-\beta}^{\beta} \alpha_g(l,k)\,\hat{G}(m+l,n+k) + \varepsilon_g(m,n) \qquad (2)$$

$$B(m,n) = \sum_{l,k=-\beta}^{\beta} \alpha_b(l,k)\,\hat{B}(m+l,n+k) + \varepsilon_b(m,n) \qquad (3)$$

where, R, G, and B denotes three channels of de-mosaicked image I, β denotes the neighborhood size used for de-mosaicking and $\varepsilon_{\{r,g,b\}}(m,n)$ denotes rounding error. However, simplicity of such algorithms comes at the cost of reduced sharpness and aliasing artifacts. Complex algorithms preserve sharpness of an image by performing interpolation in a content adaptive manner.

Table 1. Interpolation algorithms and their behavior.

Sr. No	Interpolation Algorithm	Linearity	Content Adaptiveness	Channel Interdependence
1.	Bilinear	Yes	No	No
2.	Bicubic [20]	Yes	No	No
3.	Smooth Hue Transition [21]	No	No	Yes
4.	Gradient Based [21]	No	Yes	Yes
5.	Median Filter Based [21]	No	No	Yes
6.	AHD [19]	No	Yes	Yes

As a result of CFA de-mosaicking, at every sample location, one color sample is acquired whereas other two color samples are estimated from the neighboring acquired samples. This introduces a correlation between de-mosaicked samples and acquired samples. As the Bayer pattern is periodic over a block of size 2×2, these correlations are also periodic under the assumption of non-adaptive interpolation. In the presence of content-adaptive interpolation, the periodicity of these correlations is lost to some extent. These correlations due to interpolation algorithms form the basis of CFA based forensic techniques.

CFA BASED FORENSIC TECHNIQUES

As discussed in the previous section, CFA de-mosaicking generates periodic correlations in a de-mosaicked image. Any potential manipulation in a camera-generated image may destroy these periodic correlations. Presence of such periodic correlations consistently throughout the image indicates that image is generated by a single-sensor camera, and has not undergone any manipulations. Whereas, absence or inconsistency of periodic correlations indicates that image may have undergone some manipulation or is not even generated by a single-sensor camera. Detecting the presence or absence of correlation due to CFA de-mosaicking may help a forensic investigator to comment on the authenticity of a given image. Among the wide range of imaging devices including cell phones to DSLR cameras, CFA configuration and de-mosaicking algorithms are usually fixed for all the cameras of a particular make and model but may vary from model to model, and so does the CFA de-mosaicking fingerprint. Hence, differentiating between different CFA configurations and de-mosaicking algorithms may also help to solve the problem of device classification/identification.

Depending on these two types of problems targeted by CFA forensics, previous works in this field can be divided in two major classes, i) detecting the presence of CFA de-mosaicking for tampering detection and ii) estimating the type of CFA pattern and/or CFA de-mosaicking schemes (assuming the image has undergone CFA de-mosaicking) for source classification/identification.

Detecting Presence of CFA De-mosaicking

Forensic techniques presented in this section generally assume that a camera's original images will always have CFA de-mosaicking. Under this assumption, the absence of CFA de-mosaicking indicates that image is tampered. In a given image, a given sample can belong to exactly one of the two models, i) M_1 when the sample is de-mosaicked ii) M_2 when the sample is acquired by sensor array. Thus, the problem of detecting presence of CFA de-mosaicking can be seen as a two-class classification problem where every sample needs to be classified in one of the two models M_1 and M_2. If the final assignment of samples to model M_1 and M_2 follows a specific periodic pattern, image is said to be de-mosaicked, otherwise not. Authors in [12] addressed this problem by an iterative expectation maximization (EM) approach. Assignment of samples to model M_1 and M_2 is given in terms of a probability map W, each value of which denotes the probability of a particular sample being de-mosaicked. Starting with a randomly chosen de-mosaicking kernel α, and assuming a linear non adaptive de-mosaicking algorithm, prediction error is calculated (Equation (4)) in expectation step and then, a cost function (Equation (5)) $E(\alpha)$ is minimized in maximization step, to get better estimate of de-mosaicking kernel.

$$e(m,n) = C(m,n) - \sum_{l,k=-\beta}^{\beta} \alpha_{l,k} C(m+l,n+k) \tag{4}$$

$\forall\, C \in \{R,G,B\}$ representing one color channel

$$E(\alpha) = \sum_{m,n} W(m,n) \times e^2(m,n) \tag{5}$$

This estimate of de-mosaicking kernel is then used to update variance σ^2 of rounding error and the probability map W (Equation (7)).

$$W(m,n) = Pr\{C(m,n) \in M_1 \mid C(m,n)\} \tag{6}$$

$$W(m,n) = \frac{Pr\{C(m,n) \mid C(m,n) \in M_1\} \times Pr\{C(m,n) \in M_1\}}{\sum_{i=1}^{2} Pr\{C(m,n) \mid C(m,n) \in M_i\} \times Pr\{C(m,n) \in M_i\}} \tag{7}$$

$$Pr\{C(m,n) \mid C(m,n) \in M_1\} = \frac{1}{\sigma\sqrt{2\pi}} \times exp\left| \frac{-e^2(m,n)}{2\sigma^2} \right|$$

$$Pr\{C(m,n) \mid C(m,n) \in M_2\} = \frac{1}{\text{range of possible values of } C(m,n)}$$

Each sample $W(m,n)$ of this posterior probability map, is the estimated probability of sample at location (m,n) being de-mosaicked. The updated de-mosaicking kernel and probability map are used again to re-calculate prediction error and cost function in expectation step, which is minimized in maximization step to get a new estimate of de-mosaicking kernel. This sequence of expectation followed by maximization goes on iteratively until a stable solution of de-mosaicking kernel is obtained. Since the Bayer pattern is periodic, probability map obtained after convergence of EM algorithm is also periodic (only when image is de-mosaicked), and this periodicity can be seen in the form of peaks in Fourier transform of estimated probability map (Fig. **6**).

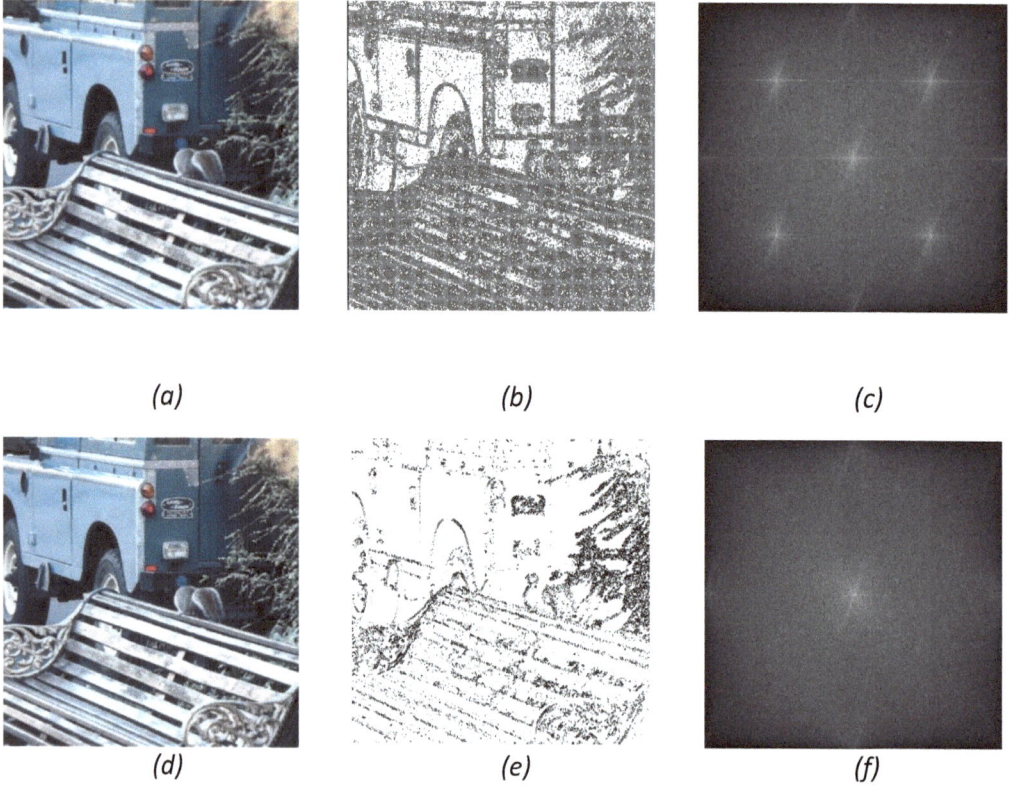

(a)   *(b)*   *(c)*

(d)   *(e)*   *(f)*

Fig. (6). From left to right: given image, probability map, fourier transform of probability map. from top to bottom: image with de-mosaicking, image without de-mosaicking.

Presence of peaks in Fourier transform indicates the presence of CFA de-mosaicking and their absence indicates absence of CFA de-mosaicking. For detection of localized forgeries in images, the same procedure is applied on small non-overlapping blocks to get a local block level decision. This EM algorithm based method proposed in [12] assumes a strictly linear, non-adaptive, channel independent de-mosaicking kernel. However, in practical scenarios, these assumptions do hold as de-mosaicking algorithms are often adaptive, channel interdependent and non-linear. To incorporate channel interdependent and adaptive behavior of de-mosaicking algorithms, authors in [22] introduced another EM algorithm based approach termed as a hybrid model for detecting

CFA de-mosaicking. Based on the study of a number of de-mosaicking algorithms, diverse behavior of these de-mosaicking algorithms is incorporated in a single hybrid model. Authors proposed that the green channel is usually de-mosaicked either in bilinear fashion or in a content adaptive fashion so as to avoid smoothening of edges.

To avoid smoothening, de-mosaicking is done along the edges and not across the edges. Depending on these two possible ways of de-mosaicking green channel, authors described two models for green channel, one bilinear (Equation (8)) and other content adaptive (Equation (9)).

$$G(m,n) = \sum_{l,k=-\beta}^{\beta} \alpha_{l,k} \hat{G}(m+l,n+k) \tag{8}$$

$$G(m,n) = \begin{cases} \sum_{k=-\beta}^{\beta} \alpha_k \hat{G}(m,n+k), & \text{for horizontal edge} \\ \sum_{l=-\beta}^{\beta} \alpha_l \hat{G}(m+l,n), & \text{for horizontal edge} \\ \sum_{l,k=-\beta}^{\beta} \alpha_{l,k} \hat{G}(m+l,n+k), & \text{for smooth region} \end{cases} \tag{9}$$

Prediction errors are estimated for these two models separately. These two prediction errors are fed separately in EM algorithms discussed previously to get two probability maps, and two estimated de-mosaicking kernel. The de-mosaicking kernel giving minimum error is chosen as estimated de-mosaicking kernel, and corresponding probability map is used for calculating a similarity measure Y given by Equation (10). In smooth regions of an image, the neighboring samples are similar, and thus every sample seems to be correlated with its neighbor. This creates false alarms in detection of CFA de-mosaicking. To avoid such false alarms, vector v in Equation (10) contains only those samples from the probability map for which corresponding samples in image have local variance greater than certain threshold.

$$Y(v,s) = \frac{\sum_{i=1}^{X}\left(v(i)-\bar{v}\right)\times\left(s(i)-\bar{s}\right)}{\sum_{i=1}^{X}\left(s(i)-\bar{s}\right)^{2}}$$

(10)

Here, v represents a one dimensional vector obtained by raster order scanning of probability map, and s represents a similar vector obtained from a synthetic map (which represents ground truth). Unlike the similarity measure presented in [12] which was insensitive to phase, this measure Y proposed in [22] is sensitive to phase as well as amplitude scaling. For red/blue channels authors proposed three de-mosaicking models depending on adaptiveness and dependence on green channel of de-mosaicking algorithms. Prediction errors for these three models are fed in EM algorithm and best model is chosen in similar manner as it done in case of green channel.

In [12] and [22], starting with a random guess, de-mosaicking kernel is updated iteratively to get the best estimate. In some other works including [23-27], this de-mosaicking kernel is kept fixed, say a bilinear kernel, and features are extracted from the prediction error obtained with this bilinear kernel. These features are then used to differentiate photo-graphic images (PIM) from photorealistic computer generated (PRCG) images and to detect local forgeries. Here it is assumed, that PIM are always CFA de-mosaicked, while PRCG images are not CFA de-mosaicked.

Authors in [23] proposed a formulation similar to the one proposed in [12] but limited the search space of Bayer pattern to the four depicted in Fig. (**4c**). In these four patterns, green channel has only two variations. For bilinear de-mosaicking scheme, a de-mosaicked green sample is obtained from neighboring acquired green samples according to Equation (11). Prediction error e for these two variants of CFA configuration is estimated according to Equation (12), and variance of error corresponding to de-mosaicked samples is computed separately for the two configurations. The configuration giving minimum variance is chosen as estimated CFA configuration, and variance of error corresponding to both de-mosaicked samples $(\sigma_{M_1}^2)$ and acquired samples $(\sigma_{M_2}^2)$ is computed for this configuration. These two variances are then used to estimate prior probabilities given by Equation (13) and (14).

$$G(m,n) = \frac{1}{4}\left(\hat{G}(m-1,n) + \hat{G}(m,n-1) + \hat{G}(m+1,n) + \hat{G}(m,n+1)\right) \qquad (11)$$

$$e(m,n) = G(m-1,n) + G(m,n-1) + G(m+1,n) + G(m,n+1) - 4 \times G(m,n) \qquad (12)$$

$$Pr\{C(m,n) \mid C(m,n) \in M_1\} = \frac{1}{\sigma_{M_1}^2 \sqrt{2\pi}} \times exp\left| \frac{-e^2(m,n)}{2\sigma_{M_1}^2} \right| \qquad (13)$$

$$Pr\{C(m,n) \mid C(m,n) \in M_2\} = \frac{1}{\sigma_{M_2}^2 \sqrt{2\pi}} \times exp\left| \frac{-e^2(m,n)}{2\sigma_{M_2}^2} \right| \qquad (14)$$

Substituting Equation (13) and (14) in Equation (7) gives the probability of each sample being de-mosaicked. Finally, three features are extracted from the magnitude of Fourier transform of this probability map to differentiate PIM from PRCG images.

In [24], authors assumed, that the acquired green samples are drawn from a uniform *iid* distribution with variance σ_g^2, the variance of a de-mosaicked green sample (assuming bilinear de-mosaicking) becomes:

$$var\{G(m,n)\} = \frac{1}{4^2} \times \left(\sigma_g^2 + \sigma_g^2 + \sigma_g^2 + \sigma_g^2\right)$$

$$var\{G(m,n)\} = \frac{\sigma_g^2}{4}$$

If the given image is de-mosaicked, error $e(m_0, n_0)$ corresponding to an acquired sample at location (m_0, n_0) can be obtained by substituting m by m_0 and n by n_0 in Equation (12). Because of the specific structure of Bayer pattern (Fig. (4c)), if a green sample at location (m_0, n_0) is acquired, green samples at location $(m_0 \pm 1, n_0)$ and $(m_0, n_0 \pm 1)$ must be de-mosaicked, and these de-mosaicked samples can be expressed in terms of its neighboring acquired samples according to Equation (11). Substituting Equation (11) in Equation (12), prediction error e at an acquired sample location (m_0, n_0), and a de-mosaicked sample location, say (m_i, n_i) is given by Equation (15) and (16) respectively.

$$
e(m_0, n_0) = \frac{1}{4}\left(\hat{G}(m_0 - 2, n_0) + \hat{G}(m_0, n_0 - 2) + \hat{G}(m_0 + 2, n_0) + \hat{G}(m_0, n_0 + 2)\right) + ...
$$
$$
\frac{1}{2}\left(\hat{G}(m_0 - 1, n_0 - 1) + \hat{G}(m_0 - 1, n_0 + 1) + \hat{G}(m_0 + 1, n_0 - 1) + \hat{G}(m_0 + 1, n_0 + 1)\right) + ... \quad \textbf{(15)}
$$
$$
(1 - 4) \times \hat{G}(m_0, n_0)
$$

$$
e(m_i, n_i) = \hat{G}(m_i - 1, n_i) + \hat{G}(m_i, n_i - 1) + \hat{G}(m_i + 1, n_i) + \hat{G}(m_i, n_i + 1) - ...
$$
$$
4 \times G(m_i, n_i) \quad \textbf{(16)}
$$

According to Equation (15), prediction error at a location corresponding to an acquired sample is obtained by weighted sum of nine neighboring acquired samples, four with weight 1/4, four with weight 1/2, and one with weight −3. Consequently, the variance of prediction error e at location corresponding to acquired samples is given by Equation (17).

$$
\sigma_0^2 = 4\left(\frac{1}{4}\right)^2 \sigma_g^2 + 4\left(\frac{1}{2}\right)^2 \sigma_g^2 + (-3)^2 \sigma_g^2 \quad \textbf{(17)}
$$

Similarly, in accordance with Equation (16), variance of prediction error at location corresponding to de-mosaicked samples is given by Equation (18).

$$
\sigma_i^2 = \left(\sigma_g^2 + \sigma_g^2 + \sigma_g^2 + \sigma_g^2\right) - 4^2 \times \frac{\sigma_g^2}{4} \quad \textbf{(18)}
$$

In case when the actual de-mosaicking kernel is bilinear, without any post-processing (ignoring rounding error) after de-mosaicking, the ratio σ_0^2/σ_i^2 becomes infinite, but in practical scenarios, with some post processing, the ratio will be a large finite value. A large value of σ_0^2/σ_i^2 indicates that the image has undergone CFA de-mosaicking.

In summary, when the predicted de-mosaicking kernel is close to the actual de-mosaicking kernel, variance of prediction error is much higher at locations corresponding to acquired samples in comparison to that at locations corresponding to de-mosaicked samples. However, the assumption made earlier that acquired samples are *iid* is not always true. Authors in [25] proposed that acquired samples will be *iid* only locally and its variance will be stationary only locally. Thus, variance of prediction error should be evaluated on small sections of image, and it is expected to vary depending on the image content. Consequently, a feature based on local variance of prediction error for fine-grained analysis of CFA de-mosaicking artifacts to detect local forgeries in images was proposed in [25]. Assuming that prediction error is locally stationary in a region of size $(2K+1)\times(2K+1)$, local variance of prediction error is defined according to Equation (19)

$$\sigma_e^2(m,n) = \frac{1}{c}\left|\left(\sum_{l,k=-K}^{K} w_{l,k}\, e^2(m+l,n+k)\right) - \mu_e^2\right| \tag{19}$$

where weights $w_{i,j}$ make sure that summation in Equation (19) is over either acquired samples or de-mosaicked samples, μ_e is mean of those samples, and c is scale factor for making estimator unbiased. Given an image, it is analyzed by considering non-overlapping blocks of size $D\times D$. A feature $L(p,q)$ is calculated at every block location (p,q) according to Equation (20)

$$L(p,q) = log\left|\frac{GM^2(p,q)}{GM^1(p,q)}\right| \tag{20}$$

where,

$$GM^1(p,q) = \left[\prod_{i,j\in B_{p,q}^1} \sigma_e^2(i,j)\right]^{1/|B_{p,q}^1|} \tag{21}$$

$$GM^2(p,q) = \left[\prod_{i,j\in B_{p,q}^2} \sigma_e^2(i,j)\right]^{1/|B_{p,q}^2|} \tag{22}$$

$B_{p,q}^1$ and $B_{p,q}^2$ are two disjoint sets containing de-mosaicked and acquired samples respectively from block $B_{p,q}$. If given image is de-mosaicked, the quantity GM^2 is higher than GM^1 and thus feature L is non-zero positive. Whereas, if the image is not de-mosaicked, because of local stationarity of image content, GM^2 and GM^1 would be nearly same and feature L would be near zero. The inference about presence of CFA de-mosaicking is based on these two observations. Based on the feature L, a likelihood map is created. Value at each pixel of this likelihood map is likelihood ratio $\Gamma(.)$ of L, defined by Equation (23).

$$\Gamma(L(p,q)) = \frac{Pr\{L(p,q)\,|\,M_2\}}{Pr\{L(p,q)\,|\,M_1\}} \tag{23}$$

Small values of likelihood ratio indicate absence of CFA de-mosaicking, and hence corresponding block of image is said to be tampered. It must be noted here, that the knowledge of Bayer pattern is must while calculating the feature L, however the same is not always available.

While the methods discussed so far extract features from variance of error, techniques proposed in [26] and [27] extracts features directly from the prediction error. These methods also restrict the search space of possible Bayer patterns to the four presented in Fig. (**4c**), and search among them to find the best match. First, the image is divided into non-overlapping blocks of size $D \times D$, then assuming a bilinear de-mosaicking kernel, total prediction error E is calculated for all four Bayer patterns and three color channels at each non-smooth block. The prediction error of ith block B_i for green channel (similar equations hold for red and blue channels by replacing G with R and B respectively, in the right hand side of the equation) of bth Bayer pattern is given by Equation (24).

$$E_i(k,c) = \frac{1}{D \times D} \sum_{m,n \in B_i} \left(G(m,n) - \sum_{l,k=-\beta}^{\beta} \alpha_{l,k} G(m+l,n+k) \right), \text{ for } c = 2 \tag{24}$$

where α is bilinear de-mosaicking kernel. For every i^{th} block B_i, E_i can be seen as a 4×3 matrix, where rows correspond to Bayer patterns and columns correspond to color channels ($c = 1$ for red, 2 for green, and 3 for blue).

The relative error between different color channels is obtained by normalizing E_i as in Equation (25).

$$E_i^{(2)}(k,c) = 100 \times \frac{E_i(k,c)}{\sum_{l=1}^{3} E_i(k,l)}, \quad \forall \, c = 1,...,3 \tag{25}$$

Since green color is sampled on Bayer pattern at twice the sampling rate of red and blue color, prediction error for green color has maximum information about the CFA pattern. Thus, a vector $V_i(k)$ is defined for every block which is then used to extract features for detecting the presence of CFA de-mosaicking. In [26], vector $V_i(k)$ is chosen to be the column of $E_i^{(2)}$ corresponding to green channel (Equation (26)). Four features for every image are extracted using this vector V_i. The first and second features capture information about CFA pattern giving minimum and second minimum prediction errors respectively. Third feature captures the uniformity of vector V_i. Fourth feature captures total prediction error of green channel all over the image.

$$V_i(k) = E_i^{(2)}(k,2) \quad \text{for} \quad k = 1,2,3,4 \tag{26}$$

In [27], two features have been proposed, the first feature F_1' is estimated according to Equation(28) using normalized vector $V_i'(k)$ (Equation (27)). This feature captures uniformity of CFA pattern over an image.

$$V_i'(k) = 100 \times \frac{E_i^{(2)}(k,2)}{\sum_{\substack{l=1 \\ l \neq k}}^{4} E_i^{(2)}(l,2)} \tag{27}$$

$$F_1' = \underset{i=1,2,...,N}{median}\left\{\sum_{l=1}^{4}\left|V_i'(l) - 25\right|\right\} \tag{28}$$

And, the second feature F_2' is based on changes in sensor noise power due CFA de-mosaicking. If a given sample is de-mosaicked, the sensor noise is suppressed due to low pass nature of de-mosaicking algorithms. Hence, variance of sensor noise at de-mosaicked samples becomes less than the variance of sensor noise at acquired samples. To estimate sensor noise dual tree wavelet based denoising is used and feature F_2' is calculated according to Equation (29).

$$F_2' = \max \left\{ \frac{var(A_1)}{var(A_2)}, \frac{var(A_2)}{var(A_1)} \right\} \tag{29}$$

here, A_1 and A_2 are two vectors containing de-mosaicked and acquired samples respectively. As discussed in this section, to detect presence of de-mosaicking, some methods *e.g.* [25], require knowledge of Bayer pattern, while others do not. However, these methods that do not require knowledge of Bayer pattern are valid under the assumption of a limited search space of possible Bayer patterns.

Estimating CFA Pattern and de-mosaicking Scheme

Techniques discussed in this section assume that incoming image is always de-mosaicked, and different camera models may have different CFA configurations and de-mosaicking algorithms. Under these assumptions, the task is to estimate some fingerprints based on CFA de-mosaicking so as to differentiate between different CFA configurations and de-mosaicking algorithms. Whereas most of the methods for estimating CFA pattern or de-mosaicking scheme assume the image is de-mosaicked, there are some techniques which do not require this assumption. Two such techniques are presented in [12] and [22], discussed in the previous section, which are capable of estimating the presence of CFA de-mosaicking as well as de-mosaicking kernel simultaneously and hence they may also be used for classifying de-mosaicking schemes. After the convergence of EM algorithm, obtained de-mosaicking coefficients are used for classifying de-mosaicking algorithms, and Fourier transform of probability map is used to detect presence of de-mosaicking.

Extension of this EM algorithm based technique for identification of commercial cameras is proposed in [28-30]. Features from smooth and non-smooth regions are extracted separately. For non-smooth regions EM algorithm is used with de-mosaicking kernel sizes $3 \times 3, 4 \times 4$, and 5×5. After convergence of EM algorithm, the obtained de-mosaicking kernel coefficients, locations, and magnitudes of peaks in Fourier transform of probability map are used as features for classification. Experimental results showed that kernel size 5×5 gives the best classification accuracy. For smooth regions, features are based on the phenomena proposed in [31] that, low-order de-mosaicking produces periodicity in the second order derivative of de-mosaicked signal. Hence for smooth regions, row average of second-order derivative of each row is estimated, and then locations and magnitudes of peaks in frequency domain reveal kernel size and de-mosaicking algorithm. Irrespective of the content adaptive behavior of actual de-mosaicking algorithm, EM algorithm based approach [28-30] assumes a simple, linear, channel independent de-mosaicking model. While authors in [32, 33] have considered the content adaptive behavior of de-mosaicking algorithms, and proposed to divide the given image into three regions *viz.* R_1 with horizontal edge, R_2 with vertical edge and R_3 with smooth region, depending on horizontal and vertical gradients defined by Equation (30) and Equation (31) respectively.

$$H(m,n) = |\, C(m,n-2) + C(m,n+2) - 2C(m,n)\,| \tag{30}$$

$$V(m,n) = |\, C(m-2,n) + C(m+2,n) - 2C(m,n)\,| \tag{31}$$

Any sample $C(m,n)$ of a given color channel C of an image can be classified into region R_1 if $V(m,n) - H(m,n) > T$, region R_2 if $H(m,n) - V(m,n) > T$, or region R_3 otherwise, where T is a suitably chosen threshold. Then the estimation of de-mosaicking kernel is done separately for each region. Under the assumption that most commercial cameras have RGB type of CFA periodic over block size 2×2, where each color sample should be acquired at-least once, 36 possible CFA patterns are considered. For each pattern, the locations of acquired and de-mosaicked samples are known, using this information a set of nine linear equations (one for each combination of color channel and region) is obtained for each one of 36 CFA patterns. This set of linear equations which gives interpolated samples in terms of acquired samples and de-mosaicking coefficients, is used to estimate de-mosaicked coefficients for all 36 patterns independently. The estimated de-mosaicking coefficients are then used to find prediction error for each one of the 36 patterns. Pattern with minimum prediction error is chosen as the estimated pattern and corresponding coefficients are used as feature for classification of de-mosaicking algorithm and hence the source camera.

Above mentioned techniques assume an intra-channel de-mosaicking model, where the de-mosaicking of one color channel depends on that particular color channel only. However, in complex de-mosaicking algorithms, green channel is first de-mosaicked in a content adaptive manner, and then red and blue channels are de-mosaicked using samples from green channel. Such inter-channel de-mosaicking model is considered in [34-37], where authors proposed, that second-order derivative of de-mosaicked image along the direction of de-mosaicking at a location corresponding to a de-mosaicked sample is same as the weighted sum of samples from sensor before de-mosaicking along the same direction. Since, depending on the image content and location of de-mosaicked sample, direction of de-mosaicking is different for different samples, hence de-mosaicked samples are grouped into different de-mosaicking groups depending on the direction of de-mosaicking. Considering the direction of de-mosaicking to be vertical, mathematical formulation for second-order derivative of de-mosaicked green sample and its relation with acquired samples is given by Equation (33) and Equation (32), respectively.

$$G^{mm}(m,n) = w_{gm1}\hat{I}^{mm}(m-2,n) + \ldots + w_{gmq}\hat{I}^{mm}(m+2,n) \qquad (32)$$

$$\text{where, } G^{mm}(m,n) = G(m-1) + G(m+1,n) - 2G(m,n) \qquad (33)$$

$$\hat{I}^{mm}(m,n) = \hat{I}(m-2) + \hat{I}(m+2,n) - 2\hat{I}(m,n) \qquad (34)$$

Here, the weights w_{gmi} (for $i = 1, \ldots, q$) are the unique characteristics of a particular de-mosaicking algorithm. The same mathematical formulation is valid for all color channels and de-mosaicking groups, only direction of de-mosaicking will vary among different de-mosaicking groups. For p number of de-mosaicked samples in a de-mosaicking group, a set of p linear equations is obtained as given by Equation (35).

$$Q = \begin{bmatrix} \hat{I}(m_1-2,n_1) & \cdots & \hat{I}(m_1+2,n_1) \\ \vdots & \ddots & \vdots \\ \hat{I}(m_p-2,n_1) & \cdots & \hat{I}(m_p+2,n_1) \end{bmatrix} w = \begin{bmatrix} w_{gm1} \\ \vdots \\ w_{gmq} \end{bmatrix} b = \begin{bmatrix} G_m''(m_1,n_1) \\ \vdots \\ G_m''(m_p,n_p) \end{bmatrix} \qquad (35)$$

$$w = argmin_{w}\left(\| Qw - b \|_2\right) \tag{36}$$

Solution of Equation (36) gives the de-mosaicking coefficients which are used for classification of de-mosaicking schemes. In [36] an expectation-maximization reverse classification (EMRC) is employed to classify de-mosaicked samples among different de-mosaicking groups, and then the de-mosaicking coefficients are estimated in a similar manner. In [37] the same approach is used for classification of mobile phones.

Another approach for estimating CFA pattern is proposed in [38] based on the count of intermediate values. Value at a sample location (m, n) is said to be an intermediate value if it lies between the maximum and minimum value of neighborhood around the sample location (m, n). For example, a value V is an intermediate value if

$$\min\{C(m+l, n+k)\} \leq V \leq \max\{C(m+l, n+k)\} \quad \forall \ l, k \in [-\beta, \beta] \tag{37}$$

Since a de-mosaicked sample is obtained from a weighted sum of its neighbors, it satisfies the condition mentioned in Equation (37). Under the assumption of only four possible Bayer patterns (Fig. (4c), method proposed in [38] counts the number of intermediate values present in a given image in a specific manner given by Equation (38) (for green channel).

$$CFA_g(i, j) = \begin{cases} CFA_g(i, j) + 1, & if \ \min\{C(xi+l, yj+k)\} \leq C(xi, yj) \leq \max\{C(xi+l, yj+k)\} \\ CFA_g(i, j), & otherwise \end{cases} \tag{38}$$

$$\forall \ i, j \in \{1, 2\}, \ x \in \{1, \ldots, M/2\}, \ y \in \{1, \ldots, N/2\}, \ l, k \in \{-\beta, \beta\}$$

Here, CFA_g is a 2×2 block resembling one of the Bayer patterns shown in Fig. (4c), $M \times N$ is size of image. A higher value of $CFA_g(i, j)$ indicates that location (i, j) in the 2×2 block corresponds to de-mosaicked sample and a smaller value of $CFA_g(i, j)$ indicates that location (i, j) corresponds to acquired sample. Similar counts are obtained for red and blue channel as well. Since in most of the de-mosaicking algorithms, green channel is de-mosaicked first, followed by red and blue, intermediate counts for green channel are estimated first. Once location of acquired and de-mosaicked green samples is obtained from the intermediate counts, locations of acquired samples of red and blue channels are decided depending on their corresponding intermediate counts.

In addition to the methods discussed so far in this chapter, there are numerous works in literature including [39] and [40]. For the sake of brevity, it is not possible to cover all minute details, but a short overview can be given. In [39], an efficient method for CFA pattern estimation based on synthesis of CFA [41] is proposed. And in [40], correlations due to CFA de-mosaicking are expressed in quadratic form in terms of a quadratic pixel correlation model, followed by principal component analysis to remove false correlation due to the scene. The decision between de-mosaicked and non de-mosaicked class is made by a back propagation neural network followed by a majority voting scheme.

EXPERIMENTAL ANALYSIS AND DISCUSSION

This section presents an experimental comparison of some of the prominent works available in literature targeted at detecting presence of CFA de-mosaicking. As this chapter aims to describe mathematics of handcrafted features rather than the classification techniques proposed in various works, results presented here are obtained by extracting features from green channel of a given image in accordance with different works and feeding them to same classifier setup to classify images into two classes *viz.* CFA de-mosaicked and not CFA de-mosaicked.

The classifier setup used is a support vector machine (SVM) with Gaussian kernel. Eighty percentage of images from each of the two classes are used for training the SVM classifier and remaining 20 percent of images from each class are used for testing purpose. Results are presented in terms of classification accuracy and receiver operating characteristic (ROC) curve.

Dataset Description

In order to assess the performance of different works under constrained scenarios (*i.e.,* without effects of camera post-processing operations), experiments were carried out on a synthetically created dataset where CFA de-mosaicking is performed artificially on a computer system without any post-processing after CFA de-mosaicking. And, to assess the performance under real-life scenarios, experiments were carried out on a real dataset comprising of camera-generated images with in-camera CFA de-mosaicking and post-processing.

Synthetic Dataset

Synthetic dataset consists of de-mosaicked and non de-mosaicked images generated from publicly available UCID database [42]. The UCID database consists of 1338 uncompressed images of varying genre, each of size 512×384 or 384×512. These images are first cropped to 384×384 size and then used as base images to generate images without CFA de-mosaicking signatures and images with CFA de-mosaicking signatures. Images without CFA de-mosaicking signatures are generated following the procedure utilized in [25]. Each image of size 384×384 is first upsampled by a factor of 2, median filtered with a kernel of size 7×7, and then downsampled back to 384×384. This sequence of upsampling followed by median filtering and downsampling removes the periodic pattern of correlations that is acquired due to CFA de-mosaicking and generates a set of 1338 images without CFA de-mosaicking signatures. In order to generate images with CFA de-mosaicking signatures, these 1338 images without CFA de-mosaicking signatures are first resampled on a Bayer array, then de-mosaicked with six de-mosaicking algorithms mentioned in Table **1**. Resulting synthetic dataset consists of 9366 images, out of which 1338 are without CFA de-mosaicking signatures, and 8028 are with CFA de-mosaicking signatures (1338 from each of the six de-mosaicking algorithms).

Real Dataset

In real scenarios, an image captured with a single-sensor camera is usually de-mosaicked within the camera. To evaluate the performance under such scenarios, experiments were carried out on a dataset that can mimic real scenarios. This real dataset consist CFA de-mosaicked images obtained directly from commercial cameras with CFA de-mosaicking done within the camera when the image is being captured.

To simulate absence of CFA de-mosaicking, most of the prior works including [24], [26] and [27], used photorealistic computer generated (PRCG) images. Unlike images generated by single-sensor cameras, PRCG images are not CFA de-mosaicked. But these PRCG images may differ from camera-generated images in other aspects also, such as chromatic aberration [26], hence while evaluating performance on PRCG *vs.* camera generated image classification, one may question, whether the algorithm is detecting presence/absence of CFA de-mosaicking or some other difference between PRCG and camera generated images.

To have unbiased experimental setup, images belonging to both the classes (*i.e.,* with CFA de-mosaicking, and without CFA de-mosaicking) must be either all camera generated or all computer generated. With the availability of commercial three-sensor cameras, it is now possible to easily get camera generated images without CFA de-mosaicking. Real dataset used for performance evaluation presented in this chapter consists of images captured with five cameras belonging to two classes, *viz.* single-sensor camera and three-sensor camera. Images with CFA de-mosaicking were captured using three different single-sensor cameras set to capture images in lossless format. Images without CFA de-mosaicking came from two different three-sensor cameras and were downloaded from an online source [43] in native RAW format and converted to lossless format with a software provided by the camera manufacturer. These images in lossless format obtained from five different cameras were divided into smaller blocks of 512×512 pixels, out of these, blocks having variance less than a predefined threshold are discarded, as they are mostly constant patches without significant visual information. Finally, the real dataset consists of 3800 camera-generated images, each of size 512×512 half of which are CFA de-mosaicked and remaining half are not CFA de-mosaicked.

Performance Evaluation under Lossless Compression

This section presents a comparative performance evaluation of some prominent works aimed at detecting presence of CFA de-mosaicking fingerprints in given image under lossless compression. Table **2** gives the classification accuracies achieved by different methods for detecting CFA de-mosaicking in green channel of images from synthetic dataset. These images were artificially de-mosaicked with algorithms mentioned in Table **1** and saved in lossless compression format. Since the assumption of linear, non-adaptive de-mosaicking kernel made in various works holds good for bilinear interpolation, all these methods give nearly 100 % accuracy for bilinear de-mosaicking. In smooth hue transition algorithm, which is not linear, not content-adaptive and channel interdependent (Table **1**), green channel is first de-mosaicked with bilinear de-mosaicking, then red and blue channels are de-mosaicked using information from green channel. Since green channel is de-mosaicked in bilinear fashion, results for smooth hue transition are similar to that for bilinear de-mosaicking algorithm. Bicubic de-mosaicking deviates slightly from bilinear by increasing the size of de-mosaicking kernel from 3×3 to 7×7, whereas kernel size assumed in detection algorithms is 3×3, hence the classification accuracies decrease slightly for bicubic de-mosaicking algorithm.

Although methods proposed in [12] and [22] both are based on EM algorithm, while [12] considers a simple bilinear de-mosaicking kernel, [22] considers a wide range of de-mosaicking kernels including nonlinear, content adaptive, and channel interdependent kernels. Hence, for simple bilinear and smooth hue transition algorithms, both [12] and [22] perform equally well, but for complex de-mosaicking algorithms such as AHD and median filter based, [22] performs better than [12]. As the EM algorithm converges to a locally optimal solution closest to the initial guess of de-mosaicking kernel, results obtained by EM algorithm based approach depend on the initial guess of de-mosaicking kernel and may correspond to a globally sub-optimal solution. While these two approaches based on EM algorithm consider all samples of the image at once and minimize an error function (similar to one given by Equation (5)) to estimate de-mosaicking kernel and presence of de-mosaicking, methods in [26] and [27] estimate the presence of de-mosaicking in small blocks of images independently.

Table 2. Classification accuracy (%) for images from synthetic dataset with lossless compression.

	Bilinear	Bicubic	Gradient Based	Smooth Hue Transition	Median Filter Based	AHD	All
Popescu *et al.* [12]	100	98.1	53.4	100	58	55.4	73.2
Dirik *et al.* [26]	100	100	100	100	100	99.1	99.7
Method 1 in [27]	99.8	100	100	100	100	96.6	99.3
Method 2 in [27]	100	99.8	100	99.8	91.4	99.6	97.9
Dirik *et al.* [27]	100	100	100	100	100	99.4	99.8
Li *et al.* [23]	100	99.6	97.6	100	90.1	90.3	94.9
Verma *et al.* [22]	100	100	99.8	100	86.9	97.6	96.6

The first method proposed in [27] uses prediction error to search over space of possible Bayer patterns for all three color channels, while the second method proposed in [27] uses noise features due to CFA de-mosaicking to decide between two possible patterns for green channel only. For most of the de-mosaicking algorithms, method based on noise features (method 2) either outperforms or performs as good as prediction error based method (method 1) (Table **2**, rows 3 and 4). As median filtering destroys these noise features, first method performs better than the second method for median filter based de-mosaicking (Table **2**, rows 3 and 4, column 6, 100% *vs.* 91.4%).

Last column of Table **2** gives the classification accuracies when first class contains 8028 images de-mosaicked with six de-mosaicking algorithms, and second class contains 1338 images without CFA de-mosaicking. In this case, SVM is trained on 1070 images randomly chosen from 1338 images without CFA de-mosaicking and another 1070 images randomly chosen from 8028 de-mosaicked images. All the remaining images from each of these two classes are used for testing. As evident by values in last column of Table **2**, [12] is least accurate for the combined classification problem while all other methods have very similar performance. These results can help us conclude that if a priori knowledge of de-mosaicking algorithm is available in some forensic settings, one should choose a detection method giving highest classification accuracy for that particular algorithm. While in absence of any a priori knowledge of de-mosaicking algorithm, a forensic examiner may combine the classification decisions given by different methods (decision fusion).

Fig. (**7**) shows the performance of different forensic detection methods for a real dataset. Performance of different methods is compared by plotting the ROC curves corresponding to various methods for lossless compressed images from real dataset. Since the images in real dataset have undergone in-camera post-processing, and de-mosaicking algorithms used in cameras are also not restricted to those mentioned in

Table **1**, the trend observed in this figure is similar to that presented in the last column of Table **2**. Method proposed in [26, 27] performs better than methods in [12, 22], and [23]. Zoomed in view of top left corner of ROC curves shows that method [26] gives better performance than [27]. Note that [26] extracts four features from given image while [27] uses only two features to detect presence of CFA de-mosaicking.

Performance Evaluation under Lossy Compression

As discussed previously, post-processing operations after CFA de-mosaicking affect the detection accuracy. Different cameras may have a number of different post-processing operations, among which JPEG compression is extremely likely post-processing operation, and most camera images are stored directly in JPEG format. Hence it becomes necessary to evaluate the performance on JPEG compressed images. This section presents results obtained by different methods on synthetic as well as real dataset images (Fig. **8** and Table **3** respectively) compressed at different JPEG quality factors. As expected, post-processing after de-mosaicking destroys correlations due to CFA de-mosaicking to some extent, and hence classification accuracy drops down.

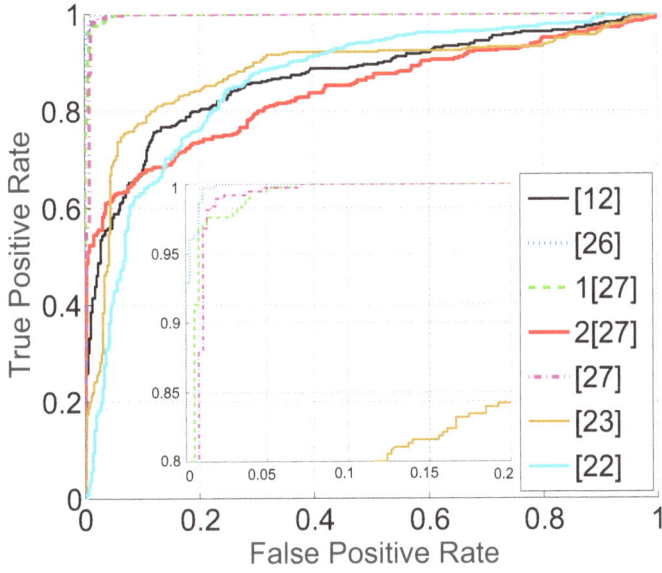

Fig. (7). ROC curves for real dataset with lossless compression.

Fig. (**8**) shows classification accuracies on synthetic dataset at different JPEG quality factors. For simple de-mosaicking algorithms (Fig. **8 a-b**), method in [23] is most robust to JPEG compression and second method in [27] is least robust, but as the de-mosaicking algorithms become more complex (Fig. **8 c-f**), [26] performs best against heavy JPEG compression and [12] performs worst compared to other methods. As observed from Fig. (**8**), second method in [27], which is noise based, is affected more by JPEG compression in comparison to the first method in [27]. It might be because JPEG compression itself introduces some *imperceptible* noise in image which interferes with the noise pattern due to CFA de-mosaicking.

Table **3** gives the performance variation with JPEG quality factor on real dataset in terms of classification accuracy. As the de-mosaicking algorithms implemented in commercial DSLR cameras are not very simple, classification accuracy follows the similar trends as it was in case of complex de-mosaicking algorithms for synthetic dataset. These comparative results of the state-of-art CFA detection methods on lossy compressed images, particular at high compression or low quality factor clearly indicate the need for developing new methods robust to JPEG compression.

Table 3. Classification accuracy (%) on images from real dataset compressed at different jpeg quality factors.

JPEG Q Factor →	100	90	80	70	60	50	40
Popescu *et al.* [12]	80.2	83.4	69.6	64.3	63.3	61.8	61.4
Dirik *et al.* [26]	98.1	86.8	76.8	71.8	63.8	61.7	60.1
Method 1 in [27]	96.8	82.6	67.1	60.8	56.7	54.3	56.0
Method 2 in [27]	82	73.4	61.5	56.2	52.1	55	50.9
Dirik *et al.* [27]	96.6	80.4	73.0	61.7	57.1	52.9	55.9
Li *et al.* [23]	83.7	77	69	66.2	64	63.1	58.3
Verma *et al.* [22]	82.4	68.1	67.0	63.7	57.7	58.0	53.1

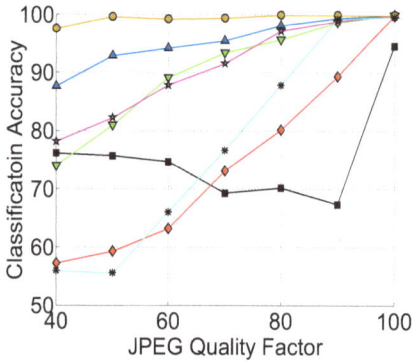

(a)   Bilinear De-mosaicking

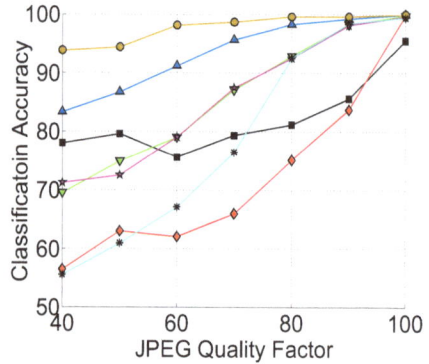

(b)   Bicubic De-mosaicking

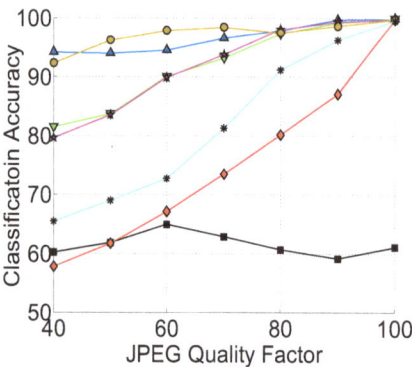

(c)   Gradient Based De-mosaicking

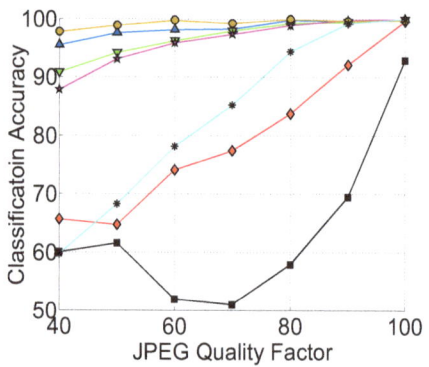

(d)   Smooth Hue Transition De-mosaicking

Fig. 8 cont.....

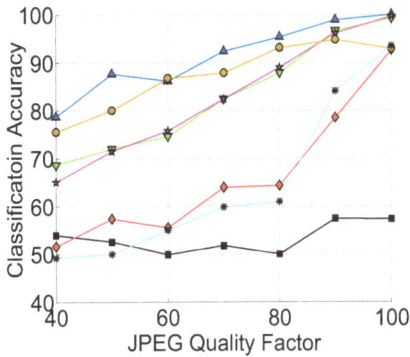

(e)   Media Filter based De-mosaicking   (f)   AHD De-mosaicking

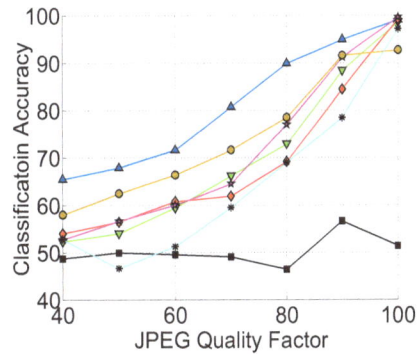

Legends: ▬■▬ [12]   ─★─ [27]
              ─▲─ [26]   ─●─ [23]
              ─▽─ 1[27]   ─*─ [22]
              ─◆─ 2[27]

Fig. (8). Variation of classification accuracy with jpeg quality factor for images from synthetic dataset de-mosaicked with different algorithms.

CONCLUSION

The concept of information sharing dates back to the evolution of human race when our ancestors used to communicate *via* visual/audible signs or symbols. But, the field of information security came into existence only when we realized potential threats to existing information and communication systems. It has been more than a century since information is being transmitted wirelessly. With the advent of networking technologies and handheld wireless devices, sharing a piece of information be it an audio, image, or a video, with billions of individuals, is now a matter of seconds. Millions of terabytes of sensitive and personal information is stored there on the so-called "web servers". This gives rise to the field of information security which provides procedures, and policies for security and reliability of these digital information and communication systems. Today in the 21st century, our understanding of events is highly dependent on audio and visual clues, and hence a very prevalent and user-friendly form of information sharing is done *via* multimedia, especially images. Not only our lifestyles are becoming dependent on digital images but also the availability of technology that can be used to easily modify these images is not rare. With this, the trust we put on digital images is at risk. Digital image forensics aims to strengthen this trust by introducing techniques and tools to keep digital images secure and reliable.

This chapter provided an introduction to the field of digital image forensics, its place in the world of information security and presented a mathematical overview of some of the prominent techniques and developments in this field. Some of these techniques are based on signatures of imaging devices, some on signatures of DSP algorithms, while others on traces left by any manipulation done after capturing the image. This chapter focused mainly on techniques based on CFA de-mosaicking signatures, and their application in solving tampering detection and source camera identification problems. Among various techniques, some are computationally complex, while some are not, some perform better under lossy compression, while some under lossless compression. Techniques which are computationally efficient pay the cost in terms of some assumptions that limit their practical applicability. In addition to this, there are some counter-attacks that may mislead some forensic techniques, including those discussed in this chapter. And hence, the research in this field is continuing to develop computationally efficient and robust tools that can assure us the trust we keep on digital images and help us identify breach of it whenever that happens.

Looking forward in future, as three-sensor technology is becoming common in commercial cameras, CFA based techniques that detect presence of CFA de-mosaicking may not be used for PIM *vs.* PRCG classification. However, these techniques can still be used to support source classification/identification problem by reducing search space to one of the two classes (*viz.* single-senor and three-sensor). Also, the techniques used for classifying/identifying the type of CFA pattern and/or de-mosaicking can be used for camera classification within the single-sensor class. In addition to this, even if in future, single-sensor cameras are replaced by three-sensor cameras, millions of billions of images that are already generated by single-sensor cameras and are present over the internet or somewhere else may always need these kinds of techniques for authentication. Consequently, the path for research in this field remains open for researchers, enthusiasts and forensic experts to contribute to the advancements in this emerging field.

CONSENT FOR PUBLICATION

Not applicable.

CONFLICT OF INTEREST

The authors confirm that there is no conflict of interest to declare for this publication.

ACKNOWLEDGEMENT

This research was supported by a grant from the Department of Science and Technology (DST), New Delhi, India, under Award Number ECR/2015/000583 and Indian Institute of Technology Gandhinagar internal research grant IP/IITGN/EE/NK/201516-06. Any opinions, findings, and conclusions or recommendations expressed in this material are those of the author(s) and do not necessarily reflect the views of the funding agencies.

REFERENCES

[1]　English Dictionary, Thesaurus, & grammar help | Oxford Dictionaries [homepage on the Internet]. Oxford: Oxford University Press; c2018 [cited: 13th Jan 2017]. Available from: https://en.oxforddictionaries.com/

[2]　R.F. Churchhouse, *Codes and Ciphers: Julius Caesar, The Enigma, and The Internet..* Cambridge University Press: Cambridge, UK, 2002.

[3]　R. Böhme, F.C. Freiling, T. Gloe, and M. Kirchner, "Multimedia Forensics is Not Computer Forensics", Z Geradts, KY Franke, and CJ Veenman, Eds., *Proceedings of the 3rd International Workshop on Computational Forensics,* pp. 90-103 Netherlands

[4]　M. Casey Does this photo of Ulysses S. Grant look strange to you?. Fox News, 30th Oct 2015. [cited: 25th Feb 2017]. Available from: http://www.foxnews.com/science/2015/10/30/can-guess-whether-this-grant-image-has-been-photoshopped.html

[5]　I. Sparks, Charlie Hebdo: Female world leaders AIRBRUSHED out of Paris march picture for Jewish newspaper. UK Mirror, 14th Jan 2015. [cited: 25th Feb 2017]. Available from: http://www.mirror.co.uk/news/world-news/charlie-hebdo-female-world-leaders-4976457

[6]　BBC News. Chennai floods: Edited Modi photo sparks online mockery. BBC, 4th Dec 2015. [cited: 28th Feb 2017]. Available from: http://www.bbc.com/news/world-asia-india-34991822

[7]　A. Pareene, http://www.salon.com/2011/04/07/birther_photoshop_fail/

[8]　V.P. Kivimaki, *Russian State Television Shares Fake Images of MH17 Being Attacked.,* https://www.bellingcat.com/ news/2014/11/14/russian-state-television-shares-fake-images-of-mh17-being-attacked/

[9]　Photo Tampering throughout History [homepage on the Internet]. Fourandsix Technologies Inc. [cited: 28th Feb 2017]. Available from: http://pth.izitru.com/

[10]　Z. Fan, and R.L. De Queiroz, "Identification of Bitmap Compression History: JPEG Detection and Quantizer Estimation", *IEEE Trans. Image Process.,* vol. 12, no. 2, pp. 230-235.

[11]　A. Swaminathan, M. Wu, and K.J.R. Liu, "Optimization of Input Pattern for Semi Non-intrusive Component Forensics of Digital Cameras", *Proceedings of the IEEE International Conference on Acoustics, Speech and Signal Processing,* pp. II-225-II-228 Honolulu, HI, USA

[12]　A.C. Popescu, and H. Farid, "Exposing Digital Forgeries in Color Filter Array Interpolated Images", *IEEE Trans. Signal Process.,* vol. 53, no. 10, pp. 3948-3959.

[13]　M. Kirchner, and J. Fridrich, "On Detection of Median Filtering in Digital Images", *Proceedings of SPIE Media Forensics and Security II,* pp. 754110-754110-12 California, US

[14]　S. Bayram, H.T. Sencar, and N. Memon, "An Efficient and Robust Method for Detecting Copy-Move Forgery", *Proceedings of the IEEE International Conference on Acoustics, Speech and Signal Processing,* pp. 1053-1056 Taipei, Taiwan

[15]　M. Chen, J. Fridrich, M. Goljan, and J. Lukáš, "Determining Image Origin and Integrity using Sensor Noise", *IEEE Trans. Inf. Forensics Security,* vol. 3, no. 1, pp. 74-90.

[16]　M.K. Johnson, and H. Farid, "Exposing Digital Forgeries through Chromatic Aberration", *Proceedings of the 8th workshop on Multimedia and Security,* pp. 48-55 Geneva, Switzerland

[17] R. Lukac, and K. Plataniotis, "Color Filter Arrays: Design and Performance Analysis", *IEEE Trans. Consum. Electron.,* vol. 51, no. 4, pp. 1260-1267.

[18] G. Sharma, and R. Bala, *Digital Color Imaging Handbook..* CRC Press: Florida, 2002.

[19] K. Hirakawa, and T.W. Parks, "Adaptive Homogeneity-Directed Demosaicing Algorithm", *IEEE Trans. Image Process.,* vol. 14, no. 3, pp. 360-369.

[20] R. Keys, "Cubic Convolution Interpolation for Digital Image Processing", *IEEE Trans. Acoust. Speech Signal Process.,* vol. 29, no. 6, pp. 1153-1160.

[21] T. Acharya, and A.K. Ray, *Image Processing: Principles and Applications..* John Wiley & Sons: New Jersey, 2005.

[22] H.K. Verma, A. Saikia, and N. Khanna, "A Hybrid Model for CFA Interpolation Detection", *Proceedings of the IEEE International Conference on Identity, Security and Behavior Analysis,* pp. 1-8 New Delhi, India

[23] L. Li, J. Xue, X. Wang, and L. Tian, "A Robust Approach to Detect Digital Forgeries by Exploring Correlation Patterns", *Pattern Anal. Appl.,* vol. 18, no. 2, pp. 351-365.

[24] A.C. Gallagher, and T. Chen, "Image Authentication by Detecting Traces of Demosaicing", *Proceedings of the IEEE Computer Society Conference on Computer Vision and Pattern Recognition Workshops,* , pp. 1-8 New Jersey

[25] P. Ferrara, T. Bianchi, A.D. Rosa, and A. Piva, "Image Forgery Localization via Fine-Grained Analysis of CFA Artifacts", *IEEE Trans. Inf. Forensics Security,* vol. 7, no. 5, pp. 1566-1577.

[26] A.E. Dirik, S. Bayram, H.T. Sencar, and N. Memon, "New Features to Identify Computer Generated Images", *Proceedings of the IEEE International Conference on Image Processing,* pp. IV-433-IV-436 San Antonio, TX, USA

[27] A.E. Dirik, and N. Memon, "Image Tamper Detection based on Demosaicing Artifacts", *Proceedings of the IEEE International Conference on Image Processing,* pp. 1497-1500 Cairo, Egypt

[28] S. Bayram, H.T. Sencar, N. Memon, and I. Avcibas, "Source Camera Identification Based on CFA Interpolation", *Proceedings of the IEEE International Conference on Image Processing,* 2005pp. III-69-72 Genova, Italy

[29] S. Bayram, H.T. Sencar, and N. Memon, Improvements on Source Camera-Model Identification Based on CFA Interpolation. Proceedings of the IFIP Working Group 11.9 International Conference on Digital Forensics; 2006 Jan; Orlando, FL. Laxenburg, Austria: IFIP 2006; pp. 24-27

[30] S. Bayram, H.T. Sencar, and N. Memon, "Classification of Digital Camera-Models Based on Demosaicing Artifacts", *Digit. Invest.,* vol. 5, no. 1, pp. 49-59.

[31] A.C. Gallagher, "Detection of Linear and Cubic Interpolation in JPEG Compressed Images", *Proceedings of the Second Canadian Conference on Computer and Robot Vision,* pp. 65-72 Victoria, BC, Canada

[32] A. Swaminathan, M. Wu, and K.J.R. Liu, "Nonintrusive Component Forensics of Visual Sensors Using Output Images", *IEEE Trans. Inf. Forensics Security,* vol. 2, no. 1, pp. 91-106.

[33] A. Swaminathan, M. Wu, and K.J.R. Liu, "Component Forensics of Digital Cameras: A Non-Intrusive Approach", *Proceedings of the 40th Annual Conference on Information Sciences and Systems,* pp. 1194-1199 Princeton, NJ, USA

[34] H. Cao, and A.C. Kot, "A Generalized Model for Detection of Demosaicing Characteristics", *Proceedings of the IEEE International Conference on Multimedia and Expo,* pp. 1513-1516 Hannover, Germany

[35] H. Cao, and A.C. Kot, "Accurate Detection of Demosaicing Regularity from Output Images", *Proceedings of the IEEE International Symposium on Circuits and Systems,* pp. 497-500 Taipei, Taiwan

[36] H. Cao, and A.C. Kot, "Accurate Detection of Demosaicing Regularity for Digital Image Forensics", *IEEE Trans. Inf. Forensics Security,* vol. 4, no. 4, pp. 899-910.

[37] H. Cao, and A.C. Kot, "Mobile Camera Identification using Demosaicing Features", *Proceedings of the IEEE International Symposium on Circuits and Systems,* pp. 1683-1686 Paris, France

[38] C.H. Choi, J.H. Choi, and H.K. Lee, "CFA Pattern Identification of Digital Cameras using Intermediate Value Counting", *Proceedings of the 13th workshop on Multimedia and Security,* pp. 21-26 Buffalo, NY, USA

[39]   M. Kirchner, "Efficient Estimation of CFA Pattern Configuration in Digital Camera Images", *Proceedings of SPIE Media Forensics and Security II,* pp. 754111-754111-12 California, US

[40]   Y. Huang, and Y. Long, "Demosaicking Recognition with Applications in Digital Photo Authentication based on a Quadratic Pixel Correlation Model", *Proceedings of the IEEE Conference on Computer Vision and Pattern Recognition,* , pp. 1-8 New Jersey

[41]   M. Kirchner, and R. Böhme, "Synthesis of Color Filter Array Pattern in Digital Images", *Proceedings of SPIE Media Forensics and Security,* pp. 72540K-72540K-14 California, US

[42]   G. Schaefer, and M. Stich, "UCID: An Uncompressed Color Image Database", *Proceedings of SPIE Storage and Retrieval Methods and Applicatoins for Multimedia,* 2004pp. 472-480 California, US

[43]   http://www.imaging-resource.com/PRODS/sigma-dp2-quattro/sigma-dp2-quattroGALLERY.HTM

CHAPTER 5

Ranking the IT Based Technologies to Enhance the Safety and Security of Food Using AHP Approach

Yogesh K. Sharma[1,*], Sachin K. Mangla[2], Pravin P. Patil[1], Alok K. Yadav[1] Suresh K. Jakhar[3], Sunil Luthra[4]

[1]*Department of Mechanical Engineering, Graphic Era Deemed to be University, Dehradun-248002, Uttarakhand, India*
[2]*Plymouth Business School (PBS), University of Plymouth, United Kingdom*
[3]*Indian Institute of Management, Lucknow, India*
[4]*Department of Mechanical Engineering, Government Polytechnic, Jhajjar-124103, India*

Abstract: Food safety and security is a growing research area due to increasing demand of food across the globe. Customers now-a-days are more conscious about their health. In the past, many cases regarding food containment and adulteration raised the concern about safety and security of the food supply companies. To minimize these concerns, IT based technologies can play an important role. In the present chapter, nine such IT based technologies were identified through review of the extant literature. Furthermore, the analytic hierarchy process (AHP) approach is used to rank the identified IT technologies based on their priority. Sensitivity analysis is also performed to check the robustness of the model. Radio frequency identification technology holds the first rank on the priority list.

Keywords: 3D printing, Analytic hierarchy process (AHP), Artificial intelligence, Bio sensors, Food industry, High power ultrasound, High pressure processing, Information Technology (IT), Nano technology, Pathogens, Radio frequency identification, Safety and security, Sensitivity Analysis (SA), Traceability, Vibrational & fluorescence spectroscopy.

INTRODUCTION

In the present era, mankind faces enormous challenges, out of which food safety and security can be placed on top of the list [1]. Food security means that individuals have enough amount of nutrition and hygienic food without compromising social, economic and environmental resources.

*Corresponding author Yogesh K. Sharma: Department of Mechanical Engineering, Graphic Era Deemed to be University, Dehradun-248002, Uttarakhand, India; Tel: 0135 264 2727; Fax: 0135-2644025; E-mail: yogeshsharmamc355@gmail.com

Mangey Ram (Ed.)

Food safety includes market to consumer practices, starting from supplier selection to manufacturing, quality control, packaging, handling, and storage of food. It involves whole processes from production to consumption. Food security incorporates ideas that not only has access to nutrient foods, but also does not face societal barriers to feed himself [2]. Globally, one third of the produced food is being wasted by humans who can feed an additional 200 million people, as per the report given by the Food and Agricultural organization (FAO) of United Nations statistics. In many FAO projects, it has been estimated that cereal demand will gradually increase to 70% by 2050 [3, 4]. However, the challenge of learning, how to feed the fast growing world population cannot be left to the private sector, government policy, *etc.* A couple of years ago, the objective of food was that food should be safe and contain nutrients. Now-a-days, this objective has been changed. Now consumers want tasty and fresh palatable food which also contain sufficient amount of nutrients [5]. Due to the huge demand of consumers, a number of technological innovations are required to fulfill the demand of our global consumers. In developing countries like India, food borne diseases are increasing, especially due to environmental as well as demographic changes. To reduce the challenges in food security and safety, new methods need to be applied for monitoring, identifying and assessment of many food hazards [6].

In the present chapter, we focused on technological innovation like RFID, nano technology, and hand held devices and cloud computing, *etc.* to cope up with this problem. In the present study, we focused on the importance of IT based technologies in safety and security of food products. AHP approach deals with decision making problems and is mainly used for ranking the identified IT based technologies on priority basis and relative weights. The objective of this research is to improve the safety and security of food by implementing IT based technologies. The findings of this research work help managers and stakeholders to invest in the installation of IT based technologies in the organization for the better future. For the validation of ranking obtained through AHP, sensitivity analysis is also performed in this chapter. The findings of this chapter suggest that Radio frequency identification (RFID) is the most important technology in the safety and security of food.

LITERATURE REVIEW

This section explores the literature on safety and security, the importance of IT based technologies and AHP approach applications and its importance in the food sector. IT is very essential now-a-days, due to increasing demand and awareness among the people related to the safety and security of food.

Food Safety and Security

According to FAO, food security is defined as a "situation that exists when all people, at all times, have physical, social, and economic access to sufficient, safe, and nutritious food that meets their dietary needs and food preferences for an active and healthy life" [7]. The theme of the Universal Exposition held in Milan in 2015 [8] was 'Feeding the Planet.' Expo 2015 focused on the urgency of providing sufficient food and nutrition to a population likely to reach about 8 billion in 2020 and nearly 10 billion by the middle of the century [9]. However, it has been initiated on relevant literature that many public health authorities do not produce food as per the guidelines. Food borne illness remains a real and challenging problem [10, 11]. There are approximately millions of people, who have deficiencies, as well as there are an equal number of people who have developed diseases of surplus energies, also 2 billion people suffer from many micronutrient deficiencies. Hence, numerous number of the world's population is malnourished. The increasing proportion of malnourished or hungry people is prevalent due to the environmental and demographic changes. In addition, the increased age of the human population changes in food habits [6]. There are many factors which increase the food insecurity like increased population, more demand for dairy and meat products [1]. Weather conditions are also constantly changing which also affects the quality of food. Cyclones, heat waves, floods, hailstorms and droughts are the worst conditions of environment which worsen the stability of food [7]. Innovation, investment and efforts by populations will be necessary for developing a food organization which adapts to weather change and ensures food security [12]. To achieve the aim of our second goal of the UN (United Nations) sustainable development goals that are zero hunger, we have to go through the technological innovations to optimization of food safety and security. Innovation is also the key for the sustained growth of the food industries [5].

IT Importance in Food Safety and Security

The global magnitude of health and nutrient problem is caused by unsafe food, but still it is hard to determine. Now, everyone knows that it has taken the size of giant [13]. Many new technologies have been proposed and develop to improve conventional technologies for better and superior quality food and its products [5]. Some modern technologies such as irradiation, information, genetic modifications, *etc.* along with conventional methods must be useful in dealing with these imperative challenges [10]. One major challenge is that the short shelf-life of food, can be reduced by using radio frequency identification based data [14]. However, with new trends of IT (*e.g.*, cloud computing and cheapest devices with a higher performance like a hand held devices), IT has become awfully efficient and user-friendly. In the coming years, the prospective of IT in food safety is tremendous [15]. Genomics assimilated technologies also play an important role in food safety by cross breeding, the genetic makeup of crops, gene interaction and gene function [16]. With the help of technology, we can also advance the food supply chain which is obligatory for food safety and security. To achieve a maximum profit, the technology needs to be properly embedded into the food chain, which is currently not well addressed in research [17]. However now-a-days, so many technologies used in India like SKYMET (it tells about the information of weather condition, which is very useful for farmers), MITRA (Machines Information, Technology, Resources for Agriculture) is used for enhancement of horticulture farm, ERUVAKA TECHNOLOGIES (used in aquaculture field, it tells about water health, whether water is good or not for survival of fish and shrimp), EKGAON technologies (it is an IT information based technology and offers a range of services to the farmer in rural area including financial, agricultural inputs and government assistance).

IT BASED TECHNOLOGIES IN SAFETY AND SECURITY OF FOOD

Information Technology (IT) has a major role to play in all facets of the food industry. Information technology is expanding rapidly and touches almost all areas of human activity. IT based technologies play a crucial role to improve the safety and security of food. These technologies help the organization to trace their process or product at every level. Additionally, IT based technologies made a huge difference between organizations in this competitive world. The purpose of food traceability is to permit the full backward and forward track of a product and its life history. Based on literature survey, we identified nine such technologies that give more impact on the food safety and security in the current scenario.

High Pressure Processing (ITT1)

This technology is a cold pasteurization technique which is done before final packaging of food products. In this technique, products are subjected to high level of pressure, which is transmitted by water. It is mainly used for the production of jams, soups, fruit juice and processed meat. High pressure can also be applied to food during their packaging, which stands as an important advantage of HPP as the possibility of post treatment contamination can be eliminated [18]. It activates some microorganisms or viruses and some enzymes also increases the shelf life of meat products. It also destructs the pathogens which can cause food spoilage [19]. It is important for food safety and security.

Radio Frequency Identification ITT2

It uses electromagnetic fields to mechanically detect and track tags pasted to objects. RFID tags use a storage device for storing data like the price of the product, manufacturing date, product identification number, *etc.* This data can be easily read by a scanner, thus RFID can work on the huge amounts of data at the same time, hence improving the efficiency of work [20]. RFID tags have been extensively applied to many traceability systems because of their ability to categorize, identify and manage the flow of [21]. The RFID technology offers the retailers, many benefits throughout the whole cycle for production of food, including traceability and food safety regulation [22, 23]. It is very important from the managerial point of view in the present days, because every Wall Mart having this technology in place of the bar code to enhance the security and safety of food products. Keep in mind that this technology is very expensive.

Nanotechnology (ITT3)

It is a technology in which the size of the particle varies between1 to 100 nanometers. It is the growing technology which has been extensively applied in many fields like food, dairy, cosmetics, medicines and agriculture. It is used to understand the uniqueness of nano particles which can modify the substance structure, texture and quality [24]. Nanotechnology in biotechnology and information technology has developed nano-biosensors which can be used for the identification of pathogens in the food sector. Nanomaterials are also used in food packaging. Regardless of food packaging, food preservation is also important. Nano sensors can detect the food spoilages [25, 26]. It is useful for improving safety and security of food products. This technology is useful for the managers to implement in the organization. The Nano particles are very small in size, which if inhaled can cause respiratory problems and take precautions before using it.

Vibrational & Fluorescence Spectroscopy (ITT4)

It is a photon emission process that involves the transfer of photons from one excited state to another. In this process, there is a conversion from electronic and vibrational states of polyatomic fluorescent molecules. Due to people awareness regarding food safety and quality, food authentication is becoming a most important field. Food authentication is the process that verifies that a food is in compliance with its label description. This is an environmentally clean technique. It also increases the safety and security of food [27]. Spectroscopy, in particular vibrational spectroscopy, is a fast and inexpensive method for both the assessment of food quality and food authenticity [28]. This technique is also useful for managers to implement it in the industry.

Artificial Intelligence (ITT5)

Development of computer systems normally requires individual intelligence, such as, speech detection, visual observation and management. The food manufacturing industry is said to be one of the most affected sectors by the implementation of artificial intelligence technologies. The report indicates that early adopters of it can expect revenue increases of 39% by 2020, while still retaining or retraining 80% of their existing employees [29]. It uses fuzzy systems which deal with uncertainty and noisy data. The models based on fuzzy logic deals with inaccurate information and knowledge which are impossible in conventional systems [30]. TOMRA, manufacturers of food sorting machines; advocate the use of artificial intelligence during the food sorting stage of the production line. It requires time and energy for the development of the the system and its implementation [31]. This technology helps managers to secure the safety of food products.

Bio Sensors (ITT6)

A machine which uses a living being or biological molecules, particularly enzymes or antibodies, to spot the occurrence of chemicals. In food technology, the sensors are and will be playing an an important role. Many sensor based equipments are manufactured, which can easily detect the contaminants present in the food. Water bee is a system, which is used to reduce water waste by collecting data on environmental factors and soil content using wireless sensors. They are small, portable instruments and are inexpensive than other systems. These can be used by agro businessman [32]. Biosensors play an important role in the detection of food pathogens. Many toxic compounds and heavy metals are detected by using enzyme inhibition sensors. It is also useful to improve the safety and security of food products and also helps managers to implement it in the the food sector.

3D Printing (ITT7)

It is also known as additive manufacturing. This technique is used to manufacture a three dimensional object in which consecutive layers of material are formed. It is one of the growing and new fields in the food industry. One of the most talked contributions of this technology in the the food industry is 3D systems candy, which is made up of pure [33]. The leader of the 3D printing industry has recently joined with Hershey's. NASA also uses this technology for making pizza, which can use as a meal for astronauts in the space. The use of 3D printer saves both time and energy. It designs cracker-like yeast structure, which is a healthy food containing spores and seeds [34]. It supplies the food in the growing population area as compared to conventional food manufacturing systems [35]. It also minimizes the food wastage by using hydrocolloid cartridges, which form gels when combined with water. The example of a 3D printer is Foodini, which is designed for the the home kitchen. The Foodini has produced many food items like pizzas, burgers and desserts.

Traceability (ITT8)

It can be defined as the ability to observe history, applications and the position of any product based on the recorded identification. Food products can be tracked by their ID which is travelling the longest routes. Traceability also includes bar coding and many imprinting tools which can be used to track the products and also their production history. Barcodes also provide other information regarding the ingredients, expiry date *etc.* thus helping in the improvement of food safety and security [36]. It is used for the prevention or reduction of food hazards. Products can be traced at each level. It is crucial for manufacturing firms to maintain their product quality. It also reduces the contamination of the dairy foods as well as aquatic products [37].

High Power Ultrasound (ITT9)

Ultra sound waves having a frequency above 20 kHz (higher than the normal limit), are used in many different fields like medical, food and manufacturing. Technologies are used for pasteurization of many fruit juices. It is mainly used in food preservation and processing which includes consumption of energy, increases in homogeneity, minimum loss of flavor in juices and breakdown of agglomerates of bacteria [38]. Microorganisms can be inactivated by using low-frequency high-power ultrasound and taste of the juices is maintained [39].It also checks the quality assurance in food manufacturing. It detects the changes in the food which include inactivation of microorganism and release of oil or fats [40]. It is useful for safety and security of food and also forces the mangers to implement it in the food sector for better future of the organization.

SOLUTION METHODOLOGY

AHP is the most commonly used and result oriented approach for formulating and decision making. It was developed so as to solve many problems and prioritization of alternate solutions. This can be achieved through pair wise comparisons between criteria elements and sub-criteria elements [41].

AHP Technique

This section contains a concise introduction of AHP along with common methodology. This method was introduced by [42-44] in which the "analytic" break down the problem into its constitutive parts and the "hierarchy" tells about the relation of consecutive or main objective [45] The AHP is used for selecting an alternative, decision making or particular process and also used for optimization. It is useful in the field of food, dairy, education, manufacturing and engineering *etc.* [46-49]. To find out the highest-ranking parameters for IT based technologies in the food sector, AHP is the best option, however this technique has some limitations, which depend on decision maker(s) and individual judgment. However, the next steps of AHP method for decision making are as follows:

1. Formulation of the work goal: Evaluating the IT based technologies in order to recognize their associated priority in the successful implementation of safety and security in food.

2. Forming pair wise assessment matrix: Pair wise assessment matrixes were formed from the literature review. The pair wise assessment matrix among the IT based technologies is accomplished through a Saaty's scale as shown in Table **1**.

3. Determination of the Eigen values and Eigen vectors and comparative importance weights: The framed pair wise comparison matrices were operated to establish the Eigen values and Eigen vectors, which were further analyzed to calculate the relative importance weights of the factors.

Table 1. Scales in pair wise comparisons (Saaty 1980).

Score	Definition
1	Equivalent importance of both factors
3	Limited importance of one factor over another
5	Strong importance of one factor over another
7	Very strong importance of one factor over another
9	Extreme importance of one factor over another
2, 4, 6, 8	Intermediate value between two close judgments

4. Assessment of the consistency ratio: The consistency ratio (CR) is calculated to ensure the reliability of pair wise comparisons. Mathematical

expression for calculating the CR is given as, CR = CI/RI, where the consistency index is denoted by (CI) = $(\lambda_{max} - n) / (n - 1)$, ($\lambda_{max}$ is the max. average value) and the value of the random consistency index (RI) explained in Table **2**, depends upon the value of (n). The value of CR must be less than 0.10 to have an improved level of consistency [50-52].

Table 2. Random Index.

N	1	2	3	4	5	6	7	8	9
R.I.	0	0	0.58	0.98	1.12	1.24	1.32	1.41	1.52

Sensitivity Analysis (SA)

SA permits us to validate the results of the judgment. It can be created to see how sensitive the alternatives are to modify with the weight of the criteria. The implementation of AHP gives four types of analysis like gradient, dynamic two dimensional analyses and performance [53]. Alternative performance is directly related to increase or decrease importance of criteria that is depicted by this technique. Regarding the previous context, main criteria affect each sub criteria on the basis of their importance. If the criterion is not sensitive, we can remove it from the AHP model.

RESULTS AND DISCUSSION

In this study, the results obtained from AHP analysis and validated by sensitivity analysis have been discussed (to show the purpose of the method described in Section 4).

AHP Analysis

Pair-wise assessment matrices which were finalized are shown in Table **3** (Saaty's1980) Nine-point scale was used for evaluating the interactions among IT based technologies for the effective use of IT in safety and security of food.

Table 3. Pair-wise assessment matrix for IT based technologies.

	ITT1	ITT2	ITT3	ITT4	ITT5	ITT6	ITT7	ITT8	ITT9	Weigh	Rank
ITT1	1.000	0.143	0.500	0.333	0.143	0.333	0.333	0.143	1.000	0.032	9
ITT2	7.000	1.000	8.000	5.000	0.500	6.000	8.000	2.000	4.000	0.267	1
ITT3	2.000	0.125	1.000	0.250	0.200	0.500	0.500	0.250	0.250	0.032	8
ITT4	3.000	0.200	4.000	1.000	0.200	1.000	0.500	0.500	0.500	0.061	6
ITT5	7.000	2.000	5.000	5.000	1.000	6.000	6.000	2.000	2.000	0.264	2
ITT6	3.000	0.167	2.000	1.000	0.167	1.000	1.000	1.000	0.333	0.059	7

(Table 3) cont.....

ITT7	3.000	0.125	2.000	2.000	0.167	1.000	1.000	1.000	0.500	0.065	5
ITT8	7.000	0.500	4.000	2.000	0.500	1.000	1.000	1.000	0.500	0.106	4
ITT9	1.000	0.250	4.000	2.000	0.500	3.000	2.000	2.000	1.000	0.114	3
SUM	34.000	4.510	30.500	18.583	3.376	19.833	20.333	9.893	10.083	1.000	

Max. Eigen value= 9.8736;   Consistency ratio= 0.0753

Calculated weights of the IT based technologies were used for giving the preferences among them which is given in Table **3**. The IT based technologies were listed on the basis of the priorities of their preference weights and it is useful for attaining the safety and security in the food sector. The current work is mainly focused on improving the safety and security of food with the help of IT based technologies. IT is a driving tool for all the technologies and also helps the companies to overcome the manual methods. The data was collected by literature survey and expert's views related to the particular area, nine technologies were selected. IT based technologies were further analyzed by AHP approach. In addition, validation of the results was done using sensitivity analysis. The collected data were analyzed for ascertaining the priorities among them. In AHP approach, the pair-wise assessment matrices (Table **3**) were developed for the IT based technologies. The order of the IT based technologies is given as (ITT1>ITT2>ITT3>ITT4>ITT5>ITT6>ITT7>ITT8>ITT9) in (Section 3). The new priority order after analysis by AHP approach according to their relative weight is (ITT2>ITT5>ITT9>ITT8>ITT7>ITT4>ITT6>ITT3>ITT1). ITT2 technology holds the first position in the priority list having the weight 0.267. ITT2 is used widely by different industries to improve the quality of their products. ITT5 comes at the second position in the priority list; it has the applications in the field of the food industry to improve their safety and security. ITT9 having the third rank in the list, is also used to reduce the possibilities of flavor change in the food products. Similarly ITT8, ITT7, ITT4, ITT6, ITT3 and ITT1 have fourth, fifth, sixth, seventh, eighth and ninth rank in the priority list respectively.

Sensitivity Analysis

The results attained by sensitivity analysis, validate the results of AHP approach. RFID technology is the most important technology among all, having the maximum weight. If there is a small change in the relative weight, it will affect the final ranking according to Chang [54]. In the AHP approach, human involvement/judgment is required for validating the ranking, and it also varies according to the weights of all the factors [55, 56]. To validate the ranking, sensitivity analysis plays an essential role in validating the ranking and causes factors for a successful implementation of IT based technologies. To demonstrate the sensitivity analysis, the impact of an incremental change should range from 0.1 to 0.9 as shown in (Table **4**). Ranking of IT based technologies on the basis of sensitivity analysis is shown in Fig (**1**). From this test, it may be concluded that RFID technology is very crucial in implementing an effective IT based technologies concept, and therefore requires major managerial concern.

Table 4. IT based technologies values.

IT Technologies	Values of preference weights for listed IT based technologies								
ITT1	0.0388	0.0345	0.0302	0.0259	0.0216	0.0172	0.0129	0.0086	0.0043
ITT2	0.1005	0.2005	0.3005	0.4001	0.5003	0.6001	0.7000	0.8002	0.9002
ITT3	0.0398	0.0354	0.0309	0.0265	0.0221	0.0177	0.0133	0.0088	0.0044
ITT4	0.0752	0.0669	0.0585	0.0502	0.0418	0.0334	0.0251	0.0167	0.0084
ITT5	0.3240	0.2880	0.2520	0.2161	0.1800	0.1440	0.1081	0.0720	0.0360
ITT6	0.0719	0.0639	0.0559	0.0480	0.0400	0.0320	0.0240	0.0160	0.0080
ITT7	0.0803	0.0713	0.0624	0.0535	0.0446	0.0357	0.0268	0.0178	0.0089
ITT8	0.1300	0.1156	0.1011	0.0867	0.0722	0.0578	0.0434	0.0289	0.0144
ITT9	0.1394	0.1239	0.1084	0.0929	0.0774	0.0619	0.0465	0.0309	0.0153
Total Weight	1	1	1	1	1	1	1	1	1

Source: Sensitivity Analysis

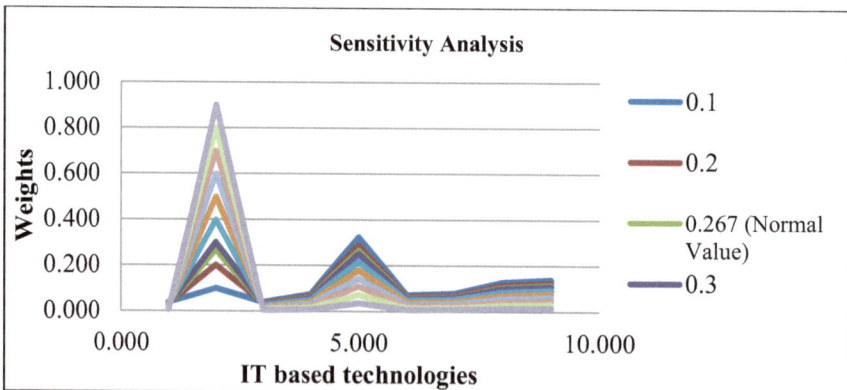

Fig. (1). Sensitivity Analysis.

CONCLUSION, LIMITATIONS AND FUTURE OPPORTUNITIES

IT based technologies play a crucial role in minimizing the costs and customer demands. It is also important to maintain their standards and position in the competitive market. In the present work, we discussed IT based technologies and their applications in the food sector.

The findings of the chapter help managers and stakeholders to know more about these technologies as well as their limitations for the implementation of the technologies in the food sector. Technologies also have their negative effects which include high costs of installation and the expertise in the particular field. RFID attains the highest position in the priority list having the weight of 0.267. Each technology has its own benefits and drawbacks for example, RFID has many limitations such as its high cost, requires more trained people and lack of hardware. Managers take precautions before implementing the IT based technologies. In food industries, people are using older technologies and it is difficult for them to adopt and implement new technologies. As discussed above, technologies directly affect the profitability and efficiency of the industry. As there is a competition between industries and individual organization, technologies play an essential role. For better understanding, we apply AHP approach for finding their relative weights among them. On the basis of their relative weights, managers easily found the best technology for their organization. Handling of these technologies is also an issue for the managers; these results give clear and exact views about the implementation and adoption of these IT based technologies. Finally, the result of sensitivity analysis shows that the ranking, comes out from AHP analysis is acceptable. Results give a clear idea for the successful implementation of IT technologies in the food industry. The suggested model has its own limitations and care should be taken for evaluation of IT based technologies execution. Although some mistakes may be there due to human incorrectness. Some other methods are also available like Best Worst Method (BWM), decision-making trial and evaluation laboratory (DEMATEL), Interpretive Structural Modeling (ISM) are used for Multiple-criteria decision-making (MCDM).

CONSENT FOR PUBLICATION

Not applicable.

CONFLICT OF INTEREST

The authors confirm that there is no conflict of interest to declare for this publication.

ACKNOWLEDGEMENTS

The authors acknowledge and express the gratitude for the support of the research facilities and funds provided by the Department of Mechanical Engineering, Graphic Era University, Dehradun, India.

REFERENCES

[1]   T Lang, D Barling, and M. Caraher, Food policy: integrating health, environment and society. OUP Oxford; 2009 Mar 19

[2]   S. Narayanan, "Food security in India: the imperative and its challenges", *Asia Pac. Policy Stud.,* vol. 2, no. 1, pp. 197-209.

[3]   I. Iuss, *FAO, 2006. World base reference for soil resources. Report on World Soil Resources..* FAO: Rome, Italy, 2006.

[4]   S.J. Vermeulen, P.K. Aggarwal, A. Ainslie, C. Angelone, B.M. Campbell, A.J. Challinor, J.W. Hansen, J.S. Ingram, A. Jarvis, P. Kristjanson, and C. Lau, "Options for support to agriculture and food security under climate change", *Environ. Sci. Policy,* vol. 15, no. 1, pp. 136-144.

[5]   K. Knoerzer, P. Juliano, G.W. Smithers, Eds., *Innovative Food Processing Technologies: Extraction, Separation, Component Modification and Process Intensification..* Woodhead Publishing, 2016.

[6]   F. Käferstein, and M. Abdussalam, "Food safety in the 21st century", *Bull. World Health Organ.,* vol. 77, no. 4, p. 347.

[7]   J. Schmidhuber, and F.N. Tubiello, "Global food security under climate change", *Proc. Natl. Acad. Sci. USA,* vol. 104, no. 50, pp. 19703-19708.

[8]   G. Locatelli, and M. Mancini, "Risk management in a mega-project: the Universal EXPO 2015 case", *Int. J. Project Organ. Manage.,* vol. 2, no. 3, pp. 236-253.

[9]   P. Ferranti, Food Sustainability, Security, and Effects of Global Change. 2018 Mar 5:1-5

[10]   "Foodborne Diseases-A Global Public Health Challenge", *Biosci. Microflora,* vol. 18, no. 1, pp. 11-15.

[11]   K. Boratyńska, and R.T. Huseynov, "An innovative approach to food security policy in developing countries", *Journal of Innovation & Knowledge.,* vol. 2, no. 1, pp. 39-44.

[12]   JR Beddington, M Asaduzzaman, A Fernandez, M Clark, M Guillou, M Jahn, L Erda, T Mamo, NV Bo, CA Nobre, and R Scholes, Achieving food security in the face of climate change: Final report from the Commission on Sustainable Agriculture and Climate Change. 2012, Mar: 1-64

[13]   R.S. Khare, "Food safety at home: some sociocultural criteria for research and application", *Information,* vol. 27, no. 4, pp. 607-622. [International Social Science Council].

[14]   M. Kärkkäinen, "Increasing efficiency in the supply chain for short shelf life goods using RFID tagging", *Int. J. Retail Distrib. Manag.,* vol. 31, no. 10, pp. 529-536.

[15]   A Vandeplas, and MP Squicciarini, 7 Food Safety Standards for Domestic and International Markets: The Case of Dairy. International Trade and Food Security: The Future of Indian Agriculture. 2016 Jul 8:96

[16]   J Singh, S Kaur, and H Majithia, Emerging genetic technologies for improving the security of food crops. Emerging technologies for promoting food security: Overcoming the world food crisis. 2015 Nov 13:23-41

[17]   C.N. Verdouw, J. Wolfert, A.J. Beulens, and A. Rialland, "Virtualization of food supply chains with the internet of things", *J. Food Eng.,* vol. 176, pp. 128-136.

[18]   J.H. Chen, Y. Ren, J. Seow, T. Liu, W.S. Bang, and H.G. Yuk, "Intervention technologies for ensuring microbiological safety of meat: current and future trends", *Compr. Rev. Food Sci. Food Saf.,* vol. 11, no. 2, pp. 119-132.

[19]   R. Buckow, and V. Heinz, "High pressure processing–a database of kinetic information", *Chemieingenieurtechnik (Weinh.),* vol. 80, no. 8, pp. 1081-1095.

[20]   B. Bilgen, and I. Ozkarahan, "Strategic tactical and operational production-distribution models: a review", *Int. J. Technol. Manag.,* vol. 28, no. 2, pp. 151-171.

[21]   V.P. Valdramidis, and K.P. Koutsoumanis, "Challenges and perspectives of advanced technologies in processing, distribution and storage for improving food safety", *Curr. Opin. Food Sci.,* vol. 12, pp. 63-69.

[22]   S. Li, J.K. Visich, B.M. Khumawala, and C. Zhang, "Radio frequency identification technology: applications, technical challenges and strategies", *Sens. Rev.,* vol. 26, no. 3, pp. 193-202.

[23]   P. Jones, C. Clarke-Hill, D. Comfort, D. Hillier, and P. Shears, "Radio frequency identification and food retailing in the UK", *Br. Food J.,* vol. 107, no. 6, pp. 356-360.

[24]   Q. Chaudhry, M. Scotter, J. Blackburn, B. Ross, A. Boxall, L. Castle, R. Aitken, and R. Watkins, "Applications and implications of nanotechnologies for the food sector", *Food Addit. Contam.,* vol. 25, no. 3, pp. 241-258.

[25]   M. Reza Mozafari, C. Johnson, S. Hatziantoniou, and C. Demetzos, "Nanoliposomes and their applications in food nanotechnology", *J. Liposome Res.,* vol. 18, no. 4, pp. 309-327.

[26]   N. Sozer, and J.L. Kokini, "Nanotechnology and its applications in the food sector", *Trends Biotechnol.,* vol. 27, no. 2, pp. 82-89.

[27]   E. Li-Chan, J. Chalmers, P. Griffiths, Eds., Applications of vibrational spectroscopy in food science. John Wiley & Sons; 2011 Jan 18, Vol.1: Instrumentation and fundamental applications

[28]   D. Cozzolino, "Recent trends on the use of infrared spectroscopy to trace and authenticate natural and agricultural food products", *Appl. Spectrosc. Rev.,* vol. 47, no. 7, pp. 518-530.

[29]   Switzerland. 2018 Jan 23-26

[30]   T. Eerikäinen, P. Linko, S. Linko, T. Siimes, and Y.H. Zhu, "Fuzzy logic and neural network applications in food science and technology", *Trends Food Sci. Technol.,* vol. 4, no. 8, pp. 237-242.

[31]   X. Zhang, J. Zhang, F. Liu, Z. Fu, and W. Mu, "Strengths and limitations on the operating mechanisms of traceability system in agro food, China", *Food Control,* vol. 21, no. 6, pp. 825-829.

[32]   I.E. Tothill, "Biosensors developments and potential applications in the agricultural diagnosis sector", *Comput. Electron. Agric.,* vol. 30, no. 1, pp. 205-218.

[33]   D.M. Kirchmajer, and R. Gorkin III, "An overview of the suitability of hydrogel-forming polymers for extrusion-based 3D-printing", *J. Mater. Chem. B Mater. Biol. Med.,* vol. 3, no. 20, pp. 4105-4117.

[34]   D Sher, and X. Tutó,

[35]   J. Sun, W. Zhou, D. Huang, J.Y. Fuh, and G.S. Hong, "An overview of 3D printing technologies for food fabrication", *Food Bioprocess Technol.,* vol. 8, no. 8, pp. 1605-1615.

[36]   T. Bosona, and G. Gebresenbet, "Food traceability as an integral part of logistics management in food and agricultural supply chain", *Food Control,* vol. 33, no. 1, pp. 32-48.

[37]   "Abela D, McElhatton A, Valdramidis VP. Assisted ultrasound applications for the production of safe foods", *J. Appl. Microbiol.,* vol. 116, no. 5, pp. 1067-1083.

[38]   S. Gao, G.D. Lewis, M. Ashokkumar, and Y. Hemar, "Inactivation of microorganisms by low-frequency high-power ultrasound: 1. Effect of growth phase and capsule properties of the bacteria", *Ultrason. Sonochem.,* vol. 21, no. 1, pp. 446-453.

[39]   H. Feng, G.V. Barbosa-Cánovas, and J. Weiss, *Ultrasound technologies for food and bioprocessing..* Springer: New York, 2011.

[40]   TL Saaty, and KP Kearns, "Analytical planning: The organization of system", *Elsevier.* 2014 May 17

[41]   Y. Wind, and T.L. Saaty, "Marketing applications of the analytic hierarchy process", *Manage. Sci.,* vol. 26, no. 7, pp. 641-658.

[42]   T.L. Saaty, (1980). The analytic hierarchy process, planning, priority setting, resource allocation, Mc-Graw Hill, New York, USA. ISBN 10: 0070543712

[43]   T.L. Saaty, "Decision making with the analytic hierarchy process", *Int. J. Serv. Sci.,* vol. 1, no. 1, pp. 83-98.

[44]   M.J. Sharma, I. Moon, and H. Bae, "Analytic hierarchy process to assess and optimize distribution network", *Appl. Math. Comput.,* vol. 202, no. 1, pp. 256-265.

[45]   P. Chaudhary, S.K. Chhetri, K.M. Joshi, B.M. Shrestha, and P. Kayastha, "Application of an Analytic Hierarchy Process (AHP) in the GIS interface for suitable fire site selection: A case study from Kathmandu Metropolitan City, Nepal", *Socioecon. Plann. Sci.,* vol. 53, pp. 60-71.

[46]   O.S. Vaidya, and S. Kumar, "Analytic hierarchy process: An overview of applications", *Eur. J. Oper. Res.*, vol. 169, no. 1, pp. 1-29.

[47]   H. Veisi, H. Liaghati, and A. Alipour, "Developing an ethics-based approach to indicators of sustainable agriculture using analytic hierarchy process (AHP)", *Ecol. Indic.*, vol. 60, pp. 644-654.

[48]   Y. Pan, and J. Wang, "Research on Selection of Logistics Supplier in the Process of Housing Industrialization", *Proceedings of the 20th International Symposium on Advancement of Construction Management and Real Estate,* 2016pp. 697-708

[49]   J Madaan, and S Mangla, Decision modeling approach for eco-driven flexible green supply chain. InSystemic Flexibility and Business Agility. 2014 17 Dec: 343-364

[50]   HD Jun, DH Min, and HK Yoon, Determination of Monitoring Systems and Installation Location to Prevent Debris-Flow through Web-Based Database and AHP. Marine Georesources & Geotechnology. 2017 Jan 25(just-accepted)

[51]   C. Padmavathy, and V.J. Sivakumar, "Adopting analytic hierarchy process to prioritise banks based on CRM effectiveness-the customers perspective", *International Journal of Business Innovation and Research.*, vol. 12, no. 1, pp. 80-93.

[52]   D.H. Byun, "The AHP approach for selecting an automobile purchase model", *Inf. Manage.*, vol. 38, no. 5, pp. 289-297.

[53]   C.W. Chang, C.R. Wu, C.T. Lin, and H.C. Chen, "An application of AHP and sensitivity analysis for selecting the best slicing machine", *Comput. Ind. Eng.*, vol. 52, no. 2, pp. 296-307.

[54]   K. Govindan, M. Kaliyan, D. Kannan, and A.N. Haq, "Barriers analysis for green supply chain management implementation in Indian industries using analytic hierarchy process", *Int. J. Prod. Econ.*, vol. 147, pp. 555-568.

[55]   A. Saltelli, K. Chan, E.M. Scott, Eds., *Sensitivity analysis..* Wiley: New York, 2000.

[56]   L. Simar, and P.W. Wilson, "Sensitivity analysis of efficiency scores: How to bootstrap in nonparametric frontier models", *Manage. Sci.*, vol. 44, no. 1, pp. 49-61.

Frontiers in Information Systems, 2018, Vol. 2, 123-167

CHAPTER 6

Mathematics and Examples of the Modern Syllogistic Method of Propositional Logic

Ali Muhammad Rushdi[1,*], and Muhammad Ali Rushdi[2]

[1]Department of Electrical and Computer Engineering, Faculty of Engineering, King Abdulaziz University, P.O. Box 80204, Jeddah, 21589, Kingdom of Saudi Arabia
[2]Department of Biomedical and Systems Engineering, Faculty of Engineering, Cairo University, Giza, 12613, Arab Republic of Egypt

Abstract: We describe the mathematical steps and the main features of the Modern Syllogistic Method (MSM), which is a relatively recent technique of deductive inference in propositional logic. This method ferrets out from a set of premises all that can be concluded from it, with the resulting conclusions cast in the simplest or most compact form. We demonstrate the applicability of the method in a variety of problems via eight examples that illustrate its mathematical details and exhibit the nature of the truth-preserving conclusions it can come up with. The method is shown to be particularly useful for detecting inconsistency within a set of given premises or hypotheses and it helps its user in penetrating to the heart of the problem and in confronting fallacious or fallacy-based argumentation. The method is also demonstrated to yield fruitful results that can aid in exploring, and maybe resolving, complex problems such as ethical dilemmas. The method is also shown to have a prominent application in the analysis of relational databases, wherein it offers a variety of algorithms for deriving the closure of a set of functional dependencies and the set of all candidate keys. Finally, several potential extensions and new applications of the method are outlined.

Keywords: Complete sum, Deductive inference, Ethical dilemma, Inconsistency, Modern Syllogistic Method, Prime implicant, Relational database, Switching function.

INTRODUCTION

One of the important traits of a successful problem solver is logical thinking [1]. This trait can usually be acquired, enhanced and mastered through appropriate training in logic [2-7]. Such training does not necessarily guarantee that a person

---

*Corresponding Author Ali Muhammad Rushdi: Department of Electrical and Computer Engineering, Faculty of Engineering, King Abdulaziz University, P. O. Box 80204, Jeddah, 21589, Kingdom of Saudi Arabia; Tel: +966126884035; +966554633544; Fax: +966126401686; E-mail: arushdi@kau.edu.sa

Mangey Ram (Ed.)

can reason well or correctly, but a person knowledgeable about logic techniques is more likely to reason correctly than one who is unaware of them. Historically, logic was looked upon as a part of, or companion to, philosophy. Traditional logicians applied deductive logic to contextual reasoning, and were deeply concerned with verbal fallacies. In its modern formal outlook, logic is a science of correct forms in which the study of such fallacies is irrelevant, and it has two distinctive branches of deduction and induction that are both essential as they play complementary rather than competitive roles in inference [7]. Nowadays, there are many logics, but we restrict ourselves herein to the classical propositional logic, which is a well-known formalism, widely used in philosophy, mathematics, artificial intelligence and computer science for capturing deductive reasoning.

In this chapter, we describe the steps, features, mathematics and some novel applications to problem solving of a general technique for deductive inference in propositional logic, which we call "the Modern Syllogistic Method (MSM)." A precursor to this method appeared in the work of H. McColl [8], who used multiplication to produce a *syllogistic formula* for a switching function, which is a sum-of-products formula whose products include, but are not necessarily confined to, all the prime implicants of the function. The MSM first appeared (under a different name) in the Ph.D. dissertation of A. Blake [9], who introduced and developed the iterative consensus procedure (also called the iterated consensus procedure) to produce the complete sum of a switching function by *explicit consensus generation* followed by *absorption*. Blake also provided an extensive example for iterative consnsus, and proved that it can be carried out letter by letter. For several decades, the method became virtually unknown, though its essential step of complete-sum derivation, has been gradually (re-)developed by many pioneers such as Quine [10-12], Tison [13], Reusch [14], and Muroga [15]. An incomplete (albeit interesting) attempt to reproduce the method appeared in a text on applied logic by Lynch [16]. The first popular correct description for the method is given in the wonderful book by Brown [17], who expounded and clarified the method, and nicely integrated it with or within Boolean reasoning and Boolean equation solving. Brown was also admirably keen to remind the world of Blake's forgotten contributions and to give him well-deserved due credit [17, 18]. The seminal work of Brown led the way for some enhancements, offshoots, or extensions of the MSM [19-34].

The great advantage of the MSM is that it is capable of unraveling all the truths hidden within a set of logical statements. In fact, it ferrets out from a given set of premises all that can be concluded from it, and it casts these conclusions in the simplest or most compact form. Though the domain of the MSM is the classical propositional logic (that is isomorphic to zeroth-order logic), its core step is dual to the resolution principle in first-order predicate logic [35], which is distinguished from propositional logic by its use of quantifiers. The resolution principle was developed by Robinson [35] based on the seminal work of Davis and Putnam [36]. It is used as a basis for automated reasoning employing non-procedural declarative logic programming languages such as PROLOG [37, 38].

The remainder of this chapter is organized as follows. Section II outlines the steps of the Modern Syllogistic Method, while section III lists its main features. Section IV illustrates some applications of the method to problem solving in terms of eight examples, mostly intended to be of utility to mathematicians, information and computer scientists, engineers and other professionals. Examples 1-3 present algorithmic deductions by the method in the context of a typical problem facing engineering students, a standard logical puzzle, and a usual problem facing engineers in transition to management. Examples 4 and 5 demonstrate how the method can test hypotheses or detect inconsistencies within a set of premises. This feature is very useful for problem solvers, because they can avoid falling into the trap of solving a perceived problem, which is a problem thought to be correctly defined while, in fact, it is not. The same feature is also necessary for those engaged in argumentation or debates, because it assists them to avoid being deceived by those who use inconsistent premises to validly deduce false conclusions, no matter how irrelevant these conclusions are. Example 6 illustrates using the MSM to explore a specific wicked problem, *viz.*, to provide some aid towards understanding, and maybe resolving, an ethical dilemma. Example 7 considers three variants of the problem facing a student when selecting elective courses under specific constraints. This example handles the situation when solutions of, as well as, conclusions about the problem are needed. Example 8 presents a prominent MSM application in the analysis of relational databases, wherein it offers a variety of algorithms for deriving the closure of a set of functional dependencies and the set of all candidate keys. The example covers full as well as incremental versions of the MSM. Section V concludes the paper, and presents several extensions and applications of the method. To make the chapter self-contained, it is supplemented by three Appendices. Appendix A introduces basic notions about the complete sum of a switching function and points out that both the MSM and MP (modus ponens) are complete single rules of inference in propositional logic, and explains why the MSM is a more convenient rule. Appendices B and C describe briefly two algorithmic methods that are suitable for hand-derivation of the complete sum, namely, the Improved Blake-Tison Method, and a method of multiplication of syllogistic formulas utilizing the variable-entered Karnaugh map (VEKM) [39], and hence called the Method of VEKM

Folding. Most of the examples in the main text are solved *via* one of these two methods, allowing the reader to check correctness of the results obtained. Some examples are solved twice *via* different orderings of variables, hinting at possibilities of reductions in computational complexity.

STEPS OF THE MODERN SYLLOGISTIC METHOD (MSM)

1. Each of the premises (antecedents) is converted into the form of a formula equated to 0 (which we call an equational form), and then the resulting equational forms are combined together into a single equation of the form $f = 0$. If we have n logical equivalence or coincidence relations of the form

$$T_i \equiv Q_i, \qquad 1 \leq i \leq n, \tag{1}$$

they are set in the equational form

$$T_i \overline{Q}_i \vee \overline{T}_i Q_i = 0, \qquad 1 \leq i \leq n. \tag{2}$$

We may also have $(m - n)$ logical-implication (logical-inclusion) relations of the form

$$T_i \rightarrow Q_i, \qquad (n+1) \leq i \leq m \tag{3}$$

These relations symbolize the statements "*If T_i then Q_i*" or equivalently "*T_i only if Q_i*". Conditions (3) can be set into the equational form

$$T_i \overline{Q}_i = 0, \qquad (n+1) \leq i \leq m. \tag{4}$$

The m premises in (1) and (3) finally reduce to the single equation $f = 0$, where f is given by,

$$f = \bigvee_{i=1}^{n} (T_i \overline{Q}_i \vee \overline{T}_i Q_i) \vee \bigvee_{i=(n+1)}^{m} T_i \overline{Q}_i. \tag{5}$$

Equations (1) and (3) represent the dominant forms that premises can take. Other less important forms are discussed in [40] and can be added to (5) when necessary. Note that the order of the premises has no meaning and is not meant to represent any respective importance.

2. The function f in (5) is rewritten as a complete sum (Blake canonical form), *i.e.*, as a disjunction of all the prime implicants of f. There are many manual and computer algorithms for deriving the complete sum of a switching function f [12-15, 17, 41-64]. Most of these algorithms depend on two logical operations: (a) Consensus generation (or equivalently multiplying a product of sums into a sum of products), and (b) absorption. We discuss pertinent notions and two favorite manual methods for deriving the complete sum in Appendices A, B, and C.

3. Suppose the complete sum $CS(f)$ of f takes the form

$$CS(f) = \bigvee_{i=1}^{\ell} P_i = 0, \tag{6}$$

where P_i is the i th prime implicant of f. Equation (6) is equivalent to

$$P_i = 0, \qquad 1 \le i \le \ell. \tag{7}$$

Equations (7) are called prime consequents [17]. They state in the simplest equational form all that can be concluded from the original premises. The conclusions in (7) can also be cast into implicational form. Suppose P_i is given as a conjunction of uncomplemented literals X_{ij} and complemented literals $\overline{Y}_{ij}$, *i.e.*

$$P_i = \bigwedge_{j=1}^{r} X_{ij} \wedge \bigwedge_{j=1}^{s} \overline{Y}_{ij}, \qquad 1 \le i \le \ell \tag{8}$$

then, equations (7) can be rewritten in implicational form in 2^{r+s} ways, where (r+s) is the number of literals in the product P_i. Some of these ways seem more appealing for human understanding and verbal rephrasing than others. One of the more appealing ways is one that involves only uncomplemented literals, which is obtained by writing

$$\bigwedge_{j=1}^{r} X_{ij} \to (\overline{\bigwedge_{j=1}^{s} \overline{Y}_{ij}}), \qquad 1 \le i \le \ell \tag{9}$$

and then invoking De Morgan rule to result in

$$\bigwedge_{j=1}^{r} X_{ij} \;\to\; \bigvee_{j=1}^{s} Y_{ij}\,,\quad 1 \le i \le \ell \tag{10}$$

Table **1** shows eight implicational forms each of which is equivalent to the equation $\{\overline{U}\overline{L}E = 0\}$ that involves a three-literal product $\overline{U}\overline{L}E$. The preference of one of these forms to another is just a matter of taste and personal convenience. While acknowledging that the implication $\{E \to U \vee L\}$ (with only non-complemented literals) might be generally preferable to others, we highlight in Table 1 the implication of choice in *Coincidence Analysis*, which is a new type of causal reasoning that uncovers deterministic causal structures [65-67]. In line with the fact that one equation has a multitude of equivalent implicational forms, one can understand why a conditional theorem of the form $A \to B \{A\overline{B} = 0\}$ has the same truth value as its *contrapositive* $\overline{B} \to \overline{A}\{\overline{B}A = 0\}$, but it is not necessarily equivalent to its *inverse* $\overline{A} \to \overline{B}\{\overline{A}B = 0\}$, or its *converse* $B \to A\{B\overline{A} = 0\}$, with the inverse and converse being equivalent.

Table 1. Totality of eight implicational forms equivalent to an equational form with a three-literal product.

Equational Form	Clausal (Implicational) Forms							
$\overline{U}\overline{L}E$ $= 0$	$\overline{U}\overline{L}E$ $\to 0$	$\overline{L}E \to U$	$\overline{U}E$ $\to L$	$\overline{U}\overline{L}$ $\to \overline{E}$	$\overline{U} \to$ $L \vee \overline{E}$	$\overline{L} \to$ $U \vee \overline{E}$	$E \to$ $U \vee L$	$1 \to$ $U \vee L \vee \overline{E}$

In passing, we note that the MSM has a *dual* version, in which each premise is converted into a formula equated to 1 rather than 0, and the whole set of premises reduces to a single function, again equated to 1 rather than 0 [32]. In this dual version, we deal with prime implicates rather than prime implicants, and derive the complete product rather than the complete sum of the aforementioned function [15].

IMPORTANT FEATURES OF THE MSM

➢ The MSM produces *all possible consequents*, since the complete sum $\mathcal{CS}(f)$ is a disjunction of all the prime implicants of f, and it casts these consequents in the *most compact form* (since all the implicants in $\mathcal{CS}(f)$ are prime ones). If any implicant (whether it is prime or not) of f is equated to 0, then the result is a true consequent (albeit not necessarily a prime one, i.e., one in the most compact form) [17, 24-26].

➤ To *test* the truth of any *claimed conclusions* based on a given set of premises, one just needs to cast these claimed conclusions in the form of a disjunction of terms equated to 0, and check to see if each of these terms subsumes (at least) one of the prime implicants in $CS(f)$ derived from the set of premises. There is a single major computational task required for this test, which is the generation of $CS(f)$. This task is performed only once for *all* the claimed conclusions. As it is the case with all methods of inference, the MSM can be used to check or test for the *validity* of any supposition, but it cannot serve for checking the *invalidity* of a supposition.

➤ The MSM is a method of deductive inference, whose function is to (a) govern truth-transmission ("*The set of all possible worlds that make (the conjunction of) the premises true is included in the set of possible worlds that make the conclusion true*" [68]), and (b) govern the information flow ("*The information conveyed by the conclusion is contained in the information conveyed by (the conjunction of) the premises*" [68]). There have been many attempts to justify deduction [69-71], but the consensus now is that deduction should be explained rather than justified [72].

➤ The MSM encompasses a complete set of inference rules [25, 26], and constitutes a *complete system* of truth-functional logic, in the sense that it permits the construction of a formal proof of validity for any valid truth-functional argument [7]. The interested reader is referred to [25, 26, 32], where an extensive number of popular *inference rules* are shown to be special cases of the MSM. A student of logic who masters the MSM does not have to memorize such inference rules or to get intrigued by which rule to apply in a certain situation. Besides being a complete method of inference that can infer any valid conclusion, the MSM is a *sound* method that never infers an invalid conclusion.

➤ The MSM has a built-in capability of detecting the existence of *inconsistency* within a given set of premises. The method will alert its user to the existence of concealed inconsistencies by producing $CS(f) = 1$. Once this happens, the user should refrain from making any conclusion, and should revise his set of premises to change it into a consistent one. The MSM can guide such a revision, say by identifying which premise(s) to omit. Otherwise, inconsistency might be tolerated by abandoning classical logic altogether and using other *paraconsistent* logics [73-76].

➤ The rules of inference are characterized as definitory or permissive rather than strategic, in the sense that they fail to supply their human user with a strategy or policy to successfully sequence the steps that should be followed [77]. These rules merely define what is allowable or permissible at every given step. Hence, deduction via these rules has a defensive tendency, where the user strives to make correct steps and avoid falling into the trap of logical fallacies. Therefore, deduction using the rules of inference can be described as an exploratory heuristic procedure, which is somewhat difficult to learn, and might be fallible as it might lead to lengthy unwarranted excursions or divergences. As stated earlier, the MSM relieves its users of the need to memorize many rules of inference, and it exempts them from thinking about a strategy to determine the sequence for the implementation of some of these rules.

➤ The MSM can be used in detecting and invalidating certain *purported arguments* or *formal fallacies*, such as the converse fallacy (the fallacy of affirming the consequent) or the inverse fallacy (the fallacy of denying the antecedent) [26].

➤ The MSM is very useful in the case of *selective deduction* [17, 20, 21], which is deduction with the knowledge of certain information or restrictions, or the lack thereof, about some of the pertinent variables. Selective deduction serves as a useful decision-making tool in many real-life situations [17, 22, 24], including the problem of deriving all the candidate keys of a relational database [27, 29, 34].

➤ As a technique of deduction, the MSM is a *truth-preserving* method [78] that unravels hidden truths [79], *i.e.*, it guarantees the truthfulness of the conclusions provided all the premises are true. As a formal technique of propositional logic, the MSM concerns itself only with the *form* of its premises and conclusions and has nothing to do with their subject matter. In fact, it has been known for two millennia that deductive reasoning is about structure and not about content. It is up to the user of the method to use plausible heuristics to formulate the premises and interpret the consequents. The intervening task of going from the formal premises to the formal conclusions is tackled in a completely *algorithmic* fashion by the method. By contrast, the heuristics required to formulate the premises are *fallible*, involve some linguistic and verbal ambiguities, and cannot be replaced by exact recipes.

➤ The essential step in the MSM is the derivation of the complete sum, which is illustrated herein for small or textbook examples *via* algorithmic methods that are suitable for hand calculations. Though automated methods that can cover larger problems do exist, they are not stressed herein, because of two reasons, *viz.*, (a) many of the useful MSM uses are in small or medium-sized problems, and (b) the step of complete-sum derivation is sandwiched between the two steps of premise formulation and conclusion interpretation, which crucially demand human *educated* intervention. However, the reader is warned that the problems handled by the MSM have many associated '*intractability*'' results [34].

➤ The MSM has an incremental version that properly handles the case when a set of premises is augmented by a single new premise (or a set of several premises) after completion of deduction based on the original set. The incremental MSM exploits the presence of the original solution to avoid redundant or repetitive computations [27, 29, 31, 34].

➤ There is a clear duality between the MSM and the resolution-based methodology adopted by the Artificial Intelligence (AI) community. As we pointed out earlier, the concept of "resolution" is the dual of that of "consensus" studied herein. In a sense, consensus in a switching function can be viewed as "propositional resolution" [80]. More generally, in "big" Boolean algebras, consensus might be thought of as "Boolean resolution" [81].

➤ The information obtained by the MSM is in the form of conclusions formulated as implicational statements. It does not provide specific solutions of the problem at hand. Such solutions can be obtained by writing $\bar{f}$ as a disjoint sum of products, and then setting each of the individual disjoint products to 1 [30, 39, 82].

EXAMPLES

Example 1

An engineering student will find a job when he graduates only if he is well-prepared, and he will be well-prepared only if he can read and write extremely well and has a good technical education. He will read and write extremely well if and only if he takes a lot of humanities courses, but if he takes a lot of humanities courses he will not take many technical courses, and if he does not take many technical courses then he will not have a good technical education [83]. To discuss the possible consequents of these premises, let us define:

$J =$	The student will find a job when he graduates,
$P =$	He is well-prepared,
$C =$	He can read and write extremely well,
$E =$	He has a good technical education,
$H =$	He takes a lot of humanities courses,
$T =$	He takes many technical courses.

The statements above may be translated as follows:

Conditional form	Equational form
$J \rightarrow P$	$J \bar{P} = 0$
$P \rightarrow C E$	$P(\bar{C} \vee \bar{E}) = 0$
$C \equiv H$	$C\bar{H} \vee \bar{C}H = 0$
$H \rightarrow \bar{T}$	$H T = 0$
$\bar{T} \rightarrow \bar{E}$	$\bar{T} E = 0$

Then the given data are equivalent to the propositional equation $f = 0$, where f is

$$f = J \bar{P} \vee P \bar{C} \vee P \bar{E} \vee C \bar{H} \vee \bar{C} H \vee H T \vee \bar{T} E. \tag{11}$$

Fig. **(1)** applies the Improved Blake-Tison Method (see Appendix B) to the absorptive formula (11) *w. r. t.* the biform variables P, C, E, H, and T. Finally, the complete sum of f is

$$CS(f) = P \vee J \vee C \bar{H} \vee \bar{C} H \vee H T \vee C T \vee \bar{T} E \vee H E \vee C E = 0 \tag{12}$$

There are nine prime consequents, which include in particular

$P = 0$ {The student is not well prepared},
$J = 0$ {He will not find a job when he graduates}.

This example is a very good illustration on how logic can be easily misused. All the innocent-looking premises seem plausible and not really threatening when viewed separately, but taken together they combine to produce some totally unexpected (sometimes surprising or even shocking) results. Here, the poor student discovers that he is neither well-prepared nor getting a job upon graduation. Historically, logic has been misused by being manipulated to give some sort of "proof" for false propositions. When one understands this, it is possible to identify the pitfall(s) within the whole process, which are sometimes hidden in not-so-thoroughly-investigated premises, but are occasionally due to the use of incorrect "rules" of inference [84].

Example 2

Suppose that liars always speak what is false, and truth-tellers always speak what is true. Further suppose that Amy, Bob, and Cal are each either a liar or a truth-teller. Amy says, "Bob is a liar." Bob says, "Cal is a liar." Cal says, "Amy and Bob are liars." Which, if any, of these people are truth-tellers [85]? To answer this question on the basis of these premises, let us define A, B, and C as the propositions that Amy is a truth-teller, Bob is a truth-teller, and Cal is a truth-teller, respectively. The premises above may be translated as follows:

Conditional form	Equational form
$A \equiv \bar{B}$	$AB \vee \overline{A}\,\overline{B} = 0$
$B \equiv \bar{C}$	$BC \vee \overline{B}\,\overline{C} = 0$
$C \equiv \overline{AB}$	$C(A \vee B) \vee \overline{A}\,\overline{B}\,\overline{C} = 0$

Then the given data are equivalent to the propositional equation $f = 0$, where f is

$$f = AB \vee \overline{A}\,\overline{B} \vee BC \vee \overline{B}\,\overline{C} \vee C(A \vee B) \vee \overline{A}\,\overline{B}\,\overline{C}. \tag{13}$$

To obtain the complete sum of f, we compute

$$F_1 = CS(f/A) = CS(B \vee BC \vee \bar{B}\bar{C} \vee C) = 1, \tag{14}$$

$$F_0 = CS(f/\bar{A}) = CS(\bar{B} \vee BC \vee \bar{B}\bar{C} \vee CB \vee \bar{B}\bar{C}) = \bar{B} \vee C, \tag{15}$$

and then use (C.2) to obtain

$$CS(f) = ABS\left((\bar{A} \lor F_1) \land (A \lor F_0)\right) = ABS\left((\bar{A} \lor 1) \land (A \lor \bar{B} \lor C)\right) =$$
$$A \lor \bar{B} \lor C = 0. \quad \textbf{(16)}$$

There are three prime consequents, which indicate that $A = \bar{B} = C = 0$, *i.e.*, Bob is a truth-teller, while Amy and Cal are liars. This MSM solution is somewhat analogous to the one in [85], which proves that Cal is a liar by assuming he is a truth-teller and deriving a contradiction through resolution in a way similar to that used in automated theorem proving. The MSM solution above decides the status of every person involved, once and for all, while the technique in [85] might need repetition or further substitutions.

The present example is typical of logical puzzles dealing with knights (people who always tell the truth), knaves (people who always lie), and alternators (people who always alternate between telling the truth and lying) [86, 87].

Consensuses/P	$P\bar{C}$	$P\bar{E}$	$C\bar{H}$ $\bar{C}H$ HT $\bar{T}E$
$J\bar{P}$	$J\bar{C}$	$J\bar{E}$	

Consensuses/C	$C\bar{H}$	$J\bar{P}$ $P\bar{E}$ $J\bar{E}$ HT $\bar{T}E$
$P\bar{C}$	$P\bar{H}$	
$J\bar{C}$	$J\bar{H}$	
$\bar{C}H$	--------	

Consensuses/E	$\bar{T}E$	$P\bar{C}$ $J\bar{C}$ $\bar{C}H$ $C\bar{H}$ $P\bar{H}$ $J\bar{H}$ $J\bar{P}$ HT
$P\bar{E}$	$P\bar{T}$	
$J\bar{E}$	$J\bar{T}$	

Consensuses/H	$\bar{C}H$	HT	$P\bar{E}$ $J\bar{E}$ TE $P\bar{T}$ $J\bar{T}$ $P\bar{C}$ $J\bar{C}$ $J\bar{P}$
$C\bar{H}$	--------	CT	
$P\bar{H}$	$P\bar{C}$	PT	
$J\bar{H}$	$J\bar{C}$	JT	

Consensuses/T	HT	CT	PT	JT	$C\bar{H}$ $P\bar{H}$ $J\bar{H}$ $\bar{C}H$ $P\bar{C}$ $J\bar{C}$ $P\bar{E}$ $J\bar{E}$ $P\bar{C}$ $J\bar{C}$ $J\bar{P}$
$\bar{T}E$	EH	CE	PE	JE	
$P\bar{T}$	PH	PC	P	JP	
$J\bar{T}$	JH	JC	JP	J	

Fig. (1). Steps of the Improved Blake-Tison Method for computing $CS(f)$ in Example 1.

Example 3

Consider an engineer who is either forceful (F) or creative (C) (or both). If she is forceful, then she is going to be a good executive (G). It is not possible that she is both efficient (E) and creative. If she is not efficient, then either she is forceful or she will be a good executive. What can be concluded about her? With the pertinent propositions expressed by the variables in parentheses, the given premises may be translated as follows:

Conditional form	Equational form
$F \vee C$	$\overline{F}\overline{C} = 0$
$F \to G$	$F\overline{G} = 0$
$\overline{E} \vee \overline{C}$	$EC = 0$
$\overline{E} \to F \vee G$	$\overline{E}\overline{F}\overline{G} = 0$

Then the given data are equivalent to the propositional equation $f = 0$, where f is

$$f = \overline{FC} \vee F\overline{G} \vee EC \vee \overline{E}\,\overline{FG} = 0. \tag{17}$$

To obtain the complete sum of f, we compute

$$F_1 = CS(f/F) = CS(\bar{G} \vee EC) = \bar{G} \vee EC, \tag{18}$$

$$F_0 = CS(f/\bar{F}) = CS(\bar{C} \vee EC \vee E\bar{G}) = \bar{C} \vee E \vee \bar{G}, \tag{19}$$

and then use (C.5) to obtain the complete sum of f as

$$CS(f) = \bar{G} \vee ABS((\bar{F} \vee EC) \wedge (F \vee \bar{C} \vee E)) = \bar{G} \vee ABS(\bar{F}\bar{C} \vee \bar{F}E \vee ECF \vee EC) = \bar{G} \vee \bar{F}\bar{C} \vee \bar{F}E \vee EC. \tag{20}$$

There are four prime consequents, which indicate that $\bar{G} = 0$, $\bar{F}\bar{C} = 0$, $\bar{F}E = 0$, and $EC = 0$, *i.e.*, one obtains a reecho of two of the original premises as well as two new consequents

✓ ($\overline{G} = 0$) or ($G = 1$) asserting the glad news that our engineer will be a good executive.

✓ ($\bar{F}E = 0$) indicating that if she is efficient, then she is going to be forceful.

Example 4

In [88], Fogler and LeBlance present a five-step strategy for creative problem solving. They assert that the most difficult and error-prone step in their strategy is its first step, namely, *problem definition*. They present several techniques that are highly likely to facilitate the job of problem definition, but cannot guarantee that it is done correctly. They use one of these techniques (the Present State/Desired State technique) to analyze the following situation: During WWII, some planes of the Allies were shot down while engaging enemy antiaircraft batteries in bombing missions over Germany. Many of the planes that made it back safely to base were riddled with bullets and projectile holes. The damaged areas were similar on each plane.

We demonstrate the utility of the MSM as a problem-definition technique by using it to analyze the above situation. We label the areas typically damaged in a returning plane as part "a" of the plane, depict the rest of the plane as part "b", and then introduce the following propositional variables:

$A =$	A plane is hit in its "a" part,
$B=$	A plane is hit in its "b" part,
$S =$	A plane is not shot down in its mission, and makes it back safely to its base,
$E=$	A plane engages enemy antiaircraft batteries.

According to the given scenario a plane that makes it back safely (S) could have avoided engaging enemy batteries. Otherwise, it engaged enemy batteries and is hit in part "a" but not in part "b". This means that

$$S \equiv \bar{E} \vee EA\bar{B}. \qquad (21)$$

An underlying assumption is that no plane can actively engage enemy batteries without being hit somewhere, namely

$$E \equiv A \vee B. \qquad (22)$$

Conditions (1) and (2) are equivalent to the propositional equation $f = 0$, where f is

$$
\begin{aligned}
f &= S\overline{\left(\bar{E} \vee EA\bar{B}\right)} \vee \bar{S}\left(\bar{E} \vee EA\bar{B}\right) \vee E\overline{(A \vee B)} \vee \bar{E}(A \vee B) \\
&= SE\bar{A} \vee SEB \vee \overline{SE} \vee \bar{S}EA\bar{B} \vee E\bar{A}\bar{B} \vee \bar{E}A \vee \bar{E}B
\end{aligned}
\qquad (23)
$$

The complete sum for f is obtained *via* VEKM multiplication in Fig. **(2)** (see Appendix C). It is given by

$$CS(f) = \bar{S}\bar{B} \vee SB \vee \bar{E}A \vee \bar{E}\bar{S} \vee \bar{E}B \vee E\bar{A}\bar{S} \vee E\bar{A}\bar{B} = 0. \qquad (24)$$

Equation (24) is equivalent to the totality of the following groups of consequents

$$\overline{SB} \vee SB = 0, \qquad\qquad \{S \equiv \bar{B} \ \text{ or } \ \bar{S} \equiv B\}, \qquad (25a)$$

$$\bar{E}(A \vee B \vee \bar{S}) = 0, \qquad\qquad \{\bar{E} \to \bar{A}\bar{B}S\}, \qquad (25b)$$

$$E\bar{A}(S \vee \bar{B}) = 0, \qquad\qquad \{E \to A \vee \bar{S}B\}, \qquad (25c)$$

Consequents (25a) – (25c) indicate respectively that

a) A plane returns safely if and only if (iff) it is not hit in its "b" part, *i.e.*, it is shot down iff it is hit in that part.

b) A plane that does not engage the enemy batteries is not hit anywhere and returns safely.

c) A plane that engages the enemy batteries, either gets hit in its "a" part or it is hit in its "b" part and shot down or both.

We note that condition (25a) represents all that can be deduced in the absence of any information about plane engagement with enemy antiaircraft batteries (all remaining consequents involve either E or $\bar{E}$). We can now penetrate to the heart of the real problem: A plane is shot down when it is hit in part "b" because this part encompasses critical components. Hence part "b" should be further protected, shielded, and supplemented with redundant pieces of equipment. An attempt to solve the perceived problem (by reinforcing the damaged areas (part "a") with thicker armor plating) would fail [88]. We can see that this should be the case since our consequents in (24) indicate that

$$A(\bar{E} \vee \overline{SB}) = 0, \qquad\qquad \{A \to E(S \vee B)\}, \qquad\qquad \textbf{(26)}$$

which means that if a plane is hit in its "a" part, then it is known to have engaged the enemy and to have returned safely or it is hit in the "b" part.

$\wedge$	$\bar{S}$	$\bar{A}$	B
S	....	$S\,\bar{A}$	$S\,B$
$\bar{B}$	$\bar{S}\,\bar{B}$	$\bar{A}\,\bar{B}$	....

(a) Multiplication matrix of $(\bar{S} \vee CS(f/ES)) = (\bar{S} \vee \bar{A} \vee B)$ and $(S \vee CS(f/E\bar{S})) = (S \vee \bar{B})$ to produce $CS(f/E)$

$\wedge$	$\bar{E}$	$\bar{S}\,\bar{B}$	$S\,B$	$S\,\bar{A}$	$\bar{A}\,\bar{B}$
E	....	$E\,\bar{S}\,\bar{B}$	$E\,S\,B$	$E\,S\,\bar{A}$	$E\,\bar{A}\,\bar{B}$
$\bar{S}$	$\bar{E}\,\bar{S}$	$\bar{S}\,\bar{B}$	....	....	$\bar{S}\,\bar{A}\,\bar{B}$
A	$\bar{E}\,A$	$A\,\bar{S}\,\bar{B}$	$A\,S\,B$	....	....
B	$\bar{E}\,B$	....	$S\,B$	$S\,\bar{A}\,B$	....

(b) Multiplication matrix of $(\bar{E} \vee CS(f/E))$ and $(E \vee CS(f/\bar{E})) = (E \vee \bar{S} \vee A \vee B)$ to produce $CS(f)$

Fig. (2). Derivation of the complete sum for f *via* VEKM multiplication.

Example 5

This example does not deal with an engineering problem per se, though it handles a problem of concern to many engineers and other professionals as well. It demonstrates how an engineer can confront illogical thinking and fallacious argumentation. Consider the real-life situation of a retiring engineer who has served his company for two consecutive periods of time. In the first period, the terms of employment were decided by an old set of statutes (O), but in the second period the company imposed a new set of statutes (N). Each set of statutes is self-consistent and strives to achieve its own sense of justice. According to the old statutes, the end-of-service gratuity is a full-month salary (F) per year of service, but this gratuity is only a half-month salary (H) per year of service in the new statutes. Also, the new statutes set an upper limit (L) on the gratuity, while in the old statutes there is no such limit.

If the engineer's service is considered continuous (C), the engineer receives a total gratuity (T) for his total service according to his initial contract based on the old statutes. Otherwise, he receives two split gratuities (S), one covering his first period of service and based on the old statutes, and another fresh one covering his second period and based on the new statutes. With the pertinent propositions expressed by the variables in parentheses, we now formalize the aforementioned premises as follows:

Clausal form	Conditional form
$O \rightarrow F\,\overline{L}$	$O\,\overline{F} \vee O\,L = 0$
$N \rightarrow H\,L$	$N\,\overline{H} \vee N\,\overline{L} = 0$
$C \rightarrow O\,T$	$C\,\overline{O} \vee C\,\overline{T} = 0$
$\overline{C} \rightarrow N\,S$	$\overline{C}\,\overline{N} \vee \overline{C}\,\overline{S} = 0$
$N \equiv \overline{O}$	$N\,O \vee \overline{N}\,\overline{O} = 0$
$S \equiv \overline{T}$	$S\,T \vee \overline{S}\,\overline{T} = 0$

These premises are now combined into a single equation of the form

$$f = O\,\overline{F} \vee O\,L \vee N\,\overline{H} \vee N\,\overline{L} \vee C\,\overline{O} \vee C\,\overline{T} \vee \overline{C}\,\overline{N} \vee \overline{C}\,\overline{S}$$
$$\vee N\,O \vee \overline{N}\,\overline{O} \vee S\,T \vee \overline{S}\,\overline{T} = 0,$$

(27)

Skipping the details of complete-sum derivation, we write

$$
\begin{aligned}
CS(f) =\ & O\overline{F} \vee OL \vee N\overline{H} \vee N\overline{L} \vee C\overline{O} \vee C\overline{T} \vee \overline{C}\,\overline{N} \vee \overline{C}\,\overline{S} \vee NO \\
& \vee \overline{N}\,\overline{O} \vee ST \vee \overline{S}\,\overline{T} \vee \overline{C}T \vee CS \vee \overline{O}\,\overline{S} \vee \overline{O}T \vee \overline{N}\,\overline{T} \\
& \vee \overline{N}S \vee C\overline{F} \vee CL \vee CN \vee \overline{N}\,\overline{F} \vee \overline{N}L \vee \overline{F}\,\overline{S} \vee \overline{F}T \\
& \vee L\overline{S} \vee LT \vee N\overline{S} \vee NT \vee \overline{C}\,\overline{H} \vee \overline{O}\,\overline{H} \vee \overline{T}\,\overline{H} \vee \overline{F}\,\overline{H} \\
& \vee L\overline{H} \vee \overline{C}\,\overline{L} \vee \overline{O}\,\overline{L} \vee \overline{T}\,\overline{L} \vee \overline{F}\,\overline{L} \vee \overline{C}O \vee \overline{T}O \\
=\ & 0.
\end{aligned}
\tag{28}
$$

Equation (28) ferrets out all the prime consequents that can be deduced from the original premises, and they are of a relatively huge number indeed. Each of these consequents makes sense in view of the original premises. For example, $L\overline{H}=0$ indicates that $L \to H$, i.e., if the gratuity has a limit, it is at the half-month rate. Note that if one adds a premise about the continuity of service, by asserting either C or $\overline{C}$, then more tangible and decisive conclusions can be reached. However, the "clever" lawyers at the so called "legal" department of the company deliberately refuse to settle the question of continuity and arbitrarily decide to assert T and N as additional premises. These new premises appear in equational form as $\overline{T}=0$ and $\overline{N}=0$, and when the disjunction comprising the function f is augmented by them, the formula of f includes now the three terms NT, $\overline{T}$ and $\overline{N}$ which sum up to 1, and hence

$$
CS(f) = 1,
\tag{29}
$$

which leads to the contradiction $1 = 0$. This means that the total set of premises is inconsistent, and hence it is totally worthless as a basis of deduction [7]. Such a set of inconsistent premises can be used to validly yield any conclusion, no matter how irrelevant. In fact, inconsistent premises can be used to conclude simultaneously any proposition $D\,(\overline{D}=0)$ and its denial $\overline{D}$ ($D=0$), since both the terms $\overline{D}$ and D subsume (are included in) the term 1. The "clever" lawyers are now at leisure to forward any unfair decision and disguise it as a valid consequent of their "legal" premises. The engineer should, if he can, insist on (a) showing that there is inconsistency within the given premises, (b) refusing to deduce anything from these premises, and (c) requesting a revision of the premises to ensure their consistency and truth. In other situations, inconsistency might be tolerated by abandoning classical propositional logic and using other paraconsistent logics.

Example 6

Ethical dilemmas are considered a prominent example of "wicked problems" [89-94]. They depict situations in which two or more ethical obligations, duties, rights, goods, or ideals come into conflict with one another, and it appears that not all of them can be fully respected [95]. Contemporary engineering practice makes it virtually inevitable that most engineers be confronted with ethical problems or dilemmas during their careers. This example discusses one such dilemma. A dishonest government employee would not grant work to a consulting engineer unless he pays him a bribe. Is it ethical for the consultant to pay the bribe so as to be awarded work? Let us define the propositions:

$W =$	The employee awards work to the consultant,
$D =$	The consultant deserves to be granted work,
$H =$	The employee is honest and would not ask for a bribe to allocate work appropriately,
$E =$	The behavior of the consultant is ethical,
$B =$	The consultant bribes the employee.

The situation above might be described by the premises $\overline{H}$, W, $H \rightarrow (\boldsymbol{W} \leftrightarrow \boldsymbol{D})$, $\overline{H} \rightarrow (\boldsymbol{W} \leftrightarrow \boldsymbol{B})$, $\overline{W} \rightarrow E$, $WD \rightarrow E$, $W\overline{D} \rightarrow \overline{E}$, $D\overline{B} \rightarrow \overline{W}$, and $B \rightarrow W$, which can be combined into the single function f (equal to 0), where

$$f = H \vee \overline{W} \vee H(W\overline{D} \vee \overline{W}D) \vee \overline{H}(W\overline{B} \vee \overline{W}B) \vee \overline{W}\overline{E} \vee WD\overline{E} \vee W\overline{D}E \vee D\overline{B}W \vee B\overline{W}. \tag{30}$$

This can be simplified *via* repeated application of absorption and the Reflection Law [15, 82] to obtain

$$CS(f) = H \vee \overline{W} \vee \overline{B} \vee D\overline{E} \vee \overline{D}E = 0, \tag{31}$$

and hence

$$H = \bar{W} = \bar{B} = D\bar{E} = \bar{D}E = 0, \tag{32}$$

which says that the employee is dishonest and that he is receiving a bribe from the consultant while granting him work. It also says that the behavior of the consultant is ethical if and only if he deserves to be granted work.

This conclusion is in agreement with dominant schools of jurisprudence, according to which the illegality or prohibition of bribery is relaxed for a person who definitely cannot find an alternative means to acquire his just rights. However, persons with superior moral characters, (especially those looked upon by society as leaders or examples to be followed) should refrain from using the above special permission whatever the circumstances are. For those, we must add the premise $(B \to \bar{E})$ so that (31) becomes

$$CS(f) = \bar{W} \vee \bar{B} \vee E \vee D = 0, \tag{33}$$

i.e., under these circumstances, the action of paying a bribe to secure work is definitely unethical and the work awarded through bribery is necessarily undeserved.

Of course, the answers above might differ if the issue is considered from the legal rather than the ethical point of view. It might also be more prudent for the consultant to explore other possible actions (other than just to pay or not to pay the bribe). For example, he might report the matter to the concerned authorities and help them catch and convict the corrupted employee.

Example 7

A student is pondering what elective courses to take. With a little abuse of notation, we let the symbols X, Y, and Z denote the propositions that he/she takes electives X, Y, and Z, respectively ($\{X = 1\}$ means taking the elective X and $\{X = 0\}$ means not taking it). The conditional $\{X \to Y\}$ means if elective X is taken, then elective Y is taken also. Table **2** demonstrates three different problems on selection of elective courses, with different sets of conditions required by the student stated as premises. Table **2** presents these premises in conditional form and then in equational form. It skips the details of complete-sum derivation and states conclusions in equational form and then in clausal form. Table **2** also lists possible solutions, if any. In the first problem, the MSM reproduces or reechoes some of the antecedents (highlighted in green) as conclusions, and augments these with new conclusions that were hidden in the premises (highlighted in red). The problem has two solutions, namely that the student takes all three electives or takes neither of them. In the second problem, the MSM proves that nothing new is hidden in the premises. This second problem has four solutions, suggesting that the student takes any single elective or takes no elective at all. The third problem has no solution and the MSM proves that the given set of premises is inconsistent. This set could be used to make any conclusion whatsoever, but should be rejected as a basis for deduction, and replaced by a consistent set.

Table 2. Three problems on selection of elective courses.

Problem	Conditional Premises	Equational Premises	Equational Conclusions	Conditional Conclusions	Solutions
1	$X \to Y$ $Y \to Z$ $Z \to X$	$X\bar{Y} = 0$ $Y\bar{Z} = 0$ $Z\bar{X} = 0$	$X\bar{Y} = 0$ $Y\bar{Z} = 0$ $Z\bar{X} = 0$ $Z\bar{Y} = 0$ $X\bar{Z} = 0$ $Y\bar{X} = 0$	$X \to Y$ $Y \to Z$ $Z \to X$ $Z \to Y$ $X \to Z$ $Y \to X$	$XYZ = 1$ $\{X = Y = Z = 1\}$, $\bar{X}\bar{Y}\bar{Z} = 1$ $\{X = Y = Z = 0\}$
2	$X \to \bar{Y}$ $Y \to \bar{Z}$ $Z \to \bar{X}$	$XY = 0$ $ZX = 0 \ YZ = 0$	$XY = 0$ $YZ = 0$ $ZX = 0$	$X \to \bar{Y}$ $Y \to \bar{Z}$ $Z \to \bar{X}$	$\bar{X}\bar{Y}\bar{Z} = 1$ $\{X = Y = Z = 0\}$, $\bar{X}\bar{Y}Z = 1$ $\{X = Y = 0, Z = 1\}$, $\bar{X}Y\bar{Z} = 1$ $\{X = Z = 0, Y = 1\}$, $X\bar{Y}\bar{Z} = 1$ $\{X = 1, Y = Z = 0\}$
3	$X \leftrightarrow \bar{Y}$ $Y \leftrightarrow \bar{Z}$ $Z \leftrightarrow \bar{X}$	$XY \vee \bar{X}\bar{Y} = 0$ $YZ \vee \bar{Y}\bar{Z} = 0$ $XZ \vee \bar{X}\bar{Z} = 0$	$1 = 0$	?	None

Example 8

There is an "*established equivalence between relational database functional dependencies (FDs) and a fragment of propositional logic,*" viz., a fragment of switching algebra based on Horn clauses [27]. A set S of *functional dependencies* ($A_k \rightarrow C_k$, $1 \leq k \leq n$) in a relational database can be viewed as *propositional implications*, and might further be denoted by the same symbols (again, with a presumably tolerable abuse of notation). We employ logic deduction *via* the MSM so as to cast these implications as equations

$$A_k \overline{C_k} = 0, \quad 1 \leq k \leq n. \tag{34}$$

The set of equations (34) subsequently reduce to the single equivalent equation

$$g = \bigvee_{k=1}^{n} A_k \overline{C_k} = 0. \tag{35}$$

Equation (35) can now be used to produce the equivalent result

$$\mathcal{CS}(g) = 0, \tag{36}$$

where $\mathcal{CS}(g)$ depicts the complete sum of the function g. Each of the prime implicants in $\mathcal{CS}(g) = 0$ is individually equated to 0, thereby producing an equation of the form (34), or equivalently a propositional implication leading to a functional dependency that is a member of S^+, which is the *closure* of the set S of functional dependencies. This closure might be used for obtaining all the candidate keys of the relational database [27, 29]. The candidate keys can be obtained also by studying another type of closures, namely, the closures of sets of attributes [29]. We present herein an alternative procedure for obtaining all the candidate keys without studying the closure of the set of functional dependencies or the closures of the sets of attributes. We supplement the set of FD's by an additional functional dependency of the form

$$\left(\bigwedge_{i=1}^{n} X_i\right) \rightarrow K, \tag{37}$$

where K is a new attribute that is associated with the notion of "Key". Equation (37) simply states that the product of all attributes X_i serves as a superkey (albeit typically reducible). We now replace the function g in (35) by a function f that expresses *all* dependencies, *viz.*

$$f = g \vee \left(\bigwedge_{i=1}^{n} X_i\right) \overline{K} = 0. \tag{38}$$

The current problem is one of *selective deduction* [17, 21], since we are interested only in the consequents that contain the literal $\bar{K}$. The complete sum $\mathcal{CS}(f)$ of f is given by

$$\mathcal{CS}(f) = \mathcal{CS}(g) \vee \bigvee_j \left(\bigwedge_{j \in J} X_j\right) \bar{K} = 0. \tag{39}$$

The prime implicants in $\mathcal{CS}(f) = 0$ that are of the form $\left(\bigwedge_{j \in J} X_j\right) \bar{K} = 0$ (*i.e.*, those that contain the complemented literal $\bar{K}$) correspond to the implication

$$\left(\bigwedge_{j \in J} X_j\right) \rightarrow K. \tag{40}$$

In (39) or (40), a set J contains indices of attributes whose product forms a superkey. In fact, such a superkey is a candidate key since it is irreducible, because it corresponds to a prime implicant. This suggests a method to obtain all candidate keys by deriving the complete sum $\mathcal{CS}(f)$ in (39), wherein a candidate key is the product of un-complemented literals in any prime implicant that contains the complemented literal $\bar{K}$. This method matches the one in [96]. Moreover, since K is a mono-form variable, no consensus is formed *w.r.t.* it by the Blake-Tison Method (see Appendix B), and it might be dispensed with altogether. This means that (38) could be rewritten with $\bar{K}$ deleted, *i.e.,* in the form

$$f = g \vee \left(\bigwedge_{i=1}^{n} X_i\right). \tag{41}$$

In this new scheme, the final result for $\mathcal{CS}(f)$ is again a replica of (39) but with $\bar{K}$ deleted

$$\mathcal{CS}(f) = \mathcal{CS}(g) \vee \bigvee_j \left(\bigwedge_{j \in J} X_j\right). \tag{42}$$

In (42), the prime implicants $\left(\bigwedge_{j \in J} X_j\right)$ of solely un-complemented literals constitute the candidate keys. This scheme agrees with the earlier procedure in [97].

Now, we supplement the above formula by concepts introduced by Saiedian and Spencer [98], and used implicitly by Cordero *et al.* [99]. We distinguish two sets of attributes $\mathcal{L}$ and $\mathcal{R}$. The set $\mathcal{L}$ contains the attributes that occur only on the left-hand side of some *FDs* in S, while the set $\mathcal{R}$ contains the attributes that occur only on the right-hand side of some FDs in S. Saiedian and Spencer [98] proved the fact that attributes in $\mathcal{L}$ must be a part of every candidate key, while none of those in $\mathcal{R}$ is a part of a candidate key. Base on this fact, Rushdi and Rushdi [34] utilized *switching-algebraic considerations* to replace the formula (42) by

$$CS(f') = \left(\wedge_{X_i \in \mathcal{L}} X_i\right) \wedge CS\left((g/(\wedge_{X_i \in \mathcal{L}} X_i \wedge_{X_i \in \mathcal{R}} \bar{X}_i)) \vee (\wedge_{X_i \in \mathcal{T}} X_i / \wedge_{X_i \in \mathcal{L} \cup \mathcal{R}} X_i)\right). \tag{43}$$

Though $CS(f)$ in formula (42) and $CS(f')$ in formula (43) are not necessarily the same, they both contain the disjunction of all candidate keys, which constitutes the terms without un-complemented literals in each formula. When the two sets of attributes $\mathcal{L}$ and $\mathcal{R}$ are both empty, the two functions f and f' coincide.
We now illustrate the results above *via* a small or textbook example. Consider the relation $\mathcal{R}$ with a set of attributes $\mathcal{T} = \{A, B, C, D, E, F\}$ with the following dependency set S, taken from Saiedian and Spencer [96],

$$S = \{AD \rightarrow B, AB \rightarrow E, C \rightarrow D, B \rightarrow C, AC \rightarrow F\}. \tag{44}$$

This set can be cast in equational form as

$$g = AD\bar{B} \vee AB\bar{E} \vee C\bar{D} \vee B\bar{C} \vee AC\bar{F} = 0. \tag{45}$$

Adding the extra term $ABCDEF\bar{K}$ to g, one obtains

$$f = g \vee ABCDEF\bar{K} = AD\bar{B} \vee AB\bar{E} \vee C\bar{D} \vee B\bar{C} \vee AC\bar{F} \vee ABCDEF\bar{K} = 0. \tag{46}$$

The complete sum $CS(f)$ of f is obtained *via* either of Figs. (**3** or **4**) as

$$\begin{aligned} CS(f) = &(B\bar{C} \vee B\bar{D} \vee AB\bar{E} \vee AB\bar{F}) \\ &\vee (AC\bar{B} \vee C\bar{D} \vee AC\bar{E} \vee AC\bar{F}) \\ &\vee (AD\bar{B} \vee AD\bar{C} \vee AD\bar{E} \vee AD\bar{F}) \\ &\vee (AB\bar{K} \vee AC\bar{K} \vee AD\bar{K}). \end{aligned} \tag{47}$$

Both Figs. (**3** and **4**) use the Improved Blake-Tison Method (see Appendix B) to derive $CS(f)$. Since the variable A is the only monoform variable in (45), consensuses are generated *w. r. t.* the other variables. Out of the possible 5! =120 possible orderings for these 5 variables, we use the forward alphabetic ordering (B, C, D, E, F) in Fig. (**3**), and the reverse alphabetic ordering (F, E, D, C, B) in Fig. 4. Note that the latter ordering results in a substantial computational saving compared with the former one. In fact, 26 absorptions are needed in Fig. (3), compared with only 8 absorptions in Fig. (4). In both figures, we deemphasize an absorbed term by writing it in pale ink and smaller font, and highlight a retained or remaining term by writing it in bold and larger font. The formula (47) for $CS(f)$ is a *self-checking* one, since it is a disjunction of $CS(g)$ with a sum of products containing $\bar{K}$, namely $(AB \vee AC \vee AD)\bar{K}$. These products indicate explicitly the existence of three candidate keys, *viz.*, AB, AC, and AD. The products constituting $CS(g)$ (the ones containing complemented literals other than $\bar{K}$) in $CS(f)$ can be used to *verify* or *check* that AB, AC, and AD are candidate keys indeed. For example, the top pair of parentheses in (47) can be used to deduce

$$\{B\bar{C} \vee B\bar{D} \vee AB\bar{E} \vee AB\bar{F} = 0\} \leftrightarrow$$
$$\{B \to C, B \to D, AB \to E, AB \to F\} \leftrightarrow$$
$$\{\boldsymbol{AB \to A, AB \to B}, AB \to C, AB \to D, AB \to E, AB \to F\}. \tag{48}$$

In (48), we made use of *Extended Reflexivity* $\{AB \to A, AB \to B\}$ and of *Augmentation* and *Decomposition* $\{(B \to C) \to (AB \to AC) \to (AB \to C)\}$, $\{(B \to D) \to (AB \to AD) \to (AB \to D)\}$, which correspond, respectively, to the switching-algebraic relations $\{AB\bar{A} = 0, AB\bar{B} = 0, (B\bar{C} = 0) \to (AB\bar{C} = 0), (B\bar{D} = 0) \to (AB\bar{D} = 0)\}$. Equation (48) indicates that

$$\{A, B\}^+ = \{A, B, C, D, E, F\} = \mathcal{T}, \tag{49}$$

i.e., the closure of the set of attributes $\{A, B\}$ is set of all attributes $\mathcal{T}$, or in other words AB is a key since knowledge of the two attributes A and B leads to knowledge of all attributes. The key AB is irreducible since each of the closures $\{A\}^+$ and $\{B\}^+$ fails to equal $\mathcal{T}$. In a similar fashion, we can show that the closure of either $\{A, C\}$ or $\{A, D\}$ is also minimally equal to $\mathcal{T}$.

Now, we note that we can, for this particular example, achieve a great saving by noting that attribute A is an essential one since it appears only in the L.H.S. in implications in (44), while each of attributes E and F is a superfluous one since it appears only in the R.H.S. in these implications. This means that $\mathcal{L} = \{A\}$, and $\mathcal{R} = \{EF\}$ in (44), allowing us to construct the complete sum according to (43)

$$CS(f') = A \wedge CS((g/A\bar{E}\bar{F}) \vee (ABCDEF/AEF)) = A \wedge CS(D\bar{B} \vee B \vee C\bar{D} \vee B\bar{C} \vee C \vee BCD) = A \wedge (D \vee B \vee C) = AD \vee AB \vee AC. \tag{50}$$

Therefore, we recover (in a much simpler way) our earlier result that there are three candidate keys, namely, AD, AB, and AC.

If $CS(g)$, (or, equivalently, the closure of the set of functional dependencies) is known beforehand, one should utilize its availability by rewriting (38) as

$$f = CS(g) \vee (\wedge_{i=1}^n X_i)\overline{K}, \tag{51}$$

and then computing $CS(f)$ *via* an incremental version of the Blake-Tison Method [31]. In fact, we can restrict our attention to the consensuses generated between terms containing $\overline{K}$ (initially the single term $(\wedge_{i=1}^n X_i)\overline{K}$) and various terms of $CS(g)$ w.r.t. biform variables traversed one by one. The final result of these consensuses is $\overline{K}$ ANDed with the disjunction of all candidate keys, *i.e.* $\vee_j(\wedge_{j\in J} X_j)\overline{K}$. Noting that each term in $CS(g)$ is a Horn term (one containing precisely one complemented literal), we use G_k to denote the disjunction of terms in $CS(g)$ containing the complemented literal number k, and use U_k to denote the disjunction of implicants of f containing $\overline{K}$ at step k. At each step of the incremental Blake-Tison Method U_k is updated *via*

$$U_{k+1} = ABS\big(U_k \vee Consensuses\ (U_k, G_k)\big). \tag{52}$$

Here, $ABS(F)$ is an absorptive formula for the sum-of-products formula F, which is a formula obtained from F by successive deletion or absorption of terms subsuming other terms in F [17]. The expression U_k can be interpreted as a disjunction of superkeys ANDed with $\overline{K}$. Its initial value is $(\wedge_{i=1}^n X_i)\overline{K}$, and its final value is the disjunction of all prime implicants of $CS(f)$ containing $\overline{K}$, which are the candidate keys multiplied by $\overline{K}$. Fig. (5) applies this method to our current example. Note that $CS(g)$ can be taken from (47) and then partitioned into groups of sums of products G_k containing the complemented literals $\overline{B}, \overline{C}, \overline{D}, \overline{E}$, and $\overline{F}$, respectively

$$CS(g) = G_B \vee G_C \vee G_D \vee G_E \vee G_F =$$
$$(AD\overline{B} \vee AC\overline{B}) \vee (B\overline{C} \vee AD\overline{C}) \vee (C\overline{D} \vee B\overline{D}) \vee (AB\overline{E} \vee AC\overline{E} \vee AD\overline{E})$$
$$\vee (AB\overline{F} \vee AC\overline{F} \vee AD\overline{F}). \tag{53}$$

The final value of U_k in Fig. (5) is $(AB\overline{K} \vee AC\overline{K} \vee AD\overline{K})$, again indicating the existence of three candidate keys AB, AC, and AD. Fig. (6) replicates Fig. (3) using a reverse partitioning of $CS(g)$, which results in a considerable computational saving.

Consensuses/B	$AB\bar{E}$	$B\bar{C}$	$AB\bar{D}$	$ABCDEF\bar{K}$	$C\bar{D}$ $AC\bar{F}$
$AD\bar{B}$	$AD\bar{E}$	$AD\bar{C}$	----------	$ACDEF\bar{K}$	

Consensuses/C	$C\bar{D}$	$AC\bar{F}$	$ACDEF\bar{K}$	$AB\bar{E}$ $AB\bar{D}$
$B\bar{C}$	$B\bar{D}$	$AB\bar{F}$	$ABDEF\bar{K}$	$AD\bar{B}$ $AD\bar{E}$
$AD\bar{C}$	-------	$AD\bar{F}$	$ADEF\bar{K}$	

Consensuses/D	$AD\bar{C}$	$AD\bar{F}$	$AD\bar{B}$	$AD\bar{E}$	$ADEF\bar{K}$	$AC\bar{F}$ $B\bar{C}$ $AB\bar{F}$ $AB\bar{E}$
$C\bar{D}$	-------	$AC\bar{F}$	$AC\bar{B}$	$AC\bar{E}$	$ACEF\bar{K}$	
$B\bar{D}$	$AB\bar{C}$	$AB\bar{F}$	-------	$AB\bar{E}$	$ABEF\bar{K}$	

Consensuses/E	$ABEF\bar{K}$	$ACEF\bar{K}$	$ADEF\bar{K}$	$B\bar{C}$ $B\bar{D}$
$AB\bar{E}$	$ABF\bar{K}$	$ABCF\bar{K}$	$ABDF\bar{K}$	$AB\bar{F}$ $AC\bar{B}$ $C\bar{D}$
$AC\bar{E}$	$ABCF\bar{K}$	$ACF\bar{K}$	$ACDF\bar{K}$	$AC\bar{F}$ $AD\bar{B}$
$AD\bar{E}$	$ABDF\bar{K}$	$ACDF\bar{K}$	$ADF\bar{K}$	$AD\bar{C}$ $AD\bar{F}$

Consensuses/F	$ABF\bar{K}$	$ACF\bar{K}$	$ADF\bar{K}$	$B\bar{C}$ $B\bar{D}$ $AB\bar{E}$ $AC\bar{B}$ $C\bar{D}$
$AB\bar{F}$	$AB\bar{K}$	$ABC\bar{K}$	$ABD\bar{K}$	$AC\bar{E}$ $AD\bar{B}$
$AC\bar{F}$	$ABC\bar{K}$	$AC\bar{K}$	$ACD\bar{K}$	$AD\bar{C}$ $AD\bar{E}$
$AD\bar{F}$	$ABD\bar{K}$	$ACD\bar{K}$	$AD\bar{K}$	

Fig. (3). Steps of the Improved Blake-Tison Method for computing $CS(f)$ in Example 8 using the ordering B, C, D, E, and F.

Consensuses/F	$ABCDEF\bar{K}$	$AD\bar{B}$
$AC\bar{F}$	$ABCDE\bar{K}$	$AB\bar{E}$ $C\bar{D}$ $B\bar{C}$ $AB\bar{D}$

Consensuses/E	$ABCDE\bar{K}$	$AD\bar{B}$ $AC\bar{F}$
$AB\bar{E}$	$ABCD\bar{K}$	$C\bar{D}$ $B\bar{C}$ $AB\bar{D}$

Consensuses/D	$AD\bar{B}$	$ABCD\bar{K}$	
$C\bar{D}$	$AC\bar{B}$	$ABC\bar{K}$	$AC\bar{F}$ $B\bar{C}$ $AB\bar{E}$
$AB\bar{D}$	-------	$ABC\bar{K}$	

Consensuses/C	$C\bar{D}$	$AC\bar{B}$	$AC\bar{F}$	$ABC\bar{K}$	
$B\bar{C}$	$B\bar{D}$	-------	$AB\bar{F}$	$AB\bar{K}$	$AB\bar{D}$ $AD\bar{B}$ $AB\bar{E}$

Consensuses/B	$B\bar{C}$	$B\bar{D}$	$AB\bar{E}$	$AB\bar{F}$	$AB\bar{K}$	
$AC\bar{B}$	-------	$AC\bar{D}$	$AC\bar{E}$	$AC\bar{F}$	$AC\bar{K}$	$C\bar{D}$
$AD\bar{B}$	$AD\bar{C}$	-------	$AD\bar{E}$	$AD\bar{F}$	$AD\bar{K}$	$AC\bar{F}$

Fig. (4). Steps of the Improved Blake-Tison Method for computing $CS(f)$ in Example 8 using the ordering $F, E, D, C,$ and B.

w. r. t.	G_k	U_k	Consensuses of G_k with U_k
B	$AD\bar{B} \vee AC\bar{B}$	$ABCDEF\bar{K}$	$ACDEF\bar{K} \vee ACDEF\bar{K}$
C	$B\bar{C} \vee AD\bar{C}$	$ACDEF\bar{K}$	$ABDEF\bar{K} \vee ADEF\bar{K}$
D	$C\bar{D} \vee B\bar{D}$	$ADEF\bar{K}$	$ACEF\bar{K} \vee ABEF\bar{K}$
E	$AB\bar{E} \vee AC\bar{E} \vee AD\bar{E}$	$ABEF\bar{K} \vee ACEF\bar{K} \vee ADEF\bar{K}$	$ABF\bar{K} \vee ABCF\bar{K} \vee ABDF\bar{K} \vee ABCF\bar{K} \vee ACF\bar{K} \vee ACDF\bar{K} \vee ABDF\bar{K} \vee ACDF\bar{K} \vee ADF\bar{K}$
F	$AB\bar{F} \vee AC\bar{F} \vee AD\bar{F}$	$ABF\bar{K} \vee ACF\bar{K} \vee ADF\bar{K}$	$AB\bar{K} \vee ABC\bar{K} \vee ABD\bar{K} \vee ABC\bar{K} \vee AC\bar{K} \vee ACD\bar{K} \vee ABD\bar{K} \vee ACD\bar{K} \vee AD\bar{K}$
		$AB\bar{K} \vee AC\bar{K} \vee AD\bar{K}$	

Fig. (5). Derivation of $CS(f)$ in (47) *via* the Incremental Blake-Tison Method, sing the variable ordering: $B, C, D, E,$ and F.

w. r. t.	G_k	U_k	Consensuses of G_k with U_k
F	$AB\bar{F} \vee AC\bar{F} \vee AD\bar{F}$	$ABCDEF\bar{K}$	$ABCDE\bar{K} \vee ABCDE\bar{K} \vee ABCDE\bar{K}$
E	$AB\bar{E} \vee AC\bar{E} \vee AD\bar{E}$	$ABCDE\bar{K}$	$ABCD\bar{K} \vee ABCD\bar{K} \vee ABCD\bar{K}$
D	$C\bar{D} \vee B\bar{D}$	$ABCD\bar{K}$	$ABC\bar{K} \vee ABC\bar{K}$
C	$B\bar{C} \vee AD\bar{C}$	$ABC\bar{K}$	$AB\bar{K} \vee ABD\bar{K}$
B	$AD\bar{B} \vee AC\bar{B}$	$AB\bar{K}$	$AD\bar{K} \vee AC\bar{K}$
____	____	$AB\bar{K} \vee AC\bar{K} \vee AD\bar{K}$	

Fig. (6). Derivation of $CS(f)$ in (47) *via* the Incremental Blake-Tison Method, using the variable ordering: $F, E, D, C,$ and B.

CONCLUSIONS

This chapter describes the Modern Syllogistic Method (MSM), which ferrets out from a given set of premises all the consequents that can be concluded from this set, and casts these consequents in the simplest or most compact form. The MSM encompasses, unifies, and replaces all rules of logic inference. With it, the core step of deductive reasoning, namely the transfer from formal premises to formal conclusions, becomes a purely mechanical or algorithmic procedure.

The MSM is a powerful pedagogical manual tool that can facilitate learning and provide insight. It also allows larger sizes for the deduction-reasoning problems that can be handled by a human problem solver. The importance of learning the MSM in this age of automated reasoning is similar, in a sense, to the importance of learning the decimal multiplication table in this age of electronic calculators. This could be a controversial issue, but we believe that too much reliance on machines without having enough pertinent knowledge could be occasionally misleading or embarrassing. The MSM can deal with arguments of many varieties on many different topics, but it is restricted herein to subject matter of engineering or professional interest. We believe that the MSM can serve as a useful tool for all problem solvers in general, and to engineers in particular, as it can help every professional to reason well and correctly about her or his specific discipline. Of course, we do not go to the extreme of suggesting that all professionals must now set their minds into reasoning based on the MSM.

Due to space limitations, the paper presents only a quick glimpse of the many possible applications of the method. Notable among the ones excluded here is the application of the method to problems of controllability and observability in automatic control [22], to fault-tree and fault-forest analysis [24], and to certain problems of scientific discovery [25]. No detailed discussion is given herein for the incremental version of the MSM [31], though an example of it is presented *via* Figs. 5 and 6. The chapter deals only with crisp logic, but we note that an intuitionistic fuzzy version of the MSM already exists [32], which includes an ordinary fuzzy version as a special case.

The MSM has good potential (yet unexplored) applications in logic-based arguments, *i.e.,* arguments that involve some well-formed premises (called the support of the argument) and a well-formed conclusion (called the claim of the argument) such that the support deductively entails the claim [100]. The MSM might be useful in studying, explaining, and illustrating many concepts and notions of logic-based approaches to argumentation, such as those of a *counterargument* (an argument that disagrees with another argument), a *defeater* (an argument whose claim refutes the support of another argument), or special cases of defeaters such as an *assumption attack*, an *undercut* (an argument that directly opposes the support of another), or a *rebuttal* (the most direct form of an argument conflicting with another, *i.e.*, an argument having exactly the opposite claim of that of another argument).

The MSM can be associated or integrated with various variants or offshoots of Boolean analysis (BA), including Boolean analysis of questionnaires [101-103], Boolean analysis of hierarchical data [104], Qualitative Comparative Analysis [105-108], and Coincidence Analysis [65-67]. The common practice in BA is to use Boolean minimization so as to obtain the minimal sum of the pertinent output or effect function. This practice is definitely useful since it produces a minimal-sum characterization of the function that is as compact as possible. The minimal sum covers the asserted part of the function with as few as possible prime implicants. Each of these prime implicants is a minimally-sufficient cause of the given effect. If BA imitates the MSM, it can enlarge its scope by deriving the complete sum as well as the minimal sum. The complete sum informs us explicitly about all minimally-sufficient causes, and hence its role supplements (but does not replace) that of the minimal sum which characterizes the function but does not explicitly exhaust all minimally-sufficient causes.

Though the MSM has been in existence for about eight decades, it has not yet found its way to popular introductory logic textbooks (See, *e.g.*, [6, 7, 83, 109-113]). Wide-spread knowledge of the MSM could possibly (hopefully) have a notable impact on the teaching and learning of logic. One might ponder whether there is a link between mastering logic and real-world reasoning competency. Assessment or measurement of such a link could be a formidable, if not impossible, task. Therefore, we might suggest a more accessible study, by proposing to investigate whether training in the MSM can enable cognition that secures higher scores on analytical or logical sections of standardized tests such as the GRE or LSAT. Though the results of such a study would be interesting to us, we simply cannot undertake it ourselves, and hence we delegate the job of performing it to interested psychologists and cognition analysts.

We are currently investigating the utility of the MSM in avoiding the trap of illusory inference, which is a class of erroneous deductions that are strongly compelling but still invalid [114, 115]. We are also trying to make use of the MSM in the study of enthymemes, which are arguments, or chains of argumentation, with one or more missing (implicit) premises or conclusions [116]. Enthymemes occur frequently in natural spoken and written language for a variety of reasons [6]. Our target here is to devise a general technique to fill in missing premises in an enthymeme subject to some reasonable criterion of acceptability. Work on this problem is promising, since it is quite related to the well-developed problem of finding a best-fit extension of a partially defined Boolean function [117]. We also consider applying the MSM in engineering design. We realize that design is a creative process, which cannot be completely performed by deductive reasoning. However, we propose to use the MSM to handle reasoning steps within design [118]. In another promising direction, we plan to apply the MSM in the study of probabilistic argumentation [119]. Here, the premises are no longer accepted as firm true facts, but are considered uncertain with known probabilities of being true. Finally, we hope to find applications of the MSM in teaching basics of project management via logic puzzles [120], and to adapt the methods used in [121] for constructing consensus logic programs to the study of the consensus among conclusions derived from multiple sets of premises.

APPENDIX A: THE COMPLETE SUM (BLAKE CANONICAL FORM)

The complete sum of a switching (two-valued Boolean) function f, denoted by $CS(f)$, is the sum-of-products (sop) formula whose products are all the prime implicants of f (and nothing else). It is called the *"Blake Canonical Form"* by Brown [17] in honor of A. Blake, who is believed to be the first person to study this form in his PhD dissertation [9]. The complete sum $CS(f)$ is *unique* (with the OR and AND operators being commutative) and hence stands for a *canonical* representation of the switching function [17]. It is the minimal or absorptive special case of a syllogistic formula of f. Here, a syllogistic formula is defined as a sum-of-products formula, whose terms include, but are not necessarily confined to, all the prime implicants of f. The complete-sum concept is intimately related to two switching-algebraic concepts, namely, the absorption of a term by another, and the consensus of two ORed terms [15, 17, 122].

Absorption

A term T_1 subsumes another T_2 if the set of literals of T_1 is a (not necessarily strict) superset of that of T_2. On a Karnaugh map, the loop of T_1 is completely contained within that of T_2. Note that while T_1 has the *containing* set of literals, it has the *contained* loop and it is said to imply T_2, which is denoted by $\{T_1 \leq T_2\}$ or, equivalently, by $\{T_1 \rightarrow T_2\}$. In this case, the disjunction $(T_1 \vee T_2)$ could simply be written as T_2, *viz.*

$$T_1 \vee T_2 = T_2. \tag{A.1}$$

This deletion of T_1 is called an absorption of the subsuming term T_1 in the subsumed term T_2. For example, the term $A\bar{B}C$ subsumes each of the eight terms $A\bar{B}C, A\bar{B}, AC, \bar{B}C, A, \bar{B}, C$, and 1. Hence, it could be deleted if it is ORed with any of them. The complete sum is an absorptive syllogistic formula, *i.e.*, it is a syllogistic formula in which no term subsumes (and hence can be absorbed in) another.

Consensus

Two terms T_1 and T_2 have a consensus if and only if they have exactly one opposition, *i.e.*, exactly one variable that appears complemented ($\bar{X}_m$) in one term (say T_1) and appears uncomplemented (X_m) in the other term. In such a case, the consensus is the ANDing of the remaining literals of the two terms, *i.e.*

$$consenus(T_1, T_2) = (T_1/\bar{X}_m) \wedge (T_2/X_m), \qquad \text{(A.2)}$$

where (f/t) denotes the Boolean quotient [17] of the function f by the term t, *i.e.*, the restriction of f when t is asserted, *viz.*

$$f/t = [f]_{t=1}. \qquad \text{(A.3)}$$

When two terms have a consensus, their disjunction can be augmented by this consensus, *i.e.*

$$T_1 \vee T_2 = T_1 \vee T_2 \vee consenus(T_1, T_2). \qquad \text{(A.4)}$$

For example, the terms $A\bar{B}$ and BC have a single opposition and are represented on the Karnaugh map by two disjoint loops sharing a border, and hence their disjunction can be augmented by their consensus $(A\bar{B}/\bar{B}) \wedge (BC/B) = AC$, which is a loop extending across the common border between the original loops and covering the part $A\bar{B}C$ of $A\bar{B}$ and the part ABC of BC. By contrast, the two terms A and BC have zero opposition, and consequently non-disjoint or overlapping loops, and possess zero or no consensus. The two terms $A\bar{B}$ and $\bar{A}B$ have more than one opposition, and consequently disjoint far-away loops, and possess zero or no consensus.

The complete-sum formula $CS(f)$ may be generated by the following two-step iterative-consensus procedure due to Blake [9]: (a) Find a syllogistic formula F for f by continually comparing terms and adding their consensus terms to the current formula of f and (b) Convert the resulting formula to an absorptive one $ABS(F)$, again by continually comparing terms and deleting subsuming terms by absorbing them in their subsumed terms. Tison [13] streamlined and updated iterative-consensus to what was typically called the Tison Method. We give deserved due credit to A. Blake, for introducing and developing iterative consensus in [9] by renaming streamlined iterative consensus as the Blake-Tison Method. While this method produces the complete sum of a switching function by *explicit consensus generation* followed by *absorption,* another much earlier method by H. McColl [8] produced a *syllogistic formula* for the function without explicit consensus generation through multiplying out any suitable product-of-sums expression for the function to produce a sum-of-products expression. The comparisons needed for absorptions constitute a heavy computational burden, and should be minimized [123, 124]. The methods described in Appendices B and C avoid many of the unwarranted comparisons.

Deductive inference can be based on any complete set of inference rules. The existence of so many inference rules is warranted just as a matter of convenience and not as a matter of necessity. In fact, any set of inference rules (even just a single rule) is complete in propositional logic provided it possesses a capability for complete-sum generation (or basically consensus generation). Therefore, the MSM is a complete method of inference in propositional logic, thanks to its reliance on the derivation of the complete sum. Another example of a single rule constituting a complete method in propositional logic is that of MP (modus ponens) or implication elimination, whose history dates back to antiquity. This rule starts with premises A and $A \rightarrow B$, and concludes B. In MSM terminology, MP starts from $f = \bar{A} \vee A\bar{B} = 0$, and produces $CS(f) = \bar{A} \vee A\bar{B} \vee \bar{B} = \bar{A} \vee \bar{B} = 0$ to conclude that $\bar{B} = 0$. The equivalence of the aforementioned formulas for f and $CS(f)$ is known as the Reflection Law [15, 82], and is a special primitive case of the Consensus Law. It is clear that consensus generation is inherent to MP through its capability to implement the Reflection Law. We now show that MP is capable of producing the Consensus Law (A.4), albeit with some difficulty. We assume that $(T_1/\bar{X}_m)$ and (T_2/X_m) are given, respectively, by YZ_1 and YZ_2 where Y is a product of literals shared between T_1 and T_2, while Z_1 and Z_2 are terms that do not share any literals. Therefore

$$consenus(T_1, T_2) = (T_1/\bar{X}_m) \wedge (T_2/X_m) = YZ_1 \wedge YZ_2 = YZ_1Z_2. \qquad \text{(A.5)}$$

We want to prove the Consensus Law (A.4) but we are entitled only to use MP in the form of the Reflection Law. This is achieved as follows

$$T_1 \vee T_2 = YZ_1\bar{X}_m \vee YZ_2 X_m = Y(Z_1\bar{X}_m \vee Z_2 X_m(Z_1 \vee \overline{Z_1})) =$$
$$Y(Z_1(\bar{X}_m \vee Z_2 X_m) \vee Z_2 X_m \overline{Z_1})) = Y(Z_1(\bar{X}_m \vee Z_2 X_m \vee Z_2) \vee$$
$$Z_2 X_m \overline{Z_1})) = T_1 \vee T_2 \vee YZ_1Z_2$$
$$= T_1 \vee T_2 \vee consenus(T_1, T_2). \qquad \text{(A.6)}$$

APPENDIX B: THE IMPROVED BLAKE-TISON METHOD (IBTM)

The Blake-Tison Method is a systematic streamlined version of the iterative-consensus procedure for obtaining the complete sum of a switching function f. The method consists of M ($\leq n$) steps, where n is the total number of variables, and M is the number of biform variables, *i.e.*, variables x_i that appear in the given formula of f in both forms, *i.e.*, both as a complemented literal $\overline{X}_i$ and a non-complemented one X_i. The method starts with a set of n_0 products $s_0 = \{T_1^{(0)}, T_2^{(0)}, ..., T_{n_0}^{(0)}\}$ with M biform variables X_1, X_2, ..., X_M and a Boolean function f that is expressed by disjunction of the products in s_0. Under the assumption that any absorbable terms in s_0 have been deleted, the disjunction of terms in s_0 is ensured to be an absorptive formula. For $1 \leq m \leq M$, the following 2-part step is repeated so as to replace an absorptive set of products s_{m-1} by another s_m. In the first part, we add consensuses *w.r.t.* the biform variable X_m, while in the second part, we delete absorbable terms.

1. For $1 \leq j < k \leq n_{(m-1)}$, if X_m appears complemented in one of the two products $T_j^{(m-1)}$ and $T_k^{(m-1)}$ and appears un-complemented in the other such that the two products have no other opposition, then they have a consensus with respect to X_m. Form that consensus and add it to s_{m-1}. . Finally, s_{m-1} is replaced by a superset $\bar{s}_{m-1}$ of $J_{(m-1)}$ elements, where $J_{(m-1)} \geq n_{(m-1)}$.

2. Consider every pair $\{T_j^{(m-1)}, T_k^{(m-1)}, j \neq k\}$ of (so far remaining) products in $\bar{s}_{m-1}$. If $T_j^{(m-1)}$ subsumes $T_k^{(m-1)}$, then delete $T_j^{(m-1)}$. Otherwise, if $T_j^{(m-1)}$ is subsumed by $T_k^{(m-1)}$ then delete $T_k^{(m-1)}$. Whenever all comparisons (with possible subsumptions/deletions) are exhausted, let the remaining absorptive set be $s_m = \text{ABS}(\bar{s}_{m-1}) = \{T_1^{(m)}, T_2^{(m)}, ..., T_{n_m}^{(m)}\}$. The disjunction of products in any of the sets s_m, where $1 \leq m \leq M$ is a formula of f.

Blake [9] (in his Theorems 10.6 and 10.8), and later Cutler, *et al.*, [122], formally proved that the final set s_M obtained by the Blake-Tison method above consists of all prime implicants of f (and nothing else). This asserts the central idea of the Blake-Tison method, namely that $CS(f)$ is obtained by applying iterative consensus to each of the biform variables one by one.

Rushdi and Al-Yahya [58] proposed an improvement in the Blake-Tison method in which the typical step starts by arranging a given absorptive formula for f with respect to a biform variable X_m ($1 \leq m \leq M$) in the form

$$f = g_0 \overline{X}_m \vee g_1 X_m \vee t, \qquad\qquad \textbf{(B.1)}$$

where g_0, g_1, and t are s-o-p formulas that are independent of X_m. Next, f is first augmented by all consensuses between terms in $g_0 \overline{X}_m$ and $g_1 X_m$ with respect to X_m (which turn out to be the nonzero products in $g_0 g_1$), and then f is diminished by deleting terms that subsume others. The method repeats this typical step for all biform variables ending with the *CS* of f after the last step.

Fig. (**B.1**) suggests an economic layout [27, 31, 58] for implementing the typical step in the Improved Blake-Tison Method (IBTM) with a restricted number for the comparisons needed for implementing absorptions. This typical step, which performs consensus generation with respect to a specific biform variable X_m, involves a rearrangement of the terms whose disjunction constitutes the current formula of f at this step. We construct a consensus-generation table with respect to X_m that resembles a multiplication table or matrix. The vertical keys of this table are the terms containing the un-complemented literal X_m and its horizontal keys are the terms containing the complemented literal $\overline{X}_m$, while its entries are the consensus terms generated by these keys with respect to X_m. Terms containing neither the un-complemented literal X_m nor the complemented literal $\overline{X}_m$ are set aside and naturally not included in the consensus generation of the table, but might absorb or be absorbed by the consensus terms produced by the table.

Consensuses/X_m	...	$X_m\ T_j$	...	$X_m\ T_k$	...	Set-aside terms (terms containing neither literal of the variable X_m)
...	...	...	...	...	...	
$\overline{X_m}\ P_i$	...	$\{P_i\ T_j\}$	...	$\{P_i\ T_k\}$	...	
...	...	...	...	...	...	
$\overline{X_m}\ P_r$	...	$\{P_r\ T_j\}$	...	$\{P_r\ T_k\}$	...	
...	...	...	...	...	...	

Fig. (B.1). An instance of the table employed by the Improved Blake-Tison Method, pertinent to generation of consensuses *w.r.t.* the variable X_m. The vertical keys of this table are the terms containing the un-complemented literal X_m and the horizontal keys are the terms containing the complemented literal $\overline{X_m}$ while terms containing neither X_m nor $\overline{X_m}$ are set aside.

Fig. (**2**) shows typical keys and entries of consensus-generation table, where we use the symbol $\{P_iT_j\}$ to denote the consensus of the vertical key X_mT_j with the horizontal key $\overline{X_m}P_i$, which is the product of the two terms P_i and T_j after deleting any repeated literals (thanks to the idempotency of the logical operation "AND"). Of course, if the terms P_i and T_j have at least another opposition, *i.e.*, one variable (other than X_m) that appears complemented in one of them and un-complemented in the other, then $\{P_iT_j\}$ is 0. The number of comparisons needed for implementing absorptions is restricted by the following facts [31]:

(a) There is no absorption among horizontal keys, vertical keys and set-aside terms.

(b) A table entry cannot be absorbed by a table key, but it could be absorbed by another table entry or a set-aside term. A set-aside term could be absorbed by a table entry.

(c) If a table entry $\{P_rT_k\}$ is to be ever absorbed by another table entry, then it has an absorbing product for it in the same row r or in the same column k.

(d) If a table vertical key $X_m T_k$ is to be ever absorbed by a table entry, then it has an absorbing product for it in the same column k.

(e) If a table horizontal key $\overline{X_m} P_r$ is to be ever absorbed by a table entry, then it has an absorbing product for it in the same row r.

APPENDIX C: THE VEKM-FOLDING METHOD

The basic idea of the VEKM folding method is that multiplication (ANDing) of two or more syllogistic formulas is also a syllogistic formula [58]. Therefore, such a multiplication implicitly achieves consensus generation. Consider the product-of-sums version of the Boole-Shannon expansion of the switching function $f(\boldsymbol{X})$ about a single variable X_i, namely

$$f(\boldsymbol{X}) = (\bar{X}_i \vee f_1)(X_i \vee f_0), \tag{C.1}$$

where $f_0 = f / \bar{X}_i$ and $f_1 = f/X_i$ are the Boolean quotients, subfunctions or ratios of f obtained by restricting the variable X_i in it to 0 and 1, respectively (see Equation (A.3)). If f_0, f_1 in (C.1) are given by the CS formulas F_0, F_1 , then (C.1) can be reduced to the complete-sum form

$$CS(f) = ABS\big((\bar{X}_i \vee F_1) \wedge (X_i \vee F_0)\big). \qquad \text{(C.2)}$$

This equation has the VEKM interpretation depicted by Fig. C.1. The VEKM in Fig. C.1(a) has 2 cells with CS entries and the corresponding VEKM in Fig. C.1(b) has a single cell with a *CS* entry. Now, we may view the function f in the previous discussion as a subfunction of some parent function, which leads us to suggest the following repeated folding. If the n-variable function $f(X)$ is given by a VEKM of m map variables, $0 \leq m \leq n$, with *CS* entries, then we can eliminate the map variables, one by one, by folding the VEKM with respect to the boundary of the map variable to be eliminated, X_i say. In such folding, the number of map cells is halved while each pair of map cells with opposite values of X_i and common values of the remaining map variables is replaced in accordance with Fig. C.1 by a single map cell, which is dependent only on these remaining map variables. Since the starting VEKM has *CS* entries in all its cells, each of the resulting VEKMs also has CS entries in all its cells. The procedure terminates when we obtain a VEKM of no map variables which is an algebraic expression of the complete sum.

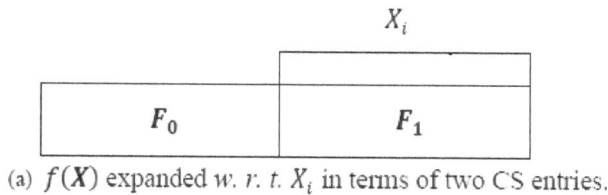

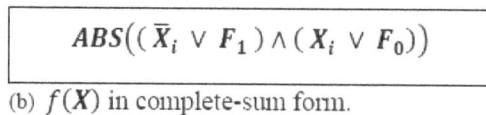

$$X_i$$

F_0	F_1

(a) $f(X)$ expanded w. r. t. X_i in terms of two CS entries.

$ABS\big((\bar{X}_i \vee F_1) \wedge (X_i \vee F_0)\big)$

(b) $f(X)$ in complete-sum form.

Fig. (C.1). The 2-cell VEKM in (a) with *CS* entries is folded into a single cell in (b) with a CS entry.

Now, we consider an important simplification for the rules of VEKM folding. Let the two CS formulas F_0 and F_1 in (C.2) have some common terms that are given by a sum-of-products (sop) formula T, namely

$$F_0 = T \vee G_0, \tag{C.3}$$

$$F_1 = T \vee G_1, \tag{C.4}$$

where G_0 and G_1 are the sop formulas that remain after excluding the common terns T from F_0 and F_1, respectively. Note that since the terms of T are a subset of those of the CS formulas F_0 and F_1, the formula T must be absorptive. In fact, it is the sum of all the prime implicants of F that are independent of X_i. No term in T subsumes a term in G_0 or G_1. Conversely, no term in G_0 or in G_1 subsumes a term in T. Now, Eq. (C.2) is replaced in accordance with (C.3) and (C.4) by

$$
\begin{aligned}
CS(f) &= ABS\big((T \vee G_1 \vee \bar{X}_i) \wedge (T \vee G_0 \vee X_i)\big) \\
&= ABS(T \vee (G_1 \vee \bar{X}_i) \wedge (G_0 \vee X_i))
\end{aligned} \tag{C.5}
$$

which can be further simplified to

$$CS(f) = T \vee ABS((G_1 \vee \bar{X}_i) \wedge (G_0 \vee X_i)). \tag{C.6}$$

Equation (C.6) can be graphically illustrated by the multiplication (ANDing) matrix shown in Fig. C.2. This matrix has some resemblance to the consensus-generating matrix of Fig. (**B.1**). However, in the current case, the keys or indices of the multiplication matrix are not (possibly) a part of the answer. The following comparisons suffice for implementing absorptions, wherein comparison continues till the compared term is absorbed or till the set of terms to which it is compared is exhausted [27].

    a. Compare every nonzero term in the matrix $G_0\,G_1$ to nonzero terms in the same row or the same column of the matrix $G_0\,G_1$ and to terms of T.

    b. Compare every nonzero term in the column vector $\bar{X}_m\,G_0$ to nonzero terms in the same row in the matrix $G_0\,G_1$.

    c. Compare every nonzero term in the row vector in $X_m G_1$ to nonzero terms in the same column in the matrix $G_0\,G_1$.

$\wedge$	$\overline{X_m}$	G_1	
X_m	......	$X_m\,G_1$	T
G_0	$\overline{X_m}\,G_0$	$G_0\,G_1$	

Fig. (C.2). A multiplication (ANDing) matrix used in VEKM folding.

CONSENT FOR PUBLICATION

Not applicable.

CONFLICT OF INTEREST

The author(s) confirm that there is no conflict of interest to declare for this publication.

ACKNOWLEDGEMENTS

The authors are gratefully indebted to Dr. Ahmad Ali Rushdi (University of California, Davis, CA, USA) for the competent technical help he generously offered during the preparation of this chapter.

REFERENCES

[1]   M.T. Holtzapple, and W. Dan Reece, *Foundations of Engineering.,* 2nd ed McGraw-Hill: Boston, MA, USA, 2003.
[2]   E. Jungwirth, "Avoidance of logical fallacies: A neglected aspect of science-education and science-teacher education", *Res. Sci. Technol. Educ.,* vol. 5, no. 1, pp. 43-58.
[3]   D.L. Hatcher, "Why formal logic is essential for critical thinking", *Informal Log.,* vol. 19, no. 1, pp. 77-89.
[4]   J. Hintikka, "Is logic the key to all good reasoning?", *Argumentation,* vol. 15, no. 1, pp. 35-57.
[5]   D. Sherry, "Formal logic for informal logicians", *Informal Log.,* vol. 26, no. 2, pp. 199-220.
[6]   P.J. Hurley, *A Concise Introduction to Logic.,* 9th ed Wadsworth/Thomson: Belmont, CA, USA, 2006.
[7]   I.M. Copi, and C. Cohen, *Introduction to Logic.,* 14th ed Prentice-Hall: Upper Saddle River, NJ, USA, 2010.
[8]   H. McColl, The calculus of equivalent statements (third paper), Proceedings of the London Mathematical Society 1878; s1-10(1): 16-28
[9]   A. Blake, Canonical Expressions in Boolean Algebra. Ph.D. Dissertation. Department of Mathematics. University of Chicago 1937
[10]   W.V. Quine, "The problem of simplifying truth functions", *Am. Math. Mon.,* vol. 59, no. 8, pp. 521-531.
[11]   W.V. Quine, "A way to simplify truth functions", *Am. Math. Mon.,* vol. 62, no. 9, pp. 627-631.
[12]   W.V. Quine, "On cores and prime implicants of truth functions", *Am. Math. Mon.,* vol. 66, no. 9, pp. 755-760.
[13]   P. Tison, Generalization of consensus theory and application to the minimization of Boolean functions. IEEE Transactions on Electronic Computers 1967. EC-16(4): 446-456, with Comments, Cutler, RB, Muroga, S. ibid. 1979. 28(7): 542-543
[14]   B. Reusch, "Generation of prime implicants from subfunctions and a unifying approach to the covering problem", *IEEE Trans. Comput.,* vol. C-24, no. 9, pp. 924-930.
[15]   S. Muroga, *Logic Design and Switching Theory..* John Wiley and Sons: New York, NY, USA, 1979.
[16]   E.P. Lynch, *Applied Symbolic Logic..* Wiley-Interscience: New York, NY, USA, 1980.
[17]   F.M. Brown, *Boolean Reasoning: The Logic of Boolean Equations. Boston, MA, USA: Kluwer Academic Publishers 1990.,* 2nd ed Dover Publications: Mineola, NY, USA, 2003.
[18]   F.M. Brown, "The origin of the method of iterated consensus", *IEEE Trans. Comput.,* vol. C-17, no. 8, p. 802.
[19]   J.R. Gregg, *Ones and Zeroes: Digital Circuits and the Logic of Sets..* Wiley/IEEE: New York, NY, USA, 1998.

[20]   A.M. Rushdi, and A.S. Al-Shehri, "Logical reasoning and its role in serving security and justice", *Security Research Journal*, vol. 11, no. 22, pp. 114-153.

[21]   A.M. Rushdi, and A.S. Al-Shehri, "Selective deduction with the aid of the variable-entered Karnaugh maps", *Magalat Game'at al-Malik Abdul Aziz. Al-U'lum al-Handasiat*, vol. 15, no. 2, pp. 21-29.

[22]   A.M. Rushdi, and O.M. Ba-Rukab, Some engineering applications of the Modern Syllogistic Method. SEC7 Paper 226, Proceedings of the Seventh Saudi Engineering Conference (SEC7), Riyadh, Saudi Arabia, Vol. 4, pp. 389-401, 2007

[23]   A.M. Rushdi, and A.O. Baz, Computer assisted resolution of engineering ethical dilemmas, SEC7 Paper 147, Proceedings of the Seventh Saudi Engineering Conference (SEC7), Riyadh, Saudi Arabia, Vol. 5, pp. 409-418, 2007

[24]   A.M. Rushdi, and O.M. Ba-Rukab, "The Modern Syllogistic Method as a tool for engineering problem solving", *Journal of Qassim University: Engineering and Computer Sciences*, vol. 1, no. 1, pp. 57-70.

[25]   A.M. Rushdi, and O.M. Ba-Rukab, "Powerful features of the Modern Syllogistic Method of propositional logic", *J. Math. Stat.*, vol. 4, no. 3, pp. 186-193.

[26]   A.M. Rushdi, and O.M. Ba-Rukab, "An exposition of the Modern Syllogistic Method of propositional logic", *Umm Al-Qura University Journal: Engineering and Architecture*, vol. 1, no. 1, pp. 1-34.

[27]   A.M. Rushdi, and O.M. Ba-Rukab, "Map derivation of the closures for dependency and attribute sets and all candidate keys for a relational database", *Magalat Game'at al-Malik Abdul Aziz. Al-U'lum al-Handasiat*, vol. 25, no. 2, pp. 3-34.

[28]   A.M. Rushdi, T.M. Alshehri, M. Zarouan, and M.A. Rushdi, "Utilization of the Modern Syllogistic Method in the exploration of hidden aspects in engineering ethical dilemmas", *Journal of King Abdulaziz University: Computers and Information Technology*, vol. 3, no. 1, pp. 73-127.

[29]   A.M. Rushdi, and O.M. Ba-Rukab, "Switching-algebraic analysis of relational databases", *J. Math. Stat.*, vol. 10, no. 2, pp. 231-243.

[30]   A.M. Rushdi, and M.A. Rushdi, "Utilization of the Modern Syllogistic Method in the service of academic advising", *Proceedings of the KAU Conference on Academic Advising in Higher Education*, , 2015pp. 228-241

[31]   A.M. Rushdi, M. Zarouan, T.M. Alshehri, and M.A. Rushdi, "The incremental version of the Modern Syllogistic Method", *Magalat Game'at al-Malik Abdul Aziz. Al-U'lum al-Handasiat*, vol. 26, no. 1, pp. 25-51.

[32]   A.M. Rushdi, M. Zarouan, T.M. Alshehri, and M.A. Rushdi, A modern syllogistic method in intuitionistic fuzzy logic with realistic tautology, The Scientific World Journal 2015, vol. 2015, Article ID 327390, 12 pages

[33]   A.M. Rushdi, and O.M. Ba-Rukab, "Pedagogical derivation of all irredundant dependency sets for relational databases", *Journal of Qassim University: Engineering and Computer Sciences*, vol. 9, no. 1, pp. 59-83.

[34]   A.M. Rushdi, and M.A. Rushdi, "Switching-algebraic algorithmic derivation of candidate keys in relational databases", *Proceedings of the IEEE International Conference on Emerging Trends in Communication Technologies (ICETCT-2016)*, 2016pp. 1-5

[35]   J.A. Robinson, "A Machine oriented logic based on the Resolution Principle", *J. Assoc. Comput. Mach.*, vol. 12, no. 1, pp. 23-41. [JACM].

[36]   M. Davis, and H. Putnam, "A computing procedure for quantification theory", *J. Assoc. Comput. Mach.*, vol. 7, no. 3, pp. 201-215. [JACM].

[37]   R.J. Schalkoff, *Artificial Intelligence: An Engineering Approach, New York.*. McGraw-Hill: NY, USA, 1990.

[38]   S. Russel, and P. Norvig, *Artificial Intelligence: A Modern Approach.*, 3rd ed Prentice-Hall: Englewood Cliffs, NJ, USA, 2010.

[39]   A.M. Rushdi, "Using variable-entered Karnaugh maps to solve Boolean equations", *Int. J. Comput. Math.*, vol. 78, pp. 23-38.

[40]   G.J. Klir, and M.A. Marin, "New considerations in teaching switching theory", *IEEE Trans. Educ.*, vol. E-12, no. 4, pp. 257-261.

[41]   E.J. McCluskey, "Minimization of Boolean functions", *Bell Labs Tech. J.*, vol. 35, no. 6, pp. 1417-1444.

[42]   M.J. Ghazala, "Irredundant disjunctive and conjunctive forms of a Boolean function", *IBM J. Res. Develop.*, vol. 1, no. 2, pp. 171-176.

[43]   E. Morreale, "Partitioned list algorithms for prime implicant determination from canonical forms", *IEEE Trans. Electron. Comput.*, vol. EC-16, no. 5, pp. 611-620.

[44]   J.R. Slagle, C-L. Chang, and R.C.T. Lee, "A new algorithm for generating prime implicants", *IEEE Trans. Comput.*, vol. C-19, no. 4, pp. 304-310.

[45]   S.R. Das, and N.S. Khabra, "Clause-column table approach for generating all the prime implicants of switching functions", *IEEE Trans. Comput.*, vol. C-21, no. 11, pp. 1239-1246.

[46]   H.R. Hwa, "A method for generating prime implicants of a Boolean expression", *IEEE Trans. Comput.*, vol. C-23, no. 6, pp. 637-641.

[47]   A. Kear, and G. Tsiknis, "An incremental method for generating prime implicants/ implicates", *J. Symbolic Comp.*, vol. 9, pp. 185-206.

[48]   J. de Kleer, "An improved incremental algorithm for generating prime implicates", *Proceedings of the Tenth National Conference on Artificial Intelligence*, , 1992pp. 780-785

[49]   P. Jackson, "Computing prime implicates incrementally", *International Conference on Automated Deduction (CADE-11)*, , 1992pp. 253-267

[50]   P. Jackson, "Computing prime implicates", *Proceedings of the*, , 1992pp. 65-72

[51]   O. Coudert, and J.C. Madre, "Implicit and incremental computation of primes and essential primes of Boolean functions", *Proceedings of the 29th ACM/IEEE Design Automation Conference*, , 1992pp. 36-39

[52]   O. Coudert, and J. Madre, "A new method to compute prime and essential prime implicants of Boolean functions", T Knight, and J. Savage, Eds., *Proceedings of MIT Conference on VLSI and Parallel Systems*, 1992pp. 113-128

[53]   T. Strzemecki, "Polynomial-time algorithms for generation of prime implicants", *J. Complexity*, vol. 8, no. 1, pp. 37-63.

[54]   T.H. Ngair, A new algorithm for incremental prime implicate generation. In IJCAI 1993 Aug 28; pp. 46-51

[55]   V.M. Manquinho, P.F. Flores, J.P. Silva, and A.L. Oliveira, "Prime implicant computation using satisfiability algorithms", *Proceedings of the Ninth IEEE International Conference on 1997 Nov 3*, , 1997pp. 232-239

[56]   L. Palopoli, F. Pirri, and C. Pizzuti, "Algorithms for selective enumeration of prime implicants", *Artif. Intell.*, vol. 111, no. 1, pp. 41-72.

[57]   P. Marquis, Consequence finding algorithms.*Handbook of Defeasible Reasoning and Uncertainty Management Systems.*, , 2000pp. 41-145

[58]   A.M. Rushdi, and H.A. Al-Yahya, "Derivation of the complete sum of a switching function with the aid of the variable-entered Karnaugh map", *Journal of King Saud University: Engineering Sciences*, vol. 13, no. 2, pp. 239-269.

[59]   A.M. Rushdi, "Prime-implicant extraction with the aid of the variable-entered Karnaugh map. Umm Al-Qura University Journal: Science", *Medicine and Engineering*, vol. 13, no. 1, pp. 53-74.

[60]   G. Alexe, S. Alexea, Y. Crama, S. Foldes, P. Hammer, and B. Simeone, "Consensus algorithms for the generation of all maximal bicliques", *Discrete Appl. Math.*, vol. 145, no. 1, pp. 11-21.

[61]   D. Ślęzak, Association reducts: Boolean representation, in G. Wang et al. (Editors), Rough Sets and Knowledge Technology, RSKT 2006, LNAI 4062, Springer, Germany: Berlin-Heidelberg 2006, pp. 305-312

[62]   Z. Pawlak, and A. Skowron, "Rough sets and Boolean reasoning", *Inf. Sci.*, vol. 177, no. 1, pp. 41-73.

[63]   Y. Crama, and P.L. Hammer, *Boolean Functions: Theory, Algorithms, and Applications..* Cambridge University Press: Cambridge, United Kingdom, 2011.

[64]   H. Ichihara, T. Inaoka, T. Iwagaki, and T. Inoue, "Logic simplification by minterm complement for error tolerant application", *Computer Design (ICCD)*, , 2015pp. 94-100

[65]   M. Baumgartner, "Uncovering deterministic causal structures: A Boolean approach", *Synthese*, vol. 170, no. 1, pp. 71-96.

[66]   M. Baumgartner, and R. Epple, "A Coincidence Analysis of a causal chain: The Swiss minaret vote", *Sociol. Methods Res.,* vol. 42, no. 2, pp. 280-312.

[67]   A.M.A. Rushdi, and R.M.S. Badawi, "Karnaugh map utilization in Coincidence Analysis", *Journal of King Abdulaziz University: Faculty of Computers and Information Technology.* in press

[68]   M. D'agostino, and L. Floridi, "The enduring scandal of deduction: Is propositional logic really uninformative?", *Synthese,* vol. 167, no. 2, pp. 271-315.

[69]   H.E. Kyburg, "The justification of deduction", *Rev. Metaphys.,* vol. 1, pp. 19-25.

[70]   M.A. Dummett, *The Justification of Deduction..* Oxford University Press: London, 1973.

[71]   S. Haack, "The justification of deduction", *Mind,* vol. 85, no. 337, pp. 112-119.

[72]   D. Prawitz, Explaining Deductive Inference. In Dag Prawitz, On Proofs and Meaning, 2015 (pp. 65-100). Springer International Publishing

[73]   B.H. Slater, "Paraconsistent logics?", *J. Philos. Log.,* vol. 24, no. 4, pp. 451-454.

[74]   W. Carnielli, M.E. Coniglio, and J. Marcos, Logics of Formal Inconsistency.*Handbook of Philosophical Logic..* Springer Netherlands, 2007, pp. 1-93.

[75]   NC Da Costa, D Krause, and O Bueno, Paraconsistent logics and paraconsistency. Philosophy of logic. 2007; 5: 655-781

[76]   A. Hunter, Paraconsistent logics.*Reasoning with Actual and Potential Contradictions..* Springer Netherlands, 1998, pp. 11-36.

[77]   J. Hintikka, *Inquiry as Inquiry: A Logic of Scientific Discovery..* Kluwer Academic Publishers: Dordrecht, The Netherlands, 1999.

[78]   S. Read, "Logical consequence as truth-preservation", *Logique et Analyse,* vol. 183, no. 4, pp. 479-493.

[79]   A. Iglesias, R. Ipanaqué, E.J. Ojeda, and F.W. Malaver, "Unravelling the hidden truth within logical statements: A computer tool", *Computational Science and Its Applications (ICCSA),* , 2013pp. 53-61

[80]   F.M. Brown, and S. Rudeanu, "A functional approach to the theory of prime implicants", *Publications De L'institut Mathématique,* vol. 40, no. 54, pp. 23-32. [BEOGRAD].

[81]   A.M. Rushdi, and H.M. Albarakati, "Prominent classes of the most general subsumptive solutions of Boolean equations", *Inf. Sci.,* vol. 281, pp. 53-65.

[82]   A.M. Rushdi, and M.A. Rushdi, Switching-Algebraic Analysis of System Reliability.*Advances in Reliability and System Engineering..* Springer International Publishing: Cham, Switzerland, 2017, pp. 139-161.

[83]   V. Klenk, *Understanding Symbolic Logic.,* 5th ed Prentice-Hall: Englewood Cliffs, NJ, USA, 2007.

[84]   I.T. Nelson, R.L. Ratliff, G. Steinhoff, and G.J. Mitchell, "Teaching logic to auditing students: Can training in logic reduce audit judgment errors", *J. Account. Educ.,* vol. 21, pp. 215-237.

[85]   T. Neller, Z. Markov, and I. Russell, "Clue deduction: Professor Plum teaches logic", *Proceedings of the 19th International FLAIRS Conference (FLAIRS-2006),* , 2006pp. 214-220

[86]   B. Averbach, and O. Chein, *Problem Solving Through Recreational Mathematics.,* 2nd ed Dover Publications: Mineola, NY, USA, 2000.

[87]   S.S. Epp, *Discrete Mathematics with Applications.,* 3rd ed Brooks/Cole-Thomson Learning: Belmont, CA, USA, 2004.

[88]   H.S. Fogler, and S.E. LeBlanc, *Strategies for Creative Problem Solving.,* 2nd ed Prentice-Hall: Upper Saddle River, NJ, USA, 2008.

[89]   H.W. Rittel, and M.M. Webber, "Dilemmas in a general theory of planning", *Policy Sci.,* vol. 4, no. 2, pp. 155-169.

[90]   R. Buchanan, "Wicked problems in design thinking", *Des. Issues,* vol. 8, no. 2, pp. 5-21.

[91]   P. Degrace, and L.H. Stahl, *Wicked Problems, Righteous Solutions: A Catolog of Modern Engineering Paradigms..* Prentice-Hall: Upper Saddle River, NJ, USA, 1998.

[92]   M.N. Wexler, "Exploring the moral dimension of wicked problems", *Int. J. Sociol. Soc. Policy,* vol. 29, no. 9/10, pp. 531-542.

[93]   A.M. Rushdi, "Engineering thinking on exploring the future", *Magalat Game'at al-Malik Abdul Aziz. Al-U'lum al-Handasiat,* vol. 20, no. 2, pp. 111-140.

[94]   J. Kasser, and Y.Y. Zhao, Wicked problems: Wicked solutions. In System of Systems Engineering Conference (SoSE), 2016 11th 2016 Jun 12 (pp. 1-6). IEEE

[95]   M.W. Martin, and R. Schinzinger, *Ethics in Engineering.,* 4th ed McGraw-Hill: Boston, MA, USA, 2005.

[96]   Y-S. Zhang, "Determining all candidate keys based on Karnaugh map", *Proceedings of the International Conference on Information Management, Innovation Management, and Industrial Engineering (ICIII),* 2009pp. 226-229

[97]   D.J. Russomano, and R.D. Bonnell, "A pedagogical approach to database design via Karnaugh maps", *IEEE Trans. Educ.,* vol. 42, no. 4, pp. 261-270.

[98]   H. Saiedian, and T. Spencer, "An efficient algorithm to compute the candidate keys of a relational database schema", *Comput. J.,* vol. 39, no. 2, pp. 124-132.

[99]   P. Cordero, M. Enciso, and A. Mora, "Automated reasoning to infer all minimal keys", *Proceedings of the Twenty-Third International Joint Conference on Artificial Intelligence,* , 2013pp. 817-823

[100]   P. Besnard, and A. Hunter, Argumentation Based on Classical Logic.*Argumentation in Artificial Intelligence. Chapter 7.* Springer-Verlag: Berlin-Heidelberg, Germany, 2009, pp. 133-152.

[101]   C. Flament, "L'analyse booléenne de questionnaires", *Math. Sci. Hum.,* vol. 12, pp. 3-10.

[102]   C. Flament, *L'analyse Booléenne de Questionnaire..* Mouton: Paris, France, 1976.

[103]   A. Degenne, and M.O. Lebeaux, "Boolean analysis of questionnaire data", *Soc. Networks,* vol. 18, no. 3, pp. 231-245.

[104]   P. Theuns, A Dichotomization Method for Boolean Analysis of Quantifiable Co-Occurrence Data.*Contributions to Mathematical Psychology, Psychometrics, and Methodology (SE-28)..* Springer: New York, NY, USA, 1994, pp. 389-402.

[105]   C.C. Ragin, *The Comparative Method: Moving Beyond Qualitative and Quantitative Strategies..* University of California Press: Berkeley, CA, USA, 1987.

[106]   AMA Rushdi, and RMS Badawi, Karnaugh map utilization in Boolean analysis: the case of war termination, Journal of Qassim University: Engineering and Computer sciences 2017, 10(1): 53-88

[107]   A.M.A. Rushdi, "Utilization of Karnaugh maps in multi-value qualitative comparative analysis, International Journal of Mathematical", *Engineering and Management Sciences,* vol. 3, no. 1, pp. 28-46. [IJMEMS].

[108]   R.A. Rushdi, and A.M. Rushdi, "Karnaugh-map utility in medical studies: The case of Fetal Malnutrition. International Journal of Mathematical", *Engineering and Management Sciences,* vol. 3, no. 3, pp. 220-244. [IJMEMS].

[109]   M.R. Cohen, E. Nagel, and J. Corcoran, *An Introduction to Logic.,* 2nd ed Hackett Publishing: Indianapolis, IN, USA, 1993.

[110]   H.K. Büning, and T. Lettmann, *Propositional Logic: Deduction and Algorithms..* Cambridge University Press: Cambridge, United Kingdom, 1999.

[111]   C. Howson, *Logic with Trees: An Introduction to Symbolic Logic..* Routledge: Milton Park, United Kingdom, 2005.

[112]   H.D. Ebbinghaus, J. Flum, and W. Thomas, *Mathematical Logic.,* 2nd ed Springer Science & Business Media: New York, NY, USA, 2013.

[113]   C.C. Leary, and L. Kristiansen, *A Friendly Introduction to Mathematical Logic..* Milne Library: Geneseo, NY, USA, 2015.

[114]   P.N. Johnson-Laird, and F. Savary, "Illusory inferences: A novel class of erroneous deductions", *Cognition,* vol. 71, no. 3, pp. 191-229.

[115]   P. Barrouillet, and J-F. Lecas, "Illusory inferences from a disjunction of conditionals: A new mental models account", *Cognition,* vol. 76, no. 2, pp. 167-173.

[116]   D. Walton, The three bases for the enthymeme: A dialogical theory. Journal of Applied Logic 2008; .6(3): 361-379

[117]   E. Boros, T. Ibaraki, and K. Makino, "Error-free and best-fit extensions of partially defined Boolean functions", *Inf. Comput.,* vol. 140, no. 2, pp. 254-283.

[118]   J. Eekels, "On the logic and methodology of engineering design", *IChemE Transactions,* vol. 80A, no. 6, pp. 615-624.

[119]   R. Haenni, "Probabilistic argumentation", *J. Appl. Log.,* vol. 7, no. 2, pp. 155-176.

[120]   H. Kerzner, *Kerzner's Project Management Logic Puzzles..* John Wiley and Sons: New York, NY, USA, 2006.

[121]   C. Sakama, and K. Inoue, Constructing Consensus Logic Programs, in Puebla, G, (Editor), Logic-Based Program Synthesis and Transformation (LOPSTR 2006), Lecture Notes in Computer Science (LNCS), Vol. 4407/2007. Berlin-Heidelberg, Germany: Springer-Verlag 2007; pp. 26–42

[122]   R.B. Cutler, K. Kinoshita, and S. Muroga, Exposition of Tison's Method to Derive all Prime Implicants and all Irredundant Disjunctive Forms for a Given Switching Function, Report No. UIUCDCS-R-79-993, Department of Computer Science, University of Illinois at Urbana-Champaign (UIUC), Urbana, Illinois, IL, USA, 1979

[123]   A. Ramesh, and N.V. Murray, "Avoiding tests for subsumption", *Proceedings AAAI,* 1994pp. 175-180 Seattle, WA, USA

[124]   R. Socher-Ambrosius, "How to avoid the derivation of redundant clauses in reasoning systems", *J. Autom. Reason.,* vol. 9, no. 1, pp. 77-97.

CHAPTER 7

Modeling of Scattering Response for Retrieval of Soil Parameters with Bistatic Radar

Rishi Prakash[1,*] and Dharmendra Singh[2]

[1]*Department of Electronics and Communication Engineering, Graphic Era Deemed to be University, Dehradun, Uttarakhand, India*
[2]*Department of Electronics and Communication Engineering, Indian Institute of Technology Rookee, Rookee, Uttarakhand, India*

Abstract: In this chapter, we will discuss the mathematical formulation of scattering in the bistatic domain. The scattering phenomenon is associated with the scattering from the soil surface. The major domain of the discussion is in the light of radar remote sensing which deals with the characterization of soil parameters with the help of mathematical modeling, empirical equations and optimization techniques. This chapter will provide an idea of scattering in the bistatic domain, scatterometer setup and retrieval methodology of various soil parameters. Soil parameters which are sensitive for radar scattering are soil texture, soil moisture and surface roughness. Information of these soil parameters is very important in various applications, such as agriculture, weather forecasting, soil erosion studies, hydrological studies and many more. Scattering from soil surface depends on two major parameters, the first one is sensor parameters and another is soil parameters. Sensor parameters are frequency, incidence angle and polarization. Role of incidence angle and polarization on scattering mechanism has been dealt in detail and it has been shown that they play a major role in the retrieval of soil parameters. The sensitivity of different soil parameters for scattering coefficient has been established with experimental observations. Kirchhoff Scalar Approximation is a theoretical approach which provides mathematical expressions for scattering coefficient based on well established electromagnetic wave theory. A soil parameter retrieval methodology relying on theoretical approach along with the experimental observation has been discussed.

Keywords: Bistatic scatterometer, Parameter retrieval, Scattering coefficient, Soil moisture, Soil texture, Surface roughness.

---

*Corresponding author Rishi Prakash:** Department of Electronics and Communication Engineering, Graphic Era Deemed to be University, Dehradun, Uttarakhand-248002, India; Tel: +91-9410371768; Fax: +91-135-2644025; E-mail: dr.rishi.prakash@ieee.org

INTRODUCTION

Remote sensing of earth's environment comprises measuring and recording of electromagnetic energy reflected from or emitted by the earth's surface and atmosphere, and relating these measurements to the nature and distribution of surface materials and atmospheric conditions. The measurement methodology in remote sensing can be characterized in two major domains, *i.e.,* passive remote sensing systems and active remote sensing systems. Remote sensing systems which measure the energy that is naturally available are called passive sensors. The passive systems mainly depend on the solar radiation (*e.g.,* optical and near infrared) and energy that is naturally emitted (*e.g.,* thermal infrared and microwave radiometer). On the other hand, an active sensing system generates and uses its own energy to illuminate the target and records the reflected energy which carries the information content. The active remote sensing systems that operate in the microwave region of electromagnetic spectrum include radiation with frequency spectrum ranges from 0.3 GHz to 300 GHz. This spectrum is subdivided into various bands, which are designated by letters. For earth observation studies, the most important bands are: L–band (f = 1–2 GHz, λ = 15–30 cm), C–band (f = 4–8 GHz, λ = 7.5–3.8 cm) and X–band (f = 8–12 GHz, λ = 3.8–2.5 cm) [1]. The active microwave sensors can generally be kept in two broad categories, *i.e.,* imaging and non–imaging. The imaging active microwave sensors include the Real Aperture Radar and Synthetic Aperture Radar (SAR). Whereas, the non–imaging active microwave sensors are Altimeter and Scatterometer. Advantages of microwave active sensors include the ability to obtain measurements anytime, regardless of the time of day or season as these systems do not rely on the solar illumination and have the capability to penetrate through the cloud, moderate rain and smoke. In addition to this, the penetration ability of microwave at low frequency is such that it can penetrate through the vegetation therefore soil characteristic, covered by vegetation, can be retrieved through the proper inclusion of scattering behavior of vegetation.

The geophysical variations in the earth surface are imaged as the spatial patterns on remote sensing images. Such variations may be vegetation, soil or water. These variations are not themselves detected directly by remote sensing images; therefore, their nature should be inferred from the measurements made. The characteristic of the measured remote sensing data is that they can be tuned so as to provide an estimate of physical properties of the targets. The most commonly used applications of the remote sensing technique are soil parameter monitoring, hydrological modeling, watershed mapping, land cover classification, fractional vegetation cover mapping, drought and flood predictions, urban modeling, weather forecasting, environmental monitoring and agriculture.

The active microwave sensors can be subdivided into two configurations based on the receiving mechanism of reflected energy. On the one hand, the transmitter and receiver are collocated or the transmitting antenna itself works as the receiving antenna and measures the radiation that is reflected back to its direction. Such kind of configuration is termed as monostatic active microwave sensor. On the other hand, the bistatic configuration foresees a passive receiver, which catches the echoes scattered by the earth surface, originating from a microwave illuminator [2]. In the last two decades, most of the satellite missions carrying active microwave sensors are of monostatic configuration. Recently launched monostatic active microwave sensors are RADARSAT–2, PALSAR–2, TerraSAR–X, RISAT. The newly launched satellite mission that operates in the bistatic domain is TanDem–X that is developed by the German Aerospace Centre (DLR) in association with the Astrium GmbH. Bistatic configuration provides the opportunity to have many receivers at different locations for their special utilization of target characterization with only one transmitter. Along with this advantage, the bistatic configuration explores the possibility of mapping the earth with the existing monostatic satellite sensors, *e.g.*, TanDEM–X that operates in association with TeraSAR–X and provides data in a bistatic mode in X–band.

In context to the active microwave remote sensing, soil moisture, surface roughness and soil texture are prominent soil parameters. The knowledge of the spatial distribution of these soil parameters is desirable in many applications. Prediction of erosion, irrigation scheduling, improving crop yield, climatology, meteorology, land use and management are some of the important applications [3, 4].

Soil parameter characterization with active microwave remote sensing has been well documented in the literature when one is interested in the monostatic domain [5-17]. Synthetic aperture radars (*e.g.*, ERS 1/2, RASARSAT 1/2, PALSAR), with the high spatial resolution capability, and scatterometers (*e.g.*, ERS 1/2, QuikSCAT, MetOp–ASCAT) are the important satellite based sensors that provide the information of soil parameters at the local scale and regional scale, respectively. Ground based as well as airborn and spaceborn experiments have been carried out to develop the relationship between scattering coefficient and soil parameters. Empirical relations as well as theoretical equations have been developed and tested for the characterization of soil parameters considering the scattering behavior in the monostatic domain [18-31]. Till date, the research is in progress to develop the more efficient and accurate tool and algorithm to access the soil parameters so that some simplified model can be developed to circumvent the complexity and the need of *apriori* information. These requirements emphasize to explore the other domain of the active microwave remote sensing. Scattering behavior in the bistatic may be exploited to investigate the characteristic of the soil parameters. The prime concern in bistatic was the complexity inherited for having transmitter and receiver on a different platform. But from the last decade, there is a renewed interest of the researchers in the field of bistatic due to the extra degree of freedom gained in remote sensing observation of natural and manmade target as well as the low cost of operation by sharing the expensive transmitter part of the system among several receivers [32, 33].

Soil moisture, surface roughness and soil texture are important soil parameters and these parameters show the feasibility to be measured with active microwave remote sensing. Soil moisture and surface roughness have gained much attention of the research community involved in soil parameter characterization. Sometimes, the prime concern is the soil moisture retrieval and researchers have applied the methodology, such as copolarization ratio to minimize the soil roughness and predict the soil moisture content [34]. However, in case of soil roughness retrieval, multi–incidence angle approach has been utilized [35, 36]. Similarly, several other techniques, such as change detection are prevalent in soil moisture and surface roughness retrieval. But in all these scenarios, more or less, the effect of soil texture has been neglected. Some of the researchers however have incorporated the effect of soil texture in soil moisture retrieval [37, 38]. In addition to this, it has been shown that soil dielectric constant is dependent on soil texture and it has been proven that the change in dielectric constant with moisture shows its dependency on soil texture [39-44]. Therefore, active microwave remote sensing, which is highly dependent on dielectric constant, may be explored to study soil texture.

Another important factor in soil parameter analysis in active microwave remote sensing is its retrieval. Scattering coefficient, that is the measured parameter in active microwave remote sensing, is a function of sensor parameters and target parameters. Sensor parameters include operating frequency, incidence angle and polarization whereas, target parameters, when interest lies in soil parameters characterization, are soil moisture, surface roughness and soil texture. Sensor parameters are known to us beforehand even though, the scattering coefficient is a function of several unknown soil parameters. Many empirical and theoretical relationships exist that determine the dependence of scattering coefficient on various soil parameters [23, 24, 29-31, 45]. But, the inversion of these relations is a cumbersome task due to the involvement of many parameters on single scattering coefficient. To solve the problem of inversion, researches have made multi–incidence, multi–frequency and multi–polarization analysis [34-36, 46-48]. Even though, the problem with empirical relations is that, they are highly data dependent and work efficiently in the environmental condition where they have been developed. Whereas, theoretical models that are based on the scattering laws are applicable for wide range of surface parameters but, these models require specifying the surface characteristic with one or more surface roughness parameter(s). The problem of defining an optimal parameter for describing surface roughness has been investigated in many studies [49-56]. Unfortunately, these models have failed to accurately account for the complex geometry of natural soil surfaces. Also, they have neglected volume scattering in the remotely sensed soil layer [1]. For these reasons, still there is a need to focus on soil parameter retrieval studies.

EXPERIMENT SETUP FOR DATA ACQUISITION

Bistatic Scatterometer

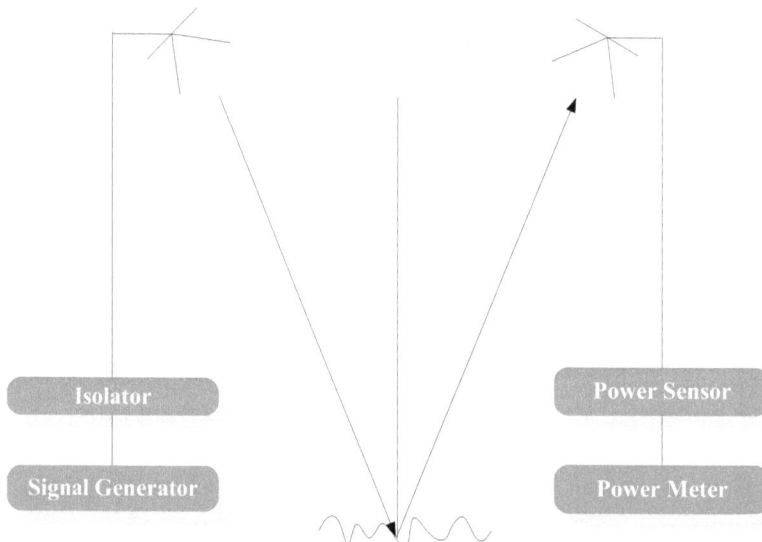

Fig. (1). Schematic diagram of the bistatic scatterometer used for the specular scattering measurement.

Fig. (**1**) shows the schematic diagram of a bistatic scatterometer that can be developed in the laboratory. It is used for collecting specular scattering data in different polarization, incidence angle and frequency. The platform on which antenna is placed should be movable so that height and distance of antenna from the target can be varied to keep the illumination from the antenna on target. Fig. (**2**) represents the coordinate system for scattering geometry. (θ, φ) define the incident direction of the transmitted power $P_p(\theta, \varphi)$ at polarization p, and (θ_s, φ_s) is the direction of the received power $P_q(\theta_s, \varphi_s)$ at polarization q. In case of specular scattering $\theta = \theta_s$, $\varphi = 0$ and $\varphi_s = 0$. Following section describe the determination of antenna location to keep the illumination from the antenna at the target location.

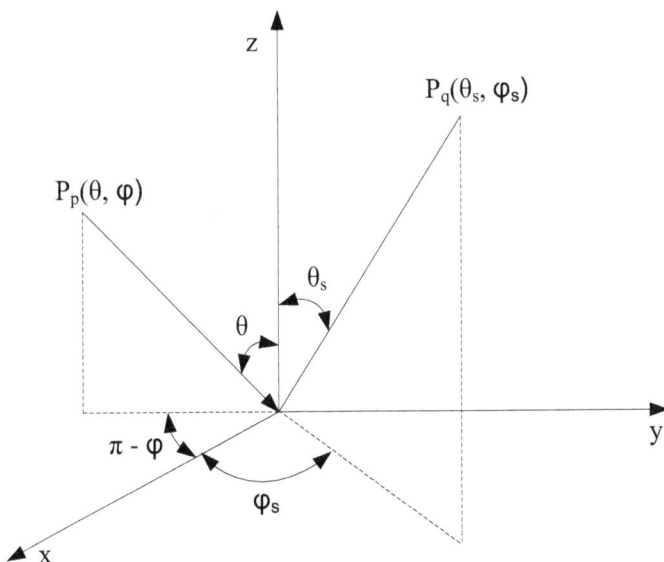

Fig. (2). Coordinate system of scattering geometry.

Determination of Point in x and y Plane

Fig. (**3**) shows the illumination geometry for a side looking antenna. It is important to keep this illumination on the target. Therefore, the location of the antenna should be determined. Following equations can be used to determine the value of x and y to position the antenna at appropriate position [57].

$$x = R\sin\theta \qquad\qquad (1)$$

and

$$y = R\cos\theta \qquad (2)$$

where R is the distance from the antenna to the center point of the ellipse and θ is the incidence angle.

The major axis of the ellipse (a) is calculated as

$$a = a_1 + a_2 \qquad (3)$$

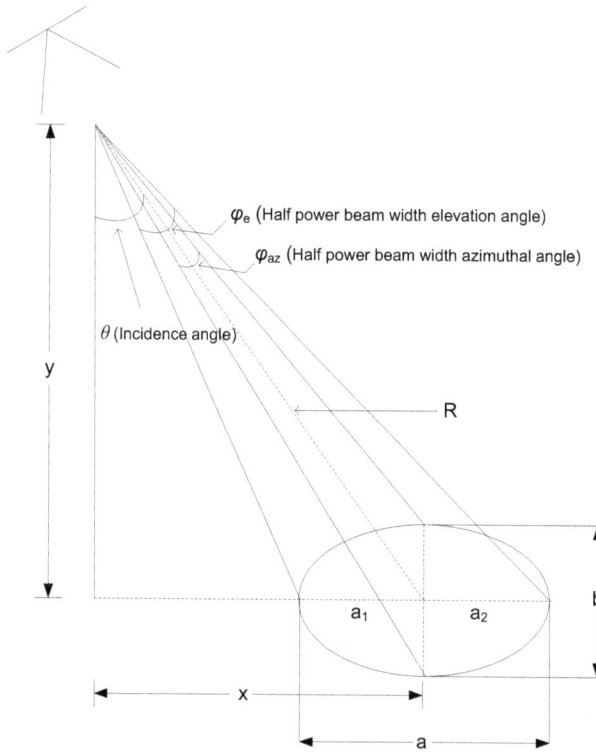

Fig. (3). Illumination geometry to calculate the antenna position in the *x–y* plane.

where

$$a_1 = R\sin\left(\frac{\varphi_e}{2}\right)\sec(\theta + \frac{\varphi_e}{2}) \qquad (4)$$

$$a_2 = R\sin\left(\frac{\varphi_e}{2}\right)\sec(\theta - \frac{\varphi_e}{2}) \qquad (5)$$

where φ_e is the elevation angle.

The minor axis (b) is calculated as

$$b = 2R\tan(\frac{\varphi_{az}}{2}) \tag{6}$$

where φ_{az} is the azimuthal angle.

The area of Illumination (I) is equal to the area of ellipse and calculated as

$$I = \pi\left(\frac{a}{2}\right)\left(\frac{b}{2}\right) \tag{7}$$

Therefore,

$$I = \frac{\pi R^2}{2}\tan\left(\frac{\varphi_{az}}{2}\right)\sin\left(\frac{\varphi_e}{2}\right)\left[\sec\left(\theta + \frac{\varphi_e}{2}\right) + \sec\left(\theta - \frac{\varphi_e}{2}\right)\right] \tag{8}$$

To determine the x and y we must first evaluate the value of R. R can be evaluated with the help of antenna parameter, *i.e.*, φ_e, φ_{az} and θ and fixing the area of illumination.

Determination of Specular Scattering Coefficient

The target we are discussing is soil parameters, *i.e.*, soil moisture, surface roughness and soil texture. Change in any of these parameters will change the specular scattering coefficient. Following steps can be used to determine the specular scattering coefficient with developed scatterometer setup.

1) Calibration plays important role in the determination of accurate data. A flat aluminum sheet can be used for calibration purposes. RCS for aluminum sheet is given as [57]

$$\sigma_{pp_{Al}}(\theta) = \frac{4\pi A^2}{\lambda^2}\left[\frac{\sin(kb\sin\theta)}{kb\sin\theta}\right]^2 \cos^2\theta \tag{9}$$

where $\sigma_{pp_{Al}}$ is RCS of aluminum sheet, A is an area of the aluminum sheet, λ is wavelength used, θ is the incidence angle, b is the dimension of the square aluminum sheet, pp employs for HH– or VV–polarization and $k = 2\pi/\lambda$.

RCS of aluminum sheet in dB can be written as

$$\sigma_{pp_{Al}}(\theta)(dB) = 10 \log_{10} \sigma_{pp_{Al}}(\theta) \qquad (10)$$

2) Now RCS of soil can be determined as

$$\sigma_{pp_{soil}}(\theta) = \left(\frac{P_{pp_{soil}}(\theta)}{P_{pp_{Al}}(\theta)} \right) \sigma_{pp_{Al}}(\theta) \qquad (11)$$

where $\sigma_{pp_{soil}}(\theta)$ is radar cross section for soil, $P_{pp_{soil}}(\theta)$ is power received for soil at various incidence angles and $P_{pp_{Al}}(\theta)$ is the corresponding power received for the aluminum sheet at various incidence angles.

Scattering coefficient is defined as "radar cross section per unit area". If the illumination cell size is kept 1 m², the division of radar cross section for soil by illumination area will provide scattering coefficient [57]. Scattering coefficient for soil is represented by $\sigma^{\circ}_{pp_{soil}}(\theta)$. Scattering coefficient of soil in decibel (dB) can be written as

$$\sigma^{\circ}_{pp_{soil}}(\theta)(dB) = 10 \log_{10} \sigma^{\circ}_{pp_{soil}}(\theta) \qquad (12)$$

Soil Texture

Soil texture is defined based on the proportionate distribution of sand, silt and clay in the soil. The diameter of sand particle varies from 2 mm to 0.05 mm, silt particle form 0.05 mm to 0.002 mm whereas the particle diameters less than 0.002 mm are classified as clay [58].

Soil Moisture

The amount of water present in soil is determined by the volumetric soil moisture content. Following equation is used to determine the volumetric soil moisture content [51].

$$m_v = \frac{w_{moist} - w_{dry}}{w_{dry}} \times \rho_b \qquad\qquad (13)$$

where w_{moist} is the weight of moist soil sample, w_{dry} is the weight of dry soil sample, and ρ_b is the soil bulk density.

Surface Roughness

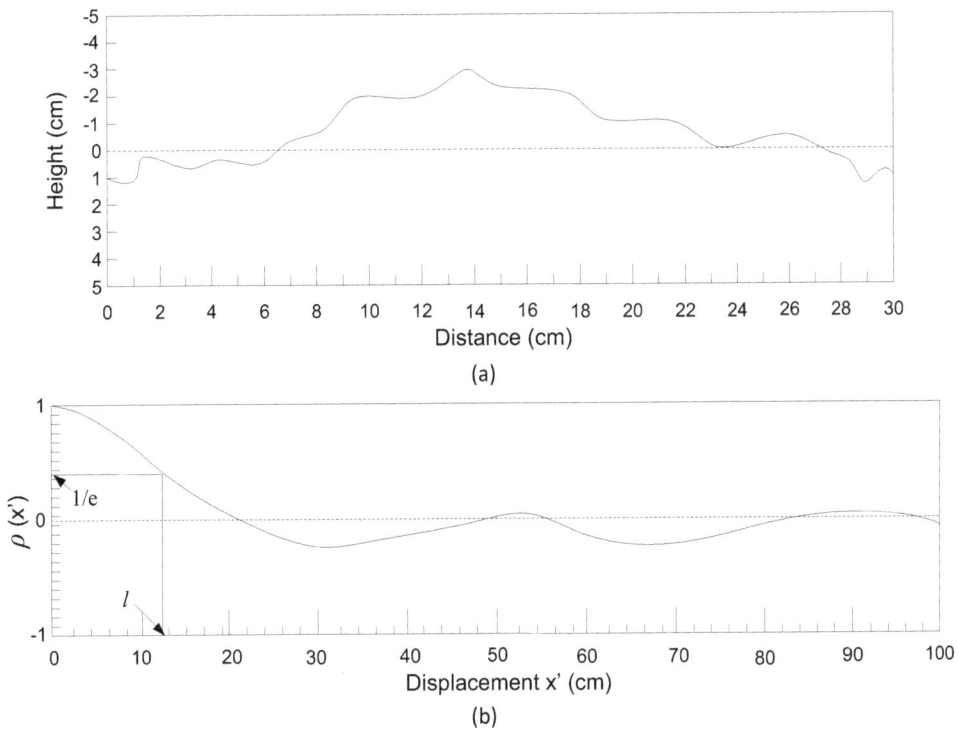

Fig. (4). (a) Surface profile (b) Autocorrelation function [31].

Soil surface roughness is generally described as a single scale process, parameterized by the root mean square (rms) height, s, the correlation length, l, and autocorrelation function [31, 50]. Surface roughness profile and autocorrelation function is shown in Fig. (**4**). Changes in surface roughness condition can be made in a controlled way with a wooden spiked harrow. The wooden spiked harrow is used to generate the periodic surface roughness [47, 53]. The characterization of soil surface roughness, *i.e.*, measurement of the rms surface height (*s*) and correlation length (*l*) was made with the help of pin profilometer. The rms surface height, *s* is defined by the mean height of the surface along with its second moment and given as

$$s = \left(\overline{z^2} - \overline{z}^2 \right)^{1/2} \tag{14}$$

The autocorrelation function measures the similarity between the height *z* at a point *x* and at a point *x'* distant from *x*. The normalized autocorrelation function in discreet case is given as

$$\rho(x') = \frac{\sum_{i=1}^{N+1-j} z_i z_{j+i-1}}{\sum_{i=1}^{N} z_i^2} \tag{15}$$

where $x' = (j - 1)\Delta x$ and *j* is an integer ≥ 1. The surface correlation length *l* is defined as the displacement *x'* for which $\rho(x')$ is equal to $1/e$. The autocorrelation length of a surface explains the statistical independence of two points on the surface; if the two points are separated by a horizontal distance greater than *l*, then their heights may be considered to be approximately statistically independent of one another [31].

BEHAVIOR OF SCATTERING COEFFICIENT WITH SENSOR AND TARGET PARAMETERS

Figs. (**5** to **8**) show behavior of specular scattering coefficient with the change is target (*i.e.*, soil) parameters and sensor parameters. The soil parameters are soil texture soil moisture and surface roughness, whereas sensor parameters for the change in specular scattering coefficient are polarization and incidence angle. Figures show the specular scattering behavior in HH and VV-polarization. Table **1** shows the soil texture of different soil fields.

Effect of soil moisture, soil texture and incidence angle on specular scattering can be clearly observed with Fig. (**5a** and **b**) for HH-polarization. Specular scattering coefficient increases with the increase in soil moisture. The major important conclusion which can be drawn from Fig. (**5**) is the differentiation among different soil texture field with the change in soil moisture. These observations clearly explain the dependency of specular scattering coefficient on soil moisture, soil texture and incidence angle in HH-polarization. Similarly, figure 6 explains the response of soil moisture, soil texture and incidence angle on specular scattering in VV-polarization. A sharp decrease in specular scattering coefficient at 60° and 65° degree in Fig. (**6**a) and (**6**b), respectively, is due to Brewster angle effect in VV-polarization. The observations in VV-polarization also explain that we can differentiate different soil texture and soil moisture based on specular scattering coefficient.

Table 1. Information of soil texture for different soil field [58].

	% of Sand	% of Silt	% of Clay	% of Gravels
Field 1	85.3	7.5	2.5	4.1
Field 2	62.6	26.1	5.3	5.2
Field 3	47.2	32.7	15.4	4.5
Field 4	24.6	20.1	48.7	6.3
Field 5	25.5	41.3	21.7	11.2
Field 6	17.4	51.2	20.8	10.4
Field 7	11.2	70.6	4.8	13.1
Field 8	12.8	29.3	51.5	5.6
Field 9	7.5	23.4	64.2	4.8
Field 10	2.3	10.3	81.6	5.6

Figs. (**7** and **8**) show the behavior of specular scattering coefficient for different soil texture, surface roughens and incidence angle in HH and VV-polarization respectively. In the previous paragraph, it was shown that with the change in soil moisture specular scattering coefficient changes. Similarly, it can be observed form Figs. (**7** and **8**) that the change in soil surface roughness also changes the specular scattering coefficient.

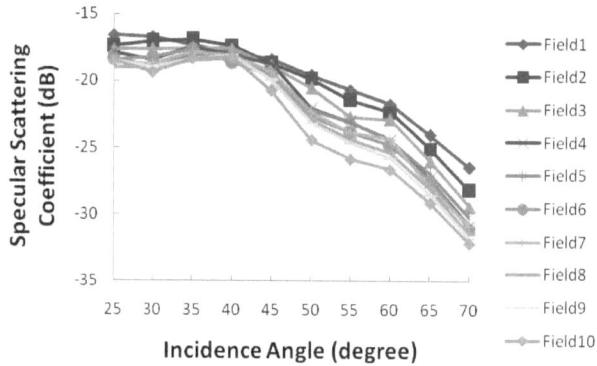

(a)

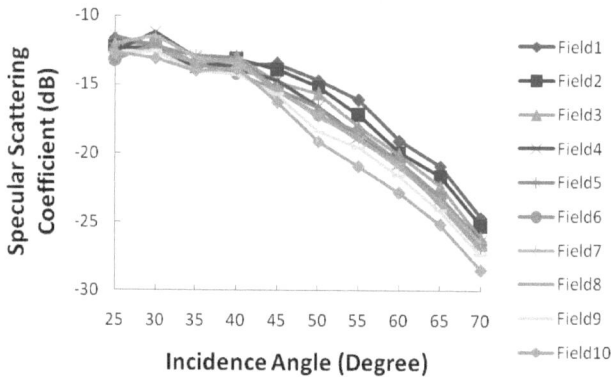

(b)

Fig. (5). Behavour of specular scattering coefficient with incidence angle for different soil texture fields in HH-polarization for the smooth surface where (a) volumetric soil moisture content is 0.027 cm^3 cm^{-3}, (b) volumetric soil moisture content is 0.188 cm^3 cm^{-3}[58].

Therefore, in conclusion we can say that specular scattering coefficient is sensitive for soil moisture, soil texture, surface roughness, incidence angle and polarization. Incidence angle and polarization which are sensor parameters are known to us *apriori* so that we can develop a methodology which can retrieve soil parameters based on known sensor parameters and specular scattering coefficient. Following sections will explain the retrieval methodology of soil texture, soil moisture and surface roughens based on sensor parameters and specular scattering coefficient.

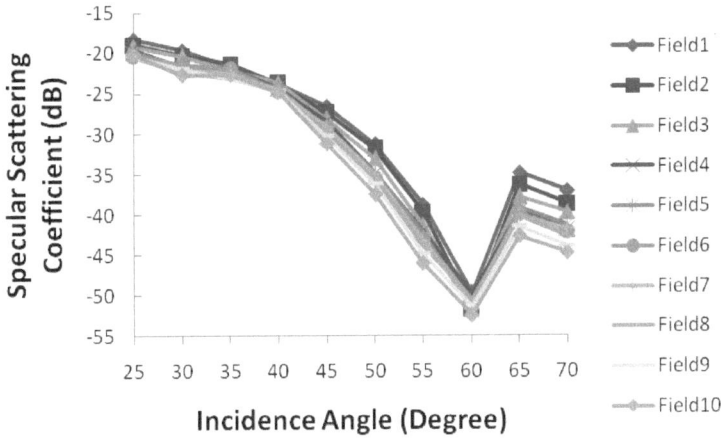

(a)

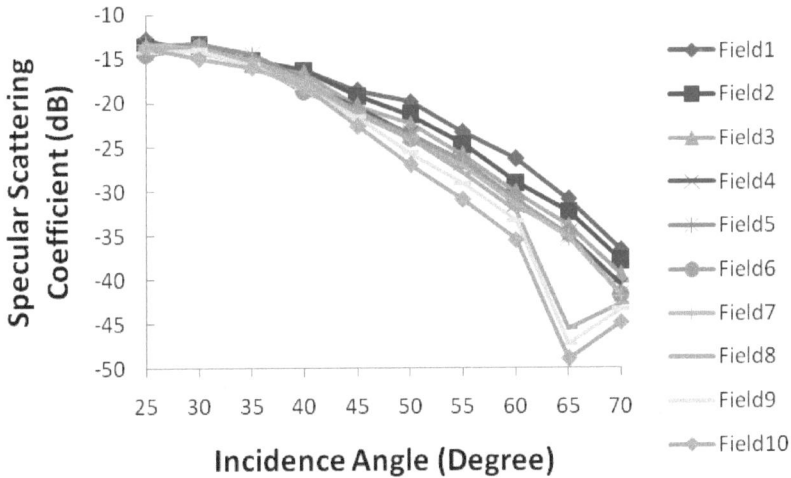

(b)

Fig. (6). Behavour of specular scattering coefficient with incidence angle for different soil texture fields in VV-polarization for smooth surface where (a) volumetric soil moisture content is 0.027 cm^3 cm^{-3}, (b) volumetric soil moisture content is 0.188 cm^3 cm^{-3}[58].

METHODOLOGY FOR RETRIEVAL OF SOIL PARAMETERS

The dependency of the specular scattering coefficient on soil parameters was discussed in the previous sections. Such observations led to the development of the relationship between specular scattering coefficient and soil parameters. This will be a kind of forward relationship which discusses the change in specular scattering coefficient with the change in soil texture, soil moisture and surface roughness and can be modeled based on the empirical developments or theoretical formulations. But, it is always a challenging task to develop an algorithm to retrieve these soil parameters with the knowledge of scattering coefficient. It is a challenging task because several soil parameters depend on single scattering coefficient value.

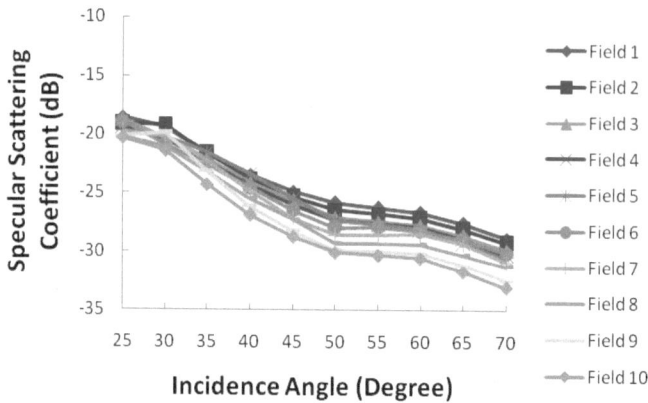

(a)

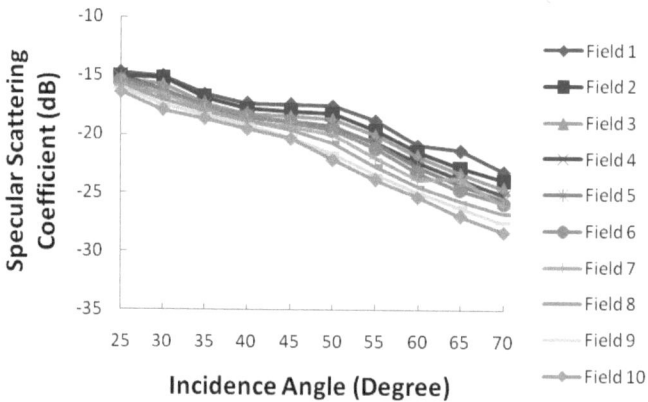

(b)

Fig. (7). Behavour of specular scattering coefficient with incidence angle for different soil texture fields in HH-polarization for volumetric soil moisture content 0.027 cm3 cm-3 where (a) rms surfcace height is 0.43 cm and correlation length is 4.68 cm (b) rms surfcace height is 0.94 cm and correlation length is 5.66 cm [58].

The developed algorithm should be efficient to provide the promising solution for retrieval of soil parameters and at the same time simple enough to apply on the data as well as require less *apriori* information. In following sections we will discuss a multi–incidence angle approach to retrieve the soil parameters with less *apriori* information.

The specular scattering coefficient is a function of a physical and dielectric property of the target, along with the frequency, polarization and incidence angel of the radar. In case of soil as the target, the parameter will be soil texture, soil moisture and surface roughness. To interpret the characteristic of soil texture, soil moisture and surface roughness from the specular scattering coefficient is difficult and generally refereed as ill posed problem. Soil parameters, *i.e.,* soil texture, soil moisture and surface roughness are nature parameter and cannot be controlled therefore, the radar parameter, *i.e.,* frequency, polarization and incidence angle can be optimized to provide the good estimate of soil parameters. In this regard we will discuss an approach that utilizes the multi–incidence angle data to retrieve surface roughness by minimizing the soil texture and soil moisture effect. This retrieved surface roughness values will be subsequently used to estimate soil texture and soil moisture.

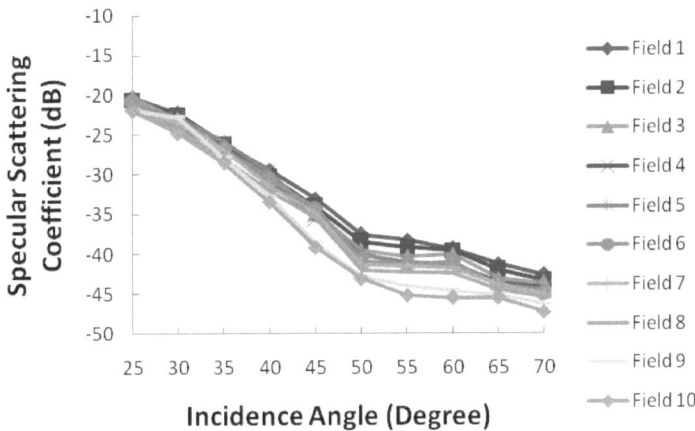

(a)

Fig. 8 cont.....

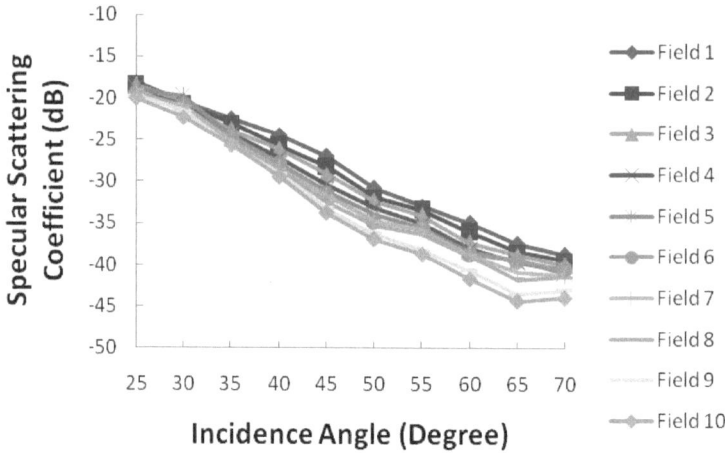

(b)

Fig. (8). Behavour of specular scattering coefficient with incidence angle for different soil texture fields in VV-polarization for volumetric soil moisture content 0.027 cm³ cm⁻³, (a) rms surfcace height is 0.43 cm and correlation length is 4.68 cm (b) rms surfcace height is 0.94 cm and correlation length is 5.66 cm [58].

Kirchhoff Scalar Approximation (SA) for Computation of Specular Scattering Coefficient

Kirchhoff Scalar Approximation can be used to retrieve scattering coefficient from soil surface in specular direction. Fig. (2) shows coordinate system used for scattering geometry. (θ, φ) define the incident direction of the transmitted power $P_p(\theta, \varphi)$ at polarization p, and (θ_s, φ_s) is the direction of the received power $P_q(\theta_s, \varphi_s)$ at polarization q. Following equation is used to evaluate scattering coefficient in specular direction with SA [31].

$$\sigma_{pq} = \sigma_{pqc} + \sigma_{pqn} + \sigma_{pqs} \qquad (16)$$

where σ_{pqc}, σ_{pqn} and σ_{pqs} represent scattering coefficient due to coherent scattering, non–coherent scattering and scattering from surface slope, respectively.

$$\sigma_{pqc} = \pi k^2 |a_\circ|^2 \delta(q_x)\delta(q_y)e^{-q_z^2 s^2} \qquad (17)$$

$$\sigma_{pqn} = \left(|a_{\circ}|kl/2\right)^2 \exp\left(-q_z^2 s^2\right)\sum_n^{\infty}\left(\frac{\left(q_z^2 s^2\right)^n}{n!n}\right)\exp\left(-\frac{\left(q_x^2 + q_y^2\right)l^2}{4n}\right) \qquad (18)$$

$$\sigma_{pqs} = -(ksl)^2\left(q_z/2\right)\exp\left(q_z^2 s^2\right)\mathrm{Re}\left\{a_{\circ}\left(q_x a_1^* + q_y a_2^*\right)\right\}$$
$$\times \sum_{n=1}^{\infty}\left(\frac{\left(q_z^2 s^2\right)^{n-1}}{n!n}\right)\exp\left[-\frac{\left(q_x^2 + q_y^2\right)l^2}{4n}\right] \qquad (19)$$

where k is wave number which is equal to $2\pi/\lambda$, λ is wavelength. s is rms surface height and l is correlation length. $\delta(q_x)$ and $\delta(q_y)$ are Dirac delta functions. $\theta = \theta_s$, $\varphi = 0$ and $\varphi_s = 0$ represent specular scattering.

$$q_x = k\left(\sin\theta_s \cos\varphi_s - \sin\theta\cos\varphi\right) = 0 \qquad (20)$$

$$q_y = k\left(\sin\theta_s \sin\varphi_s - \sin\theta\sin\varphi\right) = 0 \qquad (21)$$

$$q_z = k\left(\cos\theta_s - \cos\theta\right) = 2k\cos\theta \qquad (22)$$

Following equation provides the final expression for specular scattering coefficient.

$$\sigma_{pqc} = \pi k^2|a_{\circ}|^2\delta(0)\delta(0)e^{-q_z^2 s^2} + \left(|a_{\circ}|kl/2\right)^2\exp\left(-(2k\cos\theta)^2 s^2\right)\sum_n^{\infty}\left(\frac{\left((2k\cos\theta)^2 s^2\right)^n}{n!n}\right) \qquad (23)$$

a_o is polarization dependent. In case of HH–polarization a_o is give as

$$a_{\circ} = -R_{\perp\circ}\left(\cos\theta + \cos\theta_s\right)\cos\left(\varphi_s - \varphi\right)$$
$$= -R_{\perp\circ}\left(2\cos\theta\right) = -2R_{\perp\circ}\cos\theta \qquad (24)$$

where $R_{\perp 0}$ is the Fresnel reflection coefficient for horizontal polarization and is given as

$$R_{\perp\circ} = \frac{\cos\theta - \sqrt{\varepsilon - \sin^2\theta}}{\cos\theta + \sqrt{\varepsilon - \sin^2\theta}} \qquad (25)$$

a_o in case of VV–polarization is give as

$$a_{\circ} = R_{\|\circ}\left(\cos\theta + \cos\theta_s\right)\cos(\varphi_s - \varphi)$$
$$= R_{\|\circ}\left(2\cos\theta\right) = 2R_{\|\circ}\cos\theta \qquad (26)$$

where $R_{\|0}$ is the Fresnel reflection coefficient for vertical polarization and is given as

$$R_{\|\circ} = \frac{\varepsilon\cos\theta - \sqrt{\varepsilon - \sin^2\theta}}{\varepsilon\cos\theta + \sqrt{\varepsilon - \sin^2\theta}} \qquad (27)$$

Multi-Incidence Angle Approach to Retrieve Soil Parameters

Scattering coefficient form soil depends on target and sensor parameters. We are discussing soil surface as our target. Dielectric constant of soil and surface roughness are soil parameter which describe the scattering form soil surface. Following function can be written to represent the scattering from soil surface.

$$\sigma^{\circ} = f(\varepsilon)\, g(s, l) \qquad (28)$$

where ε, s and l are dielectric constant of soil, rms surface height and correlation length respectively. The dielectric constant of soil is described based on moisture content in soil and soil texture. Therefore, equation (28) can be modified as

$$\sigma^{\circ} = f(m_v, s, si, c)\, g(s, l) \qquad (29)$$

where s, si and c are sand, silt and clay percentage in soil.

Kirchhoff Scalar Approximation is a well known theoretical model to retrieve scattering coefficient for soil surface. Several studies have validated SA by carrying out the simulation and experimental observations [31, 33, 58].

Fig. (9a) and (9b) show the change in normalized specular scattering coefficient with rms surface height and correlation length respectively. Normalized specular scattering coefficients ($\Delta\sigma^{\circ}$) have been evaluated by taking the ratio of specular scattering coefficient at 45° and 60° incidence angle. These simulations were carried out with the help of Kirchhoff Scalar Approximation. Fig. (9a) shows the behavior of normalized specular scattering coefficient with rms surface height for different dielectric constant values. It can be clearly observed from figure that normalized specular scattering coefficient varies with rms surface height but shows negligible change with respect to the change in soil dielectric constant. These observations imply that we can develop a relationship between normalized specular scattering coefficient and rms surface height without concerning about the value of moisture content in the soil. Based on this developed empirical relationship, rms surface height can be evaluated by having the knowledge of normalized specular scattering coefficient.

Fig. (**9b**) shows the behavior of normalized specular scattering coefficient with correlation length for different soil dielectric constant. Normalized specular scattering coefficient is very less dependent of correlation length. Following section will explain the modeling approach to retrieve soil parameters with the known value of specular scattering coefficient at a different incidence angle and different polarizations.

Modeling Approach

Step 1. Regression analysis will be carried out to determine best sensor parameters (incidence angle and polarization) to analyze the soil parameters. These best sensor parameters will be used as reference parameters.

Step 2. The specular scattering coefficient values at different incidence angles will be normalized with the specular scattering coefficient values at reference incidence angle to evaluate normalized specular scattering coefficient ($\Delta\sigma^\circ$). An empirical relationship will be developed between the $\Delta\sigma^\circ$(dB), s and l.

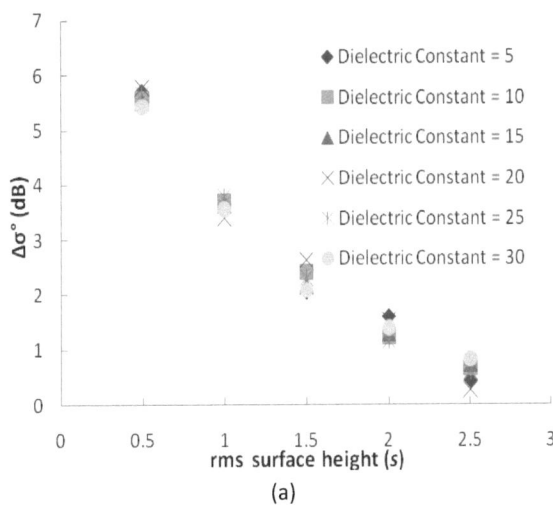

(a)

Fig. 9 cont.....

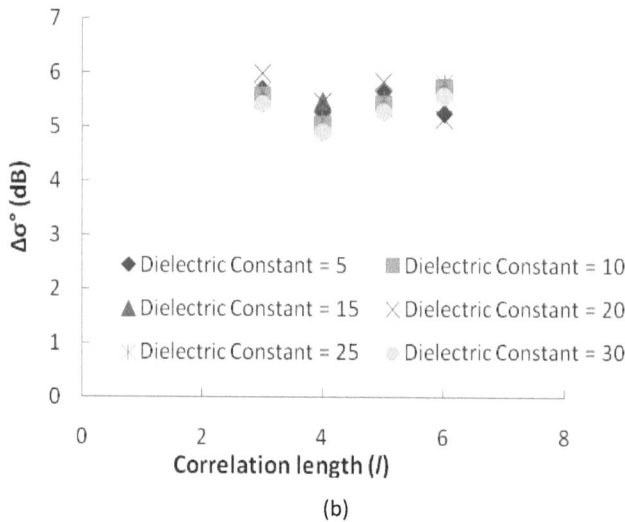

Fig. (9). Simulation result for normalized specular scattering coefficient (a) with rms surface height, s and (b) with correlation length, l. [20].

Step 3. The developed empirical relationship in step 2 will be used to evaluate s and l. These retrieved values will be used to evaluate dielectric constant of soil with the help of Kirchhoff Scalar Approximation.

Step 4. Soil moisture and soil texture will be retrieved by using Hallikainen *et al.* model [39].

Retrieval of Soil Parameters

Step 1: It was observed that specular scattering coefficient varies with sensor parameters and soil parameters. The objective of remote sensing study is to retrieve soil parameters. Therefore, the foremost objective is to decide the sensor parameters which best describe the soil parameters. In this regard, regression analysis can be carried out by considering soil parameters as independent parameter and scattering coefficient as a dependent parameter.

It was observed in various studies that higher incidence angles are more useful than lower incidence angles when the observations are made in the specular direction [20, 33, 58]. In one of the studies, it was shown that 60° is best specular incidence angle to observe soil parameters. This best incidence angle was determined based on regression analysis.

Step 2: $\Delta\sigma°$ (i.e., $\sigma°_{\theta1} - \sigma°_{\theta2}$, where θ_1 is 45°, 50°, 55°, 65°, or 70° and θ_2 is 60°) was evaluated to check the behavior of normalized specular scattering coefficient with surface roughness and soil moisture. In the development phase of the algorithm we have to select some data for developing the algorithm and rest of the date should be used to validate the algorithm. Therefore, observations which were carried out for ten different soil texture fields, five fields were used for algorithm development and the rest of the fields were used for validation. In a similar manner, soil moisture and surface roughness values were used for algorithm development and its validation. During experiment soil moisture was varied from 0.027 to 0.425, rms surface height from 0.43 cm to 2.46 cm and correlation length from 4.47 cm to 5.66 cm.

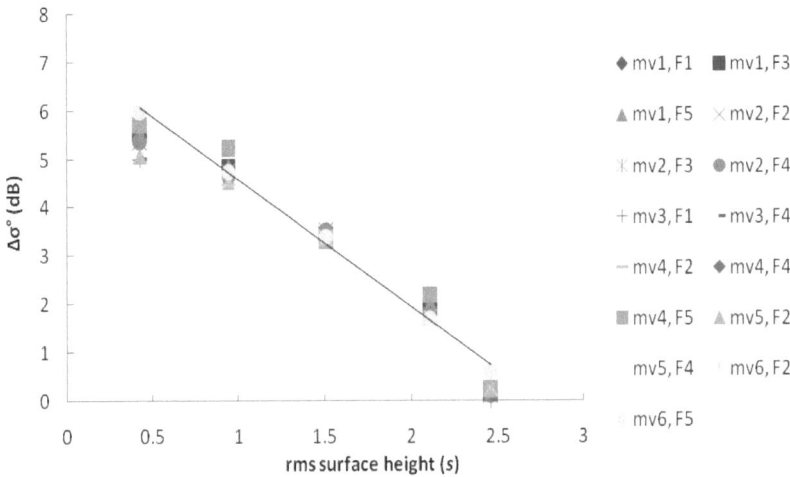

Fig. (10). Response of $\Delta\sigma°$ (dB) for rms surface height when the normalization was performed with 45° [20].

Fig. (**10**) show the change in normalized specular scattering coefficient ($\Delta\sigma°_{45-60}(dB)$) with soil surface roughness at different soil moisture and soil texture. It can be observed from these figures that the normalized specular scattering coefficient varies with the soil surface roughness while there is negligible change in the normalized specular scattering coefficient with the change in soil moisture and soil texture. Similar observations were observed for other normalized specular scattering coefficient normalized at other incident angle. A quadratic relationship between $\Delta\sigma°_{45-60}(dB)$, s and l can be observed which is given as [20].

$$\Delta\sigma°_{45-60}(dB) = a \times s + b \times l^2 + c \qquad (30)$$

where a, b, and c are the empirical constant and the value of a, b, and c are -2.4545, 0.0447 and 5.7387 respectively.

Step 3: Empirical equation developed in step 2 can be solved with any of the optimization approaches such as Nelder–Mead optimization, Gentic Algorithm or least square optimization to provide the value of s and l. The retrieved surface roughness values (s and l) can be used with Kirchhoff Scalar Approximation to retrieve soil dielectric constant. The retrieved s and l values were used in the following equation to evaluate the Fresnel reflection coefficient in HH–polarization.

$$R_{\perp 0} = \frac{1}{2\cos\theta} \times \sqrt{\frac{\sigma_{pqc}}{\pi k^2 \delta(0)\delta(0)e^{-q_z^2 s^2} + (kl/2)^2 \exp\left(-(2k\cos\theta)^2 s^2\right)\sum_{n}^{\infty}\left(\frac{\left((2k\cos\theta)^2 s^2\right)^n}{n!n}\right)}}$$

(31)

Equation 25 (Fresnel reflection coefficient in HH–polarization) was utilized to retrieve the dielectric constant of the soil by substituting the value of $R_{\perp 0}$ retrieved through Equation 31.

Step 4: The empirical relationship developed by the Hallikainen *et al.* is given by Equation 32 [39]. The retrieved soil dielectric constant value in step 4 can be utilized to determine the value of soil moisture and soil texture.

$$\varepsilon = (a_0 + a_1 S + a_2 C) + (b_0 + b_1 S + b_2 C)m_v + (c_0 + c_1 S + c_2 C)m_v^2$$

(32)

where a_i, b_i, and c_i (i=0 to 2) are empirical constants. S and C respectively are sand and clay texture component of soil in percent by weight and m_v is volumetric soil moisture content. The observed ground truth and retrieved value of soil texture, soil moisture and surface roughness are shown in Fig. (**11**).

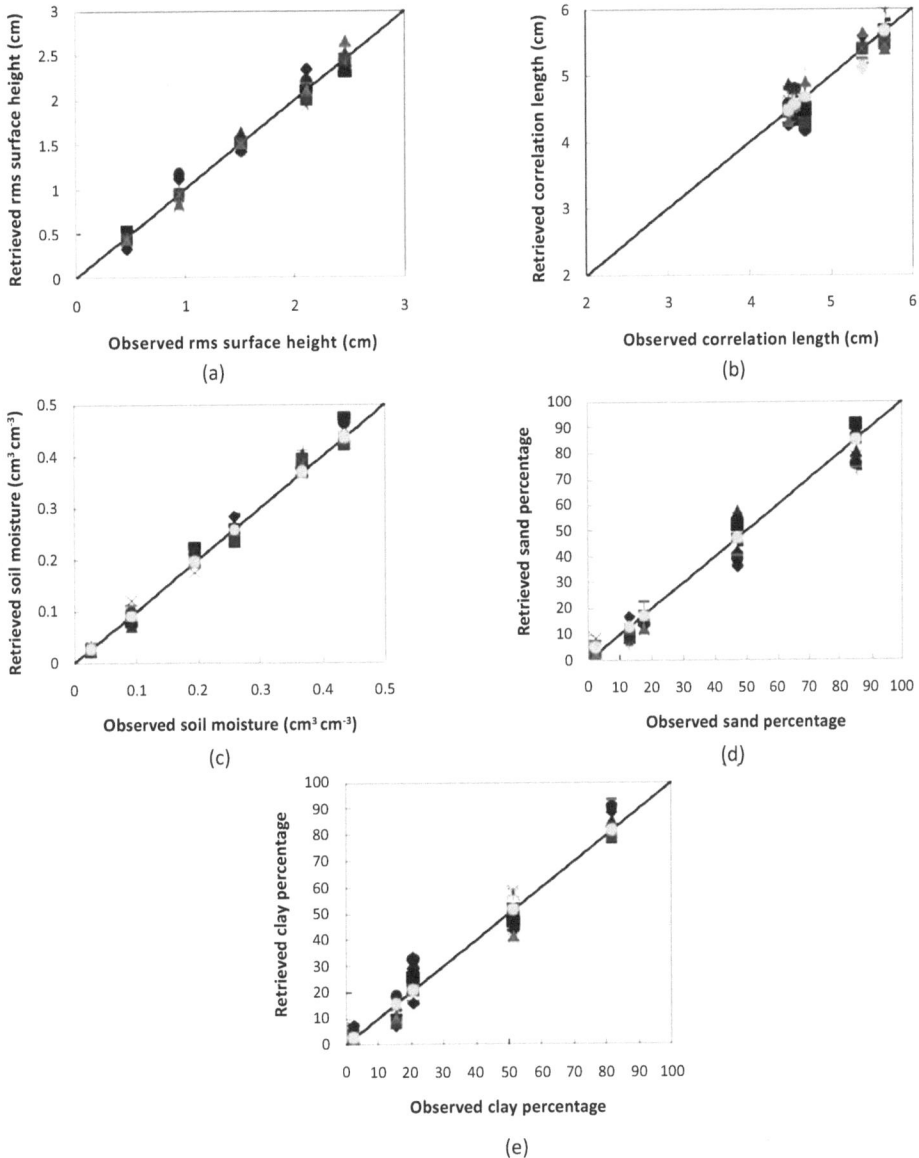

Fig. (11). Observed ground truth verses retrieved values for (a) rms surface height, (b) correlation length, (c) volumetric soil moisture, (d) percentage of sand, and (e) percentage of clay [20].

CONCLUSION

Soil moisture, soil texture and surface roughness are important soil parameters and knowledge of these parameters are needed in various applications. A bistatic scatterometer design has been discussed whose design parameters and related equations are presented in the chapter to determine the specular scattering coefficient. This designed scatterometer can be used to measure specular scattering coefficient for different values of soil parameters. The change in soil parameters can be made artificially. The soil moisture can be changed by properly irrigating the soil fields and surface roughness can be changed with the help of wooden harrow. It was established with the experimental observations and theoretical simulation that specular scattering coefficient is sensitive for the change in soil parameters. Therefore, these changes can be retrieved with the help of observed scattering coefficient at different polarization and incidence angle. A retrieval methodology has been discussed which utilizes the regression analysis to determine best sensor parameters and evaluates normalized specular scattering coefficient. This normalized specular scattering is found to be approximately independent to soil moisture and soil texture and depends on surface roughness only. Kirchhoff Scalar Approximation and Hallikainen model have been used to retrieve soil parameters. There are several other methods to retrieve soil parameters. Sometimes, when the objective is to determine only soil moisture, researchers try to minimize the effect of surface roughness on scattering coefficient by considering the copolarization ratio. Similarly, one can use the optimization technique to retrieve soil parameters. Readers are suggested to go through the references of this chapter to attain more knowledge regarding various methodologies of soil parameter retrieval.

CONSENT FOR PUBLICATION

Not applicable.

CONFLICT OF INTEREST

The author(s) confirm that there is no conflict of interest to declare for this publication.

ACKNOWLEDGEMENT

Authors are thankful to the editor of this book for inviting to write this chapter.

REFERENCES

[1]   W. Wagner, G. Bloschl, P. Panpaloni, J.C. Calvet, B. Bizzarri, J.P. Wigneron, and Y. Kerr, "Operational readiness of microwave remote sensing of soil moisture for hydrology applications", *Nord. Hydrol.,* vol. 38, pp. 1-20.

[2]   N. Pierdicca, L. Pulvirenti, F. Ticconi, and M. Brogioni, "Radar bistatic configuration for soil moisture retrieval: A simulation study", *IEEE Trans. Geosci. Remote Sens.,* vol. 46, pp. 3252-3264.

[3]   F. Bonn, and R. Dixon, "Monitoring flood extent and forecasting excess runoff risk with RADARSAT–1 data", *Nat. Hazards,* vol. 35, pp. 377-393.

[4]   T.J. Jackson, "Remote sensing of soil moisture: implications for groundwater recharge", *Hydrogeol. J.,* vol. 10, pp. 40-51.

[5]   S.K. Kweon, and Y. Oh, "Estimation of soil moisture and surface roughness from single-polarized radar data for bare soil surface and comparison with dual- and quad-polarization cases", *IEEE Trans. Geosci. Remote Sens.,* vol. 52, pp. 4056-4064.

[6]   G.G. Ponnurangam, T. Jagdhuber, I. Hajnsek, and Y.S. Rao, "Soil moisture estimation using hybrid polarimetric SAR data of RISAT-1", *IEEE Trans. Geosci. Remote Sens.,* vol. 56, pp. 2033-2049.

[7]   X. Bai, B. He, and X. Li, "Optimum surface roughness to parameterize advanced Integral Equation Model for soil moisture retrieval in Prairie Area using Radarsat-2 data", *IEEE Trans. Geosci. Remote Sens.,* vol. 54, pp. 2437-2449.

[8]   R. Prakash, D. Singh, and N.P. Pathak, "A fusion approach to retrieve soil moisture with SAR and optical data", *IEEE J. Sel. Top. Appl. Earth Obs. Remote Sens.,* vol. 5, pp. 196-206.

[9]   T.P. Anguela, M. Zribi, N. Baghdadi, and C. Loumagne, "Analysis of local variation of soil surface parameters with TerraSAR–X radar data over bare agriculture fields", *IEEE Trans. Geosci. Remote Sens.,* vol. 48, pp. 874-881.

[10]   N. Baghdadi, O. Cerdan, M. Zribi, V. Auzet, F. Darboux, M. El Hajj, and B.R. Kheir, "Operational performance of current synthetic aperture radar sensors in mapping soil surface characteristic in agricultural environments: application to hydrological and erosion modeling", *Hydrol. Processes,* vol. 22, pp. 9-20.

[11]   D.G. Blumberg, G. Ronen, J. Ben–Asher, V. Freilikher, L.D. Vulfson, and A.L. Kotlyard, "Utilizing a P–band scatterometer to assess soil water saturation percent of a bare sandy soil", *J. Hydrol. (Amst.),* vol. 318, pp. 374-378.

[12]   M.W.J. Davidson, T. Le Toan, F. Mattia, G. Satalino, T. Manninen, and M. Borgeaud, "On the characterization of agricultural soil roughness for radar remote sensing studies", *IEEE Trans. Geosci. Remote Sens.,* vol. 38, pp. 630-640.

[13]   Y. Du, F.T. Ulaby, and M.C. Dobson, "Sensitivity to soil moisture by active and passive microwave sensors", *IEEE Trans. Geosci. Remote Sens.,* vol. 38, pp. 105-114.

[14]   E.T. Eangman, and N. Chauhan, "Status of microwave soil moisture measurements with remote sensing", *Remote Sens. Environ.,* vol. 51, pp. 189-198.

[15]   N. Holah, N. Baghdadi, M. Zribi, A. Bruand, and C. King, "Potential of ASAR/ENVISAT for the characterization of soil surface parameters over bare agricultural fields", *Remote Sens. Environ.,* vol. 96, pp. 78-86.

[16]   K. Saleh, Y.H. Kerr, P. Richaume, M.J. Escorihuela, R. Panciera, S. Delwart, G. Boulet, P. Maisongrande, J.P. Walker, P. Wursteisen, and J.P. Wigneron, "Soil moisture retrievals at L–band using a two–step inversion approach (COSMOS/NAFE'05 Experiment)", *Remote Sens. Environ.,* vol. 113, pp. 1304-1312.

[17]   D. Singh, and A. Kathpalia, "An efficient modeling with GA approach to retrieve soil texture, moisture and roughness from ERS–2 SAR data", *Prog. Electromagnetics Res.,* vol. 77, pp. 121-136.

[18]   Z. Aly, F.J. Bonn, and R. Magagi, "Analysis of the backscattering coefficient of salt–affected soils using modeling and RADARSAT–1 SAR data", *IEEE Trans. Geosci. Remote Sens.,* vol. 45, pp. 332-341.

[19]   R. Tiwari, R.K. Singh, D.S. Chauhan, O.P. Singh, R. Prakash, and D. Singh, "Microwave scattering for soil texture at X-Band and its retrieval using Genetic Algorithm", *Advances in Remote Sensing,* vol. 3, pp. 120-127.

[20]   R. Prakash, D. Singh, and O.P. Singh, "Multi-incident angle approach to retrieve soil parameters for specular scattering", *IET Radar Sonar & Navigation,* vol. 3, pp. 560-568.

[21] A. Beaudoin, T.L. Toan, and Q.H.J. Gwyn, "SAR observations and modeling of the C–band backscatter variability due to multiscale geometry and soil moisture", *IEEE Trans. Geosci. Remote Sens.*, vol. 28, pp. 886-895.

[22] I. Champion, "Simple modeling of radar backscattering coefficient over a bare soil: variation with incidence angle, frequency and polarization", *Int. J. Remote Sens.*, vol. 17, pp. 783-800.

[23] P.C. Dubois, J.V. Zyl, and T. Engam, "Measuring soil moisture with imaging radars", *IEEE Trans. Geosci. Remote Sens.*, vol. 33, pp. 915-926.

[24] A.K. Fung, Z. Lee, and K.S. Chen, "Backscattering from randomly rough dielectric surface", *IEEE Trans. Geosci. Remote Sens.*, vol. 30, pp. 356-369.

[25] A. Loew, and W. Mauser, "A semiempirical surface backscattering model for bare soil surfaces based on a generalized power law spectrum approach", *IEEE Trans. Geosci. Remote Sens.*, vol. 44, pp. 1022-1035.

[26] R. Prakash, D. Singh, and N.P. Pathak, "Microwave specular scattering response of soil texture at X–band", *Adv. Space Res.*, vol. 44, pp. 801-814.

[27] Y. Wang, S. Wang, S. Yang, L. Zhang, H. Zeng, and D. Zheng, "Using a remote sensing driven model to analyze effect of land use on soil moisture in the Weihe river basin, China", *IEEE J. Sel. Top. Appl. Earth Obs. Remote Sens.*, vol. 7, pp. 3892-3902.

[28] M. Aubert, N.N. Baghdadi, M. Zribi, K. Ose, M. El Hajj, E. Vaudour, and E. Gonzalez-Sosa, "Toward an operational bare soil moisture mapping using TerraSAR-X data acquired over agricultural areas", *IEEE J. Sel. Top. Appl. Earth Obs. Remote Sens.*, vol. 6, pp. 900-916.

[29] Y. Oh, K. Sarabandi, and F.T. Ulaby, "An empirical modal and an inversion technique for radar scattering from bare soil surfaces", *IEEE Trans. Geosci. Remote Sens.*, vol. 30, pp. 370-381.

[30] D. Singh, "A Simplistic incidence angle approach to retrieve the soil moisture and surface roughness at X–Band", *IEEE Trans. Geosci. Remote Sens.*, vol. 43, pp. 2606-2611.

[31] F.T. Ulaby, R.K. Moore, and A.K. Fung, *Microwave remote sensing–active and passive–vol. 2.*, 1st ed Addison Wesley Publishing Company: Boston, USA, 1982, pp. 922-966.

[32] P.D. Fernandez, H. Cantalloube, B. Vaizan, G. Krieger, and A. Moreira, *Airborne bistatic synthetic aperture radar. In Bistatic Radar: Emerging technology.*. John Wiley & Sons Ltd.: West Sussex, 2008, pp. 159-210.

[33] A.Y. Nashashibi, and F.T. Ulaby, "MMW polarimetric radar bistatic scattering from a random surface", *IEEE Trans. Geosci. Remote Sens.*, vol. 45, pp. 1743-1755.

[34] R.D. Magagi, and Y.H. Kerr, "Estimating surface soil moisture and soil roughness over semiarid areas from the use of the copolarization ratio", *Remote Sens. Environ.*, vol. 75, pp. 432-445.

[35] M.M. Rahman, M.S. Moran, D.P. Thoma, R. Bryant, C.D.H. Collins, T. Jackson, B.J. Orr, and M. Tischler, "Mapping surface roughness and soil moisture and moisture using multi–angle radar imagery without ancillary data", *Remote Sens. Environ.*, vol. 112, pp. 391-402.

[36] M. Zribi, N. Baghdadi, N. Holah, and O. Fafin, "New methodology for soil surface moisture estimation and its application to ENVISAT–ASAR multi–incident data inversion", *Remote Sens. Environ.*, vol. 96, pp. 485-496.

[37] H.S. Srivastava, P. Patel, and R.R. Navalgund, "Incorporating soil texture in soil moisture estimation from extended low–1 beam mode RADARSAT–1 SAR data", *Int. J. Remote Sens.*, vol. 27, pp. 2587-2598.

[38] D. Wal, P.M.J. Herman, and A.W. Dool, "Characterization of surface roughness and sediment texture of intertidal flats using ERS SAR imagery", *Remote Sens. Environ.*, vol. 98, pp. 96-109.

[39]   M.T. Hallikainen, F.T. Ulaby, M.C. Dobson, M.A. El–Rayes, and L. Wu, "Microwave dielectric behavior of wet soil–Part I: empirical models and experimental observations", *IEEE Trans. Geosci. Remote Sens.,* vol. 23, pp. 25-34.

[40]   V.L. Mironov, M.C. Dobson, V.H. Kaupp, S.A. Komarov, and V.N. Kleshchenko, "Generalized refractive mixing dielectric model for moist soils", *IEEE Trans. Geosci. Remote Sens.,* vol. 42, pp. 773-785.

[41]   A.K. Sahoo, E.F. Wood, A. Al Bitar, D. Leroux, and Y.H. Kerr, "An initial assessment of SMOS derived soil moisture over the continental United States Ming Pan", *IEEE J. Sel. Top. Appl. Earth Obs. Remote Sens.,* vol. 5, pp. 1448-1457.

[42]   X. Shen, K. Mao, Q. Qin, Y. Hong, and G. Zhang, "Bare surface soil moisture estimation using double-angle and dual-polarization L-band radar data", *IEEE Trans. Geosci. Remote Sens.,* vol. 51, pp. 3931-3942.

[43]   K.C. Kornelsen, and P. Coulibaly, "Design of an optimal soil moisture monitoring network using SMOS retrieved soil moisture", *IEEE Trans. Geosci. Remote Sens.,* vol. 53, pp. 3950-3959.

[44]   J.R. Wang, and T.J. Schmugge, "An empirical model for the complex dielectric permittivity of soil as a function of water content", *IEEE Trans. Geosci. Remote Sens.,* vol. 18, pp. 288-295.

[45]   Y. Oh, "Quantitative retrieval of soil moisture content and roughness from multipolarized radar observation of bare soil surface", *IEEE Trans. Geosci. Remote Sens.,* vol. 42, pp. 596-601.

[46]   O. Bolognani, M. Mancini, and R. Rosso, "Soil moisture profiles from multi frequency radar data at basin scale", *Meccanica,* vol. 31, pp. 59-72.

[47]   D. Kuria, L. Hui, T. Koike, H. Tsutsui, and T. Graf, "Multi–frequency response to periodic roughness", *IEEE International Geoscience and Remote Sensing Symposium,* 2006pp. 1744-1747

[48]   F. Mattia, T.L. Toan, J.C. Souyris, G.D. Carolis, N. Floury, F. Posa, and G. Pasquariello, "The effect of surface roughness on multifrequency polarimetric SAR data", *IEEE Trans. Geosci. Remote Sens.,* vol. 35, pp. 954-966.

[49]   R. Bryant, M.S. Moran, D.P. Thoma, C.D.H. Collins, S. Skirvin, M. Rahman, K. Slocum, P. Starks, D. Bosch, and M.P. González–Dugo, "Measuring surface roughness height to parameterize radar backscatter models for retrieval of surface soil moisture", *IEEE Trans. Geosci. Remote Sens.,* vol. 4, pp. 137-141.

[50]   M. Callens, N.E.C. Verhoest, and M.W. Davidson, "Parameterization of tillage–induced single–scale soil roughness from 4–m profiles", *IEEE Trans. Geosci. Remote Sens.,* vol. 44, pp. 878-888.

[51]   M.W.J. Davidson, F. Mattia, G. Satalino, N.E.C. Verhoest, T. Le Toan, M. Borgeaud, J.M.B. Louis, and E. Attema, "Joint statistical properties of RMS height and correlation length derived from multisite 1–m roughness measurements", *IEEE Trans. Geosci. Remote Sens.,* vol. 41, pp. 1651-1658.

[52]   G. Franceschetti, A. Iodice, S. Maddaluno, and D. Riccio, "A fractal–based theoretical framework for retrieval of surface parameters from electromagnetic backscattering data", *IEEE Trans. Geosci. Remote Sens.,* vol. 38, pp. 641-650.

[53]   G. Mittal, and D. Singh, "Critical analysis of microwave scattering response on roughness parameter and moisture content for periodic rough surfaces and its retrieval", *Prog. Electromagnetics Res.,* vol. 100, pp. 129-152.

[54]   Y. Oh, "Effect of surface profile length on the backscattering coefficients of bare surfaces", *IEEE Trans. Geosci. Remote Sens.,* vol. 45, pp. 632-638.

[55]   M.M. Rahman, M.S. Moran, D.P. Thoma, R. Bryant, E.E. Sano, C.D.H. Collins, S. Skirvin, C. Kershner, and B.J. Orr, "A derivation of roughness correlation length for parameterizing radar backscatter models", *Int. J. Remote Sens.,* vol. 18, pp. 3995-4012.

[56]   T. Pant, D. Singh, and T. Srivastava, "The potential application of fractal approach for surface roughness retrieval: A study for simulated surfaces", *Geomatics Nat. Hazards Risk,* vol. 1, pp. 243-257.

[57]   R.N. Trebits, Radar cross section.*Radar reflectivity measurement: Technique and Applications..* Artech House: Norwood, MA, 1989, pp. 51-59.

[58]   R. Prakash, D. Singh, and N.P. Pathak, "The effect of soil texture in soil moisture retrieval for specular scattering at C–band", *Prog. Electromagnetics Res.,* vol. 108, pp. 177-204.

CHAPTER 8

Multi-Objective Non-Linear Programming Problem for Reliability Optimization in Intuitionistic Fuzzy Environment

Harish Garg*

School of Mathematics, Thapar Institute of Engineering & Technology (Deemed University) Patiala – 147004, Punjab, India

Abstract: In this chapter, multi-objective reliability-cost optimization problems have been investigated by utilizing uncertain, vague and imprecise information. During the formulation, a reliability of each component of the system is represented in the form of the triangular interval. The conflicting nature of the objectives is resolved with the help of intuitionistic fuzzy programming technique by recognizing the linear, as well as non-linear membership functions. A crisp model is formulated by using a product aggregation operator to aggregate their expected values. The resultant problem is solved with a gravitational search algorithm (GSA) and compared their results with the particle swarm optimization (PSO) and genetic algorithm (GA). Results are validated through a statistical simulation of the t-test.

Keywords: Bi-objective optimization, Gravitational search algorithm, Intuitionistic fuzzy set, Membership functions, Particle swarm optimization, Reliability-cost optimization.

INTRODUCTION

With the growing complexity of industrial systems, it is difficult for the decision makers to get an accurate decision within a predefined accuracy. In order to maintain the performance of the systems, reliability is one of the important factors. Reliability is measured as the ability of a system to perform its intended function, successfully, for a specified period, under predetermined conditions.

This attribute has far-reaching consequences on the durability, availability, and life cycle cost of a product or system and is of great importance to the end user/engineer. Typically, high-reliability targets or specifications are set for the

---

*Corresponding author Harish Garg: School of Mathematics, Thapar Institute of Engineering & Technology (Deemed University) Patiala – 147004, Punjab, India; Tel: + 9186990-31147; E-mail: harishg58iitr@gmail.com

Mangey Ram (Ed.)

system, and ways to achieve them are then examined, taking into account resource constraints. Apart from the limitations of resources, the targets set may be in dispute. For instance, high reliability generally means a high cost, weight, and volume. For a given system configuration, the individual components may have different levels of reliability and associated costs; or different component combinations [1, 2]. Thus, there is a need to optimize these parameters and formulate a general reliability optimization problem as given below.

$$Maximize \quad f(r_1, r_2, \ldots, r_m)$$
$$subject \ to \ g_j(r_1, r_2, \ldots, r_m) \leq 0 \quad ; j = 1, 2, \ldots, M$$
$$r_i^l \leq r_i \leq r_i^u \quad ; i = 1, 2, \ldots, m \tag{1}$$

This formulation is generally a continuous non-linear optimization problem, since f and g_j are typically nonlinear functions expressed in terms of the reliability of m component of a system, and the decision vector $[r_1, r_2, \ldots, r_m]^T$ is composed of continuous values representing the reliability of m components. The ith component reliability is bounded below and above by r_i^l & r_i^u. Thus, in the present scenario of global competition and faster delivery times, there is a growing interest in implementation and investigation of reliability principles for industrial systems. This study uses the tool of reliability simulation to present new work in the area of the reliability.

RELATED WORK AND BACKGROUND

In this section, a brief literature review regarding reliability analysis under optimization and the fuzzy environment is given. The gaps from literature review are also addressed in it.

Analysis Using Evolutionary Algorithms

A number of algorithms (classical and stochastic) - also categorized as approximate, exact or heuristic/meta-heuristic- have been used to find optimal solutions to the above nonlinear problems whose comprehensive analysis has been summarized in [3, 4]. But it has been observed that traditional algorithms require derivative for all constraints functions for system performance. However, for effective implementation of these methods, the variables and cost function of the generators need to be continuous. Furthermore, a good starting point is vital for these methods to be executed successfully. As an alternative to the conventional mathematical approaches, the meta-heuristic optimization techniques have been used to obtain global or near-global optimum solutions. Due to their capability of exploring and finding promising regions in the search space at an affordable time, these methods are quite suitable for global searches and furthermore alleviate the need for continuous cost functions and variables used for mathematical optimization methods. Though these are approximate methods, *i.e.*, their solution is good, but not necessarily optimal, they do not require the derivatives of the objective function and constraints and employ probabilistic transition rules instead of deterministic ones. Therefore, researchers focus on the heuristic technique that seeks the good promising solution within a reasonable time [5]. However, hybrid techniques have been used for increasing the computational efficiency, hybrid optimization algorithms have been used by achieving their individual's advantages, simultaneously. In order to avoid it, a variety of nature-inspired algorithms namely genetic algorithms (GAs) [6, 7], Particle Swarm Optimization (PSO) [8-10], Artificial Bee Colony (ABC) [11-12], Gravitational search algorithms (GSA) [13], Biogeography-based Optimization (BBO) [14] and Cuckoo search (CS) [15, 16] are convenient to solve complex computational problems in the field of reliability optimization problems during the past years.

To list a few, Coit and Smith [17] were the first to employ a genetic algorithm to solve reliability optimization problems. Later, Ravi *et al.* [18] developed an improved version of non-equilibrium simulated annealing called INESA and applied it to solve a variety of reliability optimization problems. Further, Ravi *et al.* [19] first formulated various complex system reliability optimization problems with single and multi-objective as fuzzy global optimization problems. Juang *et al.* [20] proposed a genetic algorithm based optimization model to optimize the availability for a series-parallel system where the objective is to determine the most economical policy of the component's mean time between failures and to repair. Coelho [8] presented an efficient PSO algorithm based on Gaussian distribution and chaotic sequence to solve the reliability-redundancy optimization problems. Rajpal *et al.* [21] explored the application of artificial neural networks to model the behavior of a complex, repairable system. A composite measure of reliability, availability, and maintainability (RAM) parameters called as the RAM - Index has been proposed for measuring the system performance by simultaneously considers all the three key indices which influence the system performance directly. Their index was static in nature, while Garg *et al.* [22, 23] introduced RAM-Index which was time-dependent and used historical uncertain data for its evolution.

Yeh *et al.* [24] proposed a particle swarm optimization based on the Monte Carlo Simulation approach to solving the complex network reliability optimization problems by minimizing the cost of components that constituted the network under reliability constraints. Garg and Sharma [25] had discussed the two-phase approach for analyzing the reliability and maintainability analysis of the industrial system. Garg *et al.* [26] have solved the reliability optimization problem with ABC algorithm and compared their performance with other evolutionary algorithms. For more details about the application and methodology of an evolutionary algorithm in the field of various optimization problems, we may refer [27-35].

Analysis Using Fuzzy Set Theory

Engineering systems are usually complex, involve a lot of detail, and operate in unpredictable environments thus making the job of system analysts more challenging, as they have to study, characterize, measure and analyze the uncertain systems' behavior, using various techniques, which require the component failure and repair pattern. Further, age, adverse operating conditions and the vagaries of the system, affect each unit of the system differently. Thus, one comes across the problem of uncertainty in reliability assessment. Now, in order to solve these types of nonlinear optimization problems, various researchers have assumed that the reliability of each component is a precise number which lies between zero and one. Also, in a classical optimization model, the system and element lifetimes are assumed to be random variables and the system performance, such as system reliability is evaluated by using the probability theory. Unfortunately, these assumptions are not appropriate in a wide range of situations. In many practical cases, the probability distribution function of the system and element lifetimes may be unknown or partially known. In fact, from a practical viewpoint, the fuzziness and randomness of the element lifetimes are often mixed up with each other. So one may consider ambiguous situations such as vague parameters, non-exact objectives and constraint functions in the problem. Due to these limitations, the result based on probability theory does not always provide useful information to the practitioners and hence the probabilistic approach to the conventional reliability analysis is inadequate to account for such built-in uncertainties in the data. To overcome these difficulties, methodologies based on fuzzy set theory [36] are being used in the risk analysis for propagating the basic event uncertainty. Due to incomplete and uncertain input information, mathematical models of such problems are developed in a fuzzy environment and the optimization problem under consideration becomes a fuzzy programming problem. Much successful applications of the optimization using fuzzy set theory has been reported in the literature [37 – 41] and their corresponding references in reliability optimization problems.

After their successful application of the fuzzy set theory in the field of optimization, several researchers are engaged in their extension. Since the above authors have considered only the degree of acceptance region during the analysis, but during an analysis, an equivalent degree of rejection plays a dominant role during the performance evaluation. This concept has been introduced by Atanassov [42] by extending the fuzzy set theory to intuitionistic fuzzy set (IFS) theory by adding a degree of rejection (non-membership) into the analysis. In that direction, Garg [43] had analyzed the performance of an industrial system by using a fuzzy confidence interval to handle the uncertainties in the data while PSO algorithm has been used to optimize their performance. Garg [44], further, analyzed the reliability of the series-parallel system in which IFS theory has been used for representing the data while PSO has been used for optimizing their membership function by formulating a nonlinear optimization model. In the last two decades, IFS theory has been extensively investigated in the field of reliability optimization problems which have been proven to be highly useful to deal with uncertainties and vagueness [45 – 53] and their corresponding references. Most of the authors have attempted to solve the problem as a single objective. However, the real-world problems are multidimensional and multi-objective which are often non-commensurable and conflict with each other in the optimization problem [54]. For handling such types of situations, one usually tries to search for a solution which is as close to the decision makers (DMs) expectations as possible. For this,

(i)   The problem has been solved interactive manner in which DM is initially asked to specify his or her preferences towards the objective functions.
(ii)   Based on the DM preferences, the problems have been solved and provided a possible solution.

But, during their evaluation one may tackle the problem of not getting the sufficient statistical data and hence one has to consider the situations where parameters are imprecise. Moreover, any unfortunate consequences of the unreliable behavior of such equipment or systems have led to the desire for reliability analysis. Therefore, if we consider the data as such during the analysis, then it contains a lot of uncertainties. To overcome these difficulties and to represent the data in more compromise way,

(i)   one may represent the same by interval-valued number as this representation is more appropriate among other existing representations, like a random variable representing with a known probability distribution, fixed interval value *etc.*

(ii)   Due to this, the objective functions are expressed in the form of interval numbers whose target is to maximize it.

Thus, the motivation of the work presented here is to furnish a method for solving multi-objective reliability optimization problems of a series-parallel system, under intuitionistic fuzzy set environment, in which the decision variables may have real or integer values. Keeping all the above facts in the mind, the major contribution of the present work is compiled as below.

(i)   Reliability of each component of the system has been represented in the form of a triangular fuzzy number (TFN) using the decision makers parameter I. This representation is more appropriate among other existing representations, like a random variable representing with a known probability distribution, and a fixed interval value.

(ii)   The conflicting nature of the objectives is resolved by defining the membership and non-membership functions using exponential and parabolic functions respectively.

(iii)   Due to this representation, the objective functions are in the form of interval numbers and hence their corresponding optimization problem becomes interval-valued intuitionistic fuzzy optimization problem.

(iv)   A crisp optimization problem has been formulated by considering the product operator for the degree of satisfaction of each objective and hence solves with the meta-heuristic algorithms for finding the global optimal solution and compared their results with the other existing algorithms result.

(v)   Series of reliability-cost optimization problems have been considered for demonstrating the interactive approach in which DMs have asked their preferences towards the objective in terms of their reliability interval parameter I.

ACRONYMS AND NOTATIONS

Acronyms

GSA Gravitational search algorithm.
PSOParticle swarm optimization.
GA Genetic algorithm.

DM Decision maker.
IFS Intuitionistic fuzzy set.
IFO Intuitionistic fuzzy optimization.
IFN Intuitionistic fuzzy number.
TFN Triangular fuzzy number.
EV Expected value.
MOOP Multi-objective optimization problem.

Notations

Considering m -subsystems in the system, following notations have been used for the ith subsystems $(i = 1,2,\ldots,m)$.

Mnumber of constraints.

r_i reliability of each of the components in i^{th} subsystem.

$r = (r_1,r_2,\ldots,r_m)$, the vector of component reliabilities for the system.

g_j the jth constraint function, $j = 1,2,\ldots,M$.

x_i^l lower value of each of the component's in i^{th} subsystem.

x_i^u upper value of each of the component's in i^{th} subsystem.

R_s, C_s the system reliability and cost respectively.

b number of objective functions.

S feasible search space.

$\widetilde{A}$ fuzzy set.

$\mu_{\widetilde{A}}$ membership functions of the fuzzy set $\widetilde{A}$.

$v_{\widetilde{A}}$ non- membership functions of the fuzzy set $\widetilde{A}$.

rand random number between 0 and 1.

PROBLEM   FORMULATION: RELIABILITY-OPTIMIZATION PROBLEM

Formulation of the Mathematical Model

In general, reliability optimization problem has been solved by assuming that the reliability of each component of the system is lies between zero and one in all conditions. Further, the causes may be aging, adverse operating conditions and the vagaries of manufacturing processes which affect each part/unit of the system differently, and thus the issue is subject to uncertainty. To address aforementioned, a fuzzy reliability optimization model is formulated as below.

Maximize $\tilde{R}_s(\tilde{r})$ & Minimize $\tilde{C}_s(\tilde{r})$

subject to : $g(\tilde{r}) \leq b$

$$0.5 \leq r_i \leq 1 - 10^{-6} \; ; i = 1,2,\ldots,m, \; r_i \in [0,1] \subset R \tag{2}$$

Here, $\tilde{R}_s, \tilde{C}_s$ and $\tilde{r}_i$ are defined in fuzzy numbers. Since reliability of a component/system depends on operational and environmental conditions and thus it is not possible to determine a fixed number that lies, between zero and one. Therefore, in order to handle the inaccurate parameter specified to the reliability, we have considered the reliability of each component as a TFN *i.e.*, $r_i = [a_i, b_i, c_i]$ (say) where $a_i = r_i - 1$, $b_i = r_i$ and $c_i = r_i + 1$ are the reliability of the ith component in a triangular fuzzy number and l is the triangular fuzzy function parameters of the corresponding reliability. Based on these TFNs and the structure component of the system, the system function expressions have been expressed in form of TFN. Thus reliability of each subsystem is obtained as

$$\tilde{r}_i = [r_i - 1, r_i, r_i + 1]$$

These triangular fuzzy numbers are converted to a crisp number by using the concept of expected value (EV). The expected value of system reliability $\tilde{R}_s = [A, B, C]$ is given as

$$EV_{\tilde{R}_s} = \frac{A + 2B + C}{4} \tag{3}$$

Since the cost of each component is related to its reliability and thus cost of each component, subsystem and system are in the form of the triangular fuzzy number. Therefore their system expected value $\tilde{C}_s = [D, E, F]$ is given by

$$EV_{\tilde{C}_s} = \frac{D + 2E + F}{4} \tag{4}$$

Thus in fuzzy environment, the original multi-objective reliability optimization model (2) becomes

$$\text{Maximize } EV(\tilde{R}_s) \quad \& \quad \text{Minimize } EV(\tilde{C}_s)$$

$$\text{subject to}: \quad g(\tilde{r}) \underset{\approx}{\leq} b$$

$$0.5 \leq r_i \leq 1 - 10^{-6} \quad ; i = 1, 2, \ldots, m, \quad r_i \in [0,1] \subset R \tag{5}$$

where ' $\approx$ ' indicates ambiguity.

Solution Procedure

In order to solve the above-formulated problem, the conflicts nature between the objects is handled with the help of defining the region of satisfaction using a degree of membership and non-membership functions. Finally, the so obtained objective functions are aggregated by using product aggregation operator for obtaining the optimal values of system reliability parameters. The steps for conducting the analysis have been summarized as follows.

Step 1: *Finding the ideal and anti-ideal values:* For a multi-objective nonlinear programming, considering the vague or fuzzy nature of human judgments, it is quite natural to assume that the DM may have a fuzzy goal for each of the objective function $f_t(x)$, $t = 1, 2, \ldots, b$ and b is the number of objective functions. In minimization problem, the fuzzy goal stated by the DM may be to achieve "substantially less than or equal to some value p_t". Such a fuzzy goal of the DM can be quantified by eliciting the corresponding membership function through the interaction with the DM. Here, for simplicity, the quadratic membership function is assumed for representing the fuzzy goal of the DM,

$$\mu_{f_t}(x) = \begin{cases} 0 & ; f_t(x) > f_t^0 \\ \left(\dfrac{f_t(x) - f_t^0}{f_t^1 - f_t^0} \right)^2 & ; f_t^0 \leq f_t(x) \leq f_t^1 \\ 1 & ; f_t(x) < f_t^1 \end{cases}$$

where f_t^0 and f_t^1 denotes the value of objective function f_t whose degree of membership function are 0 and 1, respectively. These values are subjectively determined through an interaction with the DM. As one of the possible way to help the DM determine f_t^0 and f_t^1, it is convenient to calculate the individual minimum m_t and maximum values M_t of each objective function under the given set of the constraint *i.e.*,

$$m_t = \min_{1 \le q \le b} f_t(x_q^*) \quad \text{and} \quad M_t = \max_{1 \le q \le b} f_t(x_q^*)$$

where x_q^*, $1 \le q \le b$ are the solutions obtained by solving the multi-objective optimization problem as a single objective cost function using one objective at a time and ignoring all the others. Then by taking account of the calculated individual minimum and maximum of each objective function, the DM is asked to access f_t^0 and f_t^1 in the closed interval $[m_t, M_t]$.

Step 2: *Formulation of the membership functions:* Based on these ideal and anti-ideal values, a fuzzy region of satisfaction has been constructed corresponding to each objective function. For this, a non-linear membership function has been used by taking exponential and quadratic functions corresponding to define the degree of acceptance and rejection respectively as follows.

$$\mu_{f_t}(x) = \begin{cases} 1 & ; f_t(x) \le m_t \\ \dfrac{\exp\left(-w\left(\dfrac{f_t(x) - m_t}{M_t - m_t}\right)\right) - \exp(-w)}{1 - \exp(-w)} & ; m_t \le f_t(x) \le M_t \\ 0 & ; f_t(x) \ge M_t \end{cases} \tag{6}$$

and

$$v_{f_t}(x) = \begin{cases} 0 & ; f_t(x) \le m_t \\ \left(\dfrac{f_t(x) - m_t}{M_t - m_t}\right)^2 & ; m_t \le f_t(x) \le M_t \\ 1 & ; f_t(x) \ge M_t \end{cases} \tag{7}$$

Step 3: *Aggregating the objective functions:* Corresponding to each objective function, the degree of satisfaction is given by $\eta_{f_j} = \mu_{f_j} - v_{f_j}$ and hence the dissatisfaction of each objective is defined as $\xi_{f_j} = 1 - \eta_{f_j}$. After obtaining the satisfaction functions of each objective, the overall satisfaction function of the objective $\eta(f)$ is expressed, by using a product operator, as a function of $b-$ sub-objectives for converting the original fuzzy problem into an equivalent crisp (non-fuzzy) model in the form as follows:

$$\text{Maximize } \eta(f) = \prod_{j=1}^{b} \eta_{f_j}$$

$$subject\ to : \mu_{f_j}(x) \geq \alpha$$

$$v_{f_j}(x) \leq \beta$$

$$\alpha \geq \beta\ ;\ \alpha + \beta \leq 1\ ;\ \alpha, \beta \geq 0 \tag{8}$$

where α denotes the minimal degree of acceptable and β denotes the maximal degree of rejection of objective(s) and constraints which can be written in the form

$$\text{Maximize } \eta(f) = \prod_{j=1}^{b} \eta_{f_j}$$

$$subject\ to : \frac{\exp\left(-w\left(\frac{f_t(x) - m_t}{M_t - m_t}\right)\right) - \exp(-w)}{1 - \exp(-w)} \geq \alpha$$

$$\left(\frac{f_j - m_j}{M_j - m_j}\right)^2 \leq \beta$$

$$\alpha \geq \beta\ ;\ \alpha + \beta \leq 1\ ;\ \alpha, \beta \geq 0 \tag{9}$$

The obtained optimization problem is solved by using one of the meta-heuristic techniques, namely gravitational search algorithm which is described in the next subsection and compared their results with a particle swarm optimization and genetic algorithm.

Step 4: *Adjustment of the preference parameters:* If the DM is satisfied with the solution obtained in Step 3, then the approach stops successfully. Otherwise, the key preference parameters, that is, decision maker's desirability functions (DF's), in terms of their ideal values, preferences of each objective function can be altered to meet the DM's choice, and the method again goes back to Step 3. The process is repeated until the DM is satisfied. We are just showing one run of the approach here as we assume that in this problem DM is satisfied by the results obtained in Step 3.

Gravitational Search Algorithm

In 2009, Rashedi *et al.* [55] developed the new heuristic algorithm called a Gravitational search algorithm (GSA) for finding the best solution in problem search space using physical rules. GSA can be considered as a collection of agents (candidate solutions) which have masses proportional to their value of the fitness function. During generations, all masses attract each other by the gravitational forces between them. The heavier the mass, the bigger the attraction forces. Therefore, the heaviest masses which are probably close to the global minimum attract the other masses in proportion to their distances. According to Rashedi *et al.* [55], suppose there are N agents (masses) in the system, whose position is represented by the candidate solution as $x_i = (x_i^1, x_i^2, ..., x_i^d, ..., x_i^n)$ where x_i^d is the position of the ith mass in the dth dimension and n is the dimension of the search space. Then, during all epochs, the gravitational forces from epoch j on agent i at a specific time t is defined as follows:

$$F_{ij}^d(t) = G(t) \frac{M_{pi}(t) \times M_{aj}(t)}{R_{ij}(t) + \in} (x_j^d(t) - x_i^d(t))$$

(10)

where M_{aj} is the active gravitational mass related to agent j, M_{pi} is the passive gravitational mass related to agent i, $\in$ is a small constant and $R_{ij}(t) = \| X_i, X_j \|_2$ is the Euclidean distance between two agents i and j, $G(t)$ is the gravitational constant at time t and is defined as $G(t) = G_0 \exp(-\alpha \times \text{iter}/\text{maxiter})$. Here α and G_0 are descending coefficient and initial values, respectively, 'iter' is the current iteration and 'maxiter' is the maximum number of iterations. The total force for d dimension that acts on agent i is calculated as

$$F_i^d(t) = \sum_{\substack{j=1 \\ j \neq i}}^{N} rand_i F_{ij}^d(t)$$

(11)

where $rand_i$ is the random number between 0 and 1.

According to the law of motion, the acceleration of an agent is proportional to the result force and inverse of its mass, so the acceleration of all agents should be calculated as follows:

$$acc_i^d(t) = \frac{F_i^d(t)}{M_{ii}(t)}$$

(12)

where d is the dimension of the problem, M_{ii} is the inertia mass of the agent i
Based on that, the velocity and position of the agent are updated as follows:

$$v_i^d(t+1) = rand_i \times v_i^d(t) + acc_i^d(t)$$

(13)

$$x_i^d(t+1) = x_i^d(t) + v_i^d(t+1)$$

(14)

The essential steps of the gravitational search algorithm are described in Algorithm 1.

Algorithm1: Template of gravitational search algorithm (GSA)
Objective function: $f(x)$
Generate an initial population
Evaluate the fitness for each agent;
While stopping criteria is not satisfied **Do**
    Update G
    Calculate the acceleration of each agent using equation (12).
    Calculate the velocity of each agent using equation (13).
    Calculate the position of each agent using equation (14).
    Evaluate the fitness of each agent
end while

ILLUSTRATIVE EXAMPLE

To demonstrate the proposed approach, the following three well-known reliability optimization problems have been considered. In these problems, the aim is to optimize simultaneously the reliability and cost of the 5 unit series system, life support system in a space capsule and complex bridge system respectively. These problems are expressed as below.

Example 1: Series System

A series system having five components, shown in Fig. **(1)** is considered [1, 39], each having component reliability r_i, $i = 1,2,3,4,5$. The system reliability R_s, unreliability Q_s and system cost C_s are given by

$$R_s = \prod_{i=1}^{5} r_i \quad or \quad Q_s = 1 - \prod_{i=1}^{5} r_i$$

$$C_s = \sum_{i=1}^{5} \left(a_i \log\left\{ \frac{1}{1-r_i} \right\} + b_i \right)$$

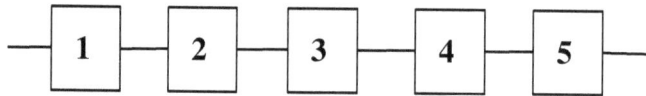

Fig. (1). Layout of the series system.

The objective of this problem is to find the decision variables r_i which minimize both Q_s and C_s, subject to $0.5 \le r_i \le 0.99$; $i = 1,2,\dots,5$. In other words, the problem can be posed as a MOOP given by

$$Minimize \quad \{EV_{Q_s}, EV_{C_s}\}$$
$$subject\,to : 0.5 \le r_i \le 0.99 \quad ; i = 1,2,\dots,5$$

where vectors of the coefficients a_i and b_i are $a=\{24, 8, 8.75, 7.14, 3.33\}$ and b $=\{120, 80, 70, 50, 30\}$ respectively [39].

Example 2: Life Support System in a Space Capsule

This problem concerns the reliability design of a life-support system in a space capsule [1,19] whose system configuration is presented in Fig. **(2)**. The system, which requires a single path for its success, has two redundant subsystems each comprising component 1 and 4. Each of the redundant subsystems is in series with component 2 and the resultant pair of series-parallel arrangement forms two equal paths. Component 3 is inserted as a third path and backup for the pair. This problem is a continuous nonlinear optimization problem and consists of four components, each having component reliability r_i, $i = 1,2,3,4$ such that their system reliability R_s, unreliability Q_s and system cost C_s are given by

$$R_s = 1 - r_3[(1 - r_1)(1 - r_4)]^2 - (1 - r_3)[1 - r_2\{1 - (1 - r_1)(1 - r_4)\}]^2$$

or

$$Q_s = 1 - R_s$$

$$C_s = 2K_1 r_1^{\alpha_1} + 2K_2 r_2^{\alpha_2} + K_3 r_3^{\alpha_3} + 2K_4 r_4^{\alpha_4}$$

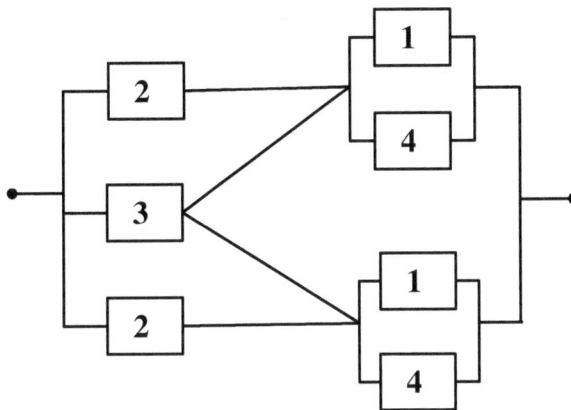

Fig. (2). Layout of space-capsule system.

Thus, the multi-objective optimization problem for the considered example is formulated as

$$Minimize \quad \{EV_{Q_s}, EV_{C_s}\}$$

$$subject\,to : 0.5 \leq r_i \leq 1.0 \quad ; i = 1,2,3,4$$

where vectors of the coefficients K_i and α_i are K={100, 100, 200, 150} and α ={0.6, 0.6, 0.6, 0.6} respectively [19].

Example 3: Complex System

The bridge network is considered as a system of the five components [1,19], each having component reliability r_i, $i = 1,2,3,4,5$, to find out the system reliability as shown in Fig. (3). The objective is to minimize the cost and reliability of the system at the same time. The algebraic expression for system reliability R_s and the cost C_s of the bridge system are given as follows:

$$R_s = r_1 r_4 + r_2 r_5 + r_2 r_3 r_4 + r_1 r_3 r_5 + 2 r_1 r_2 r_3 r_4 r_5 - r_2 r_3 r_4 r_5 - r_1 r_3 r_4 r_5 - r_1 r_2 r_3 r_5 - r_1 r_2 r_3 r_4$$

$$C_s = \sum_{i=1}^{5} a_i \exp\left\{ \frac{b_i}{1 - r_i} \right\}$$

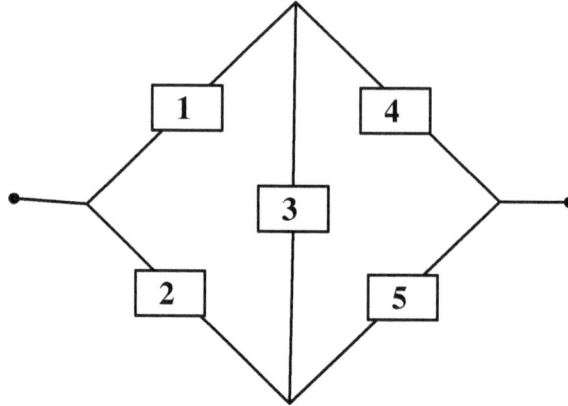

Fig. (3). Layout of the bridge system.

The problem is to find the decision variables r_i, $i = 1,2,3,4,5$ which minimize both Q_s and C_s subject to $0 \le r_i \le 1$. Hence, mathematically, the MOOP for the bridge network can be formulated as

$$Minimize \quad \{EV_{Q_s}, EV_{C_s}\}$$
$$subject\,to : 0 \le r_i \le 1.0 \quad ; i = 1,2,3,4,5$$

where $a_i = 1$ and $b_i = 0.0003$ for all $i = 1,2,3,4,5$

COMPUTATIONAL RESULTS

In this section, we have described and analyzed the results as obtained by the above stated approach for optimization.

Parameter Settings

In the experiment by the GA, PSO, and GSA, the values of the common parameters used in each algorithm such as population size and total evaluation number are chosen to be random as $20 \times d$ and 1000, respectively, where d is the dimension (number of variables) of the problem. The method has been implemented in Matlab (MathWorks) and the program has been run on a T6400 @ 2GHz Intel Core (TM) 2 Duo processor with 2GB of Random Access Memory. In order to eliminate stochastic discrepancy, 25 independent runs have been made that involved 25 different initial trial solutions with randomly chosen swarm size. The termination criterion has been set either limited to a maximum number of 1000 generations or to the order of relative error equal to 10^{-6}, whichever is achieved first. The other specific parameters of the algorithms are given below:

GA setting: In our experiment, a real-coded genetic algorithm is utilized to find the optimal values. The roulette wheel selection criterion is employed to choose better-fitted chromosomes. One point crossover with the rate of 0.9 and random point mutation with the rate of 0.01 are used in the present analysis for the reproduction of new solutions.

PSO setting: In PSO, the parameter c_1 & c_2, acceleration coefficients are taken as $c_1 = c_2 = 1.5$ while inertia weight w is represented by the linear expression

$$w = (w_1 - w_2)\left(\frac{\text{maxiter} - iter}{\text{maxiter}}\right) + w_2.$$ Here $w_1 = 0.9$ and $w_2 = 0.4$ are respectively

the initial and final values of inertia weight, 'maxiter' represents the maximum generation number (=1000) and 'iter' is used generation number.

GSA setting: In GSA, except the common parameters (population number and maximum iteration number), the gravitational constant G_0 and α are set to be 1 and 20 respectively, while the initial values of acceleration and mass are set to zero for each particle.

Results & Discussion

In order to solve above problems, the following analysis has been done for different values of reliability interval parameter I=0, 0.01, 0.03, 0.05. In it, firstly the idealism and anti-ideal values corresponding to each objective function have been computed and then desirability function values have been formulated using

Eqs. (6) and (7). Finally, by using Eq. (9), the problem is converted into its equivalent crisp model and GSA algorithm has been used to obtain their optimal parameters.

Result & Discussion for Example 1

The boundaries of the reliability and cost are taken to be [0.9, 1] and [500, 600] respectively. Based on these bounds, the desirability functions by taking non-linear membership functions corresponding for reliability are defined as below.

$$
\mu_{EV_{Rs}}(x) = \begin{cases} 0 & ;\, EV_{Rs}(x) \le 0.9 \\ \dfrac{\exp\!\left(-w\!\left(\dfrac{1 - EV_{Rs}(x)}{0.1}\right)\right) - \exp(-w)}{1 - \exp(-w)} & ;\, 0.9 \le EV_{Rs}(x) \le 1 \\ 1 & ;\, EV_{Rs}(x) \ge 1 \end{cases}
$$

(15)

and

$$
v_{EV_{Rs}}(x) = \begin{cases} 1 & ;\, EV_{Rs}(x) \le 0.9 \\ \left(\dfrac{1 - EV_{Rs}(x)}{0.1}\right)^{2} & ;\, 0.9 \le EV_{Rs}(x) \le 1 \\ 0 & ;\, EV_{Rs}(x) \ge 1 \end{cases}
$$

(16)

while for the system cost are defined as

$$
\mu_{EV_{Cs}}(x) = \begin{cases} 1 & ;\, EV_{Cs}(x) \le 500 \\ \dfrac{\exp\!\left(-w\!\left(\dfrac{EV_{Cs}(x) - 500}{100}\right)\right) - \exp(-w)}{1 - \exp(-w)} & ;\, 500 \le EV_{Cs}(x) \le 600 \\ 0 & ;\, EV_{Cs}(x) \ge 600 \end{cases}
$$

(17)

and

$$v_{EV_{Cs}}(x) = \begin{cases} 0 & ; EV_{Cs}(x) \leq 500 \\ \left(\dfrac{EV_{Cs}(x) - 500}{100}\right)^2 & ; 500 \leq EV_{Cs}(x) \leq 600 \\ 1 & ; EV_{Cs}(x) \geq 600 \end{cases} \qquad (18)$$

Using these membership functions and product aggregator operator, the single objective optimization model has been formulated as

$$\textit{Maximize } \eta(r) = \eta_{EV_{Rs}}(r) \times \eta_{EV_{Cs}}(r)$$

$$\textit{subject to : } \frac{e^{-w\left(\frac{1 - EV_{Rs}(r)}{0.1}\right)} - e^{-w}}{1 - e^{-w}} \geq \alpha$$

$$\frac{e^{-w\left(\frac{EV_{Cs}(r) - 500}{100}\right)} - e^{-w}}{1 - e^{-w}} \geq \alpha$$

$$\left(\frac{EV_{Cs}(r) - 500}{100}\right)^2 \leq \beta \qquad (19)$$

$$\left(\frac{1 - EV_{Rs}(r)}{0.1}\right)^2 \leq \beta$$

$$\eta_{EV_{Rs}}(r) = \mu_{EV_{Rs}}(r) - v_{EV_{Rs}}(r); \ \eta_{EV_{Cs}}(r) = \mu_{EV_{Cs}}(r) - v_{EV_{Cs}}(r)$$

$$\alpha \geq \beta; \ \alpha + \beta \leq 1; \ \alpha, \beta \geq 0$$

$$0.9 \leq r \leq 1$$

The above obtained optimization problem has been solved for different values of reliability interval parameter I=0, 0.01, 0.03, 0.05. Here I=0 corresponding to the parameters in which components' reliability is in the form of crisp number rather than the triangular number *i.e.*, the model has been solved under the crisp environment. Based on these data/information, the above formulated optimization problem has been solved with GSA algorithm and compared their results with PSO and GA algorithms by taking linear and nonlinear membership functions corresponding to each objective function. The computed results corresponding to it has been summarized in Table **1** for different values of I.

Table 1. Five unit series system.

When linear membership functions are taken

	I = 0.00			I = 0.01			I = 0.03			I = 0.05		
	GA	PSO	GSA	GA	PSO	GSA	GA	PSO	GSA	GA	PSO	GSA
η	0.263281	0.266683	0.272445	0.253344	0.257030	0.260199	0.167699	0.168270	0.172958	0.098146	0.092515	0.099056
r_1	0.916352	0.931820	0.926299	0.921732	0.936394	0.928281	0.936477	0.931541	0.937736	0.930934	0.929253	0.930678
r_2	0.975082	0.972316	0.974462	0.969540	0.969868	0.973082	0.958037	0.964304	0.963192	0.945399	0.947971	0.945281
r_3	0.971887	0.962334	0.971949	0.967844	0.966678	0.971205	0.960612	0.959945	0.962285	0.945347	0.942556	0.944492
r_4	0.969904	0.975737	0.976919	0.979543	0.974548	0.975524	0.967079	0.962902	0.964218	0.946490	0.948442	0.945735
r_5	0.993207	0.992389	0.989248	0.982379	0.983642	0.985239	0.967040	0.966647	0.967728	0.994374	0.992964	0.996580
EV_{Rs}	0.836542	0.844266	0.847858	0.832744	0.842026	0.843629	0.809953	0.806570	0.814979	0.793866	0.792756	0.793955
EV_{Cs}	511.9724	514.6373	515.1990	511.7282	515.0878	515.2624	515.0358	512.8192	516.7287	522.0330	522.9534	521.8307
$\mu_{EV_{Rs}}$	0.673085	0.688536	0.695718	0.665491	0.684055	0.687260	0.619908	0.613142	0.629961	0.587732	0.585514	0.587912
$\mu_{EV_{Cs}}$	0.880276	0.853625	0.848008	0.882717	0.849121	0.847375	0.849641	0.871809	0.832711	0.779672	0.770467	0.781691
$\nu_{EV_{Rs}}$	0.326914	0.311463	0.304281	0.334508	0.315944	0.312739	0.380091	0.386857	0.370038	0.412267	0.414485	0.412087
$\nu_{EV_{Cs}}$	0.119723	0.146374	0.151991	0.117282	0.150878	0.152624	0.150358	0.128190	0.167288	0.220327	0.229532	0.218308

When non-linear membership functions are taken

	I = 0.00			I = 0.01			I = 0.03			I = 0.05		
	GA	PSO	GSA	GA	PSO	GSA	GA	PSO	GSA	GA	PSO	GSA
η	0.474491	0.482934	0.485091	0.467053	0.471488	0.473326	0.376989	0.382899	0.385305	0.230820	0.231216	0.233805
r_1	0.925598	0.927801	0.925271	0.927930	0.929282	0.926643	0.932417	0.934061	0.934566	0.936501	0.937875	0.935747
r_2	0.964914	0.971762	0.973824	0.971982	0.974195	0.972601	0.958298	0.964957	0.962482	0.946341	0.947636	0.946377
r_3	0.966582	0.972727	0.971340	0.971153	0.965124	0.970720	0.962016	0.961962	0.961500	0.947935	0.943535	0.946017
r_4	0.970840	0.973293	0.976666	0.968670	0.973129	0.975259	0.964329	0.959905	0.963683	0.947474	0.946279	0.946780
r_5	0.992727	0.991969	0.988980	0.980017	0.984948	0.985139	0.962467	0.967314	0.967571	0.949221	0.949091	0.948591
EV_{Rs}	0.832008	0.846735	0.845384	0.831963	0.837901	0.840991	0.801749	0.809030	0.810391	0.766140	0.763693	0.762954
EV_{Cs}	510.5318	515.0654	514.3216	511.6051	513.3811	514.2900	511.3857	514.1918	514.4535	518.9605	517.0670	515.8284
$\mu_{EV_{Rs}}$	0.652802	0.682775	0.680024	0.652713	0.664789	0.671075	0.591499	0.606212	0.608968	0.519822	0.514914	0.513436
$\mu_{EV_{Cs}}$	0.889911	0.842875	0.850576	0.878752	0.860320	0.850903	0.881027	0.851924	0.849211	0.802637	0.822183	0.834978
$\nu_{EV_{Rs}}$	0.112885	0.093960	0.095622	0.112943	0.105101	0.101134	0.157210	0.145878	0.143804	0.218760	0.223364	0.224760
$\nu_{EV_{Cs}}$	0.011091	0.022696	0.020510	0.013468	0.017906	0.020420	0.012964	0.020139	0.020890	0.035948	0.029125	0.025054

From this table, it has been concluded that the overall objective function value $\eta(r)$ are decreasing with the increase of reliability interval value from 0 to 0.05. Similar effect has been observed from its value of membership functions *i.e.*, $\mu_{EV_{Rs}}$ and $v_{EV_{Cs}}$ are decreasing. Here, initially the solution procedure starts with I=0. The outcomes of this iteration are $EV_{Rs} = 0.845384$, $EV_{Cs} = 514.32161$ and $EV_{Rs} = 0.846735$, $EV_{Cs} = 515.06540$ and $EV_{Rs} = 0.832008$, $EV_{Cs} = 510.5318$ corresponding to the overall objective function value 0.485091, 0.482934 and 0.474491 by GSA, PSO and GA algorithms respectively when nonlinear membership functions have been taken. It has also been observed from the table that by increasing the value of reliability interval, then the expected value of the systems' reliability becomes decreases while cost will increase. On the other hand, the overall satisfaction value $\eta(r)$ of the system will also decrease. The complete Pareto optimal solutions for different values of I has been obtained for linear and nonlinear membership functions corresponding to different objective functions and are summarized in Table **1**.

Result & Discussion for Example 2

In this example, the ideal and anti-ideal values corresponding to reliability and cost are taken as [0.9, 1] and [600, 700]. Based on these bounds, the desirability functions corresponding to it have been obtained by using Eqs. (6) and (7) and hence correspondingly an equivalent objective optimization model for the considered example has been formulated as

$$\text{Maximize } \eta(r) = \eta_{EV_{Rs}}(r) \times \eta_{EV_{Cs}}(r)$$

$$\text{subject to : } \frac{e^{-w\left(\frac{1-EV_{Rs}(r)}{0.1}\right)} - e^{-w}}{1 - e^{-w}} \geq \alpha$$

$$\frac{e^{-w\left(\frac{EV_{Cs}(r)-600}{100}\right)} - e^{-w}}{1 - e^{-w}} \geq \alpha \qquad (20)$$

$$\left(\frac{EV_{Cs}(r)-600}{100}\right)^2 \leq \beta$$

$$\left(\frac{1-EV_{Rs}(r)}{0.1}\right)^2 \leq \beta$$

$$\eta_{EV_{Rs}}(r) = \mu_{EV_{Rs}}(r) - v_{EV_{Rs}}(r); \; \eta_{EV_{Cs}}(r) = \mu_{EV_{Cs}}(r) - v_{EV_{Cs}}(r)$$

$$\alpha \geq \beta; \; \alpha + \beta \leq 1; \; \alpha, \beta \geq 0$$

$$0.9 \leq r \leq 1$$

This problem has been solved previously by Ravi *et al.* [19] and reported a solution as $R_s = 0.94743$ and $C_s = 668.28$. Using an interactive method solution at different iterations by taking different levels of uncertainty for the considered problem has been summarized in Table **2**. Initially, the process has been started by taking the zero level of uncertainty in the data. In other words, the problem has been solved in the crisp environment and hence the corresponding optimum values are obtained as $R_s = 0.949667$ and $C_s = 669.78324$ with degree of acceptance is 48.42% and 49.96%, respectively, for reliability and cost.

Thus, in terms of reliability, the obtained solution is better than the solution reported in Ravi *et al.* [19]. However, for showing the results in a more realistic form, the considered optimization model has been converted into the fuzzy optimization problem by considering the reliability of each subsystem of the system in the form of triangular fuzzy number with the help of reliability interval parameter I.

The results computed corresponding to the different values of I=0.01, 0.03, 0.05 are summarized in Table **2** with the help of defining the linear as well as nonlinear membership functions corresponding to the objective functions for handling the uncertainties in the data. For instance, corresponding to I=0.01 *i.e.*, by taking $\pm 1\%$ level of uncertainties in the component's reliability of the system, the expected value of the system reliability and cost are $EV_{Rs} = 0.949855$ and $EV_{Cs} = 669.59885$ when solved with the GSA algorithm whose overall satisfaction level is 0.06285 which is still better than the solution reported by Ravi *et al.* [19].

Similar results have been computed for other values of I and compared with the results of PSO and GA algorithms. It has been observed from these results that with the increase in the interval level of the component's reliability the overall satisfaction function value is increasing.

Result & Discussion for Example 3

The idealism and anti-ideal values of the objective functions corresponding to this example are [0.99, 1] and [4.8, 5.5] respectively. Based on these bounds, a region of satisfaction is constructed corresponding to each objective function through Eqs. (6) and (7). Using these constructed membership functions, an intuitionistic fuzzy optimization model has been reformulated into its equivalent crisp optimization model as given below.

$$Maximize \ \eta(r) = \eta_{EV_{Rs}}(r) \times \eta_{EV_{Cs}}(r)$$

$$subject \ to \ : \ \frac{e^{-w\left(\frac{1-EV_{Rs}(r)}{0.01}\right)} - e^{-w}}{1-e^{-w}} \geq \alpha$$

$$\frac{e^{-w\left(\frac{EV_{Cs}(r)-4.8}{0.7}\right)} - e^{-w}}{1-e^{-w}} \geq \alpha$$

$$\left(\frac{EV_{Cs}(r)-4.8}{0.7}\right)^2 \leq \beta \qquad\qquad (21)$$

$$\left(\frac{1-EV_{Rs}(r)}{0.01}\right)^2 \leq \beta$$

$$\eta_{EV_{Rs}}(r) = \mu_{EV_{Rs}}(r) - v_{EV_{Rs}}(r); \ \eta_{EV_{Cs}}(r) = \mu_{EV_{Cs}}(r) - v_{EV_{Cs}}(r)$$

$$\alpha \geq \beta; \ \alpha + \beta \leq 1; \ \alpha, \beta \geq 0$$

$$0.9 \leq r \leq 1$$

For obtaining their corresponding non-dominant solution, the GSA has been used and compared their results with PSO and GA algorithms for different values of I = 0, 0.01, 0.03, 0.05. The results corresponding to linear and non-linear membership functions are reported in Table **3**. For instance, corresponding to I=0, the results show that $(EV_{Rs}, \ EV_{Cs}) = (0.998969, \ 5.058694)$ with membership values $(\mu_{Rs}, v_{Rs}) = (60.21\%, 14.89\%)$ and $(\mu_{Cs}, v_{Cs}) = (66.80\%, 10.30\%)$.

This result shows that 60.21% and 66.80% achievement for reliability and cost function corresponding to their acceptance region while corresponding to 14.89% and 10.30% achievement towards their rejection region goals. Hence the corresponding overall satisfaction region value of the overall objective function is 0.425626. Similar results are shown for other values of I.

Table 2: Life support system.

When linear membership functions are taken

	I = 0.00			I = 0.01			I = 0.03			I = 0.05		
	GA	PSO	GSA	GA	PSO	GSA	GA	PSO	GSA	GA	PSO	GSA
η	0.066622	0.066664	0.066738	0.068478	0.069290	0.069294	0.073244	0.073367	0.073377	0.0752589	0.075789	0.075902
r_1	0.549828	0.551576	0.558235	0.546442	0.552353	0.551959	0.556761	0.553846	0.554490	0.553212	0.560324	0.558222
r_2	0.999990	0.999990	0.991010	0.999990	0.999990	0.999990	0.999990	0.999990	0.999990	0.999990	0.999990	0.999990
r_3	0.500000	0.500000	0.500000	0.500000	0.500000	0.500000	0.500000	0.500000	0.500000	0.500000	0.500000	0.500000
r_4	0.500000	0.500000	0.500000	0.500000	0.500000	0.500000	0.500000	0.500000	0.500000	0.500000	0.500000	0.500000
EV_{Rs}	0.949333	0.949727	0.949639	0.948591	0.949914	0.949826	0.950592	0.949956	0.950097	0.949140	0.950670	0.950221
EV_{Cs}	669.5660	669.83238	669.76404	668.7379	669.6392	669.57934	669.6189	669.17604	669.2740	668.2985	669.37838	669.05991
$\mu_{EV_{Rs}}$	0.493394	0.497322	0.496442	0.485963	0.499192	0.498316	0.505976	0.499615	0.501024	0.491451	0.506759	0.502259
$\mu_{EV_{Cs}}$	0.515829	0.511316	0.512472	0.529865	0.514588	0.515604	0.514934	0.522438	0.520779	0.537313	0.519009	0.524409
$\nu_{EV_{Rs}}$	0.256648	0.252685	0.253570	0.264233	0.250808	0.251686	0.244059	0.250384	0.248976	0.258621	0.243286	0.247745
$\nu_{EV_{Cs}}$	0.234420	0.238811	0.237683	0.221026	0.235624	0.234639	0.235288	0.228064	0.229652	0.214079	0.231352	0.226186

When non-linear membership functions are taken

	I = 0.00			I = 0.01			I = 0.03			I = 0.05		
	GA	PSO	GSA	GA	PSO	GSA	GA	PSO	GSA	GA	PSO	GSA
η	0.060343	0.060361	0.060426	0.0628585	0.0628585	0.06285887	0.0665665	0.0667464	0.0667493	0.068100	0.068451	0.069155
r_1	0.550456	0.551259	0.558340	0.551979	0.552172	0.552087	0.557303	0.554292	0.554632	0.564882	0.563685	0.558379
r_2	0.999990	0.999999	0.991037	0.999990	0.999999	0.999999	0.999990	0.999999	0.999999	0.999990	0.999999	0.999999
r_3	0.500000	0.500000	0.500000	0.500000	0.500000	0.500000	0.500000	0.500000	0.500000	0.500000	0.500000	0.500000
r_4	0.500000	0.500000	0.500000	0.500000	0.500000	0.500000	0.500000	0.500000	0.500000	0.500000	0.500000	0.500000
EV_{Rs}	0.949475	0.949656	0.949667	0.949831	0.949874	0.949855	0.950710	0.950054	0.950128	0.951639	0.951386	0.950254
EV_{Cs}	669.6617	669.78410	669.7832	669.5824	669.6117	669.59885	669.7011	669.24396	669.29562	670.0677	669.8869	669.0837
$\mu_{EV_{Rs}}$	0.482313	0.484115	0.484229	0.485864	0.486293	0.486104	0.494657	0.488093	0.488836	0.503953	0.501416	0.490098
$\mu_{EV_{Cs}}$	0.501714	0.499639	0.499652	0.503060	0.502562	0.502782	0.501046	0.508806	0.507928	0.494829	0.497895	0.511527
$\nu_{EV_{Rs}}$	0.255219	0.253400	0.253285	0.251642	0.251211	0.251401	0.242896	0.249408	0.248667	0.233825	0.236282	0.247410
$\nu_{EV_{Cs}}$	0.235994	0.238012	0.237999	0.234689	0.235171	0.234959	0.236642	0.229163	0.230002	0.242726	0.239716	0.226570

Table 3: Bridge complex system.

When linear membership functions are taken

	I=0.00 GA	I=0.00 PSO	I=0.00 GSA	I=0.01 GA	I=0.01 PSO	I=0.01 GSA	I=0.03 GA	I=0.03 PSO	I=0.03 GSA	I=0.05 GA	I=0.05 PSO	I=0.05 GSA
η	0.206732	0.206191	0.207999	0.787620	0.846400	0.960015	0.677462	0.720186	0.777075	0.290953	0.365616	0.391996
r_1	0.979329	0.980055	0.977309	0.992146	0.983391	0.990151	0.980658	0.994533	0.996707	0.950026	0.984282	0.993736
r_2	0.978401	0.972828	0.977073	0.990022	0.990824	0.994136	0.989678	0.970100	0.994858	0.964161	0.994485	0.976503
r_3	0.976659	0.973394	0.977573	0.964415	0.990192	0.997901	0.970002	0.971530	0.992820	0.998591	0.985649	0.994158
r_4	0.972630	0.976509	0.977610	0.962816	0.964572	0.990423	0.990814	0.995127	0.970232	0.992359	0.950028	0.992954
r_5	0.871350	0.891034	0.880689	0.551067	0.752672	0.843300	0.984943	0.965388	0.970086	0.978326	0.976447	0.950022
EV_{Rs}	0.998795	0.998798	0.998861	0.998929	0.999222	0.999790	0.998378	0.998713	0.998876	0.997006	0.996843	0.997135
EV_{Cs}	5.054896	5.055226	5.055953	4.778061	4.799878	4.785563	4.793216	4.811421	4.685392	4.897069	4.804242	4.829880
$\mu_{EV_{Rs}}$	0.880411	0.880732	0.887039	0.893806	0.923197	0.980007	0.838730	0.872239	0.888538	0.701310	0.685049	0.714293
$\mu_{EV_{Cs}}$	0.635861	0.635391	0.634352	1.00	1.00	1.00	1.00	0.983766	1.00	0.861267	0.993941	0.957315
$\nu_{EV_{Rs}}$	0.119588	0.119267	0.112960	0.106193	0.076802	0.019992	0.161269	0.127760	0.111461	0.298689	0.314950	0.285706
$\nu_{EV_{Cs}}$	0.364138	0.364608	0.365647	0	0	0	0	0.016233	0	0.138732	0.006058	0.042684

When non-linear membership functions are taken

	I=0.00 GA	I=0.00 PSO	I=0.00 GSA	I=0.01 GA	I=0.01 PSO	I=0.01 GSA	I=0.03 GA	I=0.03 PSO	I=0.03 GSA	I=0.05 GA	I=0.05 PSO	I=0.05 GSA
η	0.424782	0.423113	0.425626	0.895133	0.952150	0.977068	0.755531	0.796965	0.853230	0.439945	0.573429	0.619348
r_1	0.975061	0.980904	0.978561	0.990165	0.996954	0.997548	0.984914	0.970152	0.976826	0.950170	0.992341	0.993073
r_2	0.976807	0.973947	0.978551	0.862928	0.990005	0.990043	0.979124	0.971156	0.994456	0.967284	0.950026	0.950013
r_3	0.979763	0.976822	0.978538	0.990958	0.939221	0.990386	0.970052	0.997419	0.993099	0.987603	0.978525	0.985699
r_4	0.978871	0.976324	0.978174	0.996593	0.984830	0.997601	0.982859	0.979696	0.980198	0.995440	0.994666	0.998658
r_5	0.871843	0.908081	0.884574	0.975581	0.990741	0.618795	0.853073	0.982794	0.970004	0.860193	0.968614	0.950492
EV_{Rs}	0.998883	0.998848	0.998969	0.999304	0.999552	0.999776	0.998017	0.998380	0.998769	0.996251	0.996882	0.997116
EV_{Cs}	5.056698	5.056463	5.058694	4.819881	4.786121	4.779205	4.771201	4.807495	4.803254	4.845446	4.809086	4.799943
$\mu_{EV_{Rs}}$	0.884248	0.594689	0.602150	0.928110	0.954071	0.977526	0.794526	0.832073	0.872371	0.614070	0.678193	0.702070
$\mu_{EV_{Cs}}$	0.621625	0.669727	0.668090	0.970197	1.0	1.0	1.00	0.988684	0.995110	0.932216	0.986365	1.00
$\nu_{EV_{Rs}}$	0.012268	0.154716	0.148963	0.004712	0.001918	0.000458	0.038994	0.025951	0.014932	0.140006	0.096737	0.082721
$\nu_{EV_{Cs}}$	0.134478	0.101978	0.103008	0.000806	0.0	0.0	0.0	0.000116	0.00002	0.004187	0.000168	0.00

From these tables, it is clearly seen that the Pareto optimal solutions of the problem with nonlinear membership functions guides the solution towards the intermediate region of the Pareto solutions. On the other hand, by taking the linear membership functions, results corresponding to it are beneficial if the decision maker (DM) does not prefer a particular objective over another objective. Based on these reported components' reliabilities, the system analysts or decision makers may plan the schedule for increasing the performance of the system.

Statistical Analysis

In order to study the performance of the proposed algorithm statistically, the simulation experiments are repeated for 25 observations. All 25 observations are generated with 25 different initial solutions. An unpaired pooled t−test assuming equal variances has been applied with significant level of 5 percent. The pooled t−test has been applied to the comparison of proposed results with PSO and GA results corresponding to different uncertainties level (I).

For instance, in case of five unit series system at I=0.01, the corresponding values of t−statistics for linear and non-linear membership functions has been computed and are shown in Table **4**. It is indicated from the table that the value of t−stat is greater than the t−critical value. Also the p−value obtained for one-tail test is less than the significance level (0.05).

Thus the mean of the proposed approach is better than the other one and this difference is statistically significant. Similar analysis has been done corresponding to different values of I and are summarized in Tables **4** - **6** which shows that the difference of their means are statistically significant.

CONCLUSION

In this chapter, we have presented a methodology for solving the reliability-cost optimization problem in an intuitionistic fuzzy environment with the assumption that reliability of each component is a triangular fuzzy number. The expected value of the functions has been used as an objective for maximizing the performance of the system under the IFS environment. The product operator has been used to reformulated the reduced problem into the single objective optimization problem and then GSA has been used for finding the optimal or near to optimal solution for different preferences of interval number I. The computed results corresponding to different values of I by the GSA are compared with the results of the PSO and GA.

Table 4. Statistical simulation results for five unit series system.

When linear membership functions are taken

	I = 0.00			I = 0.01			I = 0.03			I = 0.05		
	GA	PSO	GSA	GA	PSO	GSA	GA	PSO	GSA	GA	PSO	GSA
Mean	0.251782	0.257671	0.272425	0.238715	0.240858	0.260123	0.153925	0.161476	0.172850	0.071648	0.076886	0.097027
Std. dev.	0.00876	0.005604	2.25E−5	0.01296	0.010613	0.000106	0.006937	0.005067	0.000138	0.007615	0.007049	0.004162
observation	25	25	25	25	25	25	25	25	25	25	25	25
Degree of freedom	48	48		48	48		48	48		48	48	
Hypothetical mean difference	0	0		0	0		0	0		0	0	
t-stat	11.544	12.8972		8.0921	8.8923		13.3623	10.9927		14.3269	12.0535	
t−critical value	1.6772	1.6772		1.6772	1.6772		1.6772	1.6772		1.6772	1.6772	
$P(T \leq t)$	1.38E−11	1.38E−12		1.28E−8	2.31E−9		6.53E−13	3.75E−11		1.46E−13	5.69E−12	

When non- linear membership functions are taken

	I = 0.00			I = 0.01			I = 0.03			I = 0.05		
	GA	PSO	GSA	GA	PSO	GSA	GA	PSO	GSA	GA	PSO	GSA
Mean	0.463972	0.468021	0.485073	0.443984	0.459385	0.473286	0.343892	0.367883	0.385194	0.224728	0.218543	0.233577
Std. dev.	0.007682	0.007677	0.000017	0.005982	0.005498	0.000050	0.006582	0.006373	0.000133	0.006912	0.006227	0.000385
observation	25	25	25	25	25	25	25	25	25	25	25	25
Degree of freedom	48	48		48	48		48	48		48	48	
Hypothetical mean difference	0	0		0	0		0	0		0	0	
t-stat	13.456	10.8800		23.996	12.3859		30.734	13.304		6.262	11.805	
t−critical value	1.6772	1.6772		1.6772	1.6772		1.6772	1.6772		1.6772	1.6772	
$P(T \leq t)$	5.63E−13	4.60E−11		1.38E−18	3.23E−12		0	7.17E−13		8.97E−7	8.76E−12	

Here, E represents the exponent power

Table 5. Statistical simulation results for life support system.

When linear membership functions are taken

	I = 0.00			I = 0.01			I = 0.03			I = 0.05		
	GA	PSO	GSA	GA	PSO	GSA	GA	PSO	GSA	GA	PSO	GSA
Mean	0.064932	0.065081	0.066654	0.06478	0.065001	0.069058	0.06597	0.063416	0.073525	0.06785	0.069927	0.075842
Std. dev.	0.004711	0.001510	0.000122	0.00749	0.005778	0.000327	0.005723	0.006082	0.000143	0.005656	0.005055	0.001739
observation	25	25	25	25	25	25	25	25	25	25	25	25
Degree of freedom	48	48		48	48		48	48		48	48	
Hypothetical mean difference	0	0		0	0		0	0		0	0	
t-stat	1.79011	5.08678		2.79544	3.43430		6.46518	8.14043		6.6166	5.42064	
t-critical value	1.6772	1.6772		1.6772	1.6772		1.6772	1.6772		1.6772	1.6772	
$P(T \le t)$	0.04303	1.6683E-6		0.00501	0.00108		0.549E-6	0.115E-6		0.038E-5	0.7191E-5	

When non-linear membership functions are taken

	I = 0.00			I = 0.01			I = 0.03			I = 0.05		
	GA	PSO	GSA	GA	PSO	GSA	GA	PSO	GSA	GA	PSO	GSA
Mean	0.060127	0.060237	0.060426	0.05567	0.057394	0.062558	0.058186	0.061035	0.066728	0.06658	0.06604	0.068141
Std. dev.	0.3017E-3	0.2868E-3	0.2591E-3	0.003298	0.005896	0.000734	0.00459	0.005703	0.002833	0.002563	0.003423	0.000234
observation	25	25	25	25	25	25	25	25	25	25	25	25
Degree of freedom	48	48		48	48		48	48		48	48	
Hypothetical mean difference	0	0		0	0		0	0		0	0	
t-stat	3.6832	2.3955		9.9873	4.257		7.7582	4.3797		2.9713	2.9999	
t-critical value	1.6772	1.6772		1.6772	1.6772		1.6772	1.6772		1.6772	1.6772	
$P(T \le t)$	0.0005	0.00123		0	0.00013		0	1.005E-4		0.00332	0.0031	

Here, E represents the exponent power

Table 6. Statistical simulation results for Bridge complex system.

When linear membership functions are taken

	I = 0.00			I = 0.01			I = 0.03			I = 0.05		
	GA	PSO	GSA	GA	PSO	GSA	GA	PSO	GSA	GA	PSO	GSA
Mean	0.19421	0.194520	0.207714	0.607801	0.65782	0.874144	0.45876	0.455004	0.686854	0.2088491	0.28967	0.352414
Std. dev.	0.006783	0.005933	0.000425	0.113218	0.13092	0.064802	0.15672	0.113302	0.049911	0.050089	0.07472	0.031773
observation	25	25	25	25	25	25	25	25	25	25	25	25
Degree of freedom	48	48		48	48		48	48		48	48	
Hypothetical mean difference	0	0		0	0		0	0		0	0	
t-stat	9.7341	10.8654		10.0021	7.2547		6.7938	9.17406		11.85700	3.7857	
t-critical value	1.6772	1.6772		1.6772	1.6772		1.6772	1.6772		1.6772	1.6772	
$P(T \leq t)$	0.414E-9	0.0473E-9		0.0024E-7	0.8515E-7		0.2503E-6	0.0012E-6		0	0.00045	

When non-linear membership functions are taken

	I = 0.00			I = 0.01			I = 0.03			I = 0.05		
	GA	PSO	GSA	GA	PSO	GSA	GA	PSO	GSA	GA	PSO	GSA
Mean	0.398722	0.403254	0.425219	0.765452	0.886925	0.917505	0.566845	0.671925	0.804435	0.340844	0.471950	0.567116
Std. dev.	0.02017	0.010328	0.000442	0.074052	0.05782	0.043476	0.094679	0.05681	0.032852	0.046490	0.068291	0.042116
observation	25	25	25	25	25	25	25	25	25	25	25	25
Degree of freedom	48	48		48	48		48	48		48	48	
Hypothetical mean difference	0	0		0	0		0	0		0	0	
t-stat	6.4341	10.4093		8.67460	2.0708		11.6142	9.8920		17.6709	5.8107	
t-critical value	1.6772	1.6772		1.6772	1.6772		1.6772	1.6772		1.6772	1.6772	
$P(T \leq t)$	0.591E-6	0.111E-9		3.65E-9	0.0246		0.0122E-9	0.303E-9		0	0.27184E-5	

Here, E represents the exponent power

From the computed results, it has been concluded that the nonlinear membership functions produce a definite bias among the Pareto optimal solutions as compared to linear membership functions. Through this approach, a decision support system has been developed which helps the plant maintenance personnel in deciding his future strategy to gain optimum performance of the system.

The component's reliability corresponding to the main component of each unit is reported which may be targeted so that optimum system performance could be achieved by using the approach discussed. Thus, for different preferences suggested by decision-makers in terms of reliability interval, optimum values of systems' reliability and cost are achieved. Since each objective function is optimized, system performance under consideration is optimized automatically.

The idea presented in this study could also be applicable to many other systems like circular system, multi-state system, k-out-of-n system *etc*. The approach will be further extended and improved using other optimization tools/algorithms and artificial neural network will be used to handle the complex nature of the system. Moreover, the approach has been extended for the repairable system by considering the maintenance and repairing cost, preventive maintenance analysis *etc*. The investigations on these different systems will be carried out in our future work.

CONSENT FOR PUBLICATION

Not applicable.

CONFLICT OF INTEREST

The authors confirm that there is no conflict of interest to declare for this publication.

ACKNOWLEDGEMENT

Declared none.

REFERENCES

[1]　H. Garg, M. Rani, S.P. Sharma, and Y. Vishwakarma, "Intuitionistic fuzzy optimization technique for solving multi-objective reliability optimization problems in interval environment", *Expert Syst. Appl.*, vol. 41, no. 7, pp. 3157-3167.

[2]　H. Garg, M. Rani, S.P. Sharma, and Y. Vishwakarma, "Bi-objective optimization of the reliability-redundancy allocation problem for series-parallel system", *J. Manuf. Syst.*, vol. 33, no. 3, pp. 335-347.

[3]　W. Kuo, and V.R. Prasad, "An annotated overview of system-reliability optimization", *IEEE Trans. Reliab.*, vol. 49, no. 2, pp. 176-187.

[4]   W Kuo, and R Wan, "Recent advances in optimal reliability allocation", *Computational intelligence in reliability engineering,* vol. 39, pp. 1-36.

[5]   H. Garg, "A hybrid PSO-GA algorithm for constrained optimization problems", *Appl. Math. Comput.,* vol. 274, pp. 292-305.

[6]   T. Yokota, M. Gen, and Y.X. Li, "Genetic algorithm for non-linear mixed integer programming problems and its applications", *Comput. Ind. Eng.,* vol. 30, no. 4, pp. 905-917.

[7]   L. Painton, and J. Campbell, "Genetic algorithms in optimization of system reliability", *IEEE Trans. Reliab.,* vol. 44, no. 2, pp. 172-178.

[8]   L.S. Coelho, "An efficient particle swarm approach for mixed-integer programming in reliability-redundancy optimization applications", *Reliab. Eng. Syst. Saf.,* vol. 94, no. 4, pp. 830-837.

[9]   H. Garg, and S.P. Sharma, "Multi-objective reliability-redundancy allocation problem using particle swarm optimization", *Comput. Ind. Eng.,* vol. 64, no. 1, pp. 247-255.

[10]   W.C. Yeh, "A two-stage discrete particle swarm optimization for the problem of multiple multi-level redundancy allocation in series systems", *Expert Syst. Appl.,* vol. 36, no. 5, pp. 9192-9200.

[11]   W.C. Yeh, and T.J. Hsieh, "Solving reliability redundancy allocation problems using an artificial bee colony algorithm", *Comput. Oper. Res.,* vol. 38, no. 11, pp. 1465-1473.

[12]   H. Garg, M. Rani, and S.P. Sharma, "An efficient two phase approach for solving reliability-redundancy allocation problem using artificial bee colony technique", *Comput. Oper. Res.,* vol. 40, no. 12, pp. 2961-2969.

[13]   H. Garg, A hybrid GA-GSA algorithm for optimizing the performance of an industrial system by utilizing uncertain data. Handbook of Research on Artificial Intelligence Techniques and Algorithms 2015: 620-654

[14]   H. Garg, "An efficient biogeography based optimization algorithm for solving reliability optimization problems", *Swarm Evol. Comput.,* vol. 24, pp. 1-10.

[15]   H. Garg, "An approach for solving constrained reliability-redundancy allocation problems using cuckoo search algorithm", *Beni-Suef Uni J Basic Appl Sci.,* vol. 4, no. 1, pp. 14-25.

[16]   H. Garg, "Multi-objective optimization problem of system reliability under intuitionistic fuzzy set environment using Cuckoo Search algorithm", *J. Intell. Fuzzy Syst.,* vol. 29, no. 4, pp. 1653-1669.

[17]   D.W. Coit, and A.E. Smith, "Reliability optimization of series-parallel systems using a genetic algorithm", *IEEE Trans. Reliab.,* vol. 45, no. 2, pp. 254-260.

[18]   V. Ravi, B.S. Murty, and J. Reddy, "Nonequilibrium simulated-annealing algorithm applied to reliability optimization of complex systems", *IEEE Trans. Reliab.,* vol. 46, no. 2, pp. 233-239.

[19]   V. Ravi, P.J. Reddy, and H.J. Zimmermann, "Fuzzy global optimization of complex system reliability", *IEEE Trans. Fuzzy Syst.,* vol. 8, no. 3, pp. 241-248.

[20]   Y.S. Juang, S.S. Lin, and H.P. Kao, "A knowledge management system for series-parallel availability optimization and design", *Expert Syst. Appl.,* vol. 34, no. 1, pp. 181-193.

[21]   P.S. Rajpal, K.S. Shishodia, and G.S. Sekhon, "An artificial neural network for modeling reliability, availability and maintainability of a repairable system", *Reliab. Eng. Syst. Saf.,* vol. 91, no. 7, pp. 809-819.

[22]   H Garg, M Rani, and SP Sharma, "Fuzzy RAM analysis of the screening unit in a paper industry by utilizing uncertain data", *Int J Qual Stat Reliab,* . Article ID 203842

[23]   H. Garg, M. Rani, and S.P. Sharma, "Predicting uncertain behavior of press unit in a paper industry using artificial bee colony and fuzzy Lambda–Tau methodology", *Appl. Soft Comput.,* vol. 13, no. 4, pp. 1869-1881.

[24]   W.C. Yeh, Y.C. Lin, Y.Y. Chung, and M. Chih, "A particle swarm optimization approach based on Monte Carlo simulation for solving the complex network reliability problem", *IEEE Trans. Reliab.,* vol. 59, no. 1, pp. 212-221.

[25]   H. Garg, and S.P. Sharma, "A two-phase approach for reliability and maintainability analysis of an industrial system", *Int. J. Reliab. Qual. Saf. Eng.,* vol. 19, no. 03, p. 1250013.

[26]   H. Garg, S.P. Sharma, and M. Rani, "Cost minimization of washing unit in a paper mill using artificial bee colony technique", *Int J Syst Assur Engrg Manag.,* vol. 3, no. 4, pp. 371-381.

[27]   P. Wu, L. Gao, D. Zou, and S. Li, "An improved particle swarm optimization algorithm for reliability problems", *ISA Trans.,* vol. 50, no. 1, pp. 71-81.

[28]   E. Zio, P. Baraldi, and E. Patelli, "Assessment of the availability of an offshore installation by Monte Carlo simulation", *Int. J. Press. Vessels Piping*, vol. 83, no. 4, pp. 312-320.

[29]   H. Garg, and M. Rani, "An approach for reliability analysis of industrial systems using PSO and IFS technique", *ISA Trans.*, vol. 52, no. 6, pp. 701-710.

[30]   H. Garg, M. Rani, and S.P. Sharma, "An approach for analyzing the reliability of industrial systems using soft-computing based technique", *Expert Syst. Appl.*, vol. 41, no. 2, pp. 489-501.

[31]   H. Garg, "Reliability, availability and maintainability analysis of industrial systems using pso and fuzzy methodology", *MAPAN*, vol. 29, no. 2, pp. 115-129.

[32]   H. Garg, M. Rani, and S.P. Sharma, "Preventive maintenance scheduling of the pulping unit in a paper plant", *Jpn. J. Ind. Appl. Math.*, vol. 30, no. 2, pp. 397-414.

[33]   M. Gen, and Y. Yun, "Soft computing approach for reliability optimization: State-of-the-art survey", *Reliab. Eng. Syst. Saf.*, vol. 91, no. 9, pp. 1008-1026.

[34]   H. Garg, and S.P. Sharma, "Multi-objective optimization of crystallization unit in a fertilizer plant using particle swarm optimization", *Int J Appl Sci Eng*, vol. 9, no. 4, pp. 261-276.

[35]   M. Sheikhalishahi, V. Ebrahimipour, H. Shiri, H. Zaman, and M. Jeihoonian, "A hybrid GA–PSO approach for reliability optimization in redundancy allocation problem", *Int. J. Adv. Manuf. Technol.*, vol. 68, no. 1-4, pp. 317-338.

[36]   L.A. Zadeh, "Fuzzy sets", *Inf. Control*, vol. 8, no. 3, pp. 338-353.

[37]   M. Kumar, and S.P. Yadav, "A novel approach for analyzing fuzzy system reliability using different types of intuitionistic fuzzy failure rates of components", *ISA Trans.*, vol. 51, no. 2, pp. 288-297.

[38]   H. Garg, and S.P. Sharma, "Stochastic behavior analysis of complex repairable industrial systems utilizing uncertain data", *ISA Trans.*, vol. 51, no. 6, pp. 752-762.

[39]   H.Z. Huang, "Fuzzy multi-objective optimization decision-making of reliability of series system", *Microelectron. Reliab.*, vol. 37, no. 3, pp. 447-449.

[40]   G.S. Mahapatra, and T.K. Roy, "Fuzzy multi-objective mathematical programming on reliability optimization model", *Appl. Math. Comput.*, vol. 174, no. 1, pp. 643-659.

[41]   H. Garg, Fuzzy multiobjective reliability optimization problem of industrial systems using particle swarm optimization. J Ind Math. 2013; 2013: Article ID 872450, 9 pages

[42]   K.T. Atanassov, "Intuitionistic fuzzy sets", *Fuzzy Sets Syst.*, vol. 20, no. 1, pp. 87-96.

[43]   H. Garg, "Performance analysis of complex repairable industrial systems using PSO and fuzzy confidence interval based methodology", *ISA Trans.*, vol. 52, no. 2, pp. 171-183.

[44]   H. Garg, "An Approach for Analyzing Fuzzy System Reliability Using Particle Swarm Optimization and Intuitionistic Fuzzy Set Theory", *J Multiple-Valued Logic Soft Comput.*, vol. 21, no. 3-4, pp. 335-354.

[45]   S.M. Chen, "Analyzing fuzzy system reliability using vague set theory", *Int J Appl Sci Eng.*, vol. 1, no. 1, pp. 82-88.

[46]   H Garg, M Rani, and SP Sharma, Predicting uncertain behavior and performance analysis of the pulping system in a paper industry using PSO and Fuzzy methodology. Handbook of Research on Novel Soft Computing Intelligent Algorithms: Theory and Practical Applications. 2013 Aug 31:414-49

[47]   J.R. Chang, K.H. Chang, S.H. Liao, and C.H. Cheng, "The reliability of general vague fault-tree analysis on weapon systems fault diagnosis", *Soft Comput.*, vol. 10, no. 7, pp. 531-542.

[48]   M. Rani, S.P. Sharma, and H. Garg, "A Novel Approach for Analyzing the Behavior of Industrial Systems Using Uncertain Data", *Int. J. Perform. Eng.*, vol. 9, no. 2, pp. 201-210.

[49]   H Garg, M Rani, and SP Sharma, Reliability analysis of the engineering systems using intuitionistic fuzzy set theory. J Qual Reliab Eng. 2013; 2013: Article ID 943972, 10 page

[50]   H. Garg, "Reliability analysis of repairable systems using Petri nets and Vague Lambda-Tau methodology", *ISA Trans.*, vol. 52, no. 1, pp. 6-18.

[51]   H. Garg, "A novel approach for analyzing the reliability of series-parallel system using credibility theory and different types of intuitionistic fuzzy numbers", *J. Braz. Soc. Mech. Sci. Eng.*, vol. 38, no. 3, pp. 1021-1035.

[52]   S.M. Taheri, and R. Zarei, "Bayesian system reliability assessment under the vague environment", *Appl. Soft Comput.*, vol. 11, no. 2, pp. 1614-1622.

[53]   H. Garg, "Performance analysis of an industrial system using soft computing based hybridized technique", *J. Braz. Soc. Mech. Sci. Eng.,* vol. 39, no. 4, pp. 1441-1451.

[54]   D. Rani, T.R. Gulati, and H. Garg, "Multi-objective non-linear programming problem in intuitionistic fuzzy environment: Optimistic and pessimistic view point", *Expert Syst. Appl.,* vol. 64, pp. 228-238.

[55]   E. Rashedi, H. Nezamabadi-Pour, and S. Saryazdi, "GSA: a gravitational search algorithm", *Inf. Sci.,* vol. 179, no. 13, pp. 2232-2248.

CHAPTER 9

Modeling Quality in the Design of Supply Chains

Kanchan Das[*]

East Carolina University, College of Engineering and Technology, Greenville, North Carolina, USA

Abstract: Importance of quality in the overall supply chain management is paramount. In the current business world ensured quality product and services are the preconditions for their marketability. As such quality is the most crucial factor that will decide success and failure of the supply chain organization. Based on these facts quality should be planned for each supply chain function at the design stage. This research defines and formulates quality metrics for supply, product design and manufacturing, and customer process management with the objective of obtaining superior performance of a business system by integrating quality system of each function in the overall supply chain design and planning process. The research follows systematic steps in defining and formulating metrics for each function; and integration of the functional quality criteria in the overall supply chain design and planning model. A numerical example finally illustrates applicability of the entire approach and the models.

Keywords: Critical to quality and critical to business, Customer satisfaction attributes, Plant approval, Quality in customer management, Quality metrics, Strategic supply chain design model, Supplier affiliation.

INTRODUCTION

Quality in supply chain (SC) is a multifaceted factor, closely linked to the entire SC process. To succeed in today's highly competitive globalized business world, the quality link of the SC should be prominent to the customers and various stakeholders. Quality of inputs to the products and quality of outputs that is going to customers are the main concern in SC operations. Businesses should plan a general quality management system (QMS) giving due importance to critical-to-quality (CTQ) and critical-to-business (CTB) factors to address these concerns effectively.

*Corresponding author Kanchan Das: East Carolina University, College of Engineering and Technology, Greenville, North Carolina, USA; Tel: 252 737 1905; Fax: 252 328 1618; E-mail: dask@ecu.edu

SC should integrate QMS, CTQ, and CTB in their supply, production and distribution system planning for improving their overall performance. Defining QMS design criteria and identifying CTB and CTQ factors are the critical steps towards this end. QMS design criteria should address general quality issues for product design, input, production, safety, environment, distribution, and customer process of the SC. CTQ planning will identify the attributes and their metrics that are the determinant for the product quality assurance and are crucial for product image in the market. CTB planning will emphasize product safety, process, environment and the product user in addition to customer satisfaction indices.

This research presents a quality system based framework to create relevance of the proposed approach with the SC process. In the next step, it defines the QMS criteria by identifying the CTQ and CTB factors in a generic business setting. Finally, mathematical models are formulated to facilitate the SC manager in applying this approach in their businesses. Example problems are solved to illustrate applicability of the model and framework.

QMS criteria in any business are originated based on customer expected quality. As such businesses should select QMS standards or combinations of standards for defining required criteria in an effort to address the customer expected quality in today's globalized market.

Fig. (1). A qualitysystem based business framework.

This research proposes a performance based quality system framework as shown in Fig. (**1**), for building a QMS criteria that will coherently address global business situation. The framework will guide in defining the generic performance requirement without contradicting any QMS standard.

The quality-based SC planning literature is extremely rich and diverse. We may refer to typical supply quality studies in [1-3]; manufacturing process quality in [4-7]; or customer service quality in [8-10]. Quality is not given importance solely in literature or the academia; looking at the today's successful businesses, one might very easily choose quality as the most crucial factor that can be used for evaluating and improving performance of functions and products. Since customers care about the quality, and quality assurance covers all functions in an organization [11, 12], performance evaluation criteria of business functions should be based on the desired output quality or customer expected quality.

Considering the breadth of the quality involvement and quality planning issues in a SC, planning and design should start at input process and conclude at customer service while addressing product design, production process, and shipment or delivery to customers in between. For effectively addressing these functional steps and processes, this research proposes an integrated QMS that may be uniformly applicable for the entire global business. Current global business has turned into an extremely complex process when supply, production, and distribution nodes are located in diverse geographic locations. In global businesses, the manufacturing plants that supply to the shipping points are located in diverse geographic locations. Inputs to these manufacturing plants are procured from multilayered and multiple country-based supplier plants. These diverse locations are subject to various limitations, local regulations, and cultures. Despite the challenges posed by the complex global and logistical factors, ensuring quality at the input point and product quality and safety at the shipping point are the most crucial requirements for a global supply chain (GSC)—knowing that a small quality failure at any point in any country could mean disaster to the business.

SC QUALITY PLANNING

SC functional steps should be planned and defined based on their operational standard quality attributes to obtain expected uniform performance metrics for the entire business process. The performance metrics for the standard quality attributes that include the CTQ and CTB factors will enable management to integrate the QMS in strategic decision-making, in order to ensure uniform output quality across the global market. To oversee quality issues of the functional areas, SC needs to establish a general QMS department (defined as QM subsequently) which will function as a quality bureau for the SC to define and set standards for the quality based operational metrics. The quality attributes and metrics for the SC quality planning may be defined for the following key functional areas: supply management, product design, manufacturing system, and customer system management.

Quality in Supply Management

There are an impressive number of researches that could establish the importance and advantage of supply quality and supply management (SM) process [13-15]. The study of [11] and [13] advocated ISO 9000 QMS based SM process for obtaining improved SC performances. Kaynak and Hartley [2] proposed TQM based approach in customer and SM process. De Carvalho and Costa [3] proposed a supplier performance based SM process that considered services and cost factors of the past supplies from the suppliers. There are also several empirical researches, such as [16-18], and others that established importance of quality in SM process for improving overall business performances. But insufficient research exists that provides clear guidelines to establish quality-based SM process. To bridge this gap, this research proposes a supplier quality performance based SM process that will affiliate the supplier with the buying company based on the performance of supplier plants for CTQ and CTB factors defined by the SC QM to ensure input quality. In addition, the proposed SM process will encourage and establish continuous quality improvement process for the supplier and facilitate SCs in developing business partnership with the suppliers. The SC QM may define generic CTQ attributes for supplier plants in affiliating the suppliers. The QM may also include a weight factor scale of 1 to 5 to provide importance to attributes based on the specific business goal of the company. The following are the examples of generic CTQ attributes applicable to supplier affiliation process: We also define typical metrics scale and weight factors for the attributes.

Process Capability: average C_{pk} value for the supplier plant may be the metric. A C_{pk} value of 1.8 and above may be given 10, while a value below 1 may be given 0 in a 0 to 10 metrics scale. A weight factor 5 may be applicable here.

Scrap Rate or Rejections: average % scrap/rejection for the plant may be the metric. In a 0 to 10 scale 0% rejection may get 10 and more than 1% may get 0. A weight factor of 2 to 3 may be considered for this attribute.

ISO 9000 Certification may be the metric. A supplier plant certified recently or one to four years before may be get 10 in a 0 to 10 scale, a plant in certification process may get 5, while a score of 0 for not applying or not in process status. Considering QMS to be the most crucial in SM quality, this attribute may get 5 as weight factor.

Plant Reliability: average OEE (overall equipment effectiveness) may be the metric. OEE of 0.80 to above will get 10 while 0.65 and below may be awarded 0, in a 0 to 10 scale. A weight factor of 2 to 3 may be applicable here.

Customer Complaints average number of customer complaints per month may be the metric. In a 0 to10 scale, 10 may be awarded for 0 complaints while a 0 for 1 or more complaints per month. A weight of 3 to 4 may be awarded.

Product Approval by ABS, LLOYDS or some federal authority in USA may be the metric. A supplier plant with approved product will earn 10 while a 0 for not approved product. Weight may be 1 to 2 for this attribute.

Quality Award metric may be for obtaining Baldrige or other quality award. In a 0 to 10 scale a quality award winner supplier may get 10, and a 5 for a supplier in application process, a 0 for neither of these. Weight may be 1 to 2.

Delivery Reliability (DR) may be defined as the metric by assuming supply lead time to be normally distributed with μLT as the mean and $\sigma^2 LT$ as the variance. If

$$P(ALT \le \mu LT) = 1 - \phi(\frac{ALT - \mu LT}{\sigma LT})$$ is 95 % or more, DR may be awarded 10,

while below 75% may be awarded 0. Here ALT is the expected lead time. Weight for this factor may be 3 to 4.

The SC QM may select similar other CTQ factors, such as: JIT or lean manufacturing system follower, six sigma quality system follower, TQM system follower, inventory turnover, labor turnover, having production design and development department based on their product and business goal.

As discussed before, the SC QM should also identify CTB factors to prevent product recalls and media attention arising from consumer health, environmental hazard or such other problems created by the inputs of a supplier. CTB factors may also consider supplier's information management, standards, unit system, and others, that are vital for SC's business practices. The performance criteria in CTB may be in a 0 to 5 scale, while setting an acceptable level for the buying company. The SC should not compromise on CTB requirements. The typical CTB factors may include following:

Use of Restrictive Materials: The SC QM should devise protocol for screening the unacceptable materials, such as radioactive, toxic, lead based and such others that may create health hazard for the operator, user or community. It should similarly screen out materials that may create environmental problem in a short time interval or in the long run.

Past Product Recalls History: The suppliers should be checked for their past product recalls and the steps they have taken to restrict future repetition.

Loss Time Accidents: Supplier factory should be safe enough to ensure delivery to a SC. Acceptance criteria may be developed based on the importance the SC provides on the failure to supply due to accidents.

User of SAP or Similar Information Management System: Based on the expectation of information exchange between the supplier and the SC the acceptance criteria may be set.

In addition to the above CTBs, the SC QM may also include software adaptability, child labor use, government type, and communication for supplier affiliation process. The SC QM should create the criteria such that a supplier will be considered for CTQ evaluation only when it complies with the CTB requirements for each of the CTB attributes.

Supplier Affiliation Model

To facilitate supplier affiliation based on several CTQ and CTB attributes in a multiple input, and multiple supplier situations, this research proposes an Integer Programming (IP) model. The model considers set of CTQ attributes Q, $(q \in Q)$ and set of CTB attributes $B, (b \in B)$ identified by the SC QM for affiliating set of suppliers $S(s \in S)$ for supplying input type i $(i \in I)$ to the SC. The QM sets two threshold values, TA_i and TH_i for affiliating supplier s at acceptable quality (AQ) and high quality (HQ) level for input i. The minimum score requirement for HQ affiliated suppliers are much higher than the AQ suppliers such that the SC may accept input i supplied by HQ without inspection while supplies from AQ are subjected to inspection. Since CTB attributes carry higher strategic importance, each supplier needs to pass each CTB attribute requirements at the acceptable level before they are considered for CTQ affiliation. Let SP_{isq} is the score obtained by supplier s for CTQ attribute q; $Q'_{is}=1$ if supplier s is affiliated fulfilling minimum threshold requirements (TA_i); $Q'_{is}=0$ otherwise; and $G_{is} = 1$, when it is affiliated at the HQ level, 0 otherwise. Q_{is} identifies the AQ suppliers when HQ suppliers are separated from affiliated supplier's pool. We also assume notation SB_{sb} as the performance indices obtained by the supplier s for CTB attribute when requirement for such attribute is RB_b, and B_{sb} is the 0/1 decision variables to identify supplier s for passing or not passing the CTB requirements.

The supplier affiliation model may be defined as:

$$\textbf{maximize} \quad Z = \sum_{i \in I}{}' \sum_{s \in S}{}' \; (G_{is} + Q_{is}) \tag{1}$$

$$TA_i Q'_{is} \leq \sum_{q \in Q}{}' SP_{isq} \qquad \forall i, s \tag{2}$$

$$TH_i G_{is} \leq \sum_{q \in Q}{}' SP_{isq} \qquad \forall i, s \tag{3}$$

$$G_{is} \leq Q'_{is} \qquad \forall i, s \tag{4}$$

$$Q_{is} = Q'_{is} - G_{is} \qquad \forall i, s \tag{4.a}$$

$$Q'_{is} \leq B_{sb} \qquad \forall i, s, b \tag{5}$$

$$RB_b B_{sb} \leq SB_{sb} \qquad \forall s, b \tag{6}$$

$$G_{is}, Q'_{is}, Q_{is} \in \{0,1\}, \forall i, s \; B_{sb} \in \{0,1\}, \qquad \forall s, b \tag{7}$$

The supplier affiliation objective function (1) maximizes number of affiliated suppliers. Constraints (2) and (3) determine affiliated (in general) and HQ level suppliers based on obtained scores by the suppliers. Constraints (4) ensure affiliation of a supplier at HQ level once it is affiliated for general affiliation requirements. Constraint (4.a) identifies HQ and AQ level suppliers separately. Constraint (5) ensures consideration of a supplier for CTQ evaluation after it passes CTB screening. Constraint (6) identifies CTB passed suppliers and constraint (7) imposes integrality.

The supplier affiliation model output is integrated in the strategic model decision process such that inputs are assigned only to the quality affiliated suppliers to ensure input quality and developing partner suppliers for further improvement of quality and cost base.

Quality in Manufacturing and Design

After taking care of quality of inputs to production, the SC needs to ensure shipment quality of product in the next stage to ensure customer expected quality in the market. For a locally operated SC or a GSC, ensuring a uniform customer-expected quality for the entire market is a necessary condition to survive in the current global business process [19]. For the multiple manufacturing plants operated by a SC, a uniform product quality across global market may be ensured by creating CTQ and CTB attributes-based performance metrics, relevant to plant operations. Product design is the basis for satisfying customer needs in terms of functions and cost [20, 21]. Sohn and Choi [22] proposed a QFD (quality function deployment) based SC management approach for imparting reliability to the various product at planning stage. The approach is targeted to ensure product quality.

Kannan and Tan [23] proposed combination of JIT, TQM and SC management for improving operations performance of the businesses. Batson and McGough [24] recommended application of quality engineering in manufacturing SC design. These researches emphasized quality assurance in manufacturing and design. As mentioned earlier quality integration in manufacturing and design is crucial for ensuring product quality in the market places. An insignificant number of researches are included in the literature that provided systematic approach for integrating quality system in the product manufacturing for ensuring product quality to shipment. To ensure customer expected quality in the market places this research proposes a quality integration process in the manufacturing operations steps that first defines CTQ and CTB attributes and relevant metrics considering combined effect of product design and manufacturing on ensuring product quality. Most of the CTQ and CTB attributes defined for supplier plants will be relevant to SC's plant operations steps while transforming inputs to outputs following product design. To ensure quality in product design and overall product quality to fulfill customer requirements, the SC QM should also include following CTQ attributes in addition to the attributes considered for supplier affiliation:

Product Specification (spec) Attributes from QFD Analysis: The metrics may be defined based on the range targeted in the QFD process. Score may be 10 for the achievement of best value in the range, while a zero for not achieving within the range. Multiple QFD based spec attributes may be the candidates in this case.

Manufacturing lead time (MLT): This attribute may be the probability of achieving expected MLT. The probability and metrics may be defined taking the similar approach of delivery reliability for the supply management.

The SC QM may evaluate each plant operated by SC based on the entire set of CTB factors applicable to supplier plants and the additional requirements, such as, log-record on taking care of recent customer feedback issues; including product mix flexibility (range of product offering based on market study); capacity flexibility to accommodate demand fluctuation, and safety stock keeping ensuring desired customer service level.

Manufacturing Plant Approval Model

The following IP based manufacturing capability model will aid SC managers for effectively assigning production to quality capable plants. The model will be a vital tool, specifically, for a SC that manufactures several products using several plants. Let the SC has a set of plants M, $(m \in M)$ for producing a set of product $P, (p \in P)$. We assume same CTQ and CTB metrics notations of supplier affiliation model are applicable in this model also. The threshold value for CTQ based plant capability determination is denoted by: MT_{mp} for plant m, for producing product p. Performance score obtained by the plant m relevant to CTQ attribute q for producing product p is denoted by MP_{mpq}; $v_{mp}=1$ if the plant m has been approved as capable plant for producing product p, 0 otherwise. For the CTB attributes, each CTB requirement is a corporate decision as such a plant needs to comply with each CTB requirements to be considered for approval as capable plant. Let CB_b is the performance requirement score for CTB attribute b for each plant and ; MB_{mb} is the performance indices of plant m for CTB attributes b, and $u_{mb}=1$ if plant m complied with the CTB requirements for attribute b, 0 otherwise. The model is defined below combining CTQ and CTB requirements for design and manufacturing:

$$\textbf{maximize} \quad z = \sum_{m \in M} \sum_{p \in P} v_{mp} \tag{8}$$

$$MT_{mp} v_{mp} \leq \sum_{q \in Q} MP_{mpq} \qquad \forall m, p \tag{9}$$

$$v_{mp} \leq u_{mb} \qquad \forall m, p, b \tag{10}$$

$$u_{mb} CB_b \leq MB_{mb} \qquad \forall m, b \tag{11}$$

$$u_{mb}, v_{mp} \in \{0,1\}, \qquad \forall m, b, p \tag{12}$$

Objective function in (8) maximizes number of capable plants for product p. Constraint (9) identifies the capable plants based on the CTQ metrics score for manufacturing plants. Constraint (10) ensures compliance with CTB metrics requirements before a plant is approved for CTQ requirements. Constraint (11) checks each plant for each CTB metrics requirement. Constraint (12) imposes integrality.

The plant approval or capability model output is subsequently integrated in the strategic SC model decision such that production for a product is assigned only to CTQ capable plant. By instilling this critical step of plant capability determination following the approach described above the SC will ensure shipment quality of product that has been designed based on the customer feedback taking QFD approach.

Quality in Customer System Management

Integration of customers and customer services in the SC planning process contribute progressively towards the improvement of the SC business process [25]. Customer System Management is the final and the most crucial SC quality point. The ultimate aim of customer system management should be to provide customer satisfaction (CS) and integration of CS in the SC planning. As such, by addressing CS integration the SC would effectively address customer system management. It is often difficult to identify CS or customer integration attributes and create relevant metrics. In addition, CS factors are often business specific and quite diverse in nature to influence several business decisions by a single factor. For example, CS requirements include order fulfillment factors [26], services [27], communication [28-30], after sales services [31], product quality [8] and several others. It is apparent that most of these factors are very broad and supplement each other. The number of researches contributing in this area is insignificant in number. But there is no research that would facilitate SC managers in integrating CS factors in their decision process by defining the factors and their relevant metrics. The proposed research will define CS attributes and relevant metrics for addressing quality issues at customer system management.

Since CS is influenced by several tangible and intangible factors. SC QM may define the CS attributes and their relevant metrics in terms of effects of the factors. Considering the diverse nature of the CS factors, we define the following factors, typical attributes and relevant metrics to facilitate SCs for following similar example procedure to effectively integrate them in the strategic planning level. It may be mentioned here that the CS attribute metrics and defining of scales are business specific. The SC QM should devise the metrics/scales based on the product, business goal and other long-term perspectives of the company.

Operational: Operational factors are the most effective in providing CS [32]. CS attributes under operational factors are the core competencies of the SC that expresses market responsiveness, flexibility and includes effect of intangible factors such as customer focused policies. Operational CS attributes may include: JIT replenishment, Vendor Managed Inventory (VMI), frequent delivery, scheduled supply assurance, and such others. The SC QM may device a scale of 1 to 10 and award 10 to a JIT replenishment for any size or type of customer, and 1 to the scheduled supply. The effect of other operations attributes may be similarly defined in the customer supplier interface.

Material Management (MM): CS attributes under MM function express the capability and capacity of the SC in terms of production, quality, reliability and other relevant MM related SC competencies that provide intra-firm operational performances. These CS attributes may create foundations for influencing customer to become loyal to the SC. MM CS attributes include: (a) 100% defect free supplier, (b) six sigma quality provider, (c) warranty for product quality, (d) assurance of safety to consumer, (f) traditional quality control and such others. In a 1 to 10 scale MM CS attribute (a) may be awarded 10, while (d) may get 5.

Technological: The technological CS attributes facilitate establishing long term relationship with the customers. It creates impression for dependability of a customer on the SC capability. These attributes ultimately create partnership. Examples of such attributes: owning and sharing R&D facility, capability for virtual displaying of product feature to consumer, user of latest technology plant, e-maintenance user, user of rapid prototyping, user of ASRS for storage and quick supply. In a 1 to 10 scale, user of latest technology plant may be awarded 10 and e-maintenance may be 1.

Strategic: These CS attributes reduce the complexity of the transactions and are directed to developing long term joint venture type of relationships. Examples: production selection offer to the customer, expansion of product range based on customer's recommendations, providing flexibility in volume and product mix, investment in joint venture, supportive in customized or new product launching, offering salvage value to the customer, including recycle and remanufacture. Scale for this CS factor may be in a 5 to 10 scale. Several attributes may get 10, or little bit less important ones may get 5.

Information System (IS): Online communication and providing access to the customer on production and stock through SAP, or other software; tracking distribution, and e-business provision are examples of CS attributes for IS. In this case, online connection using SAP may be given 10 and e-business may be awarded 5 in a 5 to 10 scale.

Customer or Consumer Service: providing presale and post sale support to consumer using training or demonstration, product support in terms of repair, re-fix, and services relevant to customized products are the few CS attributes under this customer service category. Here each attribute is very valuable, as such scale may be 7 to 10, while presale or post sale support may be 7 and service relevant to customized product may be 10.

Financial Power, Link and Others: Strong financial power and link to influence policy of governments by a SC provide strong CS. The reasons for the satisfaction are the confidence of the customer in company operations. These CS attributes may be awarded 7 to 8 in a 1 to 10 scale.

The CS attribute metrics based customer system management may be used by the SC for their self evaluation in relation to existing customer/market and prospecting for growth in a market. Such evaluation will facilitate SC to determine their competency for attaining a customer/market for which they are prospecting. The CS metrics based analysis will also facilitate SC managers in identifying the attributes on which they need to improve for winning over a customer or a potential customer. The SC may take a long term continuous improvement track for their overall improvement in CS based competency. Chow *et al.* [33] confirmed that CS could be the result of SC competency achievements, in terms of quality, service, operations, distribution and design effectiveness—supporting the statement that the customer integration process leads to increased CS. In this endeavor SC may use EPSI or ACSI based indices for their benchmarking for relevant CS attributes and metrics.

SC Competency Model for Customer System Management

Based on the above discussion SC should consider several CS attributes from different functions that may influence their business performance. An IP based mathematical model is formulated to facilitate SC mangers for evaluating competency of their business considering CS attributes relevant to the multiple functions. Since most of the CS related steps have long term implications, CS based SC competency evaluation should finally be integrated in the strategic level planning. We assume a SC that markets a set of products P to a set of customers $C(c \in C)$ in diverse global market. Within the customer pool the SC has included potential customers also in addition to their existing exclusive, non-exclusive customers. Based on the requirements of customers (implied and spelled) in relation to services and performances of SC for product quality, distribution and other capabilities, the SC QM in collaboration with marketing defined a set of CS attributes $a(a \in A)$ and relevant metrics for each. Let the SC achieves the metrics score CP_{pca} for product p, for CS attributes a for supplying to the customer c. The SC QM in collaboration with marketing also determined RC_{pc}, the minimum total score for the entire set of CS attributes for supplying product p to customer c. As discussed before RC_{pc} is the parameter determined by the SC internally for their self competency evaluation to supply the customer c. We also define $SR_{pc} = 1$, if the SC achieves the required competency for supplying product p to customer c, 0 otherwise; $k_{pc} = 1$, if the SC has contractual agreement with customer c to supply product p, 0 otherwise. Also the customer c has requirements D_{pc} amount of p product and the SC has a capacity of SCP_p for supplying product p.

$$\textbf{maximize} \ \ SCcom = \sum_{p \in P} \sum_{c \in C} SR_{pc} \tag{13}$$

$$RC_{pc} SR_{pc} \leq \sum_{a \in A} CP_{pca} \qquad \qquad \forall p,c \tag{14}$$

$$D_{pc} k_{pc} \leq SCP_p \qquad \qquad \forall p,c \tag{15}$$

$$k_{pc} \leq SR_{pc} \qquad \qquad \forall p,c \tag{16}$$

$$SR_{pc}, k_{pc} \in \{0,1\} \qquad \qquad \forall p,c \tag{17}$$

The objective function in (13) maximizes the competency of SC for product-customer combinations. Constraint (14) identifies the SC competency for the product-customer combinations based on their score on the CS attributes metrics and minimum requirements relevant to customer, estimated by the SC QM. Constraint (15) limits supply to the customer based on the capacity to supply when the SC has contractual agreement with the customer. Constraint (16) ensures contractual agreement with a customer for which the SC is competent. Constraint (17) imposes integrality.

THE INTERGRATED STRATEGIC SC DESIGN MODEL

The discussed strategic SC planning and design model that integrates quality based supply management, production management, and customer system management is presented in the section. The section describes a short problem statement and explains the model equations in addition to presenting the model.

The SC problem described before in supplier affiliation, plant approval and SC competency determination model is continued here to build up the strategic SC planning and design model that will integrate decisions of previous three models and crate a SC planning and design for overall performance improvement of the SC. The model decision will design a supply chain network for ensuring quality inputs to production, quality products to shipments, and provide required customer satisfaction for overall improvement of the profit. We describe following notations in addition to the notations used in the previous three models: We include important output variables of the previous three models at the end of notations for providing ready reference.

Notations

AC_{is} is the capacity of acceptable quality supplier s for supplying input i.

$BN1$, $BN2$ are the big numbers.

b_i and βi are the auxiliary 0,1 variables for allocating input i

CD_{pj} is the capacity of DC j for warehousing product p.

CM_{pm} is the capacity of plant m for producing product p

CQM_{is} is the quality monitoring cost of affiliated supplier s for input i

CY_{pc} is the competency arrangement cost for product p to supply to customer c

D_{pc} is the demand for product p from customer c

FP_{pm} is the setup cost for producing product p in plant m

FS_{is} is fixed cost for supplying input i by supplier s

FW_j is the fixed cost for opening DC j

HC_{is} is the capacity of high quality supplier s for supplying input i.

IC_{is} is the cost of input i supplied by supplier s

IN_{is} is the inspection cost for applicable to the supply quantity by acceptable quality (AQ) suppliers

hz_{ism} is the input i supplied by high quality supplier s to plant m;

n_{mp} =1, if the plant m is set for producing product p, 0 otherwise;

o_{jc} = 1, warehouse j is assigned to customer c, 0 otherwise;

PCM_{pm} is the quality approval related cost for plant m to product p

PC_{pm} is the cost of producing product p in plant m

ρ_{ip} is the usage of inputs i to produce product p;

qz_{ism} = inputs i supplied by the acceptable quality supplier's s to plant m.

r''_{is} =1, if acceptable quality (AQ) supplier s is placed order for input i, 0 otherwise;

r'_{is} =1, if high quality(HQ) supplier s is placed order for input i, 0 otherwise;

TC_{pmj} is the cost for transporting product p from plant m to DC j

V_{pc} is the price customer c is willing to pay for product p

WC_{pjc} is the cost for distributing product p from DC j to customer c.

x_{pmj} be the production of product p in plant m and transported to DC j;

y_{pjc} is the product p distributed to customer c from DC j;

z_{ism} is the input i supplied by supplier s to plant m;

w_j =1, if DC j is open, 0 otherwise;

The following are the input parameter for Integrated Strategic Level Model that have been the output and decision variables for supplier affiliation, plant capability and SC competency models.

Q_{is}=1 if supplier s is affiliated at the AQ level; Q_{is}=0 otherwise

G_{is} = 1, when it is affiliated at the HQ level, 0 otherwise

v_{mp}=1 if the plant p has been approved as capable plant for producing product p, 0 otherwise

SR_{pc} =1, if the SC achieves the required competency for supplying product p to customer c, 0 otherwise

k_{pc} =1 when the SC has the agreement with the customer c to supply product p, 0 otherwise

The strategic planning model objective function and its components are defined in equation (18) to (21.d)

$$\textbf{maximize } \textit{Profit} \tag{18}$$

$$\textit{Profit} = \textit{Revenue (RV)} - \textit{Overall SC Cost (CST)} \tag{19}$$

$$RV = \sum_{p \in P}{}^{'} \sum_{c \in C}{}^{'} V_{pc} \sum_{j \in J}{}^{'} y_{pjc} \tag{20}$$

CST = Input cost (INC) +Production cost (PDC) +Transportation & distribution cost (TDC) +Quality cost (QSC) $\tag{21}$

$$INC = \sum_{i \in I}{}^{'} \sum_{s \in S}{}^{'} IC_{is} \sum_{m \in M}{}^{'} z_{ism} + \sum_{i \in I}{}^{'} \sum_{s \in S}{}^{'} r_{is} FS_{is} \tag{21a}$$

$$PDC = \sum_{p \in P}{}^{'} \sum_{m \in M}{}^{'} PC_{pm} \sum_{j \in J}{}^{'} x_{pmj} + \sum_{p \in P}{}^{'} \sum_{m \in M}{}^{'} FP_{pm} n_{pm} \tag{21b}$$

$$TDC = \sum_{p \in P}{}^{'} \sum_{m \in M}{}^{'} \sum_{j \in J}{}^{'} TC_{pmj} x_{pmj} + \sum_{p \in P}{}^{'} \sum_{j \in J}{}^{'} \sum_{c \in C}{}^{'} WC_{pjc} y_{pjc} + \sum_{j \in J}{}^{'} FW_j w_j \tag{21c}$$

$$QSC = \sum_{s \in S}{}^{'} \sum_{i \in I}{}^{'} CQM_{is} Q_{is} + \sum_{s \in S}{}^{'} \sum_{i \in I}{}^{'} IN_{is} qz_{ism} +$$
$$\sum_{m \in M} \sum_{p \in P} v_{pm} PCM_{pm} + \sum_{p \in P} \sum_{c \in C} SR_{pc} CY_{pc} \tag{21d}$$

The Strategic Planning Model objective function in (18) maximizes profit. Equation (19) computes profit by adjusting overall cost from the revenue. Revenue in (20) is earned by supplying products to the customer. Equation (21) defines the overall cost (*CST*) in terms of costs for inputs, production, transportation, distribution and quality. Input cost, *INC* in (21.a) includes fixed cost for ordering to supplier and cost for inputs. Production cost, *PDC* in (21.b) includes costs for production and costs for setting up a plant for production of a product. *TDC* in (21.c) computes costs for transporting product from plant to the DCs and distributing products from DCs to the customers. Quality cost, *QSC* in (21.d) includes average costs for affiliating a supplier, inspection cost for the product supplied by acceptable quality supplier, installing plant capability and achieving competency for supplying a customer.

We now define the constraints for allocating production to integrated quality capable plants, transporting products from plants to DCs and distributing products from DCs to integrated customers for which SC has the competency:

$$\sum_{j \in J}' x_{pmj} \leq PC_{pm} \eta_{mp} \qquad \forall p,m \qquad (22)$$

$$\eta_{mp} \leq v_{mp} \qquad \forall p,m \qquad (23)$$

$$\sum_{m \in M}' x_{pmj} = \sum_{c \in C}' y_{pjc} \qquad \forall p,j \qquad (24)$$

$$\sum_{m \in M}' x_{pmj} \leq w_j CD_{pj} \qquad \forall p,j \qquad (25)$$

$$\sum_{p \in P}' y_{pjc} \leq SR_{pc} D_{pc} \qquad \forall j,c \qquad (26)$$

$$o_{jc} \leq k_{pc} \qquad \forall p,j,c \qquad (27)$$

$$\sum_{p \in P}' y_{pjc} \leq o_{jc} BN3 \qquad \forall j,c \qquad (27a)$$

Constraint (22) limits production according plant capacity. Constraint (23) allocates production to a quality capable plant as decided in the *Manufacturing Plant Approval Model*. Equation (24) balances flow between plant to DC and DC to customer. Constraint (25) limits sending products to a DC based on its warehousing capacity. Constraint (26) ensures supply of product to the customer according to the SC capacity in the *SC Competency for Customer System Management* when SC has the competency. Constraint (27) assigns DCs to a customer that has an agreement with the SC as decided in the *SC Competency Model*. Constraint (27.a) confirms products from DCs to the customers according to contract.

In the next step we define the constraints for procurements of inputs from the integrated quality affiliated suppliers.

$$\sum_{s \in S}' z_{ism} = \sum_{p \in P}' \rho_{ip} \sum_{j \in J}' x_{pmj} \qquad \forall i,m \qquad (28)$$

$$z_{ism} = hz_{ism} + qz_{ism} \qquad \forall i,s,m \qquad (29)$$

$$\sum_{m \in M}' hz_{ism} \leq r'_{is} HC_{is} \qquad \forall i,s \qquad (30)$$

$$r'_{is} \leq G_{is} \qquad \forall i,s \qquad (31)$$

$$\sum_{m \in M}' qz_{ism} \leq r''_{is} AC_{is} \qquad \forall i,s \qquad (32)$$

$$r''_{is} \leq Q_{is} \qquad \forall i,s \qquad (33)$$

$$\sum_{s \in S}{}^{'} (HC_{is} - \sum_{m \in m}{}^{'} z_{ism}) \le b_i BN \qquad \forall i \tag{34}$$

$$r''_{is} \le (1 - b_i)BN \qquad\qquad\qquad \forall i, s \tag{35}$$

$$\sum_{s \in S}{}^{'} (\sum_{m \in M}{}^{'} z_{ism} - HC_{is}) \le \beta_i BN \qquad \forall i \tag{36}$$

$$\sum_{s \in S}{}^{'} (HC_{is} - \sum_{m \in m}{}^{'} hz_{ism}) \le (1 - \beta_i)BN1 \quad \forall i \tag{37}$$

$$\eta_{pm} \in \{0,1\}, \ \forall p, m; w_j, o_{jc} \in \{0,1\}, \forall j, c; r'_{is}, r''_{is} \in \{0,1\}, \forall i, s; b_i, \beta_i \in \{0,1\} \quad \forall i \tag{38}$$

Constraint (28) determines input requirements based on usage and production quantity. Constraint (29) balances inputs supply from high quality (HQ) and acceptable quality (AQ) suppliers. Constraint (30) limits procurement from HQ suppliers based on their capacity. Constraint (31) identifies HQ suppliers for supplying high quality inputs. Constraint (32) limits procurement from the acceptable quality (AQ) suppliers according to their capacity. Affiliation status of the acceptable quality (AQ) suppliers are ensured in constraint (33) before they are assigned inputs. Constraint (34) and (35) jointly ensures procurement of entire input requirements from HQ suppliers if they have the capacity to fulfill requirements for an input. Constraint (36) and (37) jointly ensures taking of input quantity from the acceptable quality (AQ) suppliers that cannot be supplied by the HQ suppliers. Constraint (38) imposes integrality.

Solution Procedure

The following solution algorithm is proposed for obtaining optimal solution of the model within reasonable time and computational resources:

Step 1: Record a) the CTQ attributes ($q = 1,2\ldots$), CTB attributes ($b=1, 2\ldots$) and relevant scale values for the supplier plant operation steps and business functions as defined and set by the SC QM; b) threshold values TA_i TH_i for affiliating suppliers at AQ and HQ level based on the overall CTQ scores for each input type and threshold value for individual CTB scores, SB_b as defined and set by SC QM for evaluating performance of supplier plant.

Step 2: Record the supplier data in terms of a) identification number (say $s=1,2$); b) capability for supplying input types ($i=1, 2\ldots$), and capacity (CS_{is}) for each input type; c) CTQ and CTB attribute metrics scores (SP_{siq} and SB_{sb} respectively); d) input cost (cost for supplying and fixed cost).

Step 3: Record the a) CTQ and CTB attributes and relevant scale similar to step 1 for manufacturing operation steps defined by the SC QM for the plants operated by SC; b) CTQ based capability threshold value, MT_{mp} for plant product combinations; c) CTB based threshold value CB_b; d) CTQ and CTB attributes metrics scores (MP_{mpq} and MB_{mb} respectively) for manufacturing plant operation.

Step 4: Record *CS* attributes ($a=1,2, ...$), relevant metrics, score value (PC_{pca}) obtained by SC, and estimated minimum CS attribute score (RC_{pc})to supply to the customers, as defined and determined jointly by marketing and SC QM.

Step 5: Solve *Supplier Affiliation Model* using information in steps 1 and 2. Record the model outcome for AQ (Q_{is}) and high quality (G_{is}) supplier –input combinations.

Step 6: Solve *Manufacturing Plant Approval Model* using data in step 3. Record the model output for capable plant –product combinations.

Step 7: Solve the *SC Competency Model for Customer System Management* using the data in Step 4. Record the model output for product-customer combinations for which the SC has been found to be competent.

Step 8: Record the costs and capacity for supplying the inputs, manufacturing the product, distributing and transporting finished products, and maintaining and improving quality.

Step 9: Record the costs related to QMS.

Step 10: solve the *Integrated Strategic SC Design Model* integrating model outcomes for supplier affiliation, manufacturing plant approval and customer competency as recorded in steps 5 to 7 into input data in steps 8 and 9 for maximizing profit ensuring product quality and targeted customer satisfaction in the market places.

Step 11: Record the model decision on assignment of inputs to suppliers, allocation of production to plants, customer–product combinations for marketing.

Numerical Example

An example problem for the strategic level planning of a SC that includes 7 production plants, 9 DCs that markets 6 products to its ultimate consumer through

10 retailers is solved for illustrating applicability of the models and solution procedure. Each product is made up of 5 to 6 inputs out of total 10 inputs procured from 8 suppliers. The QM of the SC follows a quality based supplier affiliation for ensuring quality inputs to production and plant capability evaluation for ensuring right quality product in the market places. In addition, the QM in collaboration with SC marketing department pursues customer satisfaction indices based SC competency evaluation for customer system management. In this section we include description and analysis that emphasizes quality issues of the SC functions, such as: supply, production, and customer system management. Additional information and analyses are included only to support SC functional quality issues. To solve the numerical example and illustrate applicability of the model we follow step-by step procedure outlined in **Solution Procedure.**

Step 1, part of **Step 2** and **Step 5:** The SC QM identified 15 CTQ attributes relevant to the supplier's plant operations that are responsible for input quality. The QM also defined a 0 -10 score scale and 1 - 5 weight scale for each attribute for affiliating suppliers based on their total score, ($\sum$score*weight) by comparing with the threshold value set by them. The data recorded in step 2 relevant to supplier capacity and supply cost will be used for solving the strategic level SC design model in Step 10. The data relevant to CTQ and CTB metrics score as recorded in Table 1, 2 and 3 in Step 2 are used in *Supplier Affiliation Model.*

Table 1. Typical obtained score by the suppliers (1-8) and the weight values defined by QMS for input type 1.

Suppliers	Weight values defined by the QMS for the CTQ attributes															Total score for the supplier $\sum$(score*weight)
	5	5	3	5	2	5	4	5	1	3	1	1	1	2	2	
	Score obtained by the suppliers for the **CTQ attributes**															
	1	**2**	**3**	**4**	**5**	**6**	**7**	**8**	**9**	**10**	**11**	**12**	**13**	**14**	**15**	
1	10	4	0	3	0	7	0	4	0	6	8	10	0	3	5	192
2	5	0	10	0	9	6	9	6	3	4	3	5	3	7	0	209
3	5	9	4	0	7	5	0	4	0	8	3	7	10	0	10	205
4	4	0	5	6	9	7	4	9	7	5	0	10	0	3	0	217
5	9	3	0	3	5	0	0	0	8	3	6	3	0	0	0	111
6	0	0	5	4	0	5	10	8	3	6	10	9	5	5	4	203
7	8	3	8	10	0	3	6	3	0	0	7	0	0	10	4	218
8	4	0	0	7	0	6	5	0	5	3	5	10	10	9	10	182

Table **1** presents the typical obtained score by the suppliers and the weights assigned by QM for each attribute relevant to input type 1 (Refer to **Quality in Supply Management** for definitions). The supplier 1 obtained 10 in attribute 1 and 4 in attribute 2 (in a scale of 1 to 10 defined above for the attributes), for an example, as shown in Table **1**. Table **1** also reveals that the weight assigned by QM for attributes 1 and 2 are 5 and 5. The right most column of Table **1** shows the total CTQ performance score ($\sum$(score*weight) obtained by supplier 1 is 192. Table **2** provides the total CTQ performance score obtained by each supplier relevant to the input types by considering score in each attributes and the weights assigned by the QMS. The last two rows of Table **2** also provide the threshold values set by the SC QM for each input type for affiliating suppliers at the HQ and AQ level. The total performance score obtained by supplier 1 for the input types 1 to 10 are {192, 245, 198....239, 205}. According to threshold value set by SC QM (Table **2**), each supplier should obtain total performance score of 190 for CTQ attributes to become quality affiliated as AQ suppliers for input type1, for an example.

Table 2. Total CTQ performance score ($\sum$attribute score *weight) by the suppliers (1-8) for the input types.

Suppliers	Total quality performance score by the suppliers for the **input types**									
	1	**2**	**3**	**4**	**5**	**6**	**7**	**8**	**9**	**10**
1	192	245	198	158	216	179	233	140	239	205
2	209	184	259	202	163	205	213	228	211	146
3	205	295	276	265	127	158	208	193	248	134
4	217	108	238	227	186	215	168	215	286	228
5	111	207	190	235	231	256	230	138	209	217
6	203	133	155	281	269	253	296	207	172	185
7	218	156	190	176	181	294	232	237	175	161
8	182	205	219	271	235	221	176	165	288	257
Threshold Value for HQ	208	218	215	224	215	218	218	210	215	210
Threshold Value for AQ	190	200	190	200	180	200	200	190	200	180

Table 3. Typical scores by the suppliers in the CTB attributes and the requirements for ach attribute.

Suppliers	Score for CTB attributes				
	1	**2**	**3**	**4**	**5**
1	4	5	5	4	5
2	4	5	4	4	4
3	5	5	5	4	4
4	5	4	4	4	4
...	...	...	...	...	...
Requirements	4	4	4	4	4

In addition to CTQ attributes, the QM also defined 5 CTB attributes; a 1-5 score scale and set a required score for each attribute by each supplier to become affiliated. Table **3** presents typical required scores (at the bottom most row of the Table) and the scores obtained by the suppliers for each attribute. For an example, supplier 1 obtained scores {4, 5,5, 4 and 5} for 5 CTB attributes (Table **3**).

Table **4** presents the model output for supplier affiliation. This is the first and one of the most crucial steps of SC quality planning for ensuring right quality inputs to the production such that the SC can assure quality product in the market places. The quality based supplier affiliation decisions taken in this step are integrated subsequently into the **Integrated Strategic SC Design Model** for assigning inputs only to the quality affiliated suppliers.

Table 4. Model output for quality based supplier affiliation.

	Affiliated suppliers for **Inputs**										Total number inputs
Supplier	**1**	**2**	**3**	**4**	**5**	**6**	**7**	**8**	**9**	**10**	
1	AQ	HQ	AQ	X	HQ	X	HQ	X	HQ	AQ	7
2	HQ	X	HQ	AQ	X	AQ	AQ	HQ	AQ	X	7
3	AQ	HQ	HQ	HQ	X		AQ	AQ	HQ	X	7
4	HQ		HQ	HQ	AQ	AQ		HQ	HQ	HQ	8
5		AQ	AQ	HQ	HQ	HQ	HQ	X	AQ	HQ	8
6	AQ	X	X	HQ	HQ	HQ	HQ	AQ	X	AQ	7
7	HQ	X	AQ		AQ	HQ	HQ	HQ	X	X	6
8	X	AQ	HQ	HQ	HQ	HQ	X	X	HQ	HQ	7

Based on the performance criteria defined and set by the QM, the model decided the affiliation level of the suppliers as X (not affiliated), AQ and HQ. For an example, the Model evaluated supplier 1 to be affiliated at HQ level for input types {2, 5, 7 and 9} and at AQ level for input types {1, 3, and 10}. The supplier1 has been decided to be not affiliated (X) for input types {4, 6 and 8} as shown in Table **4**. To take an example and investigate the reasons for affiliating supplier 1 as "X "for input type 4, we may Refer to Tables **2** and **3**. Based on Table **3**, supplier 1 could obtain required CTB score 4 for input type 4, but based on Table **2**, it could obtain total CTQ score 158 for input type 4, which is less than minimum required threshold value 200 (158< 200) for affiliation at AQ level. As such, the model affiliated supplier 1 as "X" for input type 4. Similar explanation may be obtained by referring to Tables **2** and **3** for each 'X' mark or non-affiliation decision by the model in Table **4**. We may also check model decision for HQ and AQ level. For example, the model decided supplier 1 to be at AQ level for input 1 while affiliated at HQ level for input type 2. Referring to Table **3**, supplier 1 could comply with CTB requirements for each input type. Now referring to Table **2**, supplier 1 obtained 192 < 208 (HQ level threshold value 208) for input 1 and 245 for input type 2, 245 > 218 (HQ level threshold value 218) for input 2. Similar explanation may be obtained for each model decision referring to Tables **2** and **3**. Based on this model, the AQ level supplier will be able to find out at which quality based operations attribute they should improve for improving their level to HQ level. Thus this model will also guide the suppliers to pursue continuous improvement steps.

Steps 3 and 6: In step 3 we record 15 CTQ and 5 CTB attributes, relevant score scale values, weight scale values, and threshold values defined and set by the SC QM for evaluating capability of the production plants operated by the SC. Table **5** records the typical CTQ attributes, score values obtained by the production plants and the weight scale set by the SC QM. Plant1 obtained scores [3,3,0, 5...3,3,3,0] for the 15 CTQ attributes for which SC QM defined weights [5,5, 3,.....1,1,2,2] as may be observed in Table **5**, for example relevant to production of product 1. Table **5** also shows the total score $\sum$(Score*Weight) =124 by plant 1 for producing product 1.

Table 5. Typical CTQ attributes score values obtained by the Plants and weight values defined by QMS for product 1.

Plants	Weight values defined and set by the QM for the CTQ attributes															Total score by the plants = $\sum$(Score*Weight)
	5	5	3	5	2	5	4	5	1	3	1	1	1	2	2	
	Metrics Scores obtained by the plants for the **CTQ Attributes**															
	1	2	3	4	5	6	7	8	9	10	11	12	13	14	15	
1	3	3	0	5	0	3	8	0	3	0	7	3	3	3	0	124
2	3	9	9	9	10	6	0	0	3	3	0	5	3	7	4	224
3	3	4	7	9	10	0	10	0	3	3	10	10	4	3	9	221
4	9	10	3	0	3	4	4	9	3	0	0	7	4	5	7	229
5	0	3	5	3	4	9	4	6	2	6	8	0	3	3	0	181
6	3	10	5	3	8	9	0	7	5	4	5	0	6	10	10	259
7	3	3	0	6	8	5	9	2	0	4	0	4	0	8	3	185

Table **6** provides the threshold values for plant capability determination and total CTQ scores obtained by the plants considering CTQ metrics scale score and weights set by the SC QM. Plant 1 could obtain total CTQ metrics scores 124 for product1, when the set threshold score by QM is 200 to become capable for product 1, for an example (Table **6**).

Table 6. Total CTQ metrics scores obtained by the plants for each product and threshold values for capability.

Plants	Total CTQ metrics scores ($\sum$score*weight) by the plants for the products					
	1	2	3	4	5	6
1	124	200	231	183	254	292
2	224	182	237	173	234	281
3	221	239	270	137	170	255
4	229	166	271	215	241	212
5	181	252	232	179	167	249
6	259	184	192	284	252	186
7	185	238	259	187	250	255
Threshold value for capability	200	180	230	175	230	210

Table **7** gives the CTB attributes scores by the plants and the requirements for individual attributes set by the SC QM. As discussed before, a plant needs to comply with each CTB attributes requirements to become a quality capable plant. Based on Table **7**, each plant operated by the example SC complied with requirements for each CTB attribute.

Table 7. Typical CTB attribute scores obtained by the Plants and the required CTB values set by the QMS.

Plants	Scores obtained by the plants for the **CTB attributes**				
	1	2	3	4	5
1	5	5	5	5	4
2	5	4	5	4	5
3	5	4	4	5	5
4	5	5	5	5	4
5	5	5	4	5	5
6	5	5	4	4	4
7	5	4	5	5	4
Requirements	4	4	4	4	4

Table **8** presents the model output for deciding plant quality capability, which is the next crucial step in integrating quality in strategic level SC planning after ensuring input quality through affiliating suppliers in Table **4**. The model output on plant quality capability is subsequently integrated in the strategic level SC design model such that production is allocated only to the quality capable plants. Based on the model output in Table **8**, plants 2, 3, 4, and 6 are quality capable for producing product 1, while plants 1, 5, and 7 could not be the quality capable for product 1, for an example. An investigation on plant 1 for not becoming quality capable plant for product 1 (Table **8**); shows that based on Table **7**, plant 1 could comply with CTB requirements but based on Table **6**, the plant could only obtain

124 as total CTQ attributes scores compared to the threshold requirements of 200 to become quality capable for product 1. The SC management will be able explore the CTQ attributes on which they need to improve for earning capability certification for plant1-product1combination. Similar explanations may be obtained from Tables **6** and **7** for each element of manufacturing plant approval model output recorded in Table **8**.

Table 8. Model outputs for plant capability determination.

Plants	Capability of the plants for the products					
	1	**2**	**3**	**4**	**5**	**6**
1	X	capable	capable	capable	capable	capable
2	capable	capable	capable	X	capable	capable
3	capable	capable	capable	X	X	capable
4	capable	X	capable	capable	capable	capable
5	X	capable	capable	capable	X	capable
6	capable	capable	X	capable	capable	X
7	X	capable	X	capable	capable	capable

Table 9. Typical score values obtained by the SC for CS attributes for Product 1.

Customers	Scores obtained by the SCs for customers – Product 1 combinations for the CS attributes																	Total
	1	**2**	**3**	**4**	**5**	**6**	**7**	**8**	**..**	**..**	**14**	**15**	**16**	**17**	**18**	**19**	**20**	
1	3	8	3	9	4	8	7	7			4	9	7	8	9	10	5	127
2	6	6	8	5	10	3	10	4	..	..	5	4	3	5	3	10	4	118
3	9	7	5	5	4	5	7	5			9	9	4	7	10	5	10	132
4	8	10	3	10	10	9	6	3			3	6	5	3	3	6	4	120
5	9	8	5	7	6	7	10	9	..	..	3	5	4	10	10	3	6	131
6	7	10	10	9	8	8	10	3			10	7	9	9	3	10	6	145
7	6	6	5	10	3	8	10	8	..	..	10	4	7	7	4	6	9	130
8	4	3	7	8	7	3	8	7			5	6	5	7	5	9	6	129
9	3	6	8	7	7	5	3	8	..	..	8	4	8	3	8	4	3	118
10	6	5	8	4	5	5	8	7			5	8	5	6	9	3	6	123

Step 4 and Step 7: Step 4 follows the definitions of CS attributes, relevant score scale and criteria for awarding the score provided jointly by the SC QM and marketing (refer to **Quality in Customer System Management**). Table 9 shows 20 CS attributes in terms of identification or code number (1, 2, 3 …), and the score obtained by the SC for a typical customer-product1 combination in the case of each attribute. For an example, the SC could obtain {3,8, 3,…..9, 10, 5} for the

CS attributes 1 to 20 in their competency evaluation for supplying product 1 to customer 1, as may be observed in Customer 1 row of Table **9**. According to the data shown in the last column of Table **9**, the SC could obtain total score 127 considering the entire set of CS attributes for customer1-Product 1 combinations. Similar explanations are applicable for competency evaluations in the case of other customer product combinations also. As covered in SC Quality Planning section, the joint team of SC QM and marketing also set the minimum required score to be earned by SC for becoming competent for the customer- product combination. Table **10** gives the typical required score value assumed for this example problem. For an example, the SC needs to obtain 126 based on the admissible criteria for the CS attributes and relevant score scale jointly set by the QM and marketing for becoming competent to supply customer 1 the product 1, as may be observed in Table 10. Following the Step 7, the SC competency model is now solved using inputs presented in Tables **9** and **10**.

Table 10. Required CS attributes score for the SC to become competent for customer-product combination.

Customer	Required total CS attributes score for becoming competent for the customers to supply the products					
	1	**2**	**3**	**4**	**5**	**6**
1	126	119	140	127	129	126
2	128	140	127	139	119	143
3	127	130	115	131	123	120
4	136	140	120	136	118	114
5	132	130	133	134	123	137
6	124	117	122	120	125	113
7	115	122	127	120	122	141
8	126	123	135	116	132	112
9	118	135	126	126	118	125
10	126	120	135	120	135	125

Table **11** presents the **SC Competency Model for Customer System Management** output. As mentioned before, SC competency model output will facilitate SC managers to evaluate their business positions in relation to satisfying existing and potential customers in terms of product performance, customer service and their business performances as expected by the customers. Based on the SC competency model output presented in Table **11**, the right-hand most columns show the competency of the SC for supplying number of products to the customers and bottom most row shows competency of SC for supplying number of customer with respect to each of the product. For an example, the SC is competent to supply products 2, 3, 4, 5 and 6 to customer 4 but not competent to supply product 1, as may be observed in Table **11** (Row for Customer 4). In Table

11 Y means competent and N means not competent. To verify why the SC could not be competent for Product 1, we may refer to Tables **9** and **10**.

Table 11. SC competency model output for supplying customers the products.

Customer	Competency of SC for relevant to customers for supplying **products**						Total # of products
	1	2	3	4	5	6	
1	Y	N	Y	Y	Y	Y	5
2	N	Y	Y	N	Y	Y	4
3	Y	Y	Y	Y	N	Y	5
4	N	Y	Y	Y	Y	Y	5
5	N	N	N	Y	Y	Y	3
6	Y	Y	Y	Y	Y	Y	6
7	Y	N	N	N	Y	N	2
8	Y	Y	Y	Y	Y	Y	6
9	Y	N	Y	Y	Y	Y	5
10	N	Y	N	Y	Y	N	3
Total customers	6	6	7	8	9	8	

According to Table **9**, total SC scores for CS attributes for **customers –Product 1** combination the SC could obtain 120 for customer 4 for supplying product 1, which is less than the 136, minimum requirement as shown in Table **10** for Customer 4 -Product 1 combinations. Similar verification for each decision of SC competency model may be obtained from information shown in Tables **9** and **10**.

Following the step by step procedure (from steps 1 to 7) we have solved the supplier affiliation model, plant capability model and SC competency model for determining quality affiliated suppliers, identifying quality capable plants and evaluating SC competency for overall customer satisfaction. As discussed before, the outputs of these models are integrated in the strategic level SC design model to ensure input quality to the production and shipment quality of products to markets and providing overall customer satisfaction in terms of quality of products, safety to the user, customer services, and business performances of the SC as expected by the customer.

Step 8: As mentioned before, this research emphasizes on the quality issues of SC and, as such, this section shall include only limited information on the costs, capacity and capability of the SC functions and operations that are needed to explain and establish quality related SC performances and requirements. Table **12** presents the demand information for the products assumed. The SC plans to satisfy the demand for the 10 customers (retailers) using quality integrated SC planning. As may be observed in Table **12**, the customer 3 has demand for 10,500 units of product 4, for an example. The information in Table **12** includes the demand information for the product- customer combinations, which the SC has been supplying historically. These customers have requirements for other products for which the SC is now contemplating to supply by first evaluating their competency. As can be seen in Table **11**, the SC has been found to be competent to supply product 1 to customer 1 in their current competency evaluation, which the SC did not supply in the past (demand for product 1 from customer 1 is zero). As such, product 1-customer 1 is a potential customer /market extension possibility for the SC. Several similar such examples may be found by studying Tables **11** and**12**.

Table 12. Typical product demand for the SC from the customers.

Product	Demand for products by the **customers**								Total demand
	1	**2**	**3**	**4**	**5**	**6, 7, 8**	**9**	**10**	
1	0	0	0	17,871	0	...	14,040	0	63,367
2	0	0	0	13,156	16,449	...	0	0	74,603
3	0	19,209	0	0	17,138	...	12,925	18,513	94,965
4	0	0	10,500	17,242	18,198	...	18,967	0	94,817
5	12,871	15,978	0	0	0	...	18,118	0	101,276
6	0	14,111	0	0	0	...	0	0	66,729

Table **13** provides the production capacity of the plants operated by the SC. For an example, plant 1 has the capacity to produce 15,583 units of product 1 (Table **13**). Table **13** also provides data for the total capacity of the SC for producing a product type using their entire capacity.

Table 13. Capacity information for the plants operated by the SC.

Plant	Production capacity of plants in units/year for the **products**					
	1	**2**	**3**	**4**	**5**	**6**
1	15,853	20,935	26,796	22,857	23,353	19,423
2	14,569	0	23,102	0	26,993	0
3	17,097	16,581	0	21,189	0	19,882
4	16,293	21,604	25,048	20,843	23,166	19,727
5	14,235	18,655	0	0	24748	0
6	0	0	22,313	21,998	23,399	0
7	0	20,445	23,696	23,032	22,944	20,495
Total	78,047	98,220	120,955	109,919	144,603	79,527

Table **14** presents the capacity of the suppliers for supplying inputs. To illustrate the information in Table **14**, supplier 1 has the capacity to supply 30,817 units of input, for an example. We would like to mention at this point that the manufacturing plants in Table **13** may not be quality capable for each of their capacity. Similarly, input suppliers in Table **14** may not be quality affiliated at the level desired by the SC for each of the capacity. We may investigate applicability of plant capacity for the plants in Table **13** and applicability of quality affiliation at various levels in Table **14** based on the decision of Quality Integrated SC design model in Step 10. In addition to product, plant capacity, supplier capacity, we also considered several other inputs information, such as usage of inputs, input costs, quality costs, production costs and others following model solution steps 2, 8, and 9 described in Section 3.1.

Table 14. Typical Capacity information of the supplier for supplying in inputs.

Supplier	Capacity of suppliers for the inputs (1 to 8 out of 10)							
	1	2	3	4	5	6	7	8
1	30,817	0	49,237	68,904	52,600	42,171	47,395	59,717
2	27,767	60,683	33,984	71,495	36,036	30,472	37,916	0
3	22,667	53,730	37,163	0	41,300	0	42,788	52,432
4	0	45,929	36,378	70,026	71,381	33,243	40,209	47,170
5	37,772	0	32,100	38,878	52,313	28,011	0	37,762
6	32,679	59351	0	46,703	49,400	40,561	0	0
7	0	0	38,368	0	65,176	38,543	48,208	36,939
8	37,233	49,176	32,106	66,835	58,827	0	40,694	51,733
Total	188,935	268,869	259,336	362,841	427,033	213,001	257,210	285,753

As mentioned before, since this research addresses quality related issues of SC, we are not providing those cost related information and limiting our discussion and analysis on the quality related issues only. Following the step 10 of the solution procedure the Quality integrated SC design model is now solved for the numerical example by using model outputs for supplier affiliation, plant capability and SC competency as the inputs in addition to the other cost related inputs discussed before.

Tables **15**, **16** and **17** shows the model decision for assigning inputs to the suppliers, allocation of production to plants and distribution products to the customers.

Table 15. Typical allocation of inputs to suppliers.

Supplier	Suppliers assigned the units of **inputs** (1 to7 out of 10)								Total
	1	**2**	**3**	**4**	**5**	**6**	**7**	...	
1					52,600		47,395		156,742
2	27,767		19,303				*2,734*		49,804
3		53,730	37,163				*42,788*		182,270
4			36,378	11,261					149,704
5				38,878	1642				274,489
6	*17,728*				49,400	1,311			68,439
7						38,543	48,208		123,690
8		*49,176*		66,835	58,827				227,519
Total	45,495	102,906	92,844	116,974	162,469	39,854	141,125		

A study of Table **15** will reveal that the Quality Integrated Model assigned inputs only to the quality affiliated (either at AQ or HQ level) suppliers, please refer to Table **4** to verify. In addition, following the constraints (34) to (37) in the integrated SC design model, the model assigned entire amount of inputs to HQ suppliers if the combined capacity of HQs for an input could fulfill the entire requirements. In the case HQs could not fulfill the requirements, only the amounts that could not be accommodated by the HQs were assigned to AQs. For an example, total requirements for input 1found by the model: 45,495 units, and there are three HQs (suppliers 2, 4 and 7) and three AQs (1, 3, and 6) affiliated for input1, please see (Table **4**). The model assigned 27,767 units to HQ supplier 2 and assigned 17,728 to AQ supplier 6. For finding an explanation whether the model complied with constrains (34) to (37), please refer to Table **14** for supplier capacity information. Other than HQ supplier 2, the other two HQ suppliers (4 and 7) do not have capacity to supply the input 1 at the period we considered. As, such the model first exhausted the capacity of HQ supplier 2 (27,767 units please see Table **14**) and assigned (45,495-27,767) =17,728 units to AQ supplier 6 (Table **15**), finding a good cost from supplier 6 compared to other AQ suppliers for the input 1. For most of the inputs, the model could assign entire amounts to HQ suppliers only. For inputs 1, 2, 7 (in italic) and 8 some amounts were assigned to AQs for the similar reasons explained for input 1. These decisions reveal that the model is quite suitable for implementing strict quality oriented planning for procuring inputs from the quality affiliated suppliers.

Table **16** presents the model decision for allocation of production to plants. It may be mentioned here that the Model decided to produce the optimal quantity shown in Table **16** based on the capacity of plants, availability of inputs, competency of supplying products to customers and capacity of DCs to maximize profits. The quantity decided by the plants are allocated only to the approved quality capable plants.

Table. 16 Allocation of the production to plants.

Plants	Plants assigned to **products.**					
	1	2	3	4	5	6
1				17,856	23,353	
2	12,105		15,703		8,409	
3	17,097					7,127
4	16,293				23,166	19,727
5						
6				21,998	23,399	
7					22,944	20,495
Total	45,495	0	15,703	39,854	101,271	47,349

For an example, the model allocated product 1 quantities to plants 2, 3, and 4 (column 1 of Table **16**), all of which are quality approved capable plants, please see (Table **8**). Similar verification may be conducted for the entire product allocation decision referring to (Table **8**). Thus the quality integrated model assigned inputs to quality affiliated suppliers and allocated production only to the quality capable plants for ensuring shipment quality of the product that is going to the customers or in the market places. We may check further integration of quality while distributing the products to the customers. Table **17** presents distribution of products from the DCs that received products from the quality capable plants in Table **16**. Just to relate, Table **17** is presented starting from last row of (Table **16**). Table **17** establishes the quality integrated decisions of **Integrated Strategic SC Design Model.** It first shows the transportation of the products from quality capable plants to DCs and then distribution from DCs to the customers. By this integrated process the model ensures shipment of quality products to the customers. To take example, 45,495 units of product 1 manufactured in quality capable plants 2, 3, 4 (Table **16**) are now transported to DCs {1, 3, 5, 7, 8, and 9}. From the DCs 45, 495 units of product is distributed to the customers7, 8, and 9 for which the SC has the appropriate competency (see Table **11**).

Table 17. Model output on transportation of products to DCs and distribution from DCs to customers.

Plants	Production of **products** by quality capable plants in Table 16					
	1	2	3	4	5	6
1 to 7						
Total	45,495	0	15,703	39,854	101,271	47,349
Transported from Plants to DCs (at the left most column)						
DCs						
1	4,233		2,933		14,119	10,023
2				11453	15155	9,218
3	9,697			4,752	14,991	1,184
4					15,291	8,058
5	8,669			13,149		
6						9261
7	7,769				13,807	27
8	5320			10500	14,426	
9	9,807		12,770		13,482	9,578
	45,495		15,703	39,854	101,271	47,349
Distributed from DCs to Customers (at the left most column)						
Customers						
1					12,871	
2			15,703		15,978	14,111
3						
4				17,242		
5				7,463		
6					16,337	18,823
7	13,989				19,359	
8	17,466			15,149	18,608	14,415
9	14,040				18,118	
10						
Total	45,495		15,703	39,854	101,271	47,349

Based on the analysis of the model output it is established that the integrated SC design model effectively integrated the quality issues of the SC by connecting and aligning entire SC planning process with the quality based supplier affiliation, plant capability determination, and customer satisfaction management process. The proposed approach will aid SC managers in effectively establishing quality based planning process for each of their business functions that will finally be integrated with the entire business process for improving overall business performances.

CONCLUSION

The research introduced a detailed approach for installing an attributes metrics based quality systems in the supply management, production management, customer systems management, and finally integrated the functions in the strategic level SC planning process for overall improvement of the business performances. The research first defined the generic operational attributes and outlined procedure for setting metrics based logical score scales and threshold values for each of the key functions applicable to any SC process. Considering the number of attributes and its multi-dimensional nature, the research then proposed a model based approach for evaluating the performances and implementing improvement steps relevant to the SC functions. Finally, the research integrated quality performance based functional planning in supply, production and customer management in the strategic level SC planning model for improving overall SC performances. To facilitate the SC managers in applying and solving the model for their specific businesses, a step-by-step solution procedure has been illustrated using a numerical example. Analysis of the model output for the numerical example clearly established the effectiveness of the model in integrating supply management, production management, and customer service management to ensure quality of inputs to production, outputs to shipment, and optimum customer satisfaction level.

The attribute metrics, decision variables, model formulation and solution procedure for supply management, manufacturing plant capability, and SC competency have been created for easy applicability of the models in a generic business setting. To the best of our knowledge this is the first research attempt where customer satisfaction management, manufacturing capability criteria and input management have been modeled and integrated in the strategic level SC model for overall business planning. By applying the proposed SC planning methodology SCs will be able to ensure desired product quality to the market places and improve customer satisfaction for the overall SC performance improvement.

CONSENT FOR PUBLICATION

Not applicable.

CONFLICT OF INTEREST

The authors confirm that there is no conflict of interest to declare for this publication.

ACKNOWLEDGEMENT

Declared none.

REFERENCES

[1]   F.E. Ouardighi, and B. Kim, "Supply quality management with wholesale price and revenue-sharing contract with wholesale price", *European Journal of Operational Research,* vol. Vol 206 , no. 2, pp. 329-340.

[2]   H. Kaynak, and J.J. Hartley, A replication and extension of the quality management into the supply chain, Journal of Operations Management. 2008; Vol 26(4), p. 468-489

[3]   R.A. De Carvalho, and H.G. Costa, Application of an integrated decision support process for supplier selection. Enterprise Information Systems. 2007; Vol 1(2), p. 197-216

[4]   M.Y. Jaber, M. Bonney, and A.L. Guiffrida, Coordinating a three level supply chain with learning - based continuous improvement. International Journal of Production Economics. 2010; Vol 127(1), p. 27-38

[5]   C.C. Hsieh, and Y.T. Liu, Quality investment and inspection policy in a supplier-manufacturer supply chain. European Journal of Operational Research. 2010; Vol 202(3), p. 717-729

[6]   J. Lyu Jr, S.Y. Chang, and T.L. Chen, Integrating RFID with quality assurance System-Framework and applications. Expert Systems with Applications. 2009; Vol 36(8), p. 10877- 10882

[7]   M. Mayer, and M. Nusswald, Improving manufacturing costs and lead times with quality oriented operating curves. Journal of Materials Processing Technology. 2001; Vol 119(1-3), p. 83-91

[8]   P.I. Karipidis, Market evaluations of dimensions of design quality. International Journal of Production Economics, 2011; Vol129(2), p.292-301

[9]   E. Rabinovich, Linking e-service quality and markups: the role of imperfect information in the supply chain. Journal of Operations Management. 2007; Vol 25(1), p. 14-41

[10]   L.L. Stanely, and J.D. Wisner, Service quality along the supply chain: implications for purchasing. Journal of Operations Management. 2001; Vol 19(3), p. 287-306

[11]   R. Sroufe, and S. Curkovic, An examination of ISO 9000:2000 and supply chain quality assurance. Journal of Operations Management. 2008; Vol 26(4), p. 503-520

[12]   D.A. Garvin, Competing on the eight dimensions of quality. Harvard Business Review. 1987; Vol 65 (6), p. 101–109

[13]   A.C.L. Yeung, Strategic supply management, quality initiatives, and organizational performance. Journal of Operations Management, 2008; Vol 26(4), p.490 -502

[14]   C. Lin, W.S. Chow, C.N. Madu, C.H. Kuei, and P.P. Yu, A structural equation model of supply chain quality management and organizational performance. International Journal of Production Economics. 2005; Vol 96(3), p. 335-365

[15]   J. Gonzalez-Benito, and A.R. Martinez-Lorente, A study of purchasing management system with respect to total quality management. Industrial Marketing Management. 2003; Vol 32(6), p. 443-454

[16]   Y. Theodorakioglou, K. Gotzamni, and G. Tsiolvas, Supplier management and its relationship to buyers' quality management. Supply Chain Management: An International Journal. 2006; Vol 11(2), p.148-159

[17]   V.H.Y. Lo, and A. Yeung, Managing Quality Effectively in Supply chain. Supply Chain Management: An International Journal. 2006; Vol 11(3), p. 208-215

[18]   R.A. Eltantawy, L. Giunipero, and G.L. Fox, A strategic skill based model of supplier integration and its effect on supply management performance. Industrial Marketing Management. 2009; Vol 38(8), p. 925-936

[19]   J. Griffiths, R. James, and J. Kempson, Focusing customer demand through manufacturing supply chains, by the use of customer focused cells: an appraisal. International Journal of Production Economics. 2000; Vol 65(1), p. 111-120

[20]   A.J.C. Trappey, and D.W. Hsiao, Applying collaborative design and modularized assembly for automotive ODM supply chain integration. Computers in Industry. 2008; Vol 59(2-3), p. 277-287

[21]   Z. Hua, X. Zhang, and X. Xu, Product design strategy in a manufacturer-retailer distribution channel. Omega, 2011; Vol 39(1), p. 23-32

[22]   S.Y. Sohn, and I.S. Choi, Fuzzy QFD for supply chain management with reliability consideration. Reliability Engineering and System Safety. 2001; Vol 72(3), p. 327-334

[23]   V. Kannan, and K.C. Tan, Just in time, total quality management, and supply chain management: understanding their linkages and impact on business performance. Omega. 2005; Vol 33(2), p. 153-162

[24]   R.G. Batson, and K.D. Mcgough, A new direction in quality engineering: supply chain quality modeling. International Journal of Production Research. 2007; Vol 35(23), p. 5455-5464

[25]   S.K. Vickery, J. Jayaram, C. Droge, and R. Calantone, The effects of an integrative supply chain strategy on customer service and financial performance: an analysis of direct versus indirect relationships. Journal of Operations Management, 2003 Vol 21(5), p.523-539

[26]   S. Thirumalai, and K.K. Sinha, Customer satisfaction with order fulfillment in retail supply chains: implications of product type in electronic B2C transactions. Journal of Operations Management. 2005; Vol 23(3-4), p. 291-303

[27]   E. Bottani, and A. Rizzi, Strategic Management of logistic service: A fuzzy QFD approach. International Journal of Production Economics. 2006; Vol 103(2), p. 585-599

[28]   W. Jammernegg, and P. Kischka, Dynamic customer oriented supply networks. European Journal of Operational Research. 2005; Vol 167(2), p. 413-426

[29]   A.E. Ellinger, P.J. Daugherty, and Q.J. Plair, Customer satisfactory and loyalty in supply chain: the role of communication. Transportation Research Part E. 1999; Vol 35(2), p. 121-134

[30]   J. Heikkila, From supply to demand chain management: efficiency and customer satisfaction. Journal of Operations Management. 2002; Vol 20(6), p. 747-767

[31]   H. Kurota, and S.H. Nam, After sales service competition in a supply chain: optimization of customer satisfaction level or profit or both. International Journal of Production Economics. 2010; Vol 127(1), p. 136-146

[32]   M. Perona, and N. Saccani, Integration techniques in customer–supplier relationships: An empirical research in the Italian industry of household appliances. International Journal of Production Economics. 2004; Vol 89, (2), p. 189–205

[33]   W.S. Chow, C.N. Madu, C.H. Kuei, and M.H. Lu, Supply Chain Management in the US and Taiwan: An empirical study. Omega. 2008; Vol 36(5), p. 665-679.

CHAPTER 10

Identification of Zonal-Wise Passenger's Issues in Indian Railways Using Latent Dirichlet Allocation (LDA): A Sentiment Analysis Approach On Tweets

Vijay Singh[1,*], Mangey Ram[2] and Bhasker Pant[1]

[1]*Department of Computer Science and Engineering, Graphic Era Deemed to be University, Dehradun, Uttarakhand, India*
[2]*Department of Mathematics; Computer Science and Engineering, Graphic Era Deemed to be University, Dehradun, Uttarakhand, India*

Abstract: Twitter is one of the effective mediums to detect the feeling of a mass. Due to the increasing penetration of this kind of social services in the society, its relevance and the credibility are also increasing. In this article, we did an analysis of 16 different Indian Railways Zonal Regions and Zonal-wise passengers issues concerning traveling, using Latent Dirichlet Allocation (LDA). The results generated by the LDA shows that the major concerns of the passengers are the sanitation, security of women, rat and bad behavior by the other passengers. These results can be used to further improve the performance of the Indian Railways and in decision making.

Keywords: Indian Railways, Latent Dirichlet Allocation (LDA), Sentiment analysis, Topic mining

INTRODUCTION

Indian railways have one of the largest railway networks in the world. Around 20 million people use services of Indian Railways every day. For this reason, the whole networks of Indian Railways are divided into sixteen Zonal- regions for better management of the services. In this research article, we collected tweets from different Zonal tweeter handles. The Zones are Central, Eastern, East Central, Northern, North Central, North Eastern, Northeast Frontier, North Western, Southern, South Central, South Eastern, South East Central, South Western, Western and West Central. In this vast network of Indian Railways and the huge numbers of passengers, it is very difficult to meet the highest satisfaction level of the passengers.

*Corresponding author Vijay Singh: Computer Science and Engineering department, Graphic Era Deemed to be University, Dehradun-248002, India; Tel/Fax: +919760322316; E-mail: vijaysingh_agra@hotmail.com

Mangey Ram (Ed.)

Review of Latent Dirichlet Allocation and Sentiment Analysis: In this section review, Latent Dirichlet Allocation [1] and Sentiment Analysis are explained for better understanding of the article.

Latent Dirichlet Allocation (LDA) is an unsupervised, generative probabilistic method used to determine the topic from the corpus or text collection in the unigram form [1]. Latent Dirichlet Allocation is one of the prominent machine learning algorithms, which are widely used in text mining, social network analysis, recommender systems, data science, bio-analysis and drug designing [2]. Latent Dirichlet Allocation in an unsupervised technique is used to maximize the probability of word assignments to the K fixed topics. The meaning of the topic is evaluated by interpretating of the top most probability word for the above mentioned topic. The goal is to infer topics that maximize the likelihood. The key concept behind the Latent Dirichlet Allocation is that the words in each document are considered as the combination of topics, where each topic is represented as the probability distribution over words [3]. In the recent years, it is observed that Latent Dirichlet Allocation outperforms well in the topic mining as well as text classification domain [4]. Suppose, there is an X independent topic in the corpus consists of D documents. Here, every topic is the polynomial probabilistic distribution of word and every document is randomly generated by X topics. In LDA, it is essential to extract the composition information (θ, Z) of the hidden topic. If Dirichlet parameters α and β are given, the distribution of random variables θ, z, and W in document d are computed as [5] shown in equation 1:

$$p(\theta, Z, W/\alpha, \beta) = p(\theta/\alpha) \prod_{i=1}^{N_m} p(\tfrac{Z_i}{\theta}) \, p(W_i/Z_i, \beta) \tag{1}$$

The graphical model of the Latent Dirichlet Allocation is shown in Fig. (**1**).

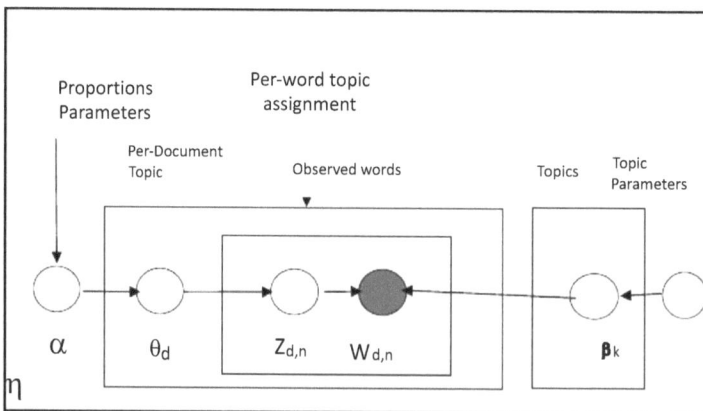

Fig. (1). Graphical model of latent dirichlet allocation (LDA).

Sentiment Analysis: Sentiment analysis is a combined approach of computational linguistics, Natural Language Processing and text analysis for finding the subjective information from the source, and in other words, it is the computational treatment of opinions [6]. Analysis of these sentiments can further be used in various application domains like customer information, marketing, books, movies, songs, conversation analysis and other similar fields of text mining [7]. Traditionally, Sentiment Analysis is used to classify the text into positive, negative and neutral, or in other terms, it is used to classify the document based on polarity. There are various challenges associated with Sentiment Analysis, it is a subfield of Natural Language Processing that is why ambiguity is a major concern of Sentiment Analysis research. Another important concern is the type and nature of data, due to the unstructured type data mostly used in sentiment analysis, which is noisy and ambiguous information, which affects the efficiency of the system. So, proper data pre-processing techniques are applied before actual algorithm implementation. Most of the researches have been carried out on sentiment analysis using Machine Learning and linguistics approaches. Walaa Medhat *et al.* [6] proposed that the classification process is divided into three levels *i.e.* document level, sentence level and aspect level. Machine Learning approach in sentiment analysis can be categorized into supervised and unsupervised methods. Most of the unsupervised methods are based on Latent Dirichlet Allocation (LDA) and they require prerequisite information making them subjective [8]. Further, supervised is classified as a decision-based approach, rule-based approach, linear classifier and probabilistic classifier. The main methods used in the linear classifier are Support Vector Machine and Neural Networks, while the main techniques used in probabilistic are Naïve Bayes, Bayesian networks and, Maximum Entropy. The classification of Machine Learning is shown in Fig. (**2**).

Related Work: Gupta and Shalini [4] proposed a system for the improvisation Experience of Indian Railway using sentimental analysis, they did the polarity calculation on the commuter's feedback. Keisuke *et al.* [5] worked on stock market analysis using the semi-supervised learning. In their study, they demonstrated bootstrapping methods for maintaining a small polarity corpus containing some initial input words. Liu *et al.* [9] worked on the various linguistic features for sentiment analysis and they performed the comparative study on blogs and review data. Zhu and Li [10] used the topic model using the Latent Dirichlet Allocation by the novel similarity measure for automatic text summarization they envisaged the similarity measure is valued. Arora and Ravindran [11] proposed a multi-document summarization by using LDA. They show that this technique is a statistically significant technique over another similar technique. Agarwal *et al.* [12] proposed POS (part of speech)-specific prior polarity feature- based system for examining sentiments. They investigated two approaches of models: tree kernel and feature based models and both outperform the unigram baseline. Srijiti *et al.* [13] worked on sub-story detection using the hierarchical Dirichlet process. They compared the hierarchical Dirichlet process with the spectral clustering and LSH (Locally Sensitive hashing) on several sub-story detections and the performance of the hierarchal Dirichlet process is better than the other techniques. Singh and Kumari [14] focused on the importance of text pre-processing in the twitter sentiment analysis. They proposed an approach of pre-processing which relies on slang words and other coexisting words to evaluate the importance of sentiment translation of slang words. Thakur and Sasi [15] worked on social media contents using the ontology-based sentiment analysis. They designed an Ontology-based method to retrieve and analyse customer's negative reviews to produce the dissatisfaction of the customer to a service. Bhradwaj *et al.* [16] demonstrated Sentiment analysis for Indian Stock market prediction using Sensex and Nifty. Devika *et al.* [17] did a comparative study on different approaches using sentiment analysis. They envisaged the advantages and disadvantages of different algorithms used in Sentiment analysis. According to them, Naïve Bayes algorithm's main disadvantages are, the algorithm is mainly used when the size of the training set is less and assumes conditional independence among the linguistic features. Preethi *et al.* [18] proposed a method for event prediction using Temporal Sentiment Analysis. They analysed the user's opinion in different time for casual rule detection. Further, these casual rules are used for event prediction. Anand and Naorem [19] worked on aspect level sentiment analysis, they proposed semi-supervised aspect based sentiment analysis for movies using review filtering. Deng *et al.* [20] performed a study of the supervised term weighting scheme for sentiment analysis. They used terms in documents and the terms for expressing sentiment. They demonstrated their evaluation on the Cornell Movie review dataset, multi-domain sentiment dataset of products by Amazon.com and Stanford large movie data set by Maas *et al.* [21]. Their experiment output envisaged that the mentioned approach outperforms the state-of-the-art unsupervised approach and produces the best accuracy. Ghiassi *et al.* [22] did a Twitter brand sentiment analysis by hybrid approach using n-gram and dynamic artificial neural networks. They used supervised feature reduction using n-gram and statistical analysis for the twitter based lexicon for Sentiment analysis. They did their experimentation on Justin Bieber Twitter corpus and find the accurate results. Li *et al.* [23] performed Sentiment analysis in an interesting domain. They demonstrated the News impact on stock price return using Sentiment analysis. They developed the generic stock price prediction framework for calculating the News impact on stock price return. Their experimental finding shows that Sentiment Analysis outperforms the bag-of-words model in validation as well as in independent testing of data. Another important finding of them, positive and negative dimensions could not bring useful prediction. Kim and Lee [24] did a Sentiment visualization and classification via semi-supervised nonlinear dimensionality reduction. They worked on semi-supervised Laplacian Eigen map for removing redundant features effectively by decreasing detection errors of sentiments.

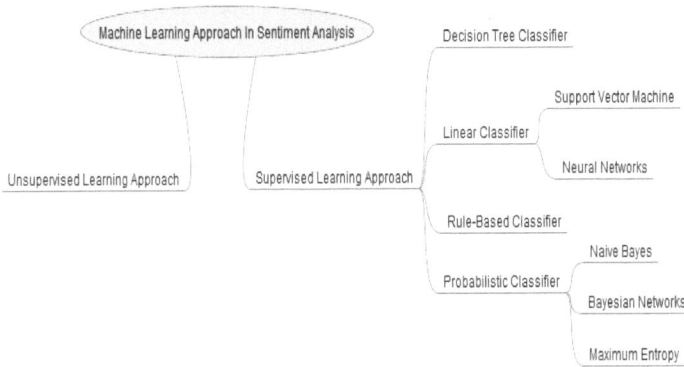

Fig. (2). Classification of machine learning approach in sentiment analysis.

Dataset Preparation: For the mentioned analysis, the dataset is collected using the twitter. Every Zone of Indian Railway has its General Manager's twitter handle, where the passenger can tweet on whatever topic they want. If they have any query, complaint or suggestions. The GMs twitter handle is shown in Table **1**. The nature of the data collected from these twitter handles is very messy and noisy. Some basic data pre-processing techniques like cleaning, transformation and filtering for noise removal and extracting the meaningful information are then applied. Sample tweets after pre-processing are shown in Table **2**.

Table 1. Twitter Handle Account of GM's at different Zonal railways.

S.No.	Zonal Railway	Twitter Handle Account
		GMs
1.	Central	@gm_crly
2.	Eastern	@EasternRailway

(Table 1) cont.....

3.	East Central	@GM_ECRly
4.	East Coast	@gmeastcoastrly
5.	Northern	@GM_NRly
6.	North Central	@GMNCR1
7.	North Eastern	@gmner_gkp
8.	Northeast Frontier	@gm_nfr
9.	North Western	@GMNWRailway
10.	Southern	@GMSRailway
11.	South Central	@Gmscrailway
12.	South Eastern	@GM/SERAILWAY
13.	South East Central	@Gmsecr
14.	South Western	@gmswr
15.	Western	@Gmwrly
16.	West Central	@Gmwcrailway

Table 2. Sample tweets after pre-processing.

S.No.	Sample Tweets
1.	Late due to Waterlogging in Tracks
2.	hats off to cleaning staff
3.	Narendramodi PMOIndia do something sir about tatkal quota
4.	I write so many times but no actionnRT Pl note change in Official Twitter Account
5.	Derailment of goods train between Ankola, Gokarna leads to disruption of
6.	suspicious activities at Railway Stations Central_Railway
7.	surge prices are OK for Railway but not OK for airlines

(Table 2) cont.....

8.	the railway is a good experiment. but hope that the facilities.....
9.	Indian Railway for the delayed train service.
10.	Why we can't pay more if we want to get more from indian railways.

METHODOLOGY USED

In this article, the concept of Sentiment Analysis and Latent Dirichlet Allocation is incorporated for better efficiency of the proposed system. We illustrate our approach using the dataset which is collected from different railway zone's General Manager's twitter handle. Sixteen Indian railway zones are identified for analysis and the individual text file is created for each railway zone, twitter handles are shown in Table **1**. The whole procedure is divided into three main sections A, B, and C, as shown in Fig. (**2**). In the first section, *i.e.* A, tweets are collected using the Twitter Archiver tool and used python programming for implementation of the Twitter API. For zonal-wise tweets collection, specific twitter handle is used. There is a huge challenge associated with the downloaded tweets, they contain various kinds of noisy data. The text quality challenges are shown in Table **3**.

Table 3. Text Quality challenge.

Challenge	Description
Stop words	Common frequency words
Text Cleaning	Removal process of unwanted contents
Clarity	There is no clarity in the text
Lemmatization	Detection of similarity in the text/words
Data Integration	It combines data from multiple source into a coherent data store.
Data Transformation	It consolidated the data into an appropriate form for mining. The techniques involve: (a) Normalization (b)Smoothing (c) Aggregation (d) Generalization of the data.
Spell correction	Correcting the spelling within the contents
Stemming	Stemming is the technique of reducing derived words to their word stem or root form.
Data Reduction	Reduction of the data set without compromising the integrity of the original data.

So, in the next section, *i.e.* B, the data pre-processing techniques are applied to the collected tweets for data preparation. The main techniques that are mainly used for data pre-processing are data cleaning, data integration, data transformation and data reduction. The complete procedure of the pre-processing involves whitespace removal, stemming, removal of stop words. Sample tweets after pre-processing are shown in Table **2**. The final step of the proposed methodology is the implementation of Latent Dirichlet Allocation in the pre-processed tweets for finding shared topics among the zone-wise collected documents as shown in Eq. (1). Fig. (**3**), shows the proposed steps of the methodology. After applying the Latent Dirichlet Allocation, the results are demonstrated and discussed in the next section.

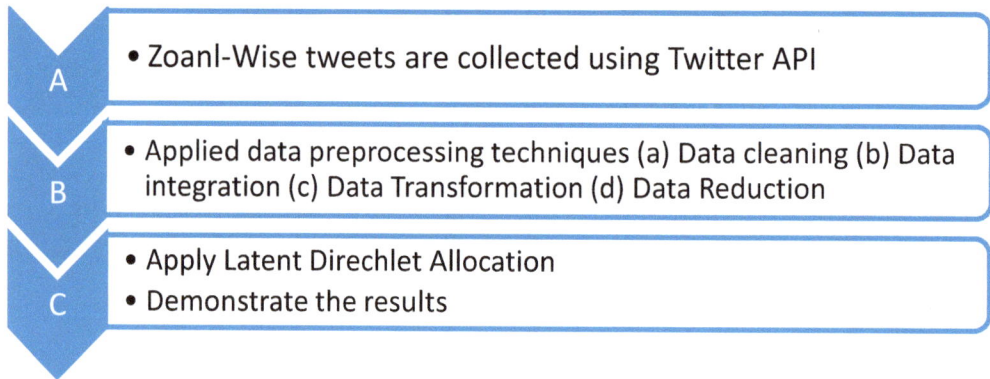

A • Zoanl-Wise tweets are collected using Twitter API

B • Applied data preprocessing techniques (a) Data cleaning (b) Data integration (c) Data Transformation (d) Data Reduction

C • Apply Latent Direchlet Allocation
       • Demonstrate the results

Fig. (3). Main steps of the framework.

RESULT AND DISCUSSION

For evaluation of the mentioned system, we used sixteen different zonal text files and applied Latent Dirichlet Allocation and the result is shown in Table **4**. The most concerned keywords are water, food, toilet, rail, security, TDR, refund etc. Which topic is associated with which document is shown in Fig. (**4**), *i.e.* Zone-wise topic identification. For example, the major concern of the eastern railway is money, TDR, and Refund. In Fig. (**5**), topic distribution is shown, the graph is generated between the document topic and probability. In the first document the probability of the first topic is 0.8 and in the second document, it is around 0.2.

Topic distribution in the corpus

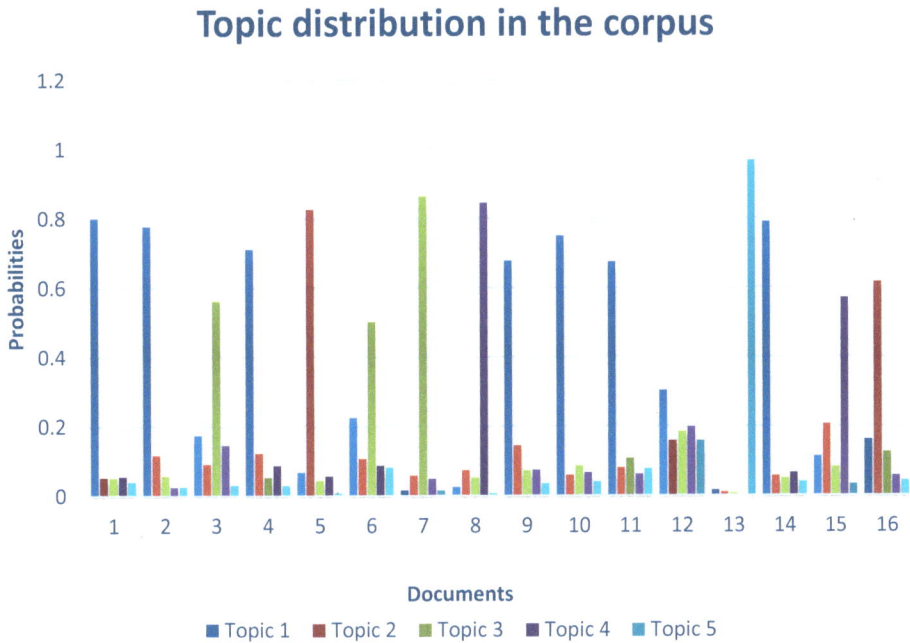

Fig. (4). Topic distribution in the corpus.

Table 4. Most discussed topics in the dataset.

	Topic 1	Topic 2	Topic 3	Topic 4	Topic 5
1	india	train	speed	tdr	cater
2	sureshpprabhu	railminindia	late	improve	travel
3	rail	sureshpprabhu	amount	sir	secure
4	money	food	clean	railminindia	quick
5	tdr	toilet	tatkal	water	system
6	refund	modi	sleep	wifi	halt

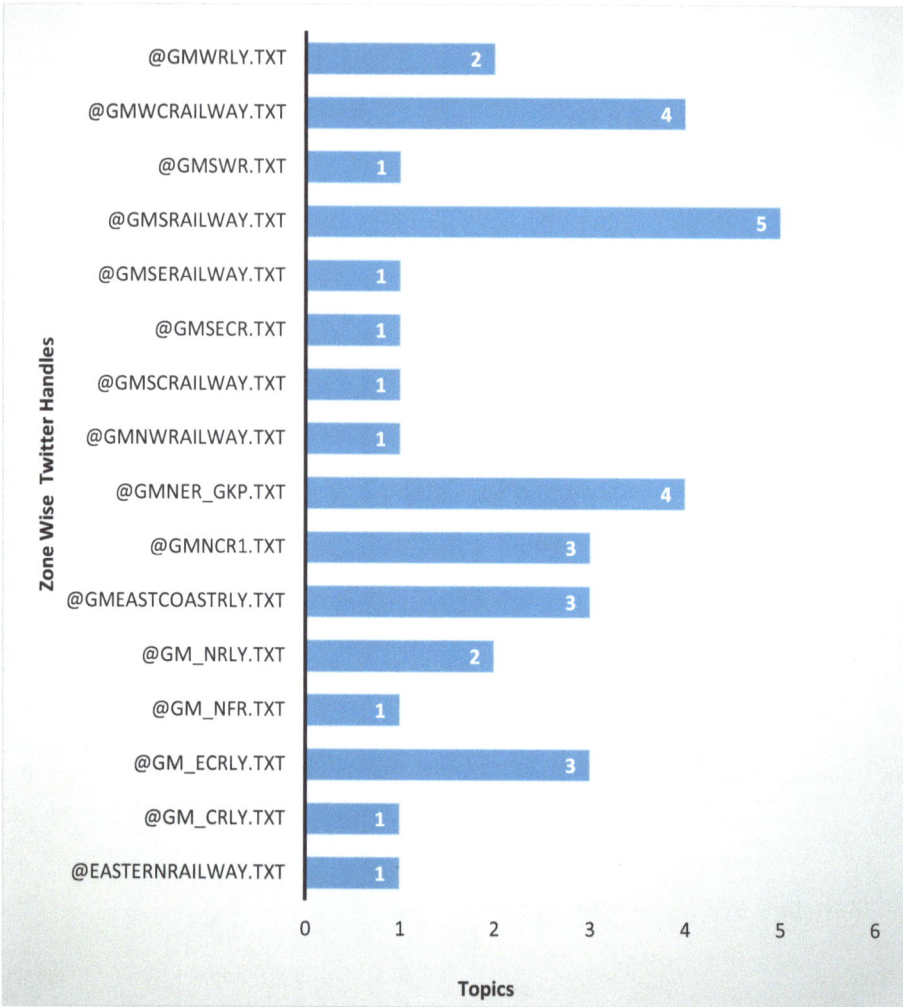

Fig. (5). Zone-wise topic identification.

CONCLUSION

Topic modeling like Latent Dirichlet Allocation is gaining popularity for finding the hidden topics shared among the documents and it is widely used in information retrieval and automatic subject indexing. This work analyse the zonal-wise passenger's issue using the Latent Dirichlet Allocation in the context of Indian scenario. They are promising and show that the major issues are very much common in all the zones like water, refund process, TDR process, security, toilet, and food. The limitation of this approach, the Latent Dirichlet Allocation, is that it works on unigrams. In future work, we would develop the methodology that can work on bi-gram or n-gram Latent Dirichlet Allocation.

CONSENT FOR PUBLICATION

Not applicable.

CONFLICT OF INTEREST

The authors declare no conflict of interest, financial or otherwise.

ACKNOWLEDGEMENTS

Declared none.

REFERENCES

[1]   D.M. Blei, A.Y. Ng, and M.I. Jordan, "Latent Dirichlet allocation", *J. Mach. Learn. Res.,* vol. 3, no. Jan, pp. 993-1022.

[2]   B. Zhang, B. Peng, and J. Qiu, "High performance lda through collective model communication optimization", *Procedia Comput. Sci.,* vol. 80, pp. 86-97.

[3]   I. Porteous, D. Newman, A. Ihler, A. Asuncion, P. Smyth, and M. Welling, "Fast collapsed Gibbs sampling for latent Dirichlet allocation", *Proceedings of the 14th ACM SIGKDD international conference on Knowledge discovery and data mining,* , 2008pp. 569-577

[4]   A.R. Gupta, and L. Shalini, "Improvisation of experience of Indian railways using sentimental analysis", *Int. J. Comput. Appl.,* vol. 66, no. 11, .

[5]   K. Mizumoto, H. Yanagimoto, and M. Yoshioka, "Sentiment analysis of stock market news with semi-supervised learning", *Computer and Information Science (ICIS),* , 2012pp. 325-328

[6]   W. Medhat, A. Hassan, and H. Korashy, "Sentiment analysis algorithms and applications: A survey", *Ain Shams Engineering Journal.,* vol. 5, no. 4, pp. 1093-1113.

[7]   D.M. Hussein, "A survey on sentiment analysis challenges", *Journal of King Saud University-Engineering Sciences..* In press

[8]   W. Ding, X. Song, L. Guo, Z. Xiong, and X. Hu, "A novel hybrid HDP-LDA model for sentiment analysis", *Proceedings of the,* vol. Volume 01, , 2013pp. 329-336

[9]   F. Liu, D. Wang, B. Li, and Y. Liu, "Improving blog polarity classification via topic analysis and adaptive methods",

[10]   T. Zhu, and K. Li, "The similarity measure based on LDA for automatic summarization", *Procedia Eng.,* vol. 29, pp. 2944-2949.

[11]   R. Arora, and B. Ravindran, "Latent Dirichlet allocation based multi-document summarization", *Proceedings of the second workshop on Analytics for noisy unstructured text data,* 2008 pp. 91-97

[12]   A. Agarwal, B. Xie, I. Vovsha, O. Rambow, and R. Passonneau, "Sentiment analysis of twitter data", *Proceedings of the workshop on languages in social media,* , 2011pp. 30-38

[13]   P.K. Srijith, M. Hepple, K. Bontcheva, and D. Preotiuc-Pietro, "Sub-story detection in Twitter with hierarchical Dirichlet processes", *Inf. Process. Manage.,* vol. 53, no. 4, pp. 989-1003.

[14]   T. Singh, and M. Kumari, "Role of text pre-processing in twitter sentiment analysis", *Procedia Comput. Sci.,* vol. 89, pp. 549-554.

[15]   P. Thakor, and S. Sasi, "Ontology-based sentiment analysis process for social media content", *Procedia Comput. Sci.,* vol. 53, pp. 199-207.

[16]   A. Bhardwaj, Y. Narayan, and M. Dutta, "Sentiment analysis for Indian stock market prediction using Sensex and nifty", *Procedia Comput. Sci.,* vol. 70, pp. 85-91.

[17]   M.D. Devika, C. Sunitha, and A. Ganesh, "Sentiment analysis: A comparative study on different approaches", *Procedia Comput. Sci.,* vol. 87, pp. 44-49.

[18]   P.G. Preethi, and V. Uma, "Temporal sentiment analysis and causal rules extraction from tweets for event prediction", *Procedia Comput. Sci.,* vol. 48, pp. 84-89.

[19]   D. Anand, and D. Naorem, "Semi-supervised Aspect Based Sentiment Analysis for Movies using Review Filtering", *Procedia Comput. Sci.,* vol. 84, pp. 86-93.

[20]   Z.H. Deng, K.H. Luo, and H.L. Yu, "A study of supervised term weighting scheme for sentiment analysis", *Expert Syst. Appl.,* vol. 41, no. 7, pp. 3506-3513.

[21]   A.L. Maas, R.E. Daly, P.T. Pham, D. Huang, A.Y. Ng, and C. Potts, Learning word vectors for sentiment analysis. In Proceedings of the 49th annual meeting of the association for computational linguistics: Human language technologies-volume 1 2011 Jun 19 (pp. 142-150). Association for Computational Linguistics

[22]   M. Ghiassi, J. Skinner, and D. Zimbra, "Twitter brand sentiment analysis: A hybrid system using n-gram analysis and dynamic artificial neural network", *Expert Syst. Appl.,* vol. 40, no. 16, pp. 6266-6282.

[23]   X. Li, H. Xie, L. Chen, J. Wang, and X. Deng, "News impact on stock price return via sentiment analysis", *Knowl. Base. Syst.,* vol. 69, pp. 14-23.

[24]   K. Kim, and J. Lee, "Sentiment visualization and classification via semi-supervised nonlinear dimensionality reduction", *Pattern Recognit.,* vol. 47, no. 2, pp. 758-768.

SUBJECT INDEX

N

Non homogeneous poisson process (NHPPs)
  1, 2, 4, 5, 6, 8, 10, 13, 14, 19, 20, 35, 38,
  40, 41, 53, 55, 56
Nonintrusive image forensics 72
Nonzero terms 161
Normalized specular scattering coefficient
  186, 187, 188, 189, 192

O

Objective function value 205, 217
Optical filters 77, 78
Optimal solutions 99, 198, 217, 222, 226
Optimization, particle swarm 197, 199, 200,
  207
Optimization problem 21, 200, 201, 202, 222
  reliability-cost 202, 222
Original premises 127, 136, 140

P

Parameter estimates 45, 49, 55
Parameter retrieval 168, 172, 192
Particle swarm optimization (PSO) 197, 199,
  200, 201, 202, 207, 212, 213, 222
Plant approval 230, 238, 239, 243, 246, 248,
  254
Plant capability determination 239, 252, 254,
  261
Plant capacity 243, 258, 260
Plant quality capability 253
Post-processing operations 77, 100
Power, exponent 223, 224, 225
PRCG images 86, 87, 97
Prediction error 83, 85, 86, 87, 88, 89, 90, 91,
  93, 99
  variance of 88, 89
Predictive log-likelihood 27, 28, 29
Predictive performance 1, 4, 21, 27, 28
Prime consequents 127, 132, 134, 136, 140
Prime implicants 123, 124, 127, 128, 129, 144,
  145, 148, 153, 154, 157, 161
Probability map 82, 83, 84, 85, 86, 87, 92
Probative facts 73, 74, 76

Problem definition 136
Product design 230, 231, 232, 237
Production cost 245, 258
Production management 243, 261, 262
Production plants 248, 252
Product quality 114, 232, 237, 239, 240, 242,
  248, 256, 262
  ensuring 237, 248
Products 6, 54, 59, 110, 111, 112, 114, 117,
  124, 127, 128, 131, 144, 145, 147, 148,
  154, 156, 157, 159, 197, 230, 232, 234,
  235, 237, 238, 239, 240, 241, 242, 243,
  244, 245, 246, 248, 249, 252, 253, 254,
  255, 256, 257, 258, 260, 261, 268
  absorbing 159
  approved 234
  customized 241
  demand for 243, 257
  meat 110, 111
  past 235
  producing 238, 243, 244, 252, 253
  shipment quality of 237, 239
  sum of 127, 147, 148
  three-literal 128
  units of 256, 257, 260
Propositional equation 132, 133, 135, 137
PSO and GA algorithms 215, 217, 218, 219

Q

Quality in customer system management 239,
  254
Quality management system (QMS) 230, 231,
  232, 233, 248, 249, 250, 252, 253
Quality metrics 230
Quality products 243, 251, 260
Quality system 230, 231, 237

R

Radio frequency identification 108, 109, 110,
  112
Real dataset 96, 97, 98, 100, 101, 102
Reflection law 141, 156
Relational databases 123, 130, 144
Release time 34, 35, 49

www.ingramcontent.com/pod-product-compliance
Lightning Source LLC
Chambersburg PA
CPIIW050014770110
41598CB00006B/207

*   9 7 8 1 6 8 1 0 8 7 1 4 6   *